Graphic Novels and Comics as World Literature

Literatures as World Literature

Can the literature of a specific country, author, or genre be used to approach the elusive concept of "world literature"? **Literatures as World Literature** takes a novel approach to world literature by analyzing specific constellations—according to language, nation, form, or theme—of literary texts and authors in their own world-literary dimensions.

World literature is obviously so vast that any view of it cannot help but be partial; the question then becomes how to reduce the complex task of understanding and describing world literature. Most treatments of world literature so far either have been theoretical and thus abstract, or else have made broad use of exemplary texts from a variety of languages and epochs. The majority of critical work, the filling in of what has been traced, lies ahead of us. **Literatures as World Literature** fills in the devilish details by allowing scholars to move outward from their own areas of specialization, fostering scholarly writing that approaches more closely the polyphonic, multiperspectival nature of world literature.

Series Editor:
Thomas O. Beebee

Editorial Board:
Eduardo Coutinho, Federal University of Rio de Janeiro, Brazil
Hsinya Huang, National Sun-yat Sen University, Taiwan
Meg Samuelson, University of Adelaide, Australia
Ken Seigneurie, Simon Fraser University, Canada
Mads Rosendahl Thomsen, Aarhus University, Denmark

Volumes in the Series
German Literature as World Literature, edited by Thomas O. Beebee
Roberto Bolaño as World Literature, edited by Nicholas Birns and Juan E. De Castro
Crime Fiction as World Literature, edited by David Damrosch, Theo D'haen and Louise Nilsson
Danish Literature as World Literature, edited by Dan Ringgaard and Mads Rosendahl Thomsen
From Paris to Tlön: Surrealism as World Literature, by Delia Ungureanu
American Literature as World Literature, edited by Jeffrey R. Di Leo

Romanian Literature as World Literature, edited by Mircea Martin, Christian Moraru, and Andrei Terian
Brazilian Literature as World Literature, edited by Eduardo F. Coutinho
Dutch and Flemish Literature as World Literature, edited by Theo D'haen
Afropolitan Literature as World Literature, edited by James Hodapp
Francophone Literature as World Literature, edited by Christian Moraru, Nicole Simek, and Bertrand Westphal
Bulgarian Literature as World Literature, edited by Mihaela P. Harper and Dimitar Kambourov
Philosophy as World Literature, edited by Jeffrey R. Di Leo
Turkish Literature as World Literature, edited by Burcu Alkan and Çimen Günay-Erkol
Elena Ferrante as World Literature, by Stiliana Milkova
Multilingual Literature as World Literature, edited by Jane Hiddleston and Wen-chin Ouyang
Persian Literature as World Literature, edited by Mostafa Abedinifard, Omid Azadibougar, and Amirhossein Vafa
Mexican Literature as World Literature, edited by Ignacio M. Sánchez Prado
Beyond English: World Literature and India, by Bhavya Tiwari
Graphic Novels and Comics as World Literature, edited by James Hodapp
African Literatures as World Literature, edited by Alexander Fyfe and Madhu Krishnan (forthcoming)
Feminism as World Literature, edited by Robin Truth Goodman (forthcoming)
Polish Literature as World Literature, edited by Piotr Florczyk and K. A. Wisniewski (forthcoming)
Taiwanese Literature as World Literature, edited by Pei-yin Lin and Wen-chi Li (forthcoming)
Pacific Literatures as World Literature, edited by Hsinya Huang and Chia-hua Lin (forthcoming)
Central American Literature as World Literature, edited by Sophie Esch (forthcoming)
Kazuo Ishiguro as World Literature, by Chris Holmes (forthcoming)

Graphic Novels and Comics as World Literature

Edited by
James Hodapp

BLOOMSBURY ACADEMIC
NEW YORK • LONDON • OXFORD • NEW DELHI • SYDNEY

BLOOMSBURY ACADEMIC
Bloomsbury Publishing Inc
1385 Broadway, New York, NY 10018, USA
50 Bedford Square, London, WC1B 3DP, UK
29 Earlsfort Terrace, Dublin 2, Ireland

BLOOMSBURY, BLOOMSBURY ACADEMIC and the Diana logo are
trademarks of Bloomsbury Publishing Plc

First published in the United States of America 2022
This paperback edition published 2023

Volume Editor's Part of the Work © James Hodapp, 2022
Each chapter © Contributors, 2022

Cover design by Simon Levy

All rights reserved. No part of this publication may be reproduced or transmitted in any form or by any means, electronic or mechanical, including photocopying, recording, or any information storage or retrieval system, without prior permission in writing from the publishers.

Bloomsbury Publishing Inc does not have any control over, or responsibility for, any third-party websites referred to or in this book. All internet addresses given in this book were correct at the time of going to press. The author and publisher regret any inconvenience caused if addresses have changed or sites have ceased to exist, but can accept no responsibility for any such changes.

Library of Congress Cataloging-in-Publication Data
Names: Hodapp, James, editor.
Title: Graphic novels and comics as world literature / edited by James Hodapp.
Description: New York : Bloomsbury Academic, 2022. |
Series: Literatures as world literature | Includes bibliographical references and index.
Identifiers: LCCN 2021052939 (print) | LCCN 2021052940 (ebook) |
ISBN 9781501373411 (hardback) | ISBN 9781501373404 (paperback) |
ISBN 9781501373428 (epub) | ISBN 9781501373435 (pdf) | ISBN 9781501373442
Subjects: LCSH: Graphic novels–History and criticism. |
Comic books, strips, etc.–History and criticism. | Narration (Rhetoric)–Social aspects. |
Literature and society. | LCGFT: Literary criticism.
Classification: LCC PN6710 .G7356 2022 (print) |
LCC PN6710 (ebook) | DDC 741.5/9–dc23/eng/20211116
LC record available at https://lccn.loc.gov/2021052939
LC ebook record available at https://lccn.loc.gov/2021052940

ISBN:	HB:	978-1-5013-7341-1
	PB:	978-1-5013-7340-4
	ePDF:	978-1-5013-7343-5
	eBook:	978-1-5013-7342-8

Series: Literatures as World Literature

Typeset by Integra Software Services Pvt. Ltd.

To find out more about our authors and books visit www.bloomsbury.com
and sign up for our newsletters.

For Alison, Logan, and Ella

Contents

List of Figures   x

Introduction: Global South Comics on Their Own Terms *James Hodapp*   1

1. Pages of Exception: Graphic Reportage as World Literature *Dominic Davies*   11
2. Latin America's *Tinta Femenina* and Its Place in Graphic "World Literature" *Jasmin Wrobel*   33
3. An Alternative Worldliness: Verbal and Visual Experimentations in *Fī shiqqat bāb el-loq* (*The Apartment in Bab El-Louk*) *Dima Nasser*   55
4. Boys Love in Latin America: The Migration of Aesthetics in Contemporary Graphic Narrative *Camila Gutiérrez*   75
5. A Sociological Approach to Francophone African Comics (1978–2016) *Sandra Federici*   97
6. Born in the "World": Leila Abdelrazaq's Writing and Art as World Literature *Allison Blecker*   123
7. Utopias Gone Wrong: Representing the Dystopic Urban in the Indian Graphic Narrative *Debadrita Chakraborty*   145
8. Opening Up a World and the Temporal–Normative Dimension: Keum Suk Gendry-Kim's *Grass* as World Literature *Jin Lee*   167
9. Between the Saltwater and the Desert: Indigenous Australian Tales from the Margins *Catherine Sly*   187
10. A Case Study of *Sita's Ramayana*, Diasporic Negotiations, COVID-19, and the Television Serial *Ramayana* *Shilpa Daithota Bhat*   213
11. Wakanda as a Sustainable Smart Society: Africanfuturism in Marvel's *Black Panther* *Jana Fedtke*   229
12. Neoliberal Ideologies in *Menggapai Bintang* (*Reach for the Stars*) *Mohd Muzhafar Idrus, Habibah Ismail and Hazlina Abdullah*   243
13. "LONG LIVE the Waste!": Junk Food Bites Back in Jung's *Approved for Adoption* *Sheng-mei Ma*   257

Notes on Contributors   269
Index   273

Figures

1.1 The double-page spread at the center of Olivier Kugler's *Escaping Wars and Waves* shows a refugee encampment in a public park on the Greek Island of Kos (Kugler 2018, 38–9). Reproduced with the permission of the artist — 12

1.2 The only double-page spread included in Kate Evans' *Threads from the Refugee Crisis* contemplates the Calais "Jungle" as a space of exception (Evans 2017, 52–3). Reproduced with the permission of the artist — 21

1.3 A double-page spread from Tings Chak's *Undocumented: The Architecture of Migrant Detention* that shows a space of exception at the heart of a Canadian detention center (Chak 2016, 52–3). Reproduced with the permission of the publisher — 23

1.4 The only double-page spread in John Sack's *La Lucha: The Story of Lucha Castro and Human Rights in Mexico* that shows Ciudad Juárez as a space of exception (Sack 2015, 9–10). Reproduced with the permission of the publisher — 26

2.1 Hilda and Uriel — 42
2.2 Uriel — 43
2.3 Diagnoses — 45
2.4 Hilda — 46
2.5 Paola's birth — 47
2.6 La adolescencia — 48
2.7 Herodotus Io — 49
3.1 and 3.2 Opening of *Fī shiqqat bāb el-loq* — 56
3.3 Page of *Fī shiqqat bāb el-loq* — 57
3.4 *Abū Naẓẓārah* (vol. 1 1878–9) — 63
3.5 Café scene of *Fī shiqqat bāb el-loq* — 65
3.6 Two-week-old newspaper with murder headline reads "Man kills brother over 50 pounds" — 67
3.7 Cat calligram — 70
4.1 Extreme close-up of Francisco when Sebastián boards the bus — 78
4.2 Francisco stares at Sebastián, captivated by his voice — 79
4.3 Juxtaposed images of a Dutch girl and a Japanese girl (right to left) in *Syōzyō* magazine — 84
4.4 Exchange between Miguel and an anonymous miner — 88

4.5	Vicente in a *sutairu ga* image that overlaps three rows of panels	89
4.6	"you're just like me"	90
4.7	The readers scroll down this long image at the end of the story. Page numbers become unclear	92
5.1	*Bingo* (1981–4)	101
5.2	*Chroniques de Lomé*	109
5.3	*La grande épopée du Tchad*	111
5.4	*Les refoulés du Katanga*	113
6.1	Map of Palestine	124
6.2	Stillborn	137
6.3	*The Fig Tree*	138
7.1	Vishwajyoti Ghosh, *Delhi Calm*	149
7.2 and 7.3	Vishwajyoti Ghosh, *Delhi Calm*	152
7.4	Sarnath Banerjee, *Corridor*	158
7.5	Sarnath Banerjee, *Corridor*	160
7.6	Sarnath Banerjee, *Corridor*	162
8.1	One of the identical bleed pages depicting Ok-sun's hometown in a realistic style (80)	173
8.2	Ok-sun on her errand for the madam of the tavern is about to meet her abductors (160)	175
8.3	Being Abducted (164)	175
8.4	Reflection in old age (167)	176
8.5	The bleed pages after Ok-sun's abduction (166–7)	177
8.6	Ok-sun tells Mija's story (274)	179
8.7	Mija gives birth to a girl at the comfort station (292)	180
8.8	… and later a boy (303).	181
8.9	Ok-sun tells her story after she came to South Korea (434).	183
9.1	*The Legend of the Phoenix Dragon* (2011)	188
9.2	*Heroes Beginnings* (2013)	189
9.3	*Return of the Dragons* (2019)	190
9.4	Final panel on page 23 of *Ubby's Underdogs: The Legend of the Phoenix Dragon*	196
9.5	Yupman Poe and his ailing niece on a boat sailing south in *Ubby's Underdogs: The Legend of the Phoenix Dragon*	197
9.6	Map of the township of Broome in *Ubby's Underdogs: The Legend of the Phoenix Dragon*	198
9.7	Panels showing the pursuit of Medinga in *Ubby's Underdogs: Heroes Beginnings*	202

9.8	Humor in this segment derives from the tourists' comments about the lack of events in Broome while Ubby and others frantically try to protect the township from the War Crown Spider in *Ubby's Underdogs: The Legend of the Phoenix Dragon*	208
10.1	Sita's abduction	216
10.2	Sita's reflections	217
10.3	Waiting	217
10.4	War	218
10.5	Image of the Ramayana serial from the Indian Doordarshan website (https://doordarshan.gov.in)	221
12.1	*Menggapai Bintang* Translation: Sophia (first page): Hey, are you blind? Our clothes are expensive, you know! You gotta pay if they get torn, you know? Cristina (first page): Stop being such a bully! It was an accident! Sophia (second page): Excuse me? How dare you … ! Emilia (second page): That's enough, Sophia. It's no use talking to them. They simply aren't sophisticated at all. Let's just go! Talking with these people will just drag us down to their level	252
12.2	Mean Girls	253
13.1	The animated *Approved for Adoption*'s adoption photo turned into the graphic novel cover	258
13.2	The animated *Approved for Adoption* skips the graphic novel's "LONG LIVE the waste!"	262
13.3	The animated *Approved for Adoption* portrays Jung's forehead drawers	264
13.4	The animated *Approved for Adoption* imagines the rendezvous with the mother in a wheat field	266
13.5	The animated *Approved for Adoption* where Jung strokes his adoption photo with his left thumb	267

Introduction: Global South Comics on Their Own Terms

James Hodapp

If a tree falls in an African forest and the west is not around to hear it, was it even a tree in the first place?
                                    Ndinda Kioko, writer and filmmaker (Nefetiti 2015)

In the past few decades literary scholars have increasingly considered the mechanisms by which texts become worldly in part to come to terms with literary circulations and the biases that inform them. More recently, some scholars have taken up questions of worldliness to reimagine a more equitable discipline that has historically been decidedly Eurocentric. Comic studies, though not absent from these conversations, have arguably lagged considerably in coming to terms with its Eurocentrism and in offering alternative and better paradigms that place non-Western comics on equal footing with their Western peers.

Picking up on the ways that influence and circulation are still highly asymmetrical between the Global North and South in literary studies, artist Ndinda Kioko above playfully critiques the ways legibility to the West is frequently decisive in determining the worldliness of non-Western literature. She argues that engagement with the preoccupations of the West unduly influence what is considered worldly, so much so that worldliness too often means either art that emanates from the West and circulates globally or non-Western art that enters the Western consciousness via translation and other modes of cultural accessibility for Western audiences. Her frustration comes from disappointment with various world literary systems such as World Literature, cosmopolitanism, the planetary, globalism, and related concepts that conceptualize equitable cultural exchange and circulation but that often result in a worldliness inflected by Western interests and narrated from Global North perspectives—updated variations on eighteenth-century teleological Eurocentrism. Literature from the non-West that does not attend to these concerns and perspectives, she argues, are in danger of being ignored outside their regions of production while their Western-orientated counterparts enjoy a seemingly seamless worldliness regularly selling back to the West its own self-aggrandizing stereotypes of child soldiers, extreme poverty, terrorist cells, religious extremism, failed states, and the like.

Through various gatekeepers such as critics, publishers, academic institutions, award committees, etc. Kioko and many other Global South artists understand that their worldliness often depends not on the nature or quality of texts they write or the responses of readers in innumerable locales around the globe, but by the acceptance of a narrow array of Western literary powerbrokers. Rather than the machinations of complex networks of global circulation that include South–South exchanges, espoused by the major architects of the most prominent theories of World Literature, their affability to cultural and linguistic translation often dictates whether they can be published and become worldly, i.e. "even a tree in the first place." Non-Western authors also understand that many works produced in the Global North are "born global" simply as a result of being written and published in Anglophone literary metropoles such as New York and London, a distinction that eludes most non-Western writers who frequently must traverse numerous real and imagined borders, be they geographical, linguistic, or cultural to be deemed worldly—a phenomenon astutely articulated for the African context by Sandra Federici in this collection.[1] A common critique of postcolonialism has been that it reifies a center-margin binary within which the complexities and positionality of non-Western actors are oversimplified and flattened. Nonetheless, the "global" study of comics contains just such centers and margins. This has been true of World Literature writ large but particularly for comic studies which has been largely Eurocentric—privileging Western texts and tokenizing particular non-Western texts under the guise of diversity, outside of Japan which acts as an alternative comic literary pole (as discussed by Camila Gutiérrez herein).[2]

Resisting this hegemony of world literary comic systems is inherently political, whether one openly acknowledges that in one's scholarship or not. To insist as authors do in this collection, for example, that Malaysian comics that have not been addressed nearly adequately enough by global comics studies or to articulate the queer Japanese–Latin American connection of "Boys Love" or the importance of out-of-print African comics that were denied worldliness (à la Kioko) by limited publication and being ignored by scholars is to articulate a resistant imaginary of Global South comics, asserting that they deserve equal consideration with Euro-American artists such as Chris Ware, Alison Bechdel, Art Spiegelman, and the like who occupy the rapidly ossifying canon of comics.

To say that Anglophone comic studies are fixated on American and European comics is at once obvious and important to acknowledge. In non-Western comic studies, it has become commonplace to argue that comics have become legitimized as literature around the world and that global comic studies as an academic field has matured into a proper discipline, while pointing out that comics and the study of

---

[1] The term "born global" is not to be confused with Rebecca Walkowitz's (2017) "born translated," which describes works that are initially published in multiple languages—a related though different kind of literary privilege.
[2] The most notable Global South comic that has become the darling of Western critics is Marjane Satrapi's *Persepolis*, in part because even though it was written by an Iranian, it is highly critical of the post-Shah Iranian regime and of many Islamic cultural norms, such as the hijab, while unabashedly embracing Western music, film, and comics.

them are not confided to the USA and Europe. Examples abound, but collections such as *Picturing Childhood: Youth in Transnational Comics* (Heimermann and Tullis, 2017), *Comics as a Nexus of Cultures* (Berninger, Ecke, and Haberkorn, 2010), and *Multicultural Comics* (Aldama, 2011) make these now standard claims, against which one would be unwise to argue. Comic studies even today frequently urges readers to accept the seriousness of comics and their international nature, perhaps because we still harbor lingering insecurities from comics previously being incorrectly defined as one-dimensional unsophisticated American pulp fare confined to children's stories and tired superhero tropes whose study stood outside (or below) literary studies.[3]

Graphic Novels and Comics as World Literature takes these two central legitimizing tenets of contemporary global comics studies as a baseline from which to expand. In other words, these notions do not require further expansion but what does necessitate advocacy are theoretical and methodological Global South comic frameworks in conjunction with culturally informed case studies steeped in regional studies and local comic traditions. We understand that comics are serious art and not the strict purview of the Western world, despite the way Western comics have been centered in the field. However, we also understand that we cannot simply ignore the Eurocentric trajectory of comic studies in Anglophone studies that we have inherited, hence this positioning of ourselves, but we would like to get on with the business of thinking about non-Western comics without constant reference to this limiting disciplinary genealogy— that is why the introduction tackles this topic while the chapters in the collection largely ignore it. In short, global comics and graphic novels offer scholars an amazing array of possibilities when analyzed by area-specific comic specialists who can tease out both the specificities of a local context *and* ties to other, including global concerns, rather than simply Western ones. Although Eurocentrism is rarely proclaimed, too often reading non-Western comics globally has simply meant reading them in reference to Western comics' influence or creating a depoliticized comics World Literature that disavows, often without acknowledging as much, the politics of representation in which non-Western comics and comic studies are steeped. These approaches often rely on an interpretation of the visuality of comics aligning with, and often explicitly citing, Will Eiser's formulation that comics are "universally understood images" (Eisner 1996, 2). This collection posits that even though one cannot deny the immediacy and power of images, comics *are* particular, informed by the cultures and traditions from which they emerge and that their universality is a Eurocentric illusion. As noted by innumerable scholars, Colonialism universalized whiteness, Western superiority, Christianity, and many other notions while otherizing and particularizing that which was outside of them, i.e. the non-Western world. This is all to say that Eurocentrism, in this case via universalism, is embedded in many of the foundational concepts and structures of comic studies, not merely because its gives most of its attention to Western subjects.

---

[3] Claiming marginalization is also a convenient rhetorical maneuver to create exigence in a field traditionally dominated by Euro-American white men who have decidedly benefited the most from marginalization in literary studies.

The task of this collection is to conceptualize non-reductive ways of reading and understanding Global South comics in and of themselves without prioritizing Western legibility. However, this collection cannot bear the burden of representing the entire world as such—producing a Global South one-size-fits-all singularity of theory and method—but rather signals the value of multifarious decentered approaches to specific comics and their traditions from the Middle East, Africa, Latin America, Asia, and indigenous Global South communities in the Global North. It does so to embrace the responsibility of understating various comic traditions around the world as equals who demand that we reshape our ways of knowing them rather than reshape them to our ways of knowing—this is, that we attempt as best we can to read them on their own terms. To wit, the articles themselves in this collection do the best work in this regard, articulating numerous ingenious approaches. Eurocentrism is defined by its narrowness while Global South reading is attendant to innumerable local forms and themes making useful analysis spectacularly diverse. However, multifariousness and capaciousness are slippery. Generalizing Global South approaches to comics is difficult, but herein they are based on an organic intellectualism that assumes localized forms, histories, representations, and related issues are best understood when studied with the locale itself centered via specialists with deep, often personal, regional and historical knowledge. This collection though does not propose itself as a comprehensive answer to the problem of how to read all the Global South comics in the world. Rather, building off of the extant, though sparse, scholarship on reading Global South comics both attuned to their cultural particularities and global solidarities this collection hopes to shift the conversation on these texts while acknowledging its participation in the system it wishes to change. As contrapuntal as this collection aims to be in some ways, it is also of this moment as World Literature is increasingly being taken to task for its Eurocentrism by scholars such as Aamir Mufti and Ian Almond and in this way hopefully contributes to a growing critical wave of politically informed examinations.

Given the solidarities we seek and the inherent limitations of reading a variety of comics from innumerable traditions, what can we say definitively about the methodology that this collection proposes? Although I am tempted to unravel the traditions from which these comics belong as internally diverse and subject to regional literary hegemonies as complex as their relationships with the rest of the world, reading globally will have to do for now. Even so, this collection does not offer a master narrative of comics as World Literature but rather offers alternative routes by getting in the weeds, or the trenches, of contextualized close reading.

One of the few literary projects of late that has truly attempted to circumvent the West in close-reading literature globally is Ian Almond's *World Literature Decentered*. His definition of reading in a worldly sense is perhaps the notion of World Literature and comics most in solidarity with *Graphic Novels and Comics as World Literature*: "A truly post-Western World Literature would need *praxis* as well as *teoria*, and would have to be willing to cross languages as well as continents, and canons as well as worlds" (Almond 2021, 14). This willingness to first acknowledge the Western bent of World Literature and then transgress both what has been legitimized as the proper subject of World Literature and comic studies along with the often ill-fitting and even arbitrary borders and disciplinary silos we find ourselves in embodies much of the spirit of this collection. Essentially, we share the above agenda and ultimately are curious to see what we get when we disavow the division of the worlds we have inherited.

Beyond how to read particular non-Western comics within their own traditions and World Literature as a stand-alone field, this collection as the title suggests is also interested in considering how graphic texts engage with the field of World Literature as a way of thinking about comic intertextuality. Prominent comic scholars, such as Hillary Chute and Frederick Luis Aldama, engage a variety of comic forms within a given non-Western literary tradition. Others address larger fields such as Denson, Meyer, and Stein's *Transnational Perspectives on Graphic Narratives* (2013) which considers "the ways that graphic narratives have been shaped by aesthetic, social, political, economic, and cultural interactions that reach across national boundaries in an interconnected globalizing world" (1).[4] *Graphic Novels and Comics as World Literature* perhaps most seamlessly compliments Mehta and Mukherji's *Postcolonial Comics* (2015) which denies "a Western priority, authority and determination" of cultural productions such as graphic novels (12). Dominic Davies, a contributor to this collection, has also previously highlighted the production of comics in emergent and globalizing urban centers. It must be said though that despite these transnational approaches most comic scholars have not addressed World Literature as a formal field, much less as one capable of subverting and problematizing comic studies' narrow Eurocentric focus. Moreover, extant scholarship that has treated comics as World Literature have frequently eschewed the intersecting notions of postcolonialism, decolonial theory, the Global South, and similar approaches that not only argue for inclusion of non-Western texts within newly forming canons and ways of reading, but critique Eurocentric literary systems. This collection, then, seeks to build off of the provocative work of these postcolonially inclined comic scholars above while engaging with the field of World Literature and its penchant to elide politics.

To date, the sparse theoretical work done to formally link World Literature and comic studies has been done primarily by Monika Schmitz-Emans (2015, 2019) and Charlotta Salmi (2018, 2020). As has become customary, both place Goethe and his *Weltliteratur* at the nexus of their discussions and contextualize non-Western comics within Goethe's concepts and their direct descendants. While this approach usefully creates epistemological geologies that dismantle the specious borders erected by national literatures for Global South comics, they also generally cordon off World Literature from the politics of representation. While innovative in their loosening of the strictures of World Literature, their analysis also represents an orthodoxy in World Literature that does not take as a primary concern the decentering of Euro-American preoccupations of comic studies—only fleetingly alluding to figures such as Edward Said when referencing the flawed Eurocentric version of World Literature currently prominent in comic studies. To their credit, Schmitz-Emans and Salmi take the initiative

---

[4] At the same time the authors explain "this volume concentrates on largely American genres and productions as an exemplary field of transnational exchange," significantly delimiting the scope of their transnational approach (3).

to consider the ways that World Literature and graphic narratives need to be thought of together, representing an important maneuver. Salmi in particular demonstrates an awareness of the value of postcolonial critical perspectives in several articles arguing that comic studies has not yet come to "grapple with the cultural mediation of the economic, cultural, and political relations of domination and subordination" (2020). Indeed, for Salmi "Comics are not just a popular art form but also an alternative, radical one" and this collection seeks to both disrupt a Western-orientated *status quo* and build off of some of these initial forays into critical Global South perspectives on comic studies (2020). Their initial forays can hopefully be mobilized along with this collection into resistant imaginaries with lateral solidarities that highlight the way Global South subjects recognize one another and view their conditions as shared.

However useful the limited initial critical interventions into pairing World Literature and Global South comic studies have been, important questions remain largely unexamined. Questions such as the role of translation that have been developed in comparative literature and World Literature are largely lacking in comic studies, as has a conceptualizing of the world as a unit of comics. Also, the particular conditions of the circulation of comics as a graphic and visual medium that often emulates the circulation of word-based texts but just as often must seek out or create different modes of circulation is underdeveloped. While not entirely resolved, these issues and many others are handled in this collection to expand on limited earlier research.

Although the large-scale theoretical and political considerations mentioned above aim to intervene in various discourses concerning comic and literary studies, the chapters themselves will demonstrate the value of this collection as they address these issues as well as innumerable others. Formulating a shared sensibility for this collection is useful in understanding its goals and ultimate trajectory, but it is the wide diversity of approaches, geographies, methodologies, languages, and genealogies borne out in the articles themselves that most clearly express the collection's character. Happily, the articles herein reflect the disparate and multifarious nature of the world of comics and use innovative methods to analyze on both the micro level by close reading individual works and images and on the macro level by considering large-scale historical and theoretical phenomena. Whether Arabic "visual poems," a Spanish Columbian–Ecuadorian coming of age story, Korean historical dramas, an indigenous narrative from Australia, innumerable Francophone African comics, or the subgenre of Japanese "Boys Love" manga in Chilean comics, this collection covers a stunning array of comics that too often fall outside the purview of Anglophone comic studies and offers equally rich critical approaches. I hesitate to coalesce them into a singularity because they reflect the disparate and fractured nature of the world but all share, whether explicitly or implicitly, in an anti-colonial global connectivity. Just as Global South subjectivity is very much in-process today, we see the value of transcending the nation state as a unit of comparative analysis without necessarily being able to fully embody and deploy that impetus. This collection imagines itself as a part of a process that takes a granular approach to often overlooked comics with an eye to their potential within the larger frameworks of south-south exchange, transculturism, and translocality.

Structurally, this collection can be perhaps best understood as bifurcated between those chapters which foreground theoretical comic concerns in the first half of the collection (Chapters 1 to 7), using individual comics to manifest those theories, and those in the collection's second half (Chapters 8 to 13) that are centered more on unpacking individual, usually marginalized, comics for their culturally specific insights with an eye towards global solidarities, World Literature, and comic theory writ large. Both these deductive and inductive, or macro and micro, approaches contribute to reading comics globally and nearly all transgress these borders even when they favor one side of this theory/practice divide. That is, all concern themselves with specificity while attuned to larger theoretical questions, type and degree being the main difference.

Opening the collection is Dominic Davies' consideration of graphic reportage, or "comic journalism." In considering comics' unique formal abilities to portray borders, Davies analyzes three separate comics about refugees that complicate the ease with which some discourses within World Literature privilege cross-border mobility as a condition of the contemporary world. For Davies, the seeming fluidity of comic narratives told via segmented comic panels uncannily reflects a world that mobilizes idyllic notions of borderless and mobile modernity while at the same time cruelly limiting the mobility of many, creating in Davies' view a "carceral terrain." Also challenging common notions of graphic narratives and World Literature, Jasmin Wrobel's article repositions Latin American women as central to South American comics. Providing expansive historical background, Wrobel describes the comic artist Powerpaola as much more than the "Latin America Marjane Satrapi" as she is sometimes referred to abroad. By examining Powerpaola's *Virus Tropical*, this article articulates the struggles of female Latin American comic artists in a traditionally male-dominated field and argues that Powerpaola and the women she has mentored are becoming essential in the study of comics in the region and beyond.

Continuing the above considerations of form, Dima Nasser's article on *The Apartment in Bab El-Louk* from Egypt examines a comic that defies easy categorization. Describing the book aptly as a series of "visual poems," Nasser points out how it resists the hegemony of the graphic novel form. Nasser argues that the graphic novel has been established as an authorizing conduit for Global South comics, particularly from the Middle Eastern, to be translated and circulated globally. The article examines how *The Apartment in Bab El-Louk* rebukes the graphic novel form and yet manages to gain success beyond Egypt. In a similarly unpredictable confluence of form and location, Camila Gutiérrez's innovative article tracks Japanese "Boys Love" tropes in Latin American comics about sexual alterity. With particular focus on Chilean artist Pía Prado Bley, Gutiérrez demonstrates how the adoption of Boys Love tropes into Latin American comics establishes a comic code for expressing queerness that while explicitly "unsaid and unseen," allows for the expression of homoeroticism that can evade censorship. She argues that comics are particularly suited for this task and that the adoption of a foreign, yet decodable, trope is essential to its success.

Although all the articles in this collection are expansive in scope, none is probably as broad and comprehensive as Sandra Federici's article on Francophone African comics. Federici's sociological approach importantly repudiates common assumptions that the lack of scholarship on African comics is due to a lack of primary texts. Beyond demonstrating that these rationales for the underrepresentation of African comics in comic studies is incorrect by meticulously documenting texts, authors, publishers, funders, and the like from all over Francophone Africa, this article articulates the complex means of production and circulation that both inhibit and enable them to become worldly texts.

Allison Blecker's focus on Palestine begins a gradual shift in the collection to more focused geographical concerns. Many of the articles in this collection rethink World Literature through place and comics, but Blecker takes on a particularly difficult notion of place and placelessness by contemplating Palestinian literature and comics as World Literature. As Palestinians are based in Palestine, and in a widely flung diaspora, Blecker questions how the assumptions of World Literature apply to Palestinian literature. She analyzes Palestinian-American comic artist Leila Abdelrazaq's *Baddawi* to argue that the comic, like much Palestinian literature, slips between categories making Palestinians superficially emblematic of a utopian stateless freedom espoused by many worldly theories but also largely incarcerated, literally and figuratively.

Also using a historical lens to highlight often elided lives in a vast community, Debadrita Chakraborty examines dystopic urban space in Indian graphic novels to unravel the myth of "India Rising" and reveals subaltern ways of being. In the process, Chakraborty usefully tracks the development of the Indian graphic novel "from adolescent fantasies to a cultural mode of artistic expression and communication" and ultimately mobilizes biopolitics and necropolitics to theorize dystopic urban space via close readings of seminal Indian comics such as *Delhi Calm* and *Corridor*.

In an entirely different manner, Jin Lee in her chapter addresses an equally vast subject: time in comics. Using Pheng Cheah's contribution to World Literature theory that stresses the temporal-normative dimension of worldliness, Lee unpacks Suk Gendry-Kim's graphic novel *Grass* that details the lives of Korean women forced into sex slavery during World War II, commonly termed "comfort women" in English. This article uses the grass of the book's title to rethink time in this comic that confronts extreme trauma with implications for addressing time in comics in the Global South at large.

Catherine Sly's analysis of *Ubby's Underdogs* by indigenous Australian Brenton E. McKenna, like Blecker and Lee, focuses on place but unpacks that place as vastly more complex than commonly understood in comic studies. Rather than representing indigenous Australians as insular as is often done, *Ubby's Underdogs*, Sly argues, situates indigenous cultures and peoples as a central nexus of post-World War II Australia. Resisting the erasure of indigenous people from the modern national narrative of Australia, as well as highlighting the role of a variety of non-white peoples, particularly Asians, Sly argues for an indigenous Global South perspective emanating from the storytelling traditions of the Yawuru people from the north western region of what is now called Australia.

Shilpa Daithota Bhat also addresses tradition and history in her chapter on the many reimaginings of the classic Indian *Ramayana* epic. In particular, she addresses

Samhita Arni's 2011 comic adaptation, *Sita's Ramayana*, that gives more agency to the classical figure of Sita in conjunction with revived interest in a television adaptation (the most watched television show in the world) that was re-aired to great fanfare during the first lockdowns of the COVID-19 pandemic in India.

What follows are chapters that all take innovative and timely approaches to individual texts of varying visibility abroad. Jana Fedke takes a popular Western comic, *Black Panther*, that represents a well-established and fairly generic superhero form and applies the newly coined term Africanfuturism to it. By approaching a familiar text type in a new way, Fedke articulates a new metric for a comic that at once is firmly American but has pretensions as a franchise to honor and represent African cultures. This Africanfuturist metric examines the ways the comic both meets and fails to fulfill its own Afro-centric promises. A text with almost no exposure beyond the borders of its country of origin, Malaysia, is *Menggapai Bintang (Reach for the Stars)*. Authors Mohd Muzhafar Idrus, Habibah Ismail, and Hazlina Abdullah highlight a text never addressed in comic studies in European languages to my knowledge to argue that the seemingly innocuous fare of school-age antics actually enacts a neoliberal agenda. By highlighting an elided dominant neoliberal ideology the article problematizes the ease with which they are usually read in favor of a critical view that imagines them as important postcolonial national narratives. Lastly, and certainly not least, Sheng-Mei Ma examines the graphic memoir of *Approved for Adoption*. Ma delineates the multiple ways in which the narrator of the comic splits himself between his Korean origins and Belgian adoptive home, never at ease as he rails against the language and culture of his adoptive land while indebted to it at the same time. As in several other chapters in this collection, this division stands as constitutive and uncomfortable, expressing itself uniquely in the comic form.

Ultimately, this collection is as dizzyingly diverse as the world of comics. The authors brought together in these pages come from an astounding array of cultural and linguistic traditions. It is their overwhelming variety that provides innumerable openings into various comic traditions. While each is a complete work, it is my hope that the broader culture of comics that they each individually gesture to becomes more prominent and available for scholars and readers on a global scale. The Global South contains multitudes and when we refuse to cater to the preoccupations of the Global North, instead delving deeply into culturally specific context, we are richly rewarded and these chapters demonstrate that.

I would be remiss not to mention that the production of this collection unfortunately took place during a pandemic and its completion feels like a triumph. While writing about worldliness and the ways we are connected via comics in different parts of the world, we often felt unease at the uncanny way a virus transgressed borders while people and literature have had a more difficult time. The irony that a virus became seamlessly worldly while this collection takes pains to explain how fraught worldliness is for Global South comics, their creators, and their subjects was not lost on us. In a very small way, the production of this collection embodies some of the difficulties of (non-viral) worldliness and I applaud everyone who brought it into existence despite significant obstacles.

References

Aldama, Frederick Luis. 2011. *Multicultural Comics: from Zap to Blue Beetle*. Austin, TX: University of Texas Press.

Almond, Ian. 2021. *World Literature Decentered: Beyond the "West" through Turkey, Mexico and Bengal*. London: Routledge.

Berninger, Mark, Ecke, Jochen, and Haberkorn, Gideon (eds.). 2010. *Comics as a Nexus of Cultures: Essays on the Interplay of Media, Disciplines and International Perspectives*. Jefferson, NC: McFarland & Co.

Denson, Shane, Meyer, Christina, and Stein, Daniel (eds.). 2014. *Transnational Perspectives on Graphic Narratives: Comics at the Crossroads*. New York: Bloomsbury.

Eisner, Will. (1996). *Graphic Storytelling and Visual Narrative*. Tamarac, FL: Poorhouse Press.

Heimermann, Mark, and Tullis, Brittany. 2017. *Picturing Childhood: Youth in Transnational Comics*. Austin, TX: University of Texas Press.

Mehta, Binita, and Mukherji, Pia. 2015. *Postcolonial Comics: Texts, Events, Identities*. New York: Routledge Taylor and Francis Group.

Nefetiti. 2015. "The State of African Literature in US Ivy League." http://grandmotherafrica.com/state-african-literature-us-ivy-league/ (accessed January 17, 2022).

Salmi, Charlotta. 2018. "The Worldliness of Graphic Narrative." In *The Cambridge Companion to World Literature*, edited by Ben Etherington and Jarad Zimbler. Cambridge, UK: Cambridge University Press, 180–96.

Salmi, Charlotta. 2020. "Sequential Art in the Age of Postcolonial Production: Comic Collectives in Israel and South Africa." In *Popular Postcolonialisms: Discourses of Empire and Popular Culture*, edited by Nadia Atia and Kate Houlden, New York: Routledge, 70–86.

Schmitz-Emans, Monika. 2015. "Graphic Narrative as World Literature." In Stein, Daniel, and Thon, Jan-Noël, eds. *Comic Strips to Graphic Novels*. Berlin: De Gruyter, 385–406.

Schmitz-Emans, Monika. 2019. "World Literature in Graphic Novels and Graphic Novels as World Literature." In Fang, Weigui, ed. *Tensions in World Literature: Between the Local and the Universal*. London: Palgrave Macmillan, 219–36.

Walkowitz, Rebecca L. 2017. *Born Translated: the Contemporary Novel in an Age of World Literature*. New York: Columbia University Press.

1

Pages of Exception: Graphic Reportage as World Literature

Dominic Davies

Introduction: Pages of Exception

At the center of Olivier Kugler's book-length work of graphic reportage, *Escaping Wars and Waves: Encounters with Syrian Refugees* (2018), is a double-page splash characteristic of the author's distinctive style (see Figure.1.1). In all of his work, Kugler does away with the conventional "narrative architecture" of comics (Chute 2008, 454), the panels and gutters of which segment space into a series of temporal units. Instead, he draws striking, double-page splash scenes of refugee camps, using other sequential techniques to nudge the readerly gaze across the borderless page. Movement is everything in Kugler's reportage: his comics are stories, certainly, the text either describing the conditions and details of camps or reproducing the real-life testimonies of those refugees Kugler has interviewed; but these stories are often conveyed in a peculiarly *immobile* visual form. As I will show in this chapter, the resulting tension between motion and stasis, image and narrative, mobility and immobility, repeats across much graphic reportage drawn to the spaces of exception—refugee camps, detention centers, slums, and other spaces of enforced non-citizenship—that arise from the legal and spatial paradoxes of the twenty-first-century's newly "carceral humanitarian" regime (Oliver, 2017; see also Rifkind 2020).

The spaces of exception depicted in pages of graphic reportage such as Kugler's challenge some of the theoretical precepts of World Literature, allowing us to think of a "carceral World Literature" instead. I am of course not the first to worry that theories of World Literature tend to lift texts into overly abstract or idealized realms, whether of cosmopolitan exchange, the marketplace, or unevenly developed world-systems. Emily Apter's *Against World Literature* challenged many such theories, insisting that— to take one of her starkest examples—for Palestinian artists and writers in the era of the checkpoint and the camp, the world's translation zones are not "porous boundar[ies]" but thresholds "of untranslatability and political blockade" (2013, Ch. V). The enclosures and blockades of carceral humanitarianism so drastically exemplified by the Palestinian case is, for Apter, the material disavowal of World Literature. This regime imprisons refugees and other displaced people in extra-legal holding pens governed

Figure 1.1 The double-page spread at the center of Olivier Kugler's *Escaping Wars and Waves* shows a refugee encampment in a public park on the Greek Island of Kos (Kugler 2018, 38–39). Reproduced with the permission of the artist.

by non-state actors, including humanitarian and aid organizations, transforming camp inhabitants into "criminals and charity cases simultaneously" (Oliver 2017, 6).

This does not mean that the critique of carceral humanitarianism is directly targeted at humanitarian organizations, who clearly perform essential life-saving work. Rather, as the architect Eyal Weizman has argued, it is when humanitarianism is "abused by state, supra-state and military action" that it becomes a "means for exercising contemporary violence and for governing the displaced, the enemy and the unwanted" (2011, 3-4). It is possible to commend humanitarian organizations for their work, while also observing that they plug in legal and territorial gaps in political governance that release national and supra-national states from their obligations under international human rights law. This situation leads philosopher Kelly Oliver to pose the question: if humanitarian organizations "are designed to mitigate and control violence and death to avoid the worst violence and death, according to calculations of lesser evils, then we must ask, what is the most evil, or the worst evil?" (2017, 14). The answer to that question is, of course, genocide, and an event as horrific as the Holocaust. But this conclusion yields yet another paradox: according to this logic, the refugee camps on the outskirts of Fortress Europe are constructed in the name of preventing the very spaces of exception that they themselves have become. As the Greek interior minister, Panagiotis Kouroublis, commented after a visit to Idomeni camp on Greece's border with Macedonia in March 2016: "I do not hesitate to say that this is a modern-day

Dachau, a result of the logic of closed borders" (Worley and Dearden 2016; see also Oliver 2017, 20).

Contemporary graphic reportage is overwhelmingly drawn to refugee stories of migration and displacement (Rifkind 2017; Parker 2018; Mickwitz 2020), and beyond that to scenes of conflict and war more generally (Chute 2016; Prorokova & Tal eds. 2018; Embury & Minichiello 2018). More often than not, it foregrounds the carceral spaces of containment and immobility that, as Apter might argue, run fluid or overly abstracted conceptions of "world" aground. Even as its images—along with the stories they tell—circulate beyond the borders of such spaces, as most definitions of World Literature would insist they do, graphic reportage continually reminds us not only of the borders that have been crossed, but also of the people who have been left behind, unable to move. It is no coincidence that, as I have argued elsewhere (Davies 2019, 3-4; 2020c, 4-6), the refugee comic's archetype and comic journalism's progenitor is Joe Sacco's *Palestine*, a work published serially during the final years of the First Palestinian Intifada (1993-5) and then published in book-form by Fantagraphics in 2001. At the very center of the book-bound edition of Sacco's well-known comic is a double-page splash (see Sacco 2001, 146-7). It stands out from the rest of the narrative because it is starkly cut away from the rhythms of Sacco's usual pages, which tend to be criss-crossed with multiple grids, text boxes, and speech bubbles—those basic visual mechanisms that propel the narrative forward. The double-page spread stands out for another reason, too: it uncharacteristically shows the Gazan refugee camp, in which much of the remainder of *Palestine* takes place, from a bird's-eye perspective—the rest of the comic is almost entirely drawn from ground-level, looking over Joe's shoulder or up from the floor. With this unusual vantage of height, we see that the camp is in a state of disarray, suffocated by the tightening Israeli occupation, though still inhabited by Palestinian refugees going about their daily lives as best they can.

The effect is clear: by drawing a splash image of the refugee camp devoid of the formal architecture of the comic's page, Sacco uses the absence of graphic narrative's most basic apparatus to suggest the camp as a "space of exception." This space of exception, a phrase developed by the philosopher Giorgio Agamben (1998) to describe Nazi concentration camps during the Holocaust, therefore turns up in both the content *and form* of Sacco's comic. It is in this sense that we can talk of a *page of exception*—a page that is cut partially away from, and yet still contained within, the rest of the graphic narrative. Partly under Sacco's influence, all of the examples of graphic reportage discussed in this chapter similarly depict different spaces of exception (a refugee camp, a detention center, a border city) in an image that is at least partly cut away from the narrative architecture of the comic.

With these pages of exception, graphic reportage insists on the borders and checkpoints that inform Apter's argument against World Literature. However, it is not my contention that graphic reportage supports Apter's politics of untranslatability: it seems to me that the very existence of the reportage itself—which circulates stories and images of refugees as neither criminals nor charity cases beyond the confined borders of the camp and detention center—is itself evidence for a contrary position. Instead, I argue that, because graphic reportage so thoroughly troubles the notions of both "world" *and* "literature," it might in fact help us to reach beyond currently hegemonic theories of World Literature for a perspective that takes account of the world's carceral spaces. In this effort, it perhaps comes closest to Timothy Brennan's recent suggestion for an "alternative to the present understanding of World Literature" (2018, 34–5). Though Brennan himself offers no textual examples in support of his proposition, graphic reportage anticipates his call for a World Literature that reinstates "a critical encounter with conflicting movements, antagonistic constituencies, hostile theories, discordant practices, unequal access, mutual epistemological incomprehension, and historically situated openings or foreclosures—in other words, the real world of peoples and texts" (2018, 34–5). Brennan's model of "World Literature," which departs from those of Damrosch, Casanova, WReC, and others, is riven with *both* movement and stasis. As I show, this (im)mobile tension turns up both in the circulation of contemporary graphic reportage and the formal techniques it deploys on the page.

To make the case for graphic reportage as a "carceral World Literature," I will draw on a series of different concrete examples. While the examples I offer are fairly distinct in their aesthetic styles and formal techniques, they all follow Sacco by orbiting their longer narratives around a central splash page that depicts a space of exception. The camp is the "pure space of exception," according to Agamben, an extra-legal territory where inhabitants are "resolutely separated from the rights of man" and, through a process of "inclusive exclusion," reduced to nothing more than "bare life" (1998, 134). It is in the camp, a space in which "humanitarianism [is] separated from politics," that the fractured terrain of carceral humanitarianism begins; it is the camp that reduces the refugee to bare life, functioning as a "limit concept that radically calls into question the fundamental categories of the nation-state" (134). Centering this space of exception allows for a carceral World Literature attuned to a geography of checkpoints and borders to be theorized, and the pages of graphic reportage—which is overwhelmingly drawn to *and from* refugee camps—presents itself as the *place* where such work should begin.

If Agamben's notion of the space of exception still feels some way from Sacco's Gazan refugee camp, we might tease out their enduring structural connections by pausing briefly to reflect on Art Spiegelman's *Maus* (1980–91). More influential even than Sacco on contemporary graphic narratives (see in't Veld 2019, 8–15; Davies 2020b, 3–8), Spiegelman's depictions of his father Vladek's memories of Auschwitz are some of the most read, discussed, and translated comics pages in the world. Vladek's time in Auschwitz is contained to roughly the third quarter of Book Two, in a chapter entitled "Auschwitz (Time Flies)" (Spiegelman 2003, 199–234). It is one of the most compelling and terrifying sections of *Maus*, and the whole narrative revolves around the concentration camp, establishing it as the comic's central horror. Spiegelman's drawings are forensic in detail, holding the unseen and "unspeakable" traumatic space of Auschwitz up to artistic scrutiny (see Mandel 2006). In particular, Spiegelman makes grim diagrammatic reproductions of the gas chambers and ovens, in which he draws their constituent parts and operating procedures in clinical detail (2003, 230). We know that Spiegelman edited drafts of Sacco's *Palestine* in the mid-1990s, but beyond this direct artistic influence there has emerged a wider trend across many graphic narratives to draw spaces of exception in the comics form and, more specifically, to break those images away from the usual comics architecture of panels and frames.

It is true that Spiegelman's drawings of Auschwitz never quite settle on a single splash page of the camp, as Sacco and his later successors do. However, there is one moment when *Maus*'s claustrophobically boxed panels—or "coffins of memory," as Spiegelman describes them (see Gorrara 2018, 120)—break away into a half-page splash. Drawn from a bird's-eye perspective, this splash shows "Auschwitz I" and "Auschwitz II, Birkenau" connected via a network of roads and train tracks, and shadowed with plumes of smoke extending from ominous chimneys. In the panels that remain scattered around the edges of this image, Vladek describes Birkenau as a space of pure death:

> Auschwitz, it was a camp where they gave you to work so they didn't finish you too fast./ Birkenau was even more bad. It was 800 people in a building made for 50 horses. There it was just a DEATH place with Jews waiting for Gas.
> (Spiegelman 2003, 211)

Significantly, the text boxes step around the splash image of this "DEATH place," both including and excluding it from the comic's narrative architecture, and thus reiterating in comics form the camp's "inclusive exclusion" and the conditions of bare life that its spatial processes make possible (Agamben 1998, 7–8). In her reading of *Maus* alongside Agamben's slightly later *Remnants of Auschwitz* (1999), Hillary Chute points to the presence of a shared paradox in both Holocaust testimony and comics grammar: just as, for Agamben, Holocaust testimony pivots on the "sayable and the unsayable" (1999, 158), the comics form operates on similar dichotomies: "inside, outside; containable, uncontainable; figurable, unfigurable" (Chute 2016, 193). In *Maus*, as in all of the examples discussed in this chapter, we find this tension between the mobility and immobility of narrative, and between the legality and extra-legality of these environments, reflected spatially on the page: it appears in the breaking down of form, such as grids, gutters, and panels, but *also* in the content of the image itself—that is, both the camp and the splash page as a space of exception.

The other examples I discuss in this chapter draw more recent and less-remembered or documented spaces of exception into view. These include refugee camps, border cities, and detention centers, all depicted in similar splash or half-splash pages that are both partially inside and outside of the main graphic narrative. My aim in highlighting this formal repetition is of course not to pit contemporary stories of suffering and states of exception against Vladek's memories of the Holocaust—quite the opposite. Rather, I draw attention to these striking continuities because they allow me to make two related points: first, it reveals the continued and growing use of the comics form to depict such spaces of exception, along with their inhabitants who are reduced to conditions of bare life; and second, it highlights the extent to which such spaces, *as well as* the comics that document them, have spread across the world through the second half of the twentieth and early twenty-first century. In this stuttering movement between incarcerated immobility and cross-national circulation, graphic reportage begins to assemble an idea—perhaps even a theory—of carceral World Literature.

Graphic Reportage as World Literature

Before turning to our examples, there remains an additional question that must be attended to here if we are to think of graphic reportage as World Literature: if graphic reportage troubles and incarcerates existing conceptions of "world," how might it challenge notions of "literature," too?

In her influential article, "Comics as Literature?," Chute took the examples of Spiegelman and Sacco to make the case to literary scholars that they should be reading graphic narratives. Describing "nonfiction comics" as "the strongest genre in the field" (2008, 452), she was cautious to separate out "comics" and "graphic narratives" from what is often called, somewhat confusingly, "the graphic novel" (453). As Chute and others have noted, "the graphic novel" emerged as a convenient marketing tool for bookstores, soothing the anxieties of middle-class readers and, indeed, academic staff in English departments concerned about comics' "lowbrow" associations (see Davies 2017a, 334–5). Katalin Orbán somewhat disdainfully describes the "partial absorption" of those comics described as graphic novels "into the category of the literary" as a process of cultural "gentrification" (2015, 123). Others have used more forceful—and peculiarly spatial—language, viewing the label "graphic novel" as a "land grab" by literary scholars that "ghettoizes" those comics "deemed unworthy of critical attention" (Labio 2011, 126). It matters little, it seems, and as Chute also observes (2008, 453), that many of the comics most often described as graphic novels—including Spiegelman's *Maus*, Sacco's *Palestine*, Marjane Satrapi's *Persepolis* (2003), and Alison Bechdel's *Fun Home* (2006)—are not in fact novels at all, but rather (auto)biographies, travelogues, and memoirs. Even Will Eisner, the artist credited with popularizing "the graphic novel," first used the term in 1978 to describe his book *A Contract with God*—not a novel, but a collection of graphic short stories. Thus the ubiquitous use of the term "graphic novel" to describe what is in fact graphic nonfiction, graphic memoir, graphic reportage, and so on, reveals the cultural work that the word "novel" performs.

In her discussion of comics as literature, Chute's immediate expansion of "literature" beyond the strictly fictional was therefore not a technical oversight, but rather central to her argument. As she stressed, one of the reasons literary scholars needed "to direct more sustained attention" to comics was precisely because the form demanded "a rethinking of narrative [and] genre" (463). Any reading of "Graphic Novels" or even "Comics" as 'World Literature,' an ambition to which *this* edited collection aspires, must therefore acknowledge the disconcerting history and historicity of its key terms. Both the novelistic and the literary are unsettled by graphic reportage, which is very much a continuation of—rather than a generic deviation from—the graphic novel's recent history. Graphic reportage takes inspiration from Sacco's pioneering work in "comics journalism," which in turn has roots in long twentieth-century histories of both underground comix and the journalistic drawing of conflict and war (see Hatfield 2005; Chute 2016; Mickwitz 2016). Of course, the term "graphic novel" has undoubtedly played a formative—rather than simply descriptive—role in the history of graphic narrative, and Chute's contention that nonfiction comics should be at the center of an emerging graphic canon did not go uncriticized (see, for example, Saunders 2009, 294). But with translations into thirty languages and fourteen languages respectively, there can be no doubt that Spiegelman's *Maus* and Sacco's *Palestine* must be at the center of any *world* literary canon of graphic novels.

If we accept the importance of nonfiction in the development of the modern graphic novel, why am I in this chapter not arguing for "graphic non-fiction as World Literature," or perhaps even "comics journalism as World Literature," instead? Let me take the latter case first. Though originally attributed to Joe Sacco's serially published and later book-bound works, the phrase "comics journalism" is increasingly used today to refer to the current surge in short journalistic webcomics (see Mickwitz 2016, 144). Just a few pages in length, and published only online via platforms such as *Cartoon Movement*, *The Cartoon Picayune*, *The Nib*, and *Drawing the Times*, this short-form journalism floats free of conventional printing and circulation markets and costs, and in some cases is more explicitly "factual" than it is visually experimental, formally innovative, or meaningfully literary. I generalize here, of course, and would be the first to point out several groundbreaking online comics (see, for example, Olle and Wallman 2014, Pourquié and Tervonen 2016). However, because it travels so freely online, comics journalism is more often described as a "transnational genre" (Banita 2014, 51), and while this might fit well with some models of World Literature, it moves away from the carceral World Literature I am outlining here.

Meanwhile, on a semantic level graphic reportage suggests a close relationship to the graphic novel, while remaining differentiated from "graphic nonfiction," which in its generality could include authors as diverse as Spiegelman, Bechdel, and Satrapi. All the examples of graphic reportage I discuss in this chapter are published in codex form, and would appear in the "graphic novel" section of any bookstore. It is important to note, however, that though they primarily circulate as material objects, in every case excerpts have also appeared. Several of Olivier Kugler's drawings were commissioned by media outlets and humanitarian organizations, and published on various websites, before they were collected together as *Escaping Wars and Waves* (2018) and published in both German and English. Kate Evans' *Threads from the Refugee Crisis* (2017) began as a blog on her website before it was picked up by left-wing publisher Verso, who commissioned a book-length graphic narrative. Tings Chak's *Undocumented: The Architecture of Migrant Detention* (2016), first published by *The Architecture Observer* in Canada, was later reissued in a special edition by *Ad Astra Comix*, and Chak features high-definition photographs of several of the comic's pages on her website. And Jon Sack's *La Lucha: The Story of Lucha Castro and Human Rights in Mexico* (2015), was published as both a physical book and an ebook by Verso, while excerpts appeared in a range of online platforms, from *The Guardian* website to the alternative comics platform, *Comics Grinder*. In this selective and partial straddling of online and offline spheres, even the modes of production and circulation of graphic reportage emulate the tension between free-flowing mobility and physical immobility that is indexed in the form and content of their pages.

In their book *Reportage Illustration*, Gary Embury and Mario Minichiello define "reportage [as] 'event-based', meaning that it is an art applied to things of significance happening in the world" (2018, 1). While the examples I include in this chapter exist at the edges of different translation and publication zones, and already have a strong claim upon the category of World Literature, I also opt here for graphic reportage over graphic nonfiction because the term emphasizes the reporting of stories *from*—rather than *about*—the spaces of exception documented in their pages. It is true that all of this graphic work is authored by artists based in the Global North. However, on the one hand, these artists have themselves inhabited the spaces of exception they draw, even if only for a temporary period; and on the other, they all capture the stories and testimonies—often in recorded, direct speech—of the dispossessed and disenfranchised who remain incarcerated in those spaces. As Chute might contend, this drawing "enters the public sphere as a form of witness that takes shape as marks and lines because no other technology could record what it depicts" (2016, 265). Graphic reportage explicitly refutes the shortened media cycles of 24-hour news channels and the objectifying photographic gaze (Orbán 2015; Davies 2020c), insisting on directly recorded testimony while deploying literary techniques that self-reflexively implicate readers—and even the authors themselves—in the politics of carceral humanitarianism (Rifkind 2020). With this eclectic blending of different literary technologies, graphic reportage deepens World Literature to break out stories from the carceral spaces of refugee camps, detention centers, and border cities.

Four Examples of Exception: Greece, France, Canada, and Mexico

In this section, I now read across four examples of graphic reportage to show in more detail how these arguments work in practice and on the page, before returning to their implications for notions of World Literature in my conclusion. I begin with Kugler's most recently published work and then move chronologically backwards in time to conclude with John Sack's drawings of Ciudad Juárez, a city on the Mexico–US border.

Let us return, then, to the central image of Kugler's *Escaping Wars and Waves: Encounters with Syrian Refugees*, briefly introduced at the beginning of this chapter (Kugler 2018, 38–9; see Figure 1.1). The "characters" that populate Kugler's graphic reportage are, as the book's subtitle suggests, "real-life" Syrian asylum seekers caught in encampments on the edges of regional, national, and supra-national territories, including Iraqi Kurdistan, Turkey, and Europe. The double-page splash I am concerned with here introduces a sequence of interviews with displaced Syrians that Kugler conducted in August 2015. Having made the dangerous crossing of the Aegean Sea from Turkey on smuggler-owned dinghies, these Syrians find themselves washed up on the Greek island of Kos, where at the time there was neither a sophisticated border infrastructure, official deportation regime, nor formal encampment. As Kugler's splash page shows, the refugees therefore camp in tents provided by Médecin Sans Frontières (MSF) on pavements and in parks, turning Greek public space at the fringes of Europe into a place of exception. With a series of cues, both textual and visual, Kugler composes a scene of informal encampment that occupies the extra-legal territory of carceral humanitarianism: the refugees are inside of both Greek and European Union territory, and yet they remain without rights, reliant instead on the benevolence of MSF, a humanitarian agency that fills the political vacuum left by the nation-state. Kugler draws both a carceral and humanitarian page of exception.

Like Sacco's image of the Gazan refugee camp, Kugler's page is not only devoid of the usual paraphernalia of comics architecture, but is drawn from a similar bird's-eye point of view. In this latter respect especially, it stands out from Kugler's other images, which tend to be ground-level portraits of individual refugees. Unlike Sacco, however, Kugler does use some techniques familiar to readers of graphic novels—such as carefully positioned speech bubbles and brief authorial captions—to nudge his narrative gently forward. The page is composed so that the reader might begin in the top left-hand corner, as is conventional for an English-speaker, but with its proliferation of detail and effacement of grids and gutters, the invocation of this Western-centric narrative direction is almost immediately subverted. Indeed, the eye is more likely to be drawn to the image's densest section that, on the right-hand side, shows a cluster of tents and the occasional limb or body of a sleeping refugee. An authorial note in the top right-hand corner of the image informs readers that it will take the police from "7–21 days" to authorize the refugees' continued journey to Athens, where their right to remain and seek asylum will be decided. On the island of Kos, the refugees occupy a spatial and legal limbo, able to do nothing but wait and survive in the meantime on extra-political humanitarian aid. It is this carceral immobility that is in turn communicated, I argue, through the indeterminate narrative direction and spatial dislocation of Kugler's graphic reportage.

Though a single image of a static scene, Kugler breathes motion into his drawing with a technique of "visual density" that has since become his trademark style. Kugler recalls developing this technique organically:

> I always returned [from time spent in refugee camps] with a lot of image and text material that I felt the urge to use. I felt that two pages are just not enough space, so, as a necessity, I crammed as many drawings and text information into the layout as I thought I could possibly get away with. [...] the visual density comes partly from the space constraints that come with the territory of editorial work and partly also with my love for including a lot of details onto the pages. When I am on location and I take my reference snaps I make sure to have shots of all the details I see in the interviewee's environment. I guess this approach allows me to create a rich and detailed picture of the people I meet and of the environment I found them in. (Jamieson 2018, n.p.)

The effect of this "visual density" is to cluster abstract, simple line drawings around the central, more detailed colored images. These simpler drawings hang like visual echoes of people or items that were once present but that have now moved on, producing an image that resembles a time-lapse: it is as though Kugler has drawn a series of comics panels split into sequential temporal units but then, rather than organizing those panels into linear succession, has instead overlaid them on top of one another. It can be seen in Figure 1.1 in the examples of passing tourists, the branches of trees, the laundry that has been hung out to dry, and, in the bottom right-hand corner, the curled bodies of sleeping refugees. The resulting paradox of temporal simultaneity allows Kugler to convey a story of both "displacement and emplacement," a doubleness that Candida Rifkind has identified in a number of "migrant detention comics" (2020, 298). This stuttering movement creates a kind of reverberation affect that invests the static depictions of the encampment—and the refugees incarcerated therein—with a strangely immanent feeling of narrative mobility.

It is significant that Kugler's technique is a consequence of his own space constraints as a commissioned journalist and artist, arising from his attempts to pack as much recorded information as possible into the necessarily confined "territory of editorial work" (Jamieson 2018, n.p.). His use of the term "territory" to describe editorial space evocatively couples the spatial confinement of the comic's eventual publication with the physical constrictions of "the interviewee's environment" that it depicts. This is not to suggest that these two spaces are somehow materially identical or of equal significance or weight—after all, as a German artist living in the UK, Kugler is able to leave Kos once his reportage work is done. However, it does point to the material processes of production that have inadvertently heightened the formal aptitude of graphic reportage to document stories from spaces of exception and circulate them beyond carceral borders. In a sense, the two spaces—the camp, and the page that depicts it—are both a consequence of carceral humanitarianism: Kugler himself has in the past been commissioned, as have many other comics journalists, by humanitarian organizations, including MSF. The same humanitarian organization that funds Kugler's reportage provides the tents that house the refugees in his drawings.

The only double-page splash included in Kate Evans' 175-page work of graphic reportage, *Threads from the Refugee Crisis*, similarly reflects on the paradoxes of carceral humanitarianism (Evans 2017, 52–3; see Figure 1.2). It shows Evans herself, identifiable by her flash of pink hair, in the foreground in the left-hand corner. She grips the metal fences of a new industrial site that has been built by the French authorities to house spillover refugees from the "Jungle" in Calais, a camp that was built in January 2015 and survived for more than eighteen months before it was demolished in late 2016. The camp appeared in Calais to house refugees waiting to travel across the Channel from mainland Europe to the UK, either by smuggling themselves onto boats and ferries or into vehicles travelling on the Channel Tunnel. It attracted much media attention and volunteers from France and the UK, including Kate Evans herself, arrived in Calais with supplies to assist refugees. Evans' *Threads* is therefore from the outset imbricated in the politics of carceral humanitarianism. Unlike Kugler, Evans is not "on the ground" simply to record and report, but to assist in the humanitarian improvement of the camp's dire conditions.

Figure 1.2 The only double-page spread included in Kate Evans' *Threads from the Refugee Crisis* contemplates the Calais "Jungle" as a space of exception (Evans 2017, 52–3). Reproduced with the permission of the artist.

Threads differs from *Escaping Wars and Waves* in other important ways, too. Kugler never draws himself into his pages, preferring an authorial transparency that allows his reportage to "perform" a documentary objectivity (Mickwitz 2016; Bake and Zöhrer 2017), even as his distinctive style betrays his deeply subjective response to refugee subjects and their environments. By contrast, Evans draws herself into almost every panel of *Threads*, highlighting the limitations of her—and implicitly, her reportage's—narrative perspective. In this explicit refusal of omniscience, she follows an artist like Sacco, though she claims there is no direct influence: "I was doing graphic reportage, and in fact I also visited Palestine and drew comics about it, before I ever read Joe Sacco's work. There are definite parallels there, but not influence" (Davies 2017b, 18). This apparent disconnect renders the similarities between Sacco's and Evans' work even more striking, implying a broader associative culture between comics and refugee camps and, within that, the compelling formal homology between spaces and pages of exception that I am tracing in this chapter. Most of Evans' pages throughout *Threads* are, like Sacco's, broken up with multiple borders and gutters. It is only in the double-page depiction of a space of exception that this formal architecture disappears and gives way to a larger splash image.

Almost two-thirds of this image is taken up by the metal bars of a thinly etched fence, which not only emphasizes incarceration and immobility, but also resembles a clustered and confined comics' grid. The accompanying text describes the carceral technologies implemented by the French authorities to contain the refugees crowding into the informal camp: "125 shipping containers. Ring-fenced. Spotlit. Biometric entry control. 12 bunks to a shipping container. No cooking facilities. No privacy. No autonomy" (Evans 2017, 52). Evans' avatar clings to the grid fence as though she is herself trapped inside the comic's architecture, trying to break out of (or into) the page. The tension of (im)mobility immanent in Kugler's drawings is also present here, though this time not in Evans' artistic style but the details the page depicts: after all, the state wishes to house refugees in shipping containers, a key technology in global supply chains purposefully designed to move goods across large distances (see Cowen 2014). Thus compared to the goods of globalization that circulate freely across borders, refugees are utterly dehumanized or reduced to bare life, their paradoxical immobility—they are caught in a "non-space" at the border between France and the UK—momentarily freezing the comic's narrative progression. Of course, we know Evans herself will eventually "get out": she has a British passport and can jump on the next ferry back to Dover, just as we readers can turn the page or put the book down. It is in the end only the refugee, inanely brushing his teeth on the right-hand side of the image, who remains incarcerated and immobile.

And yet, this refugee—who remains anonymous—recognizes the strange temporal paradox of carceral humanitarianism and the spaces and camps that it produces, quite literally pointing it out to us. With his free hand, he directs our attention away from the fence to the "Jungle" in the distance behind him: "the legal centre, the aid distribution points, the caravans, the brightly painted playground—a monument to human ingenuity and charity" (Evans 2017, 53). With this descriptive text, Evans attempts something like optimism, reluctant to criticize the humanitarian effort that has provided shelter, food, and legal advice. But the composition of the page, which bleeds from the state-sponsored space of incarceration through to the refugee camp beyond, without so much as a comics gutter to separate them, suggests a deeper acknowledgement of the carceral logics of humanitarian intervention. This reticence is registered in the refugee's only direct speech, recorded by Evans in hand-drawn pen that stands out against the rest of her type-written script: "All this … will go," the refugee offers. In this page of exception, the refugee gestures—both verbally and visually—to the camp's finite temporality. The tension of this page, which is both inside and outside of the larger graphic narrative, returns us again to the paradox of immobility: it embeds into its form the horrifying logic of carceral humanitarianism, which exists momentarily in the extra-legal space between the inevitable bulldozing of the camp and the refugee's inability to flee and exist anywhere else.

Tings Chak's *Undocumented: The Architecture of Migrant Detention* is the least conventional of the four "graphic novels" that I will discuss in this chapter. Whereas in my other examples the comic's grid only breaks away on a single splash page, Chak disrupts conventional comics architecture throughout her book. A Hong Kong-born and Toronto-raised multidisciplinary artist, trained architect, and long-time activist for migrant rights, Chak does not identify as a cartoonist, comics artist, or indeed, comics journalist, in the same way that the other authors studied in this chapter might. This different disciplinary background comes through in *Undocumented*, which could just as easily be taken as a series of architectural sketches linked by some loose narrative cues, as it could a comic or graphic novel (see Davies 2017c). Split into a series of different sections, the book begins with drawings of Canadian detention centers from the streets on which they are located (showing these in a series of four panels per page), before moving inside the centers themselves to hold these spaces of exception up to graphic scrutiny. Here, Chak's thin line-drawings of the detention center's corridors, doors, and other security apparatus operate a little like comics panels, the architecture of the carceral space itself functioning as the narrative architecture of the comics form. All of these spaces are, until the book's final section, devoid of human beings: the work as a whole is concerned to make visible in forensic detail a space of exception where photography is infamously prohibited (see Tomsky 2020). For this reason, there is no *single* page of exception as such.

However, there still remains at the center of *Undocumented* a striking double-page spread that fits into the rhythms of immobility I am identifying in this chapter. Even though Chak's graphic novel does not conform to a strict comics architecture, there remains a basic framework of panels and borders that move the narrative forward. In one particular sequence, a sustained series of such panels literally *move* the reader through drawn snapshots of the detention center's different interior rooms. Then, suddenly, the narrative pace gathered through these pages is halted and disrupted by a double-page splash, just as it is in the work of Sacco or Evans (Chak 2016, 54–5; see Figure 1.3). This page shows an anatomical depiction of "the living zone"—the space

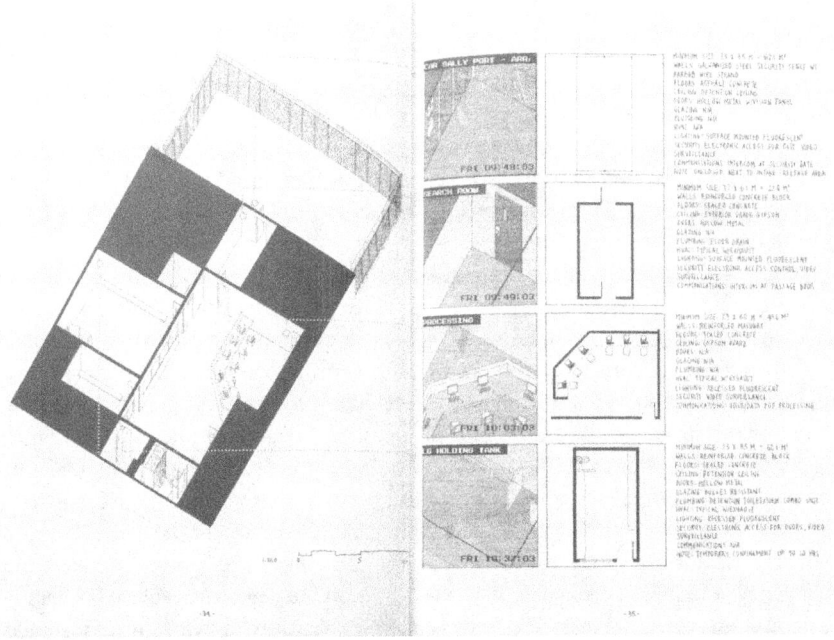

Figure 1.3 A double-page spread from Tings Chak's *Undocumented: The Architecture of Migrant Detention* that shows a space of exception at the heart of a Canadian detention center (Chak 2016, 52–53). Reproduced with the permission of the publisher.

where detained refugees wait out their incarceration. An architectural cross-section of this central kernel of the detention center hangs awkwardly in the air, at odds with the vertical and horizontal lines of the rooms and narrative grids on the pages preceding it. The result is to cut this space away from the rest of the center's architecture, just as the image is itself cut away from the graphic narrative. It details the dormitory of bunk beds where detained refugees are required to sleep; a common area, where they might congregate; and two visitation rooms, one for visitors, the other for councilors. The space is one of profound exception: refugees, deprived of their basic human rights and detained indefinitely on the rural outskirts of Canadian cities, are incarcerated here in a sinisterly sanitized architecture of confinement and isolation. Chak's clinical line drawings, along with the absence of human beings (and their rights), effectively communicate this cool institutional and extra-legal horror.

If this page of exception makes visible a space that would otherwise never be visualized beyond the detention center, with some paradox it also highlights how the refugees' rooms are built for the sole purpose of their surveillance. Within the architectural diagram, we see a one-way mirror looking onto the dormitory, where the refugees sleep, and all visitors, including councilors and lawyers, must speak with the incarcerated through panes of glass. On the right-hand side of the image, a series of squares that resemble comics panels show each of the area's rooms from two further perspectives: the architectural blueprint and the CCTV camera monitoring the refugees in real time (though unlike normal panels, neither of these moves the narrative forward). In contrast to Kugler's or Evans' spreads, the only text on this splash page also refuses to undertake narrative work, instead detailing the dimensions and surface areas of the rooms and the materials—"reinforced concrete block," "recessed fluorescent lighting," "hollow metal"—from which they have been built. There is even a to-scale reference at the bottom of the page, emphasizing the forensic accuracy of the drawing. It is hard to see this image and not be reminded of Art Spiegelman's forensic dissection of Auschwitz's architecture of extermination, and especially its gas chambers, in *Maus* (2003, 230).

On this page, Chak "rebuilds" a space of extreme exception and incarceration—we are even told that the refugees have only two drawers each for their clothes. There remains only a single instance of movement here, although this does not occur strictly within the comic itself. Chak imitates with her drawings the perspective of the architects who originally designed the detention center and the guards who now monitor the space: on the left-hand side, we have the architectural diagram, on the right, the footage from CCTV cameras. With her page of exception, Chak intervenes into this system of surveillance in order to break its images out of its closed-circuit footage. The graphic novel makes perspectives intended only for the surveillant state suddenly accessible to the reader as well—the space of incarceration once concealed from view now circulates in a public sphere beyond the detention center's borders. As Rifkind observes, this technique "recalls Sacco's imaginary drawings from forbidden viewpoints," with the effect of asking readers "to imagine the refugee lives we cannot see through the very same visual discourses that have been used to construct their confinement" (2020, 309–11). Like her fellow graphic reportage artists, Chaks "breaks" out of the comics grid, just as she breaks refugee stories out of their incarcerated spaces: as the narrative breaks down and readers find themselves "detained" by the page (Said 2001, v), a World Literature emerges that has not only communicated stories across borders, but also indexed the meaningfully material immobilities of the refugees to whom those stories belong.

I conclude this section with a final example from Jon Sack's collaboratively produced book-length piece of comics journalism, *La Lucha: The Story of Lucha Castro and Human Rights in Mexico* (2015). *La Lucha* returns us to the more conventional comic's architecture of panels, grids, gutters, and frames, using the form to document the surge in homicides—especially of women—that has plagued the Mexican border city of Juárez since George Bush's declaration of a War on Drugs in 2001. As the anthropologist Sergio González Rodríguez describes in his book *The Femicide Machine*, Juárez was through the first decade of the twenty-first century a "lawless city sponsored by a State in crisis" (2012, 7)—or in other words, in a state of exception. As the Mexican and US states retreated from a border city torn apart by gang violence, citizens were deprived of basic rights and reduced to a condition of bare life. In place of the state, a number of humanitarian organizations have arisen to try and salvage something of these rights and protect citizens, and Jon Sack's *La Lucha* documents the work of one of these: the Center for the Human Rights of Women (Centro de Derechos Humanos de las Mujeres), cofounded and coordinated by the eponymous Lucha Castro. The result is a comic about a different carceral space, though one still subject to the same humanitarian logic. If it at first appears as though the space is not so rigidly hemmed in by infrastructures of incarceration, it quickly becomes apparent that this is a carceral city: the opening scene documents the difficulty of crossing the border over into Juárez's neighboring US city of El Paso, while Juárez itself is monitored by non-state militias and riven with armed gates and electrified fences.

Although a different space of exception yet again, Sack's comic still repeats the formal technique that I have been calling throughout this chapter "pages of exception." Sack includes only one double-page spread throughout the whole of *La Lucha*, not at the center of the book but as a scene-setting device in its early pages (Sack 2015, 9–10; see Figure 1.4). As I have discussed elsewhere (Davies 2019, 264–6; 2020a, 15–16), Sack's style is similar to Sacco's and this image resembles the latter's drawing of the refugee camp in *Palestine*, though with some important differences. Most notably, of course, are the inset panels that float in the top left and bottom right-hand corners (Sacco's splash page is entirely without panels). The first of these shows the iconic graffiti emblazoned into the hillside near Juárez: "La Biblia es la Verdad, Leela" ("The Bible Is the Truth, Read It"). This floating image serves most basically as a scene setter, identifying what is at first glance a fairly generic street view as the city of Juárez. The second image appears to do little more, showing only a school bus and a few anonymous pedestrians sauntering down an empty street.

While these images at first appear rather dull and unexciting, their formal arrangement clearly constructs the city as a space of exception that is both inside and outside of the graphic narrative. Taking account of the fact that the preceding page is littered with headlines about Juárez that Sack has taken from the international

Figure 1.4 The only double-page spread in John Sack's *La Lucha: The Story of Lucha Castro and Human Rights in Mexico* that shows Ciudad Juárez as a space of exception (Sack 2015, 9–10). Reproduced with the permission of the publisher.

media, this exceptionality formally represents Juárez as a place that shifts in and out of mainstream reportage. Against this floating media representation, Sack insists on the grounded locality of his drawing: "This is Juárez," reads the spread's only scripted text, an insistence on local specificity that is also registered in the panel showing the iconic hillside graffiti. When we look more closely, it also becomes apparent that there is in fact some movement in this image, much of which is unnerving. The military vehicles carrying armed soldiers in the bottom left-hand corner tell us that this is no ordinary street. Presumably the school bus, shown almost at a stand still in the bottom right-hand panel, is the same bus that—marked "2B"—crawls away from the reader's gaze into the vanishing point at the center of the main image. It is possible, too, that the figure selling newspapers to passersby in the bottom left-hand corner is the same figure who walks through the center of the bottom right-hand panel, still holding a paper, though now with his hood pushed back.

These movements are all partial, tentative, and incomplete—they suggest that people move about this city with great hesitancy and caution, cultivating an atmosphere of insecurity that is reflected in the page's limited narrative coherence. There is a vague sense of mobility, though clearly this is restricted to those willing to risk their lives in an extra-legal territory. The only certain movement animating this page comes not from the city's inhabitants, but the weather—which, after all, always crosses borders. The gusts of sand that spiral across the bottom of the page mirror the ominous clouds that loom overhead, instilling the scene with a sense of imminent threat (the dense cross-hatching in these clouds is also the clearest visual reference to Sacco's own distinctive technique). Finally, the motion of the wind is visible in the splash-page's most prominent feature: a torn billboard advertisement for Wendy's fast food restaurant. I have argued elsewhere that the strands of the advertisement lapping "the identifiable grid of this structure" direct our attention "to the comic's own formal composition" (2020a, 16). In the context of the other pages of exception that I have identified here, however, the torn image within an image that dominates the top right-hand corner of this page seems to acknowledge—not unlike its other predecessor, *Maus*—the representational limitations of graphic reportage, which attempts (and sometimes fails) to circulate scenes and stories of exception beyond the borders and carceral spaces of our world.

Conclusion: Carceral Worlds

Comics have always crossed borders, of course, and some effort has already been made to read graphic novels as World Literature. In her chapter for *The Cambridge Companion to World Literature*, Charlotta Salmi helpfully reminds us of "the worldliness of graphic narrative," tracing the international history of the comics form as it evolved "between cartoon cultures in French-speaking Europe, America, and Japan" (2018, 180). Salmi takes as her examples the already canonical comics of Keiji Nakazawa and Marjane Satrapi, both of which are evidently world literary texts and also, we might note, nonfictional works—though Salmi does not highlight this point. Clearly, the graphic reportage studied in this chapter grows from this still-calcifying canon of graphic work, even as it is influenced by other sub-genres such as graphic memoir, newspaper cartoon strips, and comics journalism.

In another recent commentary on the relationship between graphic novels and World Literature, Monika Schmitz-Emans pursues this question of genre. Focusing on graphic adaptations of "classic" literary novels in particular allows Schmitz-Emans to explore the entangled question of World Literature *in* graphic novels, on the one hand, and graphic novels *as* World Literature, on the other. While Salmi understands graphic narrative to have developed more or less independently as "its own subset of World Literature" (2018, 182), Schmitz-Emans traces the graphic novel's cross-fertilization with world literary classics to better confront the graphic novel's tendency to transgress the conventional parameters of "dramatic or narrative fiction" (2018, 234)—the same conceptual troubling that Chute called for in her "Comics as Literature?" essay (2008, 463). It is this transgression of generic boundaries that drives graphic narrative, as Schmitz-Emans concludes, to "visualise the usually invisible" (2018, 234). Just as graphic reportage troubles our notions of "world," it similarly troubles ideas of "novels" and "literature" too, and I want to conclude by emphasizing that these two unsettlings are not simply coterminous, but fundamentally related to one another. As I have tried to show in this chapter, it is exactly their transgressive meshing of different genres that allows graphic reportage to "visualize the usually invisible" spaces of exception that carve up the contemporary world. In particular, it is through their pages of exception that these graphic narratives document and circulate refugee testimonies beyond borders *without* losing sight of, smoothing over, or abstracting away from the immobilizing carceral infrastructures that continue to contain those same refugees.

I have argued in this chapter that graphic reportage unsettles both the "world" and "literature" of "World Literature" in productive and pressingly political ways. With their shared inclusion of spaces of exception, the examples of graphic reportage analyzed here join up stories of otherwise disconnected, isolated, and imprisoned people, from the borders of Fortress Europe to the "Jungle" refugee camp in Calais, and from remote refugee detention centers in Canada to the militarized Mexican border city of Juárez. The artists surveyed in this chapter try to communicate stories from places where the rights-based legal fabric of the nation-state system has been cut away, withdrawn, or denied, and where a carceral humanitarianism has arisen in their place. Just as importantly, each artist uses a shared formal technique to communicate the partial mobilities of the testimonies included in their reportage, thereby insisting on nonfiction as literature, and thus troubling the notion of "literature" itself. Finally, by circulating through different though sometimes connected media spaces, partially online and physically offline, these pages of exception come together to form a World Literature that is not smooth or uneven, cosmopolitan or capitalist, but unforgivingly tuned into the carceral spaces that interrupt and fragment our world.

References

Agamben, Giorgio. 1998. *Homo Sacer: Sovereign Power and Bare Life*. Daniel Heller-Roazan, trans. Stanford, CA: Stanford University Press.
Agamben, Giorgio. 1999. *Remnants of Auschwitz: The Witness and the Archive*. New York: Zone Books.
Apter, Emily. 2013. *Against World Literature: On the Politics of Untranslatability*. London & New York: Verso.
Bake, Julia, and Zöhrer, Michaela. 2017. "Telling the Stories of Others: Claims of Authenticity in Human Rights Reporting and Comics Journalism." *Journal of Intervention and Statebuilding*, 11 (1): 81–97.
Banita, Georgiana. 2014. "Cosmopolitan Suspicion: Comics Journalism and Graphic Silence." In Denson, Shane, Meyer, Christina, and Stein, Daniel, eds. *Transnational Perspectives on Graphic Narratives: Comics at the Crossroads*. London: Bloomsbury, 49–65.
Bechdel, Alison. 2006. *Fun Home: A Family Tragicomic*. London: Jonathan Cape.
Brennan, Timothy. 2018. "Cosmopolitanism and World Literature." In Etherington, Ben, and Zimbler, Jared, eds. *The Cambridge Companion to World Literature*. Cambridge: Cambridge University Press, 23–36.
Chak, Tings. 2016. *Undocumented: The Architecture of Migrant Detention*. Westmount, QC: The Architecture Observer.

Chute, Hillary. 2008. "Comics as Literature: Reading Graphic Narrative?" *PMLA*, 123 (2): 452–65.
Chute, Hillary. 2016. *Disaster Drawn: Visual Witness, Comics, and Documentary Form.* Cambridge, MA: The Belknap Press of Harvard University Press.
Cowen, Deborah. 2014. *The Deadly Life of Logistics: Mapping Violence in Global Trade.* Minneapolis and London: University of Minnesota Press.
Davies, Dominic. 2017a. "'Comics on the Main Street of Culture': Alan Moore and Eddie Campbell's *From Hell* (1999), Laura Oldfield Ford's *Savage Messiah* (2011), and the Politics of Gentrification." *Urban Cultural Studies*, 4, (3): 333–60.
Davies, Dominic. 2017b. "Comics Activism: An Interview with Comics Artist and Activist Kate Evans." *The Comics Grid: Journal of Comics Scholarship*, 7: 18.
Davies, Dominic. 2017c. "Hard Infrastructures, Diseased Bodies." *Refugee Hosts*, 30 October. https://refugeehosts.org/2017/10/30/hard-infrastructures-diseased-bodies/ (accessed March 30, 2020).
Davies, Dominic. 2019. *Urban Comics: Infrastructure and the Global City in Contemporary Graphic Narratives.* London & New York: Oxford.
Davies, Dominic. 2020a. "Dreamlands, Border Zones, and Spaces of Exception: Comics and Graphic Narratives on the US-Mexico Border." *a/b: Auto/Biography Studies, Special Issue: Migration, Exile, and Diaspora in Graphic Life Narratives*, 35, (2, Spring): 1–21.
Davies, Dominic. 2020b. "Introduction: Documenting Trauma in Comics." In Davies, Dominic, and Rifkind, Candida, eds. *Documenting Trauma in Comics: Traumatic Pasts, Embodied Histories, and Graphic Reportage.* London & New York: Palgrave MacMillan, 1–26.
Davies, Dominic. 2020c. "Crossing Borders, Bridging Boundaries: Reconstructing the Rights of the Refugee in Comics." In Fiddian-Qasmiyeh, Elena, ed. *Refuge in a Moving World: Tracing Refugee and Migrant Journeys Across Disciplines.* London: UCL Press, n.p.
Eisner, Will. 2007. *A Contract with God.* New York: W.W. Norton & Company.
Embury, Gary, and Minichiello, Mario. 2018. *Reportage Illustration: Visual Journalism.* London: Bloomsbury Publishing Plc.
Evans, Kate. 2017. *Threads from the Refugee Crisis.* London & New York: Verso.
Gorrara, Claire. 2018. "Not Seeing Auschwitz: Memory, Generation and Representations of the Holocaust in Twenty-First Century French Comics." *Journal of Modern Jewish Studies*, 17 (1): 111–26.
Hatfield, Charles. 2005. *Alternative Comics: An Emerging Literature.* Jackson: University Press of Mississippi.
in't Veld, Laurike. 2019. *The Representation of Genocide in Graphic Novels: Considering the Role of Kitsch.* London & New York: Palgrave Macmillan.
Jamieson, Teddy. 2018. "Graphic Content: Olivier Kugler on Comics Journalism and the Story of Syrian Refugees." *The Herald*, September 4. https://www.heraldscotland.com/arts_ents/16686815.graphic-content-olivier-kugler-on-comics-journalism-and-the-story-of-syrian-refugees/ (accessed March 27, 2020).
Kugler, Olivier. 2018. *Escaping Wars and Waves: Encounters with Syrian Refugees.* Oxford: Myriad Editions.
Labio, Catherine. 2011. "What's in a Name?: The Academic Study of Comics and the 'Graphic Novel.'" *Cinema Journal*, 50 (3): 122–6.

Mandel, Naomi. 2006. *Against the Unspeakable: Complicity, the Holocaust, and Slavery in America*. Charlottesville & London: University of Virginia Press.

Mickwitz, Nina. 2016. *Documentary Comics: Graphic Truth-Telling in a Skeptical Age*. New York: Palgrave Macmillan.

Mickwitz, Nina. 2020. "Comics Telling Refugee Stories." In Davies, Dominic, and Rifkind, Candida, eds. *Documenting Trauma in Comics: Traumatic Pasts, Embodied Histories, and Graphic Reportage*. London & New York: Palgrave MacMillan, 277–96.

Oliver, Kelly. 2017. *Carceral Humanitarianism: Logics of Refugee Detention*. Minneapolis, MN: University of Minnesota Press.

Olle, Nick, and Wallman, Sam. 2014. "A Guard's Story". *The Global Mail*, February. http://tgm-serco.patarmstrong.net.au/ (accessed March 25, 2020).

Orbán, Katalin. 2015. "Mediating Distant Violence: Reports on Non-Photographic Reporting in the Fixer and the Photographer." *Journal of Graphic Novels and Comics*. 6 (2): 122–37.

Parker, Emma. 2018. "Refugee Comics: Personal Stories of Forced Migration Illustrated in a Powerful New Way." *The Conversation*, November 14. https://theconversation.com/refugee-comics-personal-stories-of-forced-migration-illustrated-in-a-powerful-new-way-106832 (accessed March 19, 2020).

Postema, Barbara. 2013. *Narrative Structure in Comics: Making Sense of Fragments*. New York: RIT Press.

Pourquié, Jeff, and Tervonen, Taina. 2016. "The Borders of Shame". *Drawing the Times*, Special Issue 3: "Human Rights". https://drawingthetimes.com/story/the-borders-of-shame/# (accessed February 13, 2020).

Prorokova, Tatiana, and Tal, Nimrod eds. 2018. *Cultures of War in Graphic Novels: Violence, Trauma, and Memory*. New Jersey: Rutgers University Press.

Rifkind, Candida. 2017. "Refugee Comics and Migrant Topographies." *a/b: Auto/Biography Studies*, 32(3): 648–54.

Rifkind, Candida. 2020. "Migrant Detention Comics and the Aesthetic Technologies of Compassion." In Davies, Dominic, and Rifkind, Candida, eds. *Documenting Trauma in Comics: Traumatic Pasts, Embodied Histories, and Graphic Reportage*. London & New York: Palgrave MacMillan, 297–316.

Rodríguez, Sergio González. 2012. *The Femicide Machine*. Michael Parker-Stainback trans. and ed. Los Angeles, CA: Semiotext(e).

Sacco, Joe. 2001. *Palestine*. Seattle: Fantagraphics.

Sack, Jon. 2015. *La Lucha: The Story of Lucha Castro and Human Rights in Mexico*. London & New York: Verso.

Said, Edward. 2001. "Homage to Joe Sacco." In Sacco, Joe, *Palestine*. Seattle: Fantagraphics, iiv.

Salmi, Charlotta. 2018. "The Worldliness of Graphic Narrative." In Etherington, Ben, and Zimbler, Jared, eds. *The Cambridge Companion to World Literature*. Cambridge: Cambridge University Press, 180–96.

Satrapi, Marjane. 2008. *Persepolis*. London: Vintage.

Saunders, Ben. 2009. "Divisions in Comics Scholarship." *PMLA*, 124 (1): 292–4.

Schmitz-Emans, Monika. 2018. "World Literature in Graphic Novels and Graphic Novels as World Literature." In Fang, Weigui, ed. *Tensions in World Literature: Between the Local and the Universal*. Singapore: Palgrave MacMillan, 219–38.

Spiegelman, Art. 2003. *The Complete Maus*. London & New York: Penguin Books.

Tomsky, Terri. 2020. "Seeking Asylum: Mapping the Hidden Worlds of Migrant Detention Centres in Recent Literary Representations." In Moore, Alexandra S., and Pinto, Samantha, eds. *Writing Beyond the State: Post-Sovereign Approaches to Human Rights in Literary Studies*. London & New York: Palgrave MacMillan, 223–42.

Weizman, Eyal. 2011. *The Least of All Possible Evils: Humanitarian Violence from Arendt to Gaza*. London & New York: Verso.

Worley, Will, and Dearden, Lizzie. 2016. "Greek Refugee Camp is 'as Bad as a Nazi Concentration Camp', Says Minister." *The Independent*, March 18. https://www.independent.co.uk/news/world/europe/idomeni-refugee-dachau-nazi-concentration-camp-greek-minister-a6938826.html (accessed March 27, 2020).

2

Latin America's *Tinta Femenina* and Its Place in Graphic "World Literature"

Jasmin Wrobel

> *[T]here is a new aesthetics emerging around self-representation: contemporary authors, now more than ever, offer powerful nonfiction narratives in comic form. Many, if not most, of these authors are women.*
> Hillary Chute: Graphic Women: Life Narrative and Contemporary Comics, 2010

> *¡Cuidado, contagio! [Watch out, contagious!]*
> Powerpaola: Virus Tropical, 2013

Preliminary Considerations

The subject of the present volume touches on two questions: on the one hand, whether and how graphic narratives can be read as "World Literature" and, on the other hand—as the editor, James Hodapp, pertinently problematizes the mainly Euro-American-Japanese-centric academic perspective—how graphic narratives from the Global South are arranged and intersect within this "world literary" constellation. In this article, which will focus on Latin American graphic narratives, I would like to add a third desideratum to this twofold problem: the presence and visibility of female comic artists and their participation and place(s) within (graphic) "World Literature".

In the last few decades and years, women have played an increasingly important role in the Latin American landscape of sequential art, not least related to the proliferation of autobiographical and autofictional works, so-called graphic memoirs. This bias can be traced back to a global tendency in women's comics (at least) since the publication of Marjane Satrapi's *Persepolis* (I–IV; 2014 [2000–3]) or Alison Bechdel's *Fun Home: A Family Tragicomic* (2007 [2006]), both autobiographical coming-of-age stories. While Satrapi addresses the specific female experience of coming of age in situations of political and religious oppression, migration and xenophobia, Bechdel graphically explores her childhood and adolescence in relation to family trauma, sexual orientation, and heteronormativity. The genre of the graphic memoir allows authors to discuss such matters in a serious (and in some cases, at the same time, playful) way, within complex narrative structures and combining factual and fictional storytelling.

With her expressive style, the extensive autobiographical work of comic artist Powerpaola (Paola Gaviria) stands out in the generic context of the graphic memoir in Latin America. In her probably best known and internationally widely received coming-of-age story *Virus Tropical* (2013 [2011]), the Colombian–Ecuadorian author narrates key episodes of her childhood and adolescence in Quito and Cali, addressing topics such as the absence of a father figure, the struggles to integrate herself into new environments, the insecurities of a young woman having her first relationships and sexual encounters and, finally, the autonomous decision of becoming an artist and the emancipation from her family. While these aspects are typical for the genre of graphic memoirs and coming-of-age stories, *Virus Tropical* creates a fruitful tension between the global and the local on other levels. The latter is referred to, for example, by the linguistic varieties, transmedial references or the historical background of Colombia's drug cartel warfare era of the 1980s and 1990s.

According to the three-part question of this article, the first step is to examine a supposed "formula for success" of graphic memoirs and to identify frequently appearing components. Furthermore, I seek to discuss the genre's special potential in relation to the question why graphic memoirs have become a particularly popular format especially for female comic artists. In a second step, I will give a brief overview about the history of comics in Latin America paying special attention to what extent the panel has been transformed into a venue (or even battlefield) of feminist discourse especially in the last years. These first two sections are intended to situate Powerpaola's work both within a global tendency in sequential art as well as against the background of the history of (women's) comics in Latin America. In my analysis of *Virus Tropical*, a work that I consider paradigmatic for the participation of Latin American graphic narratives in "graphic World Literature" (Schmitz-Emans 2015, 392), I will focus on mainly three aspects: the negotiation of feminist discourses, the productive tension between the global and the local, on the one hand, and between "popular" and "high culture," on the other.[1]

Graphic Memoirs and the Female Ink

Nonfictional graphic narratives—"the strongest genre in the field," according to Hillary Chute (2008, 452)—whose plot is autobiographical or autofictional and which are often

---

[1] I am very grateful to the editor, James Hodapp, for his attentive reading of my manuscript and his many helpful comments. As a German scholar of Latin American (Literary) studies, I have increasingly worked on graphic narratives from the continent in recent years, especially on the representation of social inequalities, memory discourses and the presence and visibility of female comic artists. I have hereby benefited from collaborations with colleagues from Latin America and Europe, to which I will refer explicitly in this article. However, I would like to emphasize the Latin American research network *RING. Red de investigadoras e investigadores de narrativa gráfica* (https://ringlatinoamerica.wordpress.com/; accessed November 12, 2020) and the Leverhulme-funded project *Comics and the Latin American City: Framing Urban Communities* (2016–19; https://comicsandthelatinamericancity.wordpress.com/; accessed November 12, 2020) and thank especially their coordinators, Hugo Hinojosa and Javiera Irribarren, and, respectively, James Scorer, for the fruitful exchange and support in the last years.

referred to as "graphic memoirs" (cf. Smith and Watson 2010; Pedri 2015; Schröer 2015) have made a significant contribution to the revaluation of graphic literature and to its (partial) inclusion into "literary canons."[2] First of all, it is noticeable that graphic narratives which make it onto bestseller lists and are given special consideration by (literary) critics, particularly often belong to this genre. It is also striking that in this context, four works—a small canon of its own, if you will—are discussed with remarkable frequency in research literature: Art Spiegelman's paradigmatic *Maus. A Survivor's Tale* (2003 [1986/1991]), Marjane Satrapi's *Persepolis* (2014 [2000-2003]), Craig Thompson's *Blankets* (2017 [2003]), and Alison Bechdel's *Fun Home* (2007 [2006]) (cf., for example, Versaci 2007, 34–108; García 2012, 245–300; Kukkonen 2013, 55–72; Schröer 2016, *passim*). It is therefore worth taking a closer look at these works in preparation for the analysis of Powerpaola's *Virus Tropical*. While all four works share the examination of traumatic experiences (on different levels and by means of quite different stylistic approaches), *Persepolis*, *Blankets*, and *Fun Home* have also in common that they are coming-of-age stories, presenting, for the most part, a child protagonist and an adult narrator. While in *Persepolis* and especially in *Maus* the historical background plays a significant or even protagonist role, in *Blankets* and *Fun Home* it is the religiously prudish or, respectively, pretendedly heteronormative family

---

[2] The (literary) "value" of graphic narratives and their place in (a changing notion of) World Literature have been the subject of much research in recent years (e.g. Versaci 2007; Baetens 2011; Schmitz-Emans 2015, 2018). At the same time, there have been critical voices regarding the (artificial) opposition between "World Literature" and "popular literature," evoked especially by the term "graphic novel" (coined by Richard Kyle in 1964 and later popularized by Will Eisner) and its connotation as a "marketing concept." Jan Baetens for example notes that the "age-old hegemony of the word no longer stands" and that the implicit understanding of "World Literature" as—exclusively—"word literature" is faltering (2011, 338). Hereby he conceives the graphic novel as "perfect illustration of the visual turn that has swept over the literary field" while he problematizes the "widening gap between (popular, non-literary) comics and (alternative, literary) graphic novels [as] testimony to the persistence of old-fashioned distinctions between high and low, popular and elite, mass media and elite circuits. Edward King and Joanna Page specify this problematization for the Latin American context by identifying comics (with recourse to Argentine scholar Néstor García Canclini) as an important "point of intersection between national-popular culture and global cultural structures and systems of signification" (King/Page 2017, 16; cf. Canclini 1995, 249–58). The general adoption of the term "graphic novel" in academic research would therefore not least give rise—again—to the problem of "theoretical colonization": "Waldomiro Vergueiro and Gêisa Fernandes D'Oliveira argue that the use of the term is indicative of attempts from the realm of academia to legitimize the comics medium as a serious object of study. This gesture risks obscuring the specific associations between comic book networks and popular cultures in the region. They argue that interest in comic books grows [… 'not when they become more popular but when they are incorporated into an elite culture to which the more popular classes do not have access']. According to this argument, the use of the term graphic novel is complicit in the betrayal of the national-popular and part of a process of theoretical colonization" (King/Page 2017, 17; cf. Vergueiro and Fernandes D'Oliveira 2011, 137). King and Page still opt to use the term in their study on *Posthumanism and the Graphic Novel in Latin America* to refer to "a constantly morphing medium," while considering the "points of continuity as well as divergences between comic book and graphic novel" (2017, 17–18). This is, as I see it, a necessary and differentiated problematization that could also be applied to the more specific genre term of the "graphic memoir": here, too, "memoir" refers to an "established" literary narrative form which might lead to a symbolic "elevation" of the work. Despite this objection, I find it to be more accurate in relation to competing terms (cf. Schröer 2016 263–5) in that "memoirs" usually relate to a specific period or key moments in the author's life which is the case of the works to be discussed in this article.

structures that are broken up in both cases by the protagonists (and, in *Fun Home*, by the assumed suicide of the father). With the exception of *Persepolis*, where the family structures tend to create stability (Marjane's parents are supportive of her) in otherwise highly unstable and oppressive environments, in the other narratives those structures are motives for conflicts and, partially, carry the plot. The stylistic approaches for the representation of the respective traumas are quite different: while Spiegelman, as is well known, relies on an anthropomorphic strategy of alienation, which on the one hand ethically enables him to visually approach the unspeakable and on the other hand consists in a multilayered interlacing of different references,[3] Satrapi's minimalist, childlike drawing style creates a productive tension with the complex identity conflicts she experiences. Both Craig Thompson and Alison Bechdel make use of extensive intertextual references—the Bible, in Thompson's case and (for example) Camus or Joyce, in Bechdel's case—and establish thus a complex intermedial dialogue between their own autobiographical work, the canonical texts (both visually represented in the books) and their own readings of these texts.

As already quoted in the motto preceding this text, Hillary Chute, in her study *Graphic Women: Life Narrative and Contemporary Comics*, emphasizes the significant number of female authors who work in the genre of "nonfiction narratives," calling *Persepolis* and *Fun Home* "the two biggest literary graphic narratives since Art Spiegelman's world-famous *Maus*" (2010, 1) and stressing "the enabling role of the visual in self-articulation and in representing the processes of memory, especially traumatic memory" (2010, 7) for female artists:

> The field of graphic narrative brings certain key constellations to the table: hybridity and autobiography, theorizing trauma in connection to the visual, textuality that takes the body seriously. I claim graphic narratives, as they exhibit these interests, "feminist".
>
> (2010, 3–4)

The emphasis on the body and corporeality is essential here and, not least, a (re) connection to the *underground comix* and post-underground comics which often had a strong autobiographical component, making them a kind of forerunner for graphic memoirs (cf. Kukkonen 2013, 117–18; Schröer 2016, 265; Merino 2017, *passim*). Authors such as Aline Kominsky-Crumb, Phoebe Gloeckner, or Julie Doucet counter the often sexist, misogynistic and violent depictions of their male colleagues visualizing, in an aesthetically analogous—that is taboo breaking—way, their own lust, sexual self-determination, menstruation and other bodily fluids, but also physical abuse and sexual violence. While the *underground comix* and post-underground comics' authors use obscenity as a stylistic device,[4] Satrapi's and Bechdel's examination of (female) corporeality is subtler, but crucial for the narratives' argument.

---

[3] See, in this context, the chapter "Why Mice?" in Spiegelman's *MetaMaus* (2011, 111–63).
[4] For a detailed analysis of the instrumentalization of obscenity and taboo-breaking in Aline Kominsky-Crumb see Véronique Sina 2020.

The first panel of the *Persepolis* series shows Marjane as a ten-year-old girl with a hijab, while she looks the reader discontentedly in the eyes. This first self-portrayal proves the importance of the veil—not of the hijab specifically, but the symbolic meaning of the veil as a "disguising feature"—as a kind of leitmotif for Satrapi's story (cf. Worth 2007, 155). Between adaptation and rebellion, Marjane is constantly striving to adapt to her own demands and the demands of others. She experiences the physical metamorphosis of puberty during her years in Austria, trying to compensate these uncontrollable (and somewhat asymmetrical) changes of her body with self-induced physical changes that help her to adapt to her punk environment (Satrapi 2014, 190–1).

In Alison Bechdel's *Fun Home*, corporeality is an important device to illustrate the physical and emotional distance (Bechdel 2007, 3–4) but, in some ways, also special proximity between Alison and her father: both of them, father and daughter, can be seen as "inversions of one other" according to Bechdel (98), which time and again leads to a deep, non-verbal form of understanding. The corpses that Alison is repeatedly confronted with in the funeral home underline the emotional coldness in which she partly grows up. In contrast to that stands the attraction which Alison feels—for different motives and in different ways—for female and male bodies. The ambiguous experience and exploration of her own (female) corporeality by means of masturbation, menstruation, cross-dressing, etc. leads, in the end, to her political and sexual awakening as a lesbian woman (81; 214–15). In both cases, *Persepolis* and *Fun Home*, corporeality is a central means of expression, while the performative embodiment leads to a higher investment of the readers.

Graphic Narratives in Latin America *y la tinta femenina*

The "ninth art" has a long tradition in Latin America,[5] with visual language already playing a decisive role in the pre-Hispanic cultures if we think of the Mayan logosyllabic writing system, for example, a fact that is repeatedly referred to in comics studies. Thus, in the first chapter of his key work *Understanding Comics*, Scott McCloud cites the Mixtec *Codex Zouche-Nutall* as an early example of a kind of proto-comic, showing some excerpts of the pictographic screenfold and demonstrating—briefly—the interplay between "words" and "pictures" in the scripture (McCloud 1993, 10–11).

In the nineteenth century, which marks the birth of what we understand as "comics" strictly speaking, Italian-born Brazilian Angelo Agostini created two of the first illustrated stories considered as comics worldwide—*As Aventuras de Nhô Quim ou Impressões de uma Viagem à Corte* (1869) and *As Aventuras de Zé Caipora* (1883). In the twentieth century, the Argentine sequential art can be counted among the most important comic traditions internationally, with Quino's (aka Joaquín Salvador Lavado Tejón) *Mafalda* (1964–73) becoming one of the most popular comic strips in Latin

---

[5] For a helpful overview of the history of Latin American comics, see Catalá Carrasco et al. 2017, 5–11.

America and Europe and, moreover, a universal emblem for human rights. While Quino went into Italian exile at the beginning of the Argentine military dictatorship, Héctor Germán Oesterheld—another representative of the so-called Golden Age of the Argentine Comics (mid-1940s to 1960s)—fell victim to it in 1977/1978. His masterpiece and probably most famous work, the science fiction comic *El Eternauta*, first published between 1957 and 1959 in *Hora Cero Semanal* and with artwork by Francisco Solano López,[6] is considered a pioneering graphic novel and a key work in Argentine national culture. It is the only comic that was included in Clarín's *La Biblioteca Argentina – Serie Clásicos* and thus quite explicitly integrated into a literary canon. *El Eternauta* was translated into English rather recently by Erica Mena in 2015, published by Fantagraphics Books as *The Eternaut*, while Italian and French translations were already published in 1979 and 2008, respectively. It received prestigious recognition being awarded the Eisner Award in the category "Best Archival Collection/Project – Strips" in 2016, also the year of the publication of the first German translation.

A more recent example of Latin American comic artists whose works are circulating internationally are Brazilian twin brothers Fábio Moon and Gabriel Bá. In the early 1990s, they began to self-publish their graphic narratives in Brazil, both individual and joint projects. Since 1999, they mainly publish their work in the USA and in English, which has enabled them to be read more widely. Their artistic collaborations have met with broad critical acclaim and several international awards. In particular, their work *Daytripper* (2011), a ten-issue graphic narrative loosely inspired by Brazilian writer Machado de Assis' realist novel *Memórias Póstumas de Brás Cubas* (1881), is considered a masterpiece and was awarded, among others, the Eisner Award in the category "Best Limited Series or Story Arc" in 2011. Another Eisner Award was won in 2018 by the also Brazilian comic artist Marcelo D'Salete for the translation of his graphic novel *Cumbe*, published in 2017 with the English title *Run for It: Stories of Slaves Who Fought for Their Freedom* (transl. Andrea Rosenberg), in the category Best US Edition of International Material. D'Saletes graphic narratives have been translated into seven languages in the last few years, including Turkish and Polish. The relevance of graphic narratives and their acceptance as important cultural assets has also been proven by growing scholarship in the field (cf. Catalá Carrasco et al. 2017, 3–5).[7]

With regard to the still young twenty-first century, researchers often speak of a real "boom" in the Latin American comic production, an allusion to the globally perceived and commercially extremely successful *Boom Latinoamericano*, which brought authors such as Julio Cortázar, Gabriel García Márquez, Mario Vargas Llosa, or Carlos Fuentes international recognition and a global readership (see, for example, King and Page 2017, 15). In this context, James Scorer rightfully points to

---

[6] Oesterheld rewrote *El Eternauta* in 1969, with more political references and more openly critical of dictatorial regimes, this time with artwork by Alberto Breccia. When he was already in hiding (Oesterheld and his daughters had joined the leftist organization Montoneros) in the mid-1970s, he wrote episodes for the second part of *Eternauta*, again with artwork by Francisco Solano López (*El Eternauta. Segunda Parte*, 1976). After Oesterheld's forced "disappearance" in 1977, other authors and artists attempted to continue the saga, but with less success.

[7] In relation to national comic histories, see the book series *La historieta latinoamericana* (2008), coordinated by Hernán Ostuni. See also Lent (2005) and L'Hoeste and Poblete (2009).

an analogical-conceptual link between the title of the pioneering comic anthology *El Volcán: un presente de la historieta latinoamericana*, published in 2017 by editors José Sainz and Alejandro Bidegaray, which includes comic artists from over ten Latin American countries (among them Powerpaola): "With a title suggesting an eruption not dissimilar to the explosion of the *Boom* in Latin American fiction in the 1960s and 1970s, *El Volcán* [...] reflects growing regional self-awareness of expansion, exposure and dissemination" (Scorer 2020, 1). In the context of this (now graphic) "Boom" in Latin America, female comic artists play a decisive and game-changing role as I would like to discuss in more detail in the following.

Even if it is true that also in Latin America, the history of sequential art has been (and partly still is) dominated by male artists, it is important to mention that already at the beginning of the twentieth century there were several very remarkable female caricaturists and cartoonists: the Argentineans Susana Licar and Niní Marshall, Mexican Delia Larios or Brazilian Nair de Teffé, Hilde Weber, and Patrícia Rehder Galvão ("Pagu") can be counted, among others, as the pioneers of female sequential art in Latin America, even if, for the most part, they did not dedicate themselves exclusively to the creation of caricatures or comic strips. In the second half of the twentieth century, especially in the last three decades, more and more female comic artists appeared on the scene, like Argentineans Maitena Burundarena, Patricia Brecchia, and Ana von Rebeur, Brazilian Cecília Alves Pinto ("Ciça") and Crau de Ilha, Mexican María Luisa López or Chilean Marcela Trujillo ("Maliki"; cf. Borges et al. 2018, *passim*).

In the last decades of the twentieth century, female artists begin to conquer their own space in magazines and special editions in Latin America, even if the media where they publish are, for the most part, still in the hands of men. In relation to the "female ink" one can observe a bias toward feminist topics, also the standing of women in the male-dominated comic scene begins to be questioned. Since the beginning of the new millennium at the latest, however, there is a strong increase in the number of publications of (queer) feminist sequential art, a tendency that is not least due to the emergence and establishment of new publication platforms.[8] In Latin America, the emergence of comic magazines such as *Tribuna Femenina Cómix* (Chile, 2009–2012), *Clítoris* (Argentina, 2010–2018), and *Brígida* (Chile, since 2018)—and feminist collectives like *Tetas Tristes Cómics* (Chile) or the international group *Chicks on Comics*—around founding member Powerpaola—have opened up separated and independent publishing spaces. The examination of themes related to gender, sexist and/or racist discrimination and violence, (sexual) self-determination, body image, and current political debates is thereby often taking place in dialogue with hashtag movements such as #niunamenos, #vivasnosqueremos (both referring to protests

---

[8] I would like to stress that in this short section I cannot, of course, cover the entire panorama of the extremely multifaceted and diverse productions of Latin American female comic artists; the works and authors I mention are conditioned by my own (regional) research priorities and certainly overlook important representatives. For a very helpful overview of the Argentinean, Chilean, Brazilian, and Mexican female comic production, including online formats, see Borges et al. 2018. In relation to alternative publishing forms beyond book formats, see *Comics Beyond the Page in Latin America* (2020), ed. by James Scorer.

against the huge number of femicides in several Latin American countries), #seráley, #quesealey (referring to the demand for legal abortion in Argentina, granted in December 2020), or the international #metoo.

Comic anthologies that have been published in recent years demonstrate, on the one hand, the growing recognition and relevance of the art form, but they also do now include numerous contributions by female artists. Besides the already mentioned *El Volcán: un presente de la historieta latinoamericana* (17 out of the 42 contributions are by women, approx. 40 percent), one could mention *Informe. Historieta argentina del siglo XXI* (2015), *Historieta LGBTI* (2017), *Capisci? Antología independiente de historietas* (2017), *Poder trans: historieta latinoamericana* (2019), or *Quadrinhos queer* (2020). The international anthology *Drawing Power: Women's Stories of Sexual Harassment and Survival* (2019), edited by *underground comix* artist Diane Noomin, includes two autobiographical accounts by Latin American authors: "Bailanta," by Powerpaola, and "Beehive," by Marcela Trujillo.

As already has been indicated, the genre of graphic memoirs enjoys particular popularity among female comic artists in Latin America. Marcela Trujillo, for example, plays explicitly with different autobiographical genres ("chronicles" and "diaries") and large text elements in her graphic narratives around her alter ego figure "Maliki 4 ojos": *Las crónicas de Maliki 4 ojos* (2010), *Diario íntimo de Maliki 4 ojos* (2011), *El diario iluminado de Maliki 4 ojos* (2013), and *Diario oscuro* (2019). In her work, which Spanish scholar Ana Merinos sees in dialogue with North American (post)underground artists like Julie Doucet, Aline Kominsky, or Phoebe Gloeckner (Merino 2016, 36), she addresses her time in New York as a young artist, maternity, the conflictive separation from her husband, the resulting sexophobia, her life as a single mother and autonomous artist, and, in her recent work, the rape she suffered when she was nineteen years old. Besides sexual abuse and domestic violence, psychological violence is also a current topic in Latin American graphic narratives authored by women. Argentine Sole Otero's autofictional graphic narrative *Poncho Fue* (2017) tells the story of a toxic relationship between the protagonist Lu (whom we can read as an alter ego of the author) and her boyfriend Santi. His psychologically abusive behavior towards her leads to self-denial and depression for Lu who manages to overcome this life crisis (and her boyfriend) not least because of her prospering artistic career. Furthermore, nonfictional graphic narratives that deal with the dictatorships of South America are currently experiencing—to reuse the conceptual metaphor—a real "boom" in recent years. In this context, Nacha Vollenweider's autobiographical "graphic essay" *Notas al pie*, published in 2017 both in Germany (*Fußnoten*) and Argentina, is a paradigmatic and highly acclaimed example. In *Notas al pie* Vollenweider intertwines through visual "footnotes" ("notas al pie") two narratives that encompass, on the one hand: the forced "disappearance" of her uncle during the military dictatorship in Argentina, the familiar and the national trauma; and, on the other: the search for family traces in Switzerland, her relationship with her wife Chini and the migration crisis in Europe (Wrobel 2021a). In all three examples, corporeality and the performativity of visual embodiment are decisive elements for the development of the argument. These range from the staging of "disappearing bodies" (caused by the Argentinean state terror in *Notas al pie*) to moments of self-assertion and self-empowerment in *Poncho Fue*. Vollenweider's, Otero's, and Trujillo's visual language is thus directed not least of all against a hegemonic, patriarchal, and heteronormative gaze and its visual cultures and traditions. I will come back to this aspect in the analysis of Powerpaola's *Virus Tropical*.

In relation to scholarship, as a last point, one has to mention the pioneering role of Ana Merino, who has published widely on North American, but also on Spanish and Latin American (female) comics (2003, 2011, 2016, 2017). Elisa McCausland edited an issue on "Comics and Feminism" in the Spanish electronic journal *Tebeosfera* in 2018, including a very instructive article on feminist comics in Argentina, Chile, Brazil, and Mexico authored by Gabriela Borges (Brazil), Katherine Supnem (Chile), Mariela Acevedo (Argentina), and Maira Mayola (Mexico), to my knowledge the first broader investigation that examines the female production in Latin America from a transnational perspective. Quite recently, two themed issues were published that continue and deepen this line of research: "Mulheres, Humor e Cultura de Massa," edited by Cintia Lima Crescêncio, Mara Burkart, and Maria da Conceição Francisca Pires (in *Tempo & Argumento*, 2020), and "Mujeres, Historietas y Humor Gráfico," edited by Mara Burkart, Maria da Conceição Francisca Pires, and Laura Vázquez (in *Revista de la Red de Intercátedras de Historia de América Latina Contemporánea*, 2021). Reference should also be made to the catalogs *Presentes: autoras de tebeo de ayer y hoy* (2016), *Nosotras contamos: un recorrido por la obra de autoras de historieta y humor gráfico de ayer y hoy* (Acevedo 2019), *Coordenadas gráficas. Cuarenta historietas de autoras de España, Argentina, Chile y Costa Rica* (2020), and *Mujeres chilenas en la historieta* (2021), as well as to the anthology *Mulheres e quadrinhos*, edited by Dani Marino and Laluna Machado (2019), which brings together both graphic narratives and theoretical texts.

Powerpaola's *Virus Tropical*: Coming-of-Age Between Ecuador and Colombia

Probably the best-known and most discussed work in the context of Latin American graphic memoirs is *Virus Tropical* (2009) by Colombo-Ecuadorian Powerpaola (Paola Gaviria, *1977), who is often referred to—or even "marketed"—as the "Latin American Marjane Satrapi" (e.g. Gómez Gutiérrez 2015, 89; King and Page 2017, 16; Tarifeño 2011). In fact, she has at least two things in common with Satrapi: a black and white drawing style—at least in her debut—and the fact that *Virus Tropical* was also adapted into an animated movie with the same title in 2017, directed by Santiago Caicedo and released at the German film festival Berlinale in 2018. Her visual style, however, differs greatly from Satrapi's in its detailed, sometimes confusingly crowded panels and a more expressive representation form, even though both authors partly aim at a childlike-naïve expression. *Virus Tropical* has been published so far in France (2013), Italy (2013), Brazil (2015), the USA (2016), and Germany (2022). Besides her graphic debut, she published seven more graphic memoirs: *Por dentro* (2012), *Diario* (2013), *qp* (2014), *Todo va a estar bien* (2015), *Nos vamos* (2016) *Amazonas: diario de viaje* (2016), and *Espero porque dibujo* (2019), in addition to innumerous graphic short stories that were either self-published on her blog or the *Chicks on Comics*' website[9] or integrated into international anthologies. Powerpaola can be considered one of the most important networkers in the Latin American and international female comic scene. Together with the Dutch artist Joris Bas Backer, she founded *Chicks on Comics* in 2008, an international group with a feminist agenda that includes several comic artists from Latin America, especially from Argentina.

With *Virus Tropical*, Powerpaola inscribes herself in the tradition of coming-of-age-stories, a genre, as discussed earlier, that is particularly popular in graphic literature. Thereby, *Virus Tropical* is located between the global and the local: on the one hand, the experiences Powerpaola's avatar "Paola" makes and the phases she goes through are very typical (universal) for coming-of-age stories, reflected also in some of the twelve chapter titles (e.g., "La familia," "Las despedidas" ["The farewells"], "La adolescencia," "La identidad," etc.). As in other graphic narratives of this kind (think of Satrapi's *Persepolis*, Thompson's *Blankets*, or Bechdel's *Fun Home*), the story is told by an adult first-person narrator who manifests herself in the captions as a "present voice" and who we identify with both the growing up protagonist "Paola" ("past voice") and the author/drawer of *Virus Tropical*, Powerpaola. The tacit agreement of the autobiographical pact (Lejeune) includes here, thus, three entities. As in other graphic memoirs, there are also self-reflexive moments, e.g. when, after a childhood episode, the adult Paola addresses two friends with whom she has lost contact and physically portrays herself as the present author, with short, dark hair (Powerpaola 2013, 90). Here, too, it is the family constellation that motivates the dynamics of the action: Paola's father Uriel is a former catholic priest who violated his vows by marrying her mother Hilda and having three children with her (Figure 2.1).[10] The initial splash

Figure 2.1 Hilda and Uriel

[9] *Chicks on Comics*: https://chicksoncomics.tumblr.com/ (accessed November 12, 2020).
[10] Powerpaola 2013, 5. All images courtesy Powerpaola.

page shows, thus, the procreation of Paola as a kind of "fall from grace" (even if Paola is already their third child): her parents are shown having sexual intercourse, Uriel's Bible and the rosary lie forgotten under the stool on which they copulate, the expressionless—above all affectionless—faces are turned toward each other. On the floor, we can see other objects that anticipate specific moments in *Virus Tropical*, such as the pistol (foreshadowing the drug violence Paola experiences in Cali) or a money note and dominoes (Hilda keeps her and her daughters financially afloat by reading the future from the stones, after Uriel leaves the family). The caption reads "Quito, 1976" (Figure 2.2).[11]

The father's (religious) hypocrisy is repeatedly referred to, for example on another splash page (Figure 2.2) showing Uriel in a devotional prayer; he is standing on his Bible, the cross of the rosary dangles ironically upside down. In the background an airplane can be seen, in which—according to the previous plot—Uriel's mother is traveling back to Colombia, but it also anticipates that he himself will leave the family in the following chapter. The clouds seem to be slipping away from Uriel himself, as Powerpaola represents him farting (at another point, little Paola is shown thinking: "Huele a pedo," 33),[12] satirizing, thus, the supposed opposition between religiosity and undignified behavior by the subversive potential of comics' visual language.

Figure 2.2 Uriel

---

[11] Powerpaola 2013, 25.
[12] "Smells like farts." All English translations from *Virus Tropical* are from the first US-American edition, translated by Jamie Richards (cf. Powerpaola 2016).

On the other hand, local aspects play a major role in *Virus Tropical*, which takes place during Colombia's violent drug cartel warfare era of the 1980s and 1990s. As a child, when the family is still living in Ecuador, Paola finds a cocaine spoon in her dollhouse which belongs to her older sister Claudia (42–3). At the age of fourteen, already in Cali, Colombia, she experiences a shoot-out between members of the Cali and Medellin cartels, a situation in which she also has her first kiss (111–12). The childlike-naïve drawing style stands in opposition to what is represented in these cases, also to the explicit sexual scenes (e.g. 151). Another local, historical reference that creates authenticity and highlights the factual aspects of the narrative, is the visit of Pope John Paul II to Ecuador in 1985, when Paola was seven years old (37). Even more important in relation to local aspects, however, are the linguistic details. Paola grows up in Quito and after moving to Cali she is mocked by her classmates for her Ecuadorian accent and vocabulary. Her sister Patty teaches her the regional way of speaking the "caleño" dialect to make it easier for Paola to fit in (100–1; Patty is not only the "linguistic" initiator for Paola, she also shows her how to use hygienic products and teaches her about sex). In general, however, regional (Ecuadorian or Colombian) vocabulary in *Virus Tropical* is provided with a footnote by the author, with a "translation" of the specific word into a more "standard Spanish," to ensure understanding. A third aspect are the intermedial dialogues established in the graphic narrative. The circulation of music and also TV programs in the Hispanic world is very widespread. Thus, most of the music quoted in *Virus Tropical* varies between contemporary Spanish (indie) pop (Mecano, 76; Christina y los Subterráneos, 114; Los Rodríguez, 149), Caribbean merengue and salsa (Miami Band, Juan Luis Guerra, Gilberto Santa Rosa, 117–18), or bambuco, a music tradition from the Andean region in Colombia (José A. Morales, 110), while music and lyrics often reflect Paola's feelings and emotions. When her beloved sister Patty moves back to Quito, however, Pink Floyd's "Wish You Were Here" is played at her farewell party (155): the universal experience of loss is illustrated here by a song that is globally known and listened to in similar situations.

With reference to Hillary Chute, who emphasizes nonfictional graphic narratives as a medium that "takes the body seriously" (Chute 2010, 4), I would like to conclude this chapter by highlighting two aspects or moments in *Virus Tropical* that play a key role in the negotiation of feminist discourses and create a type of "counter-gaze" (Wrobel 2021b). As mentioned before, Uriel was a priest before he married Hilda and therefore, on principle, he should not have had children at all according to the rule of celibacy. Paola's mother, on the other hand, after having two daughters with her husband, Claudia and Patty, underwent a tubal ligation. In other words, Hilda's pregnancy with Paola goes against all odds. The doctors (all men) she consults after noticing the growing belly (Figure 2.3),[13] offer different explanations for the swelling: since Hilda has been sterilized, pregnancy is ruled out from the outset. It is actually this scene from where the title *Virus Tropical* originates, as one of the doctors diagnosticates

---

[13] Powerpaola 2013, 9.

Figure 2.3 Diagnoses

Hilda with a "tropical virus" (9). Despite the quite evident symptoms of her own body's transformation—which Powerpaola also graphically depicts in all evidence—Hilda accepts the somewhat absurd diagnoses made by the doctors:

The fact that she has internalized the "male-scientific knowledge" (Gómez Gutiérrez 2015, 92)—due to the surgery she cannot be pregnant—is further highlighted when Hilda, after several consultations, meets an indigenous woman on the street selling her some corn (Figure 2.4).[14] This woman, also the mother of a child that she carries wrapped in cloth on her back, close to her body, immediately recognizes Hilda's pregnancy and asks her: "Cacerita, are you having a boy or a girl?" and Hilda answers with one of the diagnoses made by the doctors, while she looks directly at the reader: "Air." The involvement of the reader, in this case, intensifies the effect of estrangement that corresponds to Hilda's distancing from her own body. At the same time, we find our reaction reflected in the thought bubble ("?") and

[14] Powerpaola 2013, 10.

Figure 2.4 Hilda

the facial expression of the indigenous woman who, irritated, looks to the right side of the panel. Hilda accepts the fact of being pregnant only when, after meeting the woman, she consults another doctor, "recién llegado al Ecuador, después de su doctorado en México," who reveals to her: "Señora, usted tiene 5 meses de embarazo" (11).[15] Felipe Gómez Gutiérrez rightfully observes the oppositional configuration of the (supposedly masculine, Western and authorized) "medical–technological" knowledge—which fails here—and the (supposedly feminine, autochthonous and illicit) "intuitive" knowledge, while he emphasizes the fact that Paola's mother internalized the former to a degree that she ignores her own body. Paola's very existence challenges this type of knowledge in an analogous way to how Powerpaola challenges the male dominance in the field of comics with *Virus Tropical* (cf. Gómez Gutiérrez, 91–2).

[15] "just arrived in Ecuador after finishing medical school in Mexico"; "Señora, you are five months pregnant."

Paola's—quite bloody—birth (Figure 2.5)[16] marks a caesura in the (patriarchal) family structures. When Uriel learns about his wife's third pregnancy (deemed impossible), he wishes that this time he will finally become the father of "un hombrecito," "a little man" (11), a wish that will not be fulfilled. It is significant that not only is another girl born, but Hilda contradicts Uriel for the first time when he wants to name the baby after his friend, a nun with the very pious name "María Pía." With determination and an expression of irritation, Hilda answers him: "No, esta vez yo escojo el nombre, se

Figure 2.5 Paola's birth

---

[16] Powerpaola 2013, 14.

Figure 2.6 La adolescencia

va a llamar: Paola" (14),[17] transforming, thus, the birth of her third daughter into a moment of female self-empowerment.

From this scene on, the Uriel character gradually loses importance and presence in *Virus Tropical*. When he leaves the family a couple of years later, Hilda has to finance herself and her three daughters. Paola therefore grows up in a family consisting solely of women.

---

[17] "No, I'm choosing this time. She will be called: Paola."

Figure 2.7 Herodotus Io

Another image of utmost relevance in the context of corporeality and its representations in *Virus Tropical* is the splash page of the chapter dealing with Paola's adolescence (Figure 2.6).[18] In 1990, at the age of 14, Paola and her mother move from Quito to Cali. On the day of her arrival in Colombia, of all days, the protagonist gets her

---

[18] Powerpaola 2013, 91.

period for the first time, which is also reflected in the splash page. The representation of Paola, in this case, is based on complex intermedial dialogues.

The image is visually inspired by a woodcut from the first French edition of the Latin translation of Herodotus' *The Histories* (approx. 430 BC) from about 1510, which shows the abduction of Io by the Phoenicians (Figure 2.7).[19] The boat carries supposedly Io, who is depicted with a phoenix on her head, a symbol of cyclic regeneration, floating through the waters. On Powerpaola's splash page for the chapter "La adolescencia," the protagonist is being carried by the flows of her own menstruation, symbolizing the beginning of her adolescence and the process of becoming a woman (she wears a blossom on her T-shirt), as well as the move itself. In her hands, she holds tight on one of her dolls, which she plays with in one of the previous chapters. Here we can recognize parallels—as also observed by Gómez Gutiérrez (2015, 97)—with the emblematic scene of King Kong capturing Ann Darrow and holding her in his hand, while he is surrounded by helicopters. However, in this image, Paola lets go of two other dolls ("Ken" and an ALF puppet who drop into the sea) and looks down to the Barbie doll that not only resembles Ann Darrow physically, but also looks up to Paola in fear. The reference to King Kong (and ALF) can be associated with the "monstrosity" or "alienness" that adolescence implies with the perception of one's own body changes, the mood swings, and the questioning of one's own identity, while the barbie doll in her hand also represents Western beauty standards Paola is confronted with. In the background, we can see the city of Cali and an erupting volcano, also a symbol for the beginning of adolescence and sexual activity. This specific image seems particularly relevant to me for two reasons: it is proof of the complex transmedial dialogues that comics are capable of and, even more important, shows how the author creates a productive tension arising from the alleged opposition between "high culture" (Herodotus) and "popular culture" (King Kong, ALF). Secondly, because it draws attention, on a more general level, to the fact that in graphic narratives authored by women there are several cases in which menstruation blood (or other female body fluids) is somehow related to the drawing ink (Wrobel 2020). The flow of her own menstruation, depicted as a "sea of blood" in which Paola's boat floats, not least also a clear reference to Julie Doucet's graphic short story "Heavy Flow" (1993), is transformed here into a (somewhat turbulent) means of transport that takes the protagonist to a new stage in her life. In this sense, the image dialogues with that of her birth when (after the water has broken) it is the flow of "maternal blood" (actually, amniotic fluid) that brings her into the world. In the last chapter of *Virus Tropical*, it will be paint that changes her life once again.

---

[19] *Herodoti Halicarnassei Thurii Historie parentis memoratissimi Nove Muse a Laurentio Valla tralate cu Prenotamentis & additionibus non antea Impressis: nec non indice & productissimo & facilimo.* Paris: Joanne Parvo, 1510. The corresponding woodcut can be consulted on several websites, for example at https://camillesourget.com/en-607-rare-books-first-edition-precious-books-herodotus-herodote-herodoti-halicarnassei-thurii-historie-parentis-the-first-french-edition-of-.html (accessed November 12, 2020). For this reference, I would like to thank Paola Gaviria (Powerpaola) and also my student Oxana Dubova who interviewed the author in the framework of a seminar I taught in 2015 ("Comics and graphic novels in Brazil and Latin America," Freie Universität Berlin).

Conclusion

Graphic narratives have not only become suitable for literary awards, they are also impulse-giving for literary and cultural theoretical debates. Hereby, the genre of the graphic memoir plays an important role: in the autobiographical/autofictional genre, female authors in particular bring new, often still marginalized or neglected thematic impulses and perspectives. Powerpaola's *Virus Tropical* can be considered particularly relevant both within the debate on graphic narratives as "World Literature" and in relation to the negotiation of feminist discourses in comics. Her work, a coming-of-age story that problematizes religious hypocrisy and patriarchal family structures, coincides in several aspects with graphic memoirs such as *Persepolis*, *Fun Home*, or *Blankets* that were both critically acclaimed and commercially successful internationally, not least in relation to the complex intermedial dialogues Powerpaola establishes. These dialogues are composed of different elements of both "high" and "popular" culture and support the feminist tenor of the work, while at the same time creating a tension between the global and the local. Both with reference to the rape of Io by the Phoenicians and to the King Kong/Ann Darrow scene, Powerpaola converts moments in which female figures become (passive) victims of an abduction into their opposite: Paola is carried by the flow of her own menstruation (i.e., self-directedly, if you will) to the Colombian city of Cali and thus also into a new (life) chapter. The visual embodiment of Powerpaola's adolescence illustrates therefore also a powerful response to the colonial (that is Western) hegemonic gaze.

The presence of Powerpaola (against all odds, if we remember the improbability of her conception) in Latin America, but also in the global comic world, helped other women artists come forward. Paola Gaviria does not only serve as an example or role model in this context, she actively supports other women, not least as one of the co-founders of the international feminist comic collective *Chicks on Comics*. She holds, in this sense, an important networker or even gatekeeper position that previously was reserved for male creators and agents in the comic production. Applied to the idea of a global circulation of literature and against the background of the fact that this article was written during the COVID-19 pandemic, it can be stated that the female ink from Latin America is becoming increasingly widespread—or contagious, as stated on *Virus Tropical*'s 2013 book cover: "¡Cuidado, contagio!"

References

Baetens, Jan. 2011. "World Literature and Popular Literature: Toward a wordless literature?" In D'Haen, Theo, Damrosch,David, andDjelal, Kadir, eds. *The Routledge Companion to World Literature*. London: Taylor and Francis, 336–44.

Bechdel, Alison. 2007[2006]. *Fun Home: A Family Tragicomic*. Boston/New York: Mariner Books.

Borges, Gabriela, Supnem, Katherine, Mayola, Maira, and Acevedo, Mariela. 2018. "Historieta feminista en América Latina: Autoras de Argentina, Chile, Brasil y México." In *Revista Tebeosfera*. Tercera época, 6. https://www.tebeosfera.com/documentos/historieta_feminista_en_america_latina_autoras_de_argentina_chile_brasil_y_mexico.html (accessed March 1, 2020).

Canclini, Néstor García. 1995. *Hybrid Cultures: Strategies for Entering and Leaving Modernity*. Transl. by Christopher L. Chiappari and Silvia L. López. Minneapolis: University of Minnesota Press.

Catalá Carrasco, Jorge, Drinot, Paulo, and Scorer, James, eds. 2017. *Comics & Memory in Latin America*. Pittsburgh, PA: Univ. of Pittsburgh Press.

Chute, Hillary. 2008. "Comics as Literature? Reading Graphic Narrative." *PMLA*, 123 (2, Mar.): 452–65.

Chute, Hillary L. 2010. *Graphic Women: Life Narrative and Contemporary Comics*. New York: Columbia Univ. Press.

García, Santiago. 2012. *A novela gráfica*. Trans. Magda Lopes. São Paulo: Martins Fontes.

Gómez Gutiérrez, Felipe. 2015. "Virus Tropical. Presencia y relevancia del personaje autobiográfico femenino en la novela gráfica colombiana." *IBEROAMERICANA. América Latina – España – Portugal*, 15 (57), 85–102.

L'Hoeste, Héctor Fernández and Poblete, Juan, eds. 2009. *Redrawing the Nation: National Identity in Latin/o American Comics*. Basingstoke: Palgrave.

King, Edward, and Page, Joanna. 2017. *Posthumanism and the Graphic Novel in Latin America*. London: UCL Press.

Kukkonen, Karin. 2013. *Studying Comics and Graphic Novels*. Malden, MA: John Wiley & Sons Inc.

Lent, John, ed. 2005. *Cartooning in Latin America*. Cresskill, NJ: Hampton.

Marino, Dani, and Machado, Laluna, eds. 2019. *Mulheres e quadrinhos*. São Paulo: Skript.

McCloud, Scott. 1993. *Understanding Comics: The Invisible Art*. New York: Harper Perennial.

Merino, Ana. 2003. *El cómic hispánico*. Madrid: Cátedra.

Merino, Ana. 2011. "Entre el margen y el canon: pensamientos discursivos alrededor del cómic latinoamericano." *Revista Iberoamericana*, 67 (234): 13–18.

Merino, Ana. 2016. "El eje femenino americano y la consolidación de sus miradas". In *Presentes: autoras de tebeo de ayer y hoy*. Exposition catalogue. Madrid: AECID, 24–36.

Merino, Ana. 2017. *Diez ensayos para pensar el cómic*. León: Universidad de León/EOLAS.

Noomin, Diane, ed. 2019. *Drawing Power: Women's Stories of Sexual Violence, Harassment, and Survival*. Intro. by Roxane Gay. New York: Abrams Comicarts.

Otero, Sole. 2017. *Poncho Fue*. Barcelona: La Cúpula.

Pedri, Nancy. 2015. "Graphic Memoir: Neither Fact Nor Fiction." In Stein, Daniel, and Thon, Jan-Noël, eds. *From Comic Strips to Graphic Novels: Contributions to the Theory and History of Graphic Narrative*. 2nd ed. Berlin/Boston: De Gruyter, 127–54.

Powerpaola. 2013 [2011]. *Virus Tropical*. Barcelona: Mondadori.

Powerpaola. 2016. *Virus Tropical*. Transl. Jamie Richards. Minneapolis: 2dcloud.

Sainz, José, and Bidegaray, Alejandro, eds. 2017. *El Volcán: un presente de la historieta latino-americana*. Rosario, Santa Fe: e(m)r / Buenos Aires: Musaraña Editora.

Satrapi, Marjane. 2014 [2000–2003]. *Persepolis*. Transl. Stephan Pörtner. Zürich: Edition Moderne.

Schmitz-Emans, Monika. 2015. "Graphic Narrative as World Literature." In Stein, Daniel, and Thon, Jan-Noël (eds.). *From Comic Strips to Graphic Novels: Contributions to the Theory and History of Graphic Narrative*. Berlin/Boston: De Gruyter, 385–406.

Schmitz-Emans, Monika. 2018. "World Literature in Graphic Novels and Graphic Novels as World Literature." In Fang, Weigui, ed. *Tensions in World Literature: Between the Local and the Universal*. Singapore: Springer Singapore, 219–38.

Schröer, Marie. 2016. "Graphic Memoirs – autobiografische Comics." In Abel, Julia, and Klein, Christian, eds. *Comics und Graphic Novels: Eine Einführung*. Stuttgart: J.B. Metzler, 263–75.

Scorer, James, ed. 2020. *Comics Beyond the Page in Latin America*. London: UCL Press.

Sina, Véronique. 2020. "'The Good, the Bad, and the Ugly'. Obszönität und Tabubruch in den Comics von Aline Kominsky-Crumb." *Closure. Kieler e-Journal für Comicforschung*, #6.5: 99–122.

Smith, Sidonie, and Watson, Julia. 2010. *Reading Autobiography. A Guide for Interpreting Life Narratives*. 2nd ed. Minneapolis/London: University of Minnesota Press.

Spiegelman, Art. 2003 [1986/1991]: *The Complete Maus*. London: Penguin Books.

Spiegelman, Art. 2011. *MetaMaus*. New York: Pantheon Books.

Stein, Daniel, and Thon, Jan-Noël, eds. 2015. *From Comic Strips to Graphic Novels: Contributions to the Theory and History of Graphic Narrative*. Berlin/Boston: De Gruyter.

Tarifeño, Leonardo. 2011. "El Virus Powerpaola." In: *La Nación*; https://www.lanacion.com.ar/cultura/el-virus-powerpaola-nid1385136 (accessed March 1, 2020).

Thompson, Craig. 2017 [2003]. *Blankets: A Graphic Novel by Craig Thompson*. London: Faber & Faber.

Vergueiro, Waldomiro, and Fernandes D'Oliveira, Gêisa. 2011. "De discursos não competentes a saberes dominantes: reflexões sobre as histórias em quadrinhos no cenário brasileiro." *Revista Iberoamericana*, LXXVII (234): 135–48.

Versaci, Rocco. 2007 *This Book Contains Graphic Language: Comics as Literature*. New York/London: Continuum.

Vollenweider, Nacha. 2017. *Notas al pie*. Buenos Aires: Maten al Mensajero.

Worth, Jennifer. 2007. "Unveiling: *Persepolis* as Embodied Performance." *Theatre Research International*, 32 (2): 143–60.

Wrobel, Jasmin. 2020. "Tinta(s) femenina(s): La recuperación del cuerpo en la narrative latinoamericana y española." In Callsen, Berit, and Groß, Angelika, eds. *Cuerpos en oposición: representations de corporalidad en la literature y cultura hispánicas actuals*. Madrid: Iberoamericana, 15–41.

Wrobel, Jasmin. 2021a. "Entrelazamientos de memoria(s) entre Hamburgo y Argentina: la representación de la ausencia forzada en *Notas al pie*, de Nacha Vollenweider." In Buschmann, Albrecht, and Souto, Luz C., eds. *Decir desaparecido(s) II. Análisis transculturales de la desaparición forzada*. Berlin: LIT, 97–113.

Wrobel, Jasmin. 2021b. "Körper/Blicke und Selbst(be)zeichnungen bei Pagu, Laerte und Powerpaola." *Closure. Kieler e-journal für Comicforschung*, #7.5, 64–81.

3

An Alternative Worldliness: Verbal and Visual Experimentations in *Fī shiqqat bāb el-loq* (*The Apartment in Bab El-Louk*)

Dima Nasser

Picture this: wordlessly, the work opens with a framed black-and-white illustration of a bathroom sink and counter against a tiled turquoise wall suspended in the center of a blank page. The close-up angle allows for only the view of the frame's contents: cluttered creams, serums, sprays, and roll-ons next to bottles of oil, and medicinal herbs (see Figure 3.1). The viewer is immediately struck by the distance between herself and the small framed image, which appears buried in the thick white cadre of the page. The alienating effect lasts only for a moment, however, as the left half of the spread quickly presents a spatial overcorrection: the angle shifts, the distance closes, and the viewer is pulled into the enlarged panel. The gaze lifts up from the tap, as though one were standing in front of the sink and made to peer into an expected mirror, only to find it is another framed picture of a giant cockroach fastened to the wall with writing on its surface (see Figure 3.2). The oversized insect is again framed by chunks of text above and below it. The lack of space allows one no choice but to read the words inscribed on the surface, which welcome you into what is arguably the most intimate room inside this apartment in Bāb el-Loq. The words belong to a disembodied speaker that claims ownership of the private space and the clutter within, and directly addresses what is assumed to be the reader–viewer but also a prospective tenant in the narrative world. The message written on the mirror shifts gears to provide an early warning to said tenant, which only confirms the discomfort and alienation: you have stumbled upon a lonely place that resembles the estrangement one feels when moving to a new country, where you will continue to wait and watch for signs of life in a cluttered field.

The following spread offers a slanted view of this old, haunted building's exterior with part of a photograph captured at an upwards angle. The same voice returns to tell the unwitting tenant that the apartment interior is merely an extension of

---

Images from the graphic text are courtesy of the artist. Copyright © 2014 by Donia Maher and Ganzeer.

56 Graphic Novels and Comics as World Literature

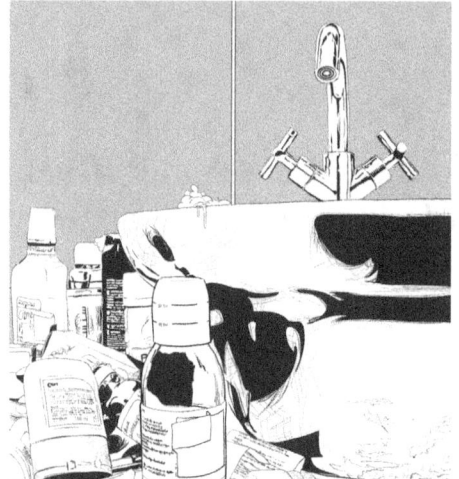 

Figure 3.1 and 3.2 Opening of *Fī shiqqat bāb el-loq*

Bāb el-Loq, a clustered and overly crowded neighborhood in downtown Cairo that fills one with a sense of dread due to the constantly watching eyes and the "many crazies" lurking under the balcony (Maher 2013, 4).[1] The voice directs the act of reading and viewing through the glass window and looks out over "the corners of Cairo that appear neglected and desolate, like a crime scene that has been deserted on purpose" (3). It advises the tenant to keep the curtains drawn in an attempt to dispel the "sad scene" and create a false barrier of protection against the paranoid neighborhood watch, which explains the tenant's impulse to always have a travel bag packed and ready to go. True to its warning, the bottom-right corner reveals part of a man's illustrated face, his disembodied head tilted slightly forward, his beady eyes cast upwards in a still sideways stare (see bottom of Figure 3.3).

These images describe the disturbing opening scenes of the 2013 Arabic graphic text titled *Fī shiqqat bāb el-loq* (translated by Elisabeth Jacquette in 2017 as *The Apartment in Bab el-Louk*) as rendered by the prominent multi-disciplinary Egyptian artist Ganzeer. An overwhelming sense of anxiety pervades the work from the beginning to the very last spread, on which the single word "تمّ" occupies a central and diminutive position in an otherwise blank page. On the one hand, *tammat*, literally meaning "it is finished" or "the end," signals the work's denouement. On the other hand, it also constitutes an imperfect paronomasia (*jinās nāqiṣ*) with *tamūt* (تموت), which means "you die," nailing shut the proverbial coffin of the random

---

[1] All translations from Arabic are my own unless otherwise indicated.

Figure 3.3 Page of *Fī shiqqat bāb el-loq*

death scene that immediately precedes the end, and cementing the mysterious atmosphere that undergirds the entire work with its cryptic neighborhood setting and the silhouetted characters who occupy it.

Fī shiqqat bāb el-loq is an album-sized[2] work in two visually dissimilar parts that are connected through the space of the apartment building: the first and longer part constitutes Ganzeer's visual documentation in black, white, and turquoise, that uses several forms of superimposed media—hand-drawn illustrations, photographs, calligrams, and newspaper clippings—set against diurnal reflections written in standard Arabic prose by Egyptian artist–writer, Donia Maher. The verbal and visual registers work together to juxtapose a new tenant's nervous experience moving into a strange apartment with equally unsettling scenes from the neighborhood. The second part of the work looks more like a conventional comic and is a brief sequence of cartoon-like illustrations in black and white made by political cartoonist Ahmad Nady and coupled with vernacular Egyptian dialogue, in which a man's death is discovered in that same apartment. Acting as a temporal device, a single black page divides, or perhaps links, the latter part as a flashback to the former, allowing the reader–viewer to conclude that the new tenant had moved into that same apartment only two weeks after the murder had taken place.

This multi-stylistic work, which won the Kahil Award for Best Graphic Novel in 2016, appears at an exciting time in the production and distribution of collaborative art projects and graphic texts in Egypt. In 2015, Cairo joined less than a handful of other Arab cities as a hub for one of the biggest and most attractive comics festivals in the region when three Egyptian comics artists launched CairoComix as a counterpoint to the *Festival International de la Bande Dessinée d'Alger*. The festival has since put Arabic comics under the spotlight by hosting sales and exhibitions of local and international comics as well as talks and workshops that attract regional and international artists and a solid popular fan base among the Egyptian youth.[3] It is curious and perhaps inspiring to think of how an art, literary, and cultural sphere could burgeon in spite of a militarized and authoritarian political environment where the notorious surveillance and print censorship laws under Gamal 'Abdel Nasser and Anwar el-Sadat have even spawned cyber-based iterations to curb freedom of speech online under el-Sisi.[4] Arabic comics have not only been successful on a local front: they have also been securing afterlives in translation shortly after or even simultaneously with the Arabic publication. And if the artist's career is any indicator, it can be argued that working in the comics form has created and received possibilities for the artist to work on projects across artistic mediums in international cities all at once. Ganzeer, for instance, became hugely successful both in Egypt and on the international art scene in the aftermath of the

---

[2] The album has an A4 standard size and format distinct from American comic books and trade paperbacks, and is usually associated with the Franco-Belgian *album de bande dessinée*.
[3] See Marcia Lynx Qualey, "CairoComix Festival Kicks Off" (2015).
[4] Egyptian President 'Abdel Fattah el-Sisi ratified the Anti-Cyber and Information Technology Crimes Law in August 2018, which allows government authorities to block websites in the name of national security and combatting extremism and terrorism. The most popular targets have been sites belonging to independent media organizations. See Miller, "Egypt leads the pack in internet censorship across the Middle East" (2018).

2011 Tahrir Revolution when his series of street artworks titled "Martyr Murals," graffiti portraits that commemorated the revolution's victims, began to proliferate as rapidly as the rising death toll on walls in public spaces.[5] He is known for being a versatile artist, working comfortably between many mediums, and is driven by producing socially engaged work. In an artist's statement from 2011, he spoke about what it means to defy the compartmentalization of artistic professions today by working across the institutionalized hierarchies of elite and popular art or high and low culture:

> I'm not exactly a graphic designer, nor am I a product designer. I am not particularly a street-artist or comic book artist, nor am I an installation artist, writer, speaker, or video-maker. But I've had the chance to assume one of those roles at different periods of time and in different locations around the world.
>
> (Ganzeer / European Culture Congress)

Ganzeer has since gone on to exhibit his work in some of the major art cities around the world including Dubai, Berlin, Brussels, Toronto, and New York, while collaborating on multiple publications and giving public talks on contemporary art practices. One of the key takeaways from the nature of his work is its interdisciplinarity and its refusal to be categorized under a conventional genre and form. Similarly, the graphic text medium is one conceived through a sense of worldliness, in that it cannot help drawing on a plurality of visual forms as well as cultural and aesthetic influences, and it lends itself well to translation and circulation especially when it opens a "window unto another culture" at a politically interesting moment. Often, however, graphic texts from the Middle East are implicitly conceived of in ready-made models like the American graphic novel to gain a worldly currency, leaving alternative or more experimental works—or even works written in a major Middle Eastern language—without much visibility beyond local or regional markets and cultural spheres.[6] It is for this reason that *Fī shiqqat bāb el-loq* presents an interesting case in point as it resists being labeled by the constraining marketing term "graphic novel" and has nevertheless succeeded outside its place of origin.

Ganzeer, Maher, and Nady's qualms with calling their collaboration a graphic novel is the perfect analogy for the very problem this paper seeks to address: the homogenization of aesthetic and literary experimentation under the assumptions of a

---

[5] Examples of Ganzeer's murals can be found on the artist's webpage: https://ganzeer.com/Martyr-Murals.

[6] See for example, Chris Reyns-Chikuma and Houssem Ben Lazreg's "The Discovery of Marjane Satrapi and the Translation of Works from and about the Middle East" (2018). It speaks about how Satrapi's *Persepolis*, considered the first Middle Eastern graphic novel, has been wildly successful because it combines all the universally known markers of the graphic narrative: black-and-white adult-oriented content, a personal memoir (a young girl's *bildungsroman*) that infuses a non-extremist telling of modern Iranian history and culture, a linear succession of small panels in the French *images d'Épinal* style, and it certainly did not hurt for it to have been originally written in French and published in France, the center of *bandes dessinées*.

standardized formal vocabulary perpetuated by the use of problematic terms that carry valences of consumerism as with "graphic novel," or colonial culture as with "*bande dessinée*," or cultural tokenization as with "manga." This important discussion on theorizing the medium itself has already begun and the lack of consensus is telling but productive. Scott McCloud, one of the foundational scholars of the field, prefers calling all output in this verbal–visual format "comics," and he posits an open-ended definition for it as a medium of sequential art that is not restricted to a singular genre, representational form, subject matter, materiality, or reading public in his theoretical work *Understanding Comics: The Invisible Art* (1993). This has been contested by proponents of the alternative term "comix," which first appeared in America in the mid-1960s to distinguish the form's history as children's entertainment from an emerging subgenre of black-and-white, adult-oriented "underground" comic books. Hillary Chute, on the other hand, who is fast becoming the foremost academic expert in the American field, offers a more specific definition of what she calls "graphic narratives" in her essay "Comics as Literature? Reading Graphic Narrative" (2008) as "a hybrid word-and-image form in which two narrative tracks, one verbal and one visual, register temporality spatially" (452). The very idea of a differentiated duality between a strictly visual medium and a strictly verbal one, however, has already been called into larger question by visual culture theorists such as W.J.T. Mitchell, who argues in "There are no Visual Media" (2005) that "all media are, from the standpoint of sensory modality, mixed media" (257). In other words, even at its purest state, visual imagery instantaneously evokes verbal and aural language for its expression. Similarly, the words on the page invariably activate pictorial, aural, and even tactile modes of perception in the engaged reader's mind. The impurity that thus constitutes the comics medium is a unique representational asset that demands a nuanced method of consuming pictures and words at the same time. Chute makes the argument that "[c]omics is an aesthetically self-consciously artificial form: panels and gutters, tiers and grids provide its grammar, which shapes the surface of the page. While all media, to some extent, do the work of framing, comics crucially makes its frames hand-drawn and *literal*, and juxtaposes them, carving temporal moments out of the space the page provides" (Chute 2012, 408).[7] It is for this reason that comics are the ideal medium for dealing with temporally aberrant and aesthetically experimental narratives. Because it is a non-transparent form, it calls attention to its own materiality and construction, and demands careful multimodal ways of reading and seeing. Going a step further, I would argue for the cautious and circumstantial use of the term "narrative," because it implies a sense of teleology and chronology that set up expectations of a linear plot developing alongside a steadily progressing timeline, one that is ultimately meant to satisfy the reader–viewer's storytelling expectations. *Fī shiqqat bāb el-loq* is one such work that defies these comfortable expectations, and instead offers the reader–viewer a visual vocabulary of alienation, a truncated model of time as well as fragmented flashes of life under surveillance in the local neighborhood. It does so by completely obliterating the grammar of panels and word bubbles that is typical of graphic novels. It therefore

---

[7] Emphasis original.

becomes imperative to break with conventional ways of seeing by privileging an inter-artistic approach to reading the aesthetic consciousness of this work, one which will challenge homeostatic understandings of visuality and textuality in the comics medium. This, in turn, foregrounds the Arabic form's emergence at the intersection of a contextualized history of modern Egyptian art and literature rather than simply reading it as an imitation of Western European and American models.

The Egyptian Graphic Text: Within and Beyond a History of Egyptian Modernism

This hybrid word-and-image medium has a long history in Egypt, which makes it difficult to speak about *Fī shiqqat bāb el-loq* in isolation from the larger tradition of literary and visual representation in Egypt. By the 1950s, the comics form had become established in the medium of glossy children's magazines such as *Sindibād* (est. 1952) and *Samīr* (est. 1956) which were extremely popular, as Lina Ghaibeh points out in her 2015 article "Telling Graphic Stories of the Region: Arabic Comics after the Revolution" (324). Their content was mainly didactic and concerned children's education and entertainment, but these same comics artists (*fannānīn/rassāmīn komiks*) were also caricaturists who had been publishing political cartoons (*karikatūr*) in Egyptian newspapers, magazines, and dailies since the 1920s (Guyer 2017). In the first half of the twentieth century we thus find a class of artists had emerged that was associated with both children's magazines and political newspapers, and we see evidence of a strong crossover aesthetic between the two. Under Nasser, children's cartoons in *Sindibād* and *Samīr* were quickly politicized to serve as subliminal nationalist and pan-Arabist propaganda and widely circulating teaching aids to indoctrinate the young nation with patriarchal iconography, Arab traditions, as well as nationalist and pan-Arab culture. The same strategy is seen again with resistance comics and anti-Israel/pro-Palestine single-frame works and sequential strips after the 1967 Arab war with Israel in addition to comics that told the story of Nasser, father of the Egyptian nation, after his death in the 1970s (Guyer 2017, 335–6). As its title suggests, John Lent's article "Egyptian Cartooning: An Overview" (2007) provides a survey of the rich history of Egyptian cartoonists, their contributions to and satirical critiques of local and regional political situations in print publications such as *Roz el-Yūsef, Megallet al-ithnayn, Akhbār al-yom, Ṣabāḥ el-kheir, al-Ahrām, al-Akhbār*, etc. Two pioneer Egyptian cartoonists, Mohamed 'Abdel-Moneim Rakhkha and Zohdi al-'Awadi, set the bar in the 1920s for political expression with cartoons, and as the decades rolled by, cartoonists themselves have agreed that though there has been relatively more freedom in expression on social media and digital platforms, especially among opposition papers and blogs, the quality of work is down in comparison with their predecessors' ingenuity in creating social archetypes (150). As Rania Saleh (2007) explains, under Sadat's *infitāḥ*/open-door policy, the medium began to develop in modern Egypt through the importation and translation of American, French, and

Belgian comics in the 1970s (203). This was quickly followed by the infiltration of regionally circulating Arabic comics into the Egyptian market, such as the UAE's *Mājed* and Lebanon's *Aḥmad* series in the 1970s and 1980s (Ghaibeh 2015, 324). But even as the Egyptian market sold translated copies of Western comics, there always was a circulation of characters from the classical Arabic tradition in comics such as *Ibn Baṭṭūṭa* and *'Antara Ibn Shaddād*. Political cartoons about more serious social and intellectual concerns aimed at adults go back even further to the late nineteenth and early twentieth centuries. Despite censorship restrictions under the British occupation and the lack of non-commercial or independent publication opportunities for young writers and artists, there was a recognition, from the start, of the form's ability to critique and subvert state-sponsored narratives of "Progression" under the hegemony of the capitalist, westward-looking nation-state, to cast a critical light on sociopolitical injustices by activating concealed symbolic representations and by using external sites of production such as Beirut, London, and Paris, as well as underground networks of circulation that were more opaque to the government.

One of the major forerunners of Egyptian caricature was Ya'qub (James) Sanua, an Italian–Egyptian Jewish journalist, playwright, and the founding editor of the first illustrated Arabic-language journal in the late nineteenth century *Nahḍah* or Arab Revival period: *Abū Naẓẓārah Zarqah* (1877–1910). This weekly anti-imperial satirical journal began issuing scathing critiques of the tension between Khedive Ismaʿīl, who was then the ruler of Egypt, and European interests in the Suez Canal. Sanua produced lithographical illustrations of political cartoons alongside columns written in Egyptian vernacular, featuring the fictional character of the "man with blue spectacles" as the people's local witness and reporter of political developments. This hybrid method quickly became popular and created a reading and viewing public comprised of the elite and the masses, earning Sanua a sentence to exile, which he chose to live out in Paris where he continued to publish the journal and have it smuggled into Cairo until his death. *Abū Naẓẓārah* is often considered an early example of the Egyptian graphic text form; its most interesting aesthetic principle acting as a bridge between art illustration and journalism as well as realist and surrealist caricatures of Egyptian subjects and the ruling political party. This early example demonstrates an already maturing aesthetic consciousness and a consistent, popular, trans-class audience open to experimental crossover forms between word and image at the turn of the century. Sanua's graphic endeavors did not take place in a void: they were at the intersection of a group of experimental styles of writing and art produced, and bore a striking resemblance to the caricatures in Europe, especially the style of the British *Punch* and French *Le Charivari* as well as Ottoman works like *Hayal* and *Istikbal* (Guyer 2017, 334). This, however, did not constitute a simple exchange with the West: artists and writers like Sanua were reviving traditional forms of writing in Arabic (rhymed prose most associated with the *Maqāmah* genre) while also creating a new vocabulary of artistic expression. They were not, in other words, bypassing the local concern to look westward. For this reason, while the French influence with disproportionately small body parts compared to an unusually large head is clear, the influence of hybrid creatures, mainly animals with human heads, from Egyptian peasant and popular culture is equally potent, as seen with the snake

Figure 3.4 *Abū Naẓẓārah* (vol. 1 1878–1879)

and the buffalo (Figure 3.4). The latter illustration is a clear example of the image as a culturally referential signifier that communicates to a local public a symbolic sociopolitical message by using the public's own iconographic knowledge of social archetypes (the military officer, the Muslim sheikh, and the peasant). It activates a visual literacy that is possessed by Egyptians across social class, regardless of their level of education or ability to read Arabic, thereby rendering the explanatory text in the caption a complementary aid at best.

Sanua's modern artistic endeavor lies at the intersection among several political, technological, and cultural factors that collided in the nineteenth century to produce the lived experience that is now called Egyptian modernism. This is a field that is just coming into its own in response to the art history academy's lack of interest in Middle Eastern art past the year 1800, with its fixation on so-called "Islamic" art as the canonical example of "original" art from the Middle East, whereas genres of art since the nineteenth century are relegated as mere applications of an encounter with modern European art. In her nuanced reading of the history of modern Egyptian art in *Modernism on the Nile* (2019), Alex Seggerman offers the term "constellational modernism" in thinking about the finite yet flexible networks between artists, artworks, movements, and exhibition centers between the mid-nineteenth and mid-twentieth centuries. Drawing on the use of the astronomical term "constellation" by Theodor Adorno (who borrows it from Walter Benjamin), Seggerman posits that "constellational modernism rejects a central core or narrative, but rather frames modernism as a series of overlapping and intersecting units as opposed to concentric circles emanating from the metropole" (8). By regarding the work of every artist as a new constellation, she effectively argues that it is the (art) historian's job to trace infinitely new paths of connection and intersection. This allows for modern Egyptian art to escape the homogenizing identifier as "global" art, which in turn, has become the conventional way of thinking of all non-Euro–American art from around the world, and to see the literary and artistic production in Cairo and Alexandria as engaged in networks of modernism far more complicated than a one-to-one relationship with Paris or London.

Seggerman further contextualizes the emergence of modern Egyptian art in the *Nahḍah* (the cultural revival) in the nineteenth century when an industrial and technological modernity inaugurated by the printing press and the advent of colonialism dovetailed with a cultural modernity in art, literature, and translation, which wanted to negotiate a presence for itself in relation to notions of tradition, colonialism, and postcolonialism. She builds on Timothy Mitchell's definition of modernity as "a creation of the interaction between the West and non-West," but she complicates it by pointing out that while the lived experience of modernity in Egypt might have been an expression of imperialistic forces, it nevertheless managed to resonate and interact in overlapping and dyssynchronous ways with non-Western hubs in Chile, Shanghai, New Mexico, and other places. It is within this complicated but vital history of graphic representation that an aesthetically experimental work like *Fī shiqqat bāb el-loq* must be read.

Fī shiqqat bāb el-loq: A Visual Documentation of Fragmented Sights and Disembodied Sounds

As suggested earlier, *Fī shiqqat bāb el-loq* is obsessed with watching, waiting, and bearing witness. In *Disaster Drawn* (2016), Chute aptly describes a global turn in the twenty-first century toward documenting history, arguing that "we are now in a kind of golden age of documentary, in which attention to myriad forms of recording and archiving is greater than ever, and the work of documentary is central to all sorts of conversations" (5). Although she is speaking about a primarily American context, this can easily apply to Egypt before, during, and after several instances of revolt which have overwhelmed the first decade of the twenty-first century. The very form of comics arguably lends itself to presenting images as evidence. Its unorthodox "spatial grammar of gutters, grids, and panels" suggests an architecture of visual testimonies in time (4). But even without a convention of frames, panels, and gutters, *Fī shiqqat bāb el-loq* executes a visual documentation of sights and sounds in an equally experimental manner. When the narrator first describes to the prospective tenant the static café culture splayed on the curb outside the apartment building, the voice comments on the days that pass by with no noticeable change in the crowd of people that hangs around the café, men and women smoking their shisha water-pipes, playing backgammon, and sipping Turkish coffee (Figure 3.5). Detailed hand-drawn illustrations of plastic chairs and tables, dice, and an enlarged coffee cup and saucer are a faded version of nineteenth-century café

Figure 3.5 Café scene from *Fī shiqqat bāb el-loq*

culture in the cosmopolitan city. The drawings are conflated with the two black-and-white photographs that reveal similarly themed street scenes. The artist here affects an easy interplay between realism and abstraction, both styles of imagery operating on the same level of factual representation while also occupying multiple planes of perspective and depth, thereby intercepting the reader's ability to exercise a methodical reading of the comics page. This effectively forces the reader–viewer to look at the entire page at once and allot equal attention to all of its components rather than perform a linear reading along horizontal and vertical lines across panels in a conventional comic strip or *bande dessinée*.

There is no shortage of objects to look at in the graphic text but none propel life in a linear, progressional direction. Instead, the work activates a disoriented sense of seeing that parallels the fragmented, stagnant, and endlessly nightmarish state of the space being represented. Morning newspapers are another outmoded product that is available to excess, begging to be consumed and put out of their misery. As the new tenant picks up a two-week-old paper and looks at the headlines of what were once "current events," they read a modern version of the Cain and Abel story where one man murders his brother over a fifty-pound bank note dispute. The tenant's involuntary reaction of uncontrollable laughter suggests the irony of having rampant and unresolved petty crimes under a militarized government that exercises extreme surveillance and yet cannot identify this one criminal. But on a darker note of social realism, it also alludes to how poor, desperate, and without means one must be to be ready to kill for an inconsequential sum of money.[8] In keeping with the absurdity, the tenant then imagines another news-story has turned into a space for their own reflections, and ponders how death can offer an uncontestable narrative to one's life. It allows one to escape justice and can turn even a sinner into a saint who can no longer be persecuted for what they've said or done, because they are no longer part of the material world (see Figure 3.6). The story is, on the one hand, another surreal consequence of living in surveilled idleness. But it also indirectly reveals the irony of looking at state-sponsored newspapers (themselves a visual medium) as sources that report objective news by showing how much they do not know, while also suggesting satirical comics as more productive alternative spaces of personal testimonials. On a formal level, deploying a public writing platform as a personal genre, and doing so by parodying the visual format of news and reportage, are signs of an activated creative imagination and a psychological dexterity that can cope with an otherwise restrictive environment. It certainly sheds new light on the notion which is taken for granted that news is objective and impersonal when actually it is made up of human stories that in turn are transformed into objects and called "events" or "incidents." This falls in line with what Chute has to say about the current need to document personal and public testimonies in visual forms, and comics being the optimal form to do so. However, it also pushes further by reminding the reader that the people have always been objects of documentation by the state, and are implicated in endlessly multiplying cyclical processes of seeing and being seen.

Fī shiqqat bāb el-loq does not waste time building toward a world where sensory experience is all that is left to go on. But it is a world where these senses might play tricks on the spectator's mind. Choosing Bāb el-Loq, with its iconic turquoise

---

[8] Fifty Egyptian pounds is equivalent today to less than four US dollars.

Figure 3.6 Two-week-old newspaper depicts tenant's hysterical reaction to absurd fratricide story.

backdrops, is no accident. Located in the heart of downtown Cairo, it was first built in the thirteenth century under the Ayyubids and used to be famous for its once vibrant open-air market. It is also mere minutes away from Egypt's Ministry of Interior and the iconic Tal'at Harb and Tahrir Squares, which make it a highly surveilled residential area. As the tenant stands on the balcony, they hear the sound of protests floating upwards and they are eventually moved to follow the sounds and participate in the nearby Tahrir Square. But once the tenant does, they find nothing there and no one, yet the screams and chants persist. On a visual level, this is translated into a two-page spread with no ethnographic content, but rather predominant white spaces and only turquoise-colored scribbles on top that capture the familiar chaotic sound of protest carried through the air. We also see the looming statue of Mohammad Tal'at Harb, the renowned twentieth-century Egyptian nationalist economist who founded Banque Misr, illustrated at an austere upwards angle, emphasizing the alienating mood in the square and the irony in the government's coopting of nationalist symbols of the country's historical struggle against imperialism.

The expressionist nature of the images so far seems to look out of place in the comics medium, which usually sets up neat expectations of discrete images within framed panels that move in a linear manner in the narrative. These images, however, are not unusual to the modernist Egyptian art scene. In fact, they grow out of a Surrealist movement in poetry and painting that gained ground in the late 1930s and 1940s with the Art and Liberty Group founded by George Henein and Ramses Yunan to promote anti-fascist and anti-imperialist art (founded in 1938 and disbanded in 1948).[9] The elements associated with Surrealism, mainly fantastical imagery and distorted realities, certainly have an impact on the themes and images we see in Egyptian comics today with the simple and playful lines that seeped into both political cartoons and paintings (Guyer 2017, 339). Many modernist artists who were trained as fine artists were also cartoonists and illustrators, like Adham Wanly and Hussein Bikar who founded the aforementioned *Sindibād*, which also explored motifs drawn from the *Alf Layla w Layla* popular-culture repertoire. The idea of the sequential narrative was also anticipated in several individual experiments including the single-frame works of Alexander Saroukhan and the illustrated collection of folk poetry by 'Abdel Hadi Gazzar, who was also associated with Art and Liberty, which resembles a proto-comic or graphic poem. Such cultural figures were cognizant of the movement's inter- and transnational nature from the get-go, as is evidenced by the following excerpt from a response Kamel el-Telmissany wrote in defense of Surrealism:

> Surrealism is not a "specifically French movement" [...] rather it is a movement that is primarily defined by the globalism of its thinking and its actions ... It is not only between the French leaders, the painter Giorgio De Chirico is Italian-Greek, Salvador Dali is Spanish just as Picasso, Paul Klee and Max Ernst are from Germany, Ben Rose is English as is Henry Moore, Paul Delvaux likewise is Belgian, and Chagall is of Russian origin, among others[.]

---

[9] For a detailed history of Art and Liberty's cultural and political imbrications with local and global discourses on fascism and freedom in the context of World War II, see Sam Bardaouil's *Surrealism in Egypt: Modernism and the Art and Liberty Group* (2017), especially the chapter titled "Fascism at Home."

Have you heard stories or poems from local, popular literature? .... All of these, Sir, are all surrealist.
Have you seen the Egyptian Museum? ... Much of pharaonic art is surrealist.
Have you seen the Coptic Museum? Much of Coptic art is surrealist.

(Seggerman 2013, 11–12)

While the Surrealist movement in Egypt attempted to engage the aesthetic formation of a national identity and championed the autonomy of art and culture as well as the freedom of thought and expression, the consecutive and long-held Sadat and Mubarak totalitarian regimes stifled the state institutions that supported art education and exhibition practices. Though the institutionalized form of Surrealism in Egypt remains locked in a mid-twentieth-century historical moment, "Egyptian artists have [nevertheless] continued to employ the aesthetic techniques, ideological attitudes, and political networks [that were] introduced by this influential group" (24). This goes to show how intricately bound histories of fine art and comics art are in Egypt, and justifies how much of it resurfaced in the aftermath of the 2011 Tahrir Revolution.

The Surrealist Aesthetic of Voyeurism in *Fī shiqqat bāb el-loq*

Ganzeer would perhaps not identify as explicitly "surrealist," but there are uncanny resemblances to the work of the twentieth-century French poet and artist who is now considered to be the forefather and coiner of the term "surrealism": Guillaume Apollinaire. Because *Fī shiqqat bāb el-loq* is a graphic text, it sets up a hybrid interplay between a verbal and visual register that are equally represented in Maher's poetic reflections and Ganzeer's superimposed multimodal art. However, it goes one step further when the two registers entirely subsume one another in the calligrams of a cat and the rain, effectively producing a likeness to Apollinaire's (1918) cat and rain poems from the early twentieth century, but alone that would be too simple a reading. In the cat's case, Maher's words are rearranged to take the shape of a feline's body in motion with an erect tail. Its head and one of its paws, however, are shaded in black, producing an incomplete calligram (Figure 3.7). Viewers have to read the poem from top to bottom and right to left in the original work, their eyes trailing along every word and falling with a gentle tip-toeing motion that mimics the cats' soundless movement on all-fours through the apartment. The cats are described as "follow[ing] you silently from place to place ... eavesdropping on your phone calls ... siz[ing] up your visitors [and] judg[ing] your every move" (2017, 21; Jacquette translation). The abstracted drawing is also juxtaposed with two photographs of cats staring straight at the viewer with luminescent eyes, waiting and watching for their next move. The impression made is that of eerie silence with a focus on the cats' voyeuristic talents. They succeed in making the tenant and reader–viewer feel like they're constantly being watched, thus exercising a powerful gaze over them. This effect is a complete departure from

Figure 3.7 Cat calligram from *Fī shiqqat bāb el-loq*

Apollinaire's configuration of his cat poem "La nuit tous les chats sont gris," which is meant to be a humorous rhyme using French idioms about cats.

In the case of the rain calligram, we have the adverse effect: Ganzeer's adaptation takes up the majority of an entire spread. Maher's words do not exactly replace the streaks of rain but rather cascade in a slanted and parallel manner above them. Something important to note is that Ganzeer's rain is portrayed as diagonal lines through the hatching technique, mimicking violent and multiple scratches on the glass surface of a window pane. In Apollinaire's "Il Pleut," the words themselves form the droplets of exactly five streaks of rain running down a window pane in a more vertical direction. Apollinaire's rain is softer, almost a drizzle, compared to Ganzeer's brash lines. While both iterations are meant to produce a sonic and visual effect of rainfall in the reader's mind, the sound of Apollinaire's rain is burdened by an atmosphere of sorrow and is exacerbated by women's voices and regretful weeping, whereas the sound of Ganzeer's rain is mixed with the shrieks of hysterical and repeated laughter coming from an unknown source outside the apartment. Ganzeer's take on the rain calligram is another visual representation that confirms the anxiety and dread pervading the Bāb el-Loq world.

The plenitude of gazing in this work raises an old question of what this form of voyeurism means. The old answer which draws on Michel Foucault's panopticon model suggests a mode of invisible surveillance that would constantly keep the behavior of a prisoner, and by extension a subject of society, in check, whether or not the surveilling apparatus is actually there. The feeling of being watched and the knowledge that criminal behavior will be punished is thus internalized, and this unconsciously dictates the subject's behavior. The newer answer, which is grounded in film studies, complicates the voyeur's desires when gazing at their victim. In his work titled *The Cinematic Society* (1995), Norman Denzin explains this as a gaze that seeks to "unravel the untruths that others tell, including their lies, violence, illicit affairs, cover-ups, murders, political assassinations, illegal acts [...] and deeply held secrets" (54). He artfully traces the evolution of the voyeur's gaze from an open and blatant stare that characterizes early cinema to the repressed gaze of modernism and ends with parodies of gazing in late modernist films, which is characterized by a "pornography of the visible" that is now everywhere as "nothing is any longer hidden" (191). In spite of this apparent transparency, it is interesting to think how there is still something to fear and there is an incessant desire to upend repressed truths in *Fī shiqqat bāb el-loq*. Its world is one in which everyone and everything has become a voyeur, not just people who watch other people, but even animals and inanimate objects, such as the rain, participate in the double cloistering effect on the tenant and the reader–viewer. In an alienated and desolate neighborhood where the state's apparatus of power is nowhere to be seen but everywhere felt, the voyeuristic effect is still palpable as every participant replicates its probing gaze. This turns the form of the comic itself into the ultimate voyeur and the narrator's voice into one coming from beyond the grave. It is the comics form, not the state's failed surveillance apparatus, which has exposed the truth of the murder through a careful arrangement of images. And it is the narrator's ethereal voice that has left the new tenant with an allusion to the truth by warning them about the spirit of death hanging around the apartment. The hybrid text has confessed that nobody is safe but everybody (including the reader–viewer) will continue to obsessively watch every spectacle unfold. This is nowhere more evident than in the final spread where we see the narrator's corpse being carried out of the building on a stretcher, and in order to avoid a lengthy investigation, the police arrest the innocent doorman in order to call the case closed, which makes newspaper headlines just two weeks before the tenant's arrival. The very impulse driving the work is, therefore, to behave as an alternative apparatus that uses surrealism to push back against the government's corruption and abuse of authority with its own documentation of sights, sounds, and gazes, which are encountered as attempts to preserve one's survival and sanity in an otherwise heavily policed environment.

Conclusion

Fī shiqqat bāb el-loq is a clear example of constellational modernism. With roots in late nineteenth- and twentieth-century avant-garde Egyptian verbal and visual arrangements and engagements with transnational artistic expressions, it is no wonder that the commercial term "graphic novel" used in the publishing industry comes across as reductive for an experimental work such as this. Its images, which convey jarring slanted, upward and downcast angles as well as fragmented scenes that dissolve into the white background, activate a multimodal sensory approach instead of a conventional reading method. One has to feel the images unfold in their layered materiality, hear the sounds and silences, while paying close attention to the sights rendered and the ones suppressed beneath the whiteness, which are left to the imagination, in order to unearth some form of truth within an authoritarian regime. Perhaps the last word is best put by Marcia Lynx Qualey (2017) who sums up this effect in her review of the work, saying: "Those hoping for news from Tahrir or a story with a clear beginning, middle and end will be disappointed. But those willing to unshackle themselves from the expectations of story and immerse themselves in a collaborative portrait of downtown Cairo will be greatly rewarded." This graphic text has defied the universalized standards set by European and American comics by drawing attention to the potentials for experimentation with the form. It has also suggested that perhaps the heterogeneity and alterity of Arabic comics is the best remedy for the quickly ossifying subcategories of graphic novels within an economy of World Literature.

References

Apollinaire, Guillaume. 1918. *Calligrammes: Poêmes de la paix et de la guerre 1913-1916*. Paris: Mercure de France.
Bardaouil, Sam. 2017. *Surrealism in Egypt: Modernism and the Art & Liberty Group*. New York: I.B. Taurus.
Chute, Hillary. 2008. "Comics as Literature? Reading Graphic Narrative." *PMLA* 123 (2): 452–65.
Chute, Hillary. 2012. "Graphic Narrative." In Bray, Joe, Gibbons, Alison, and McHale, Brian, eds. *The Routledge Companion to Experimental Literature*. London and New York: Routledge Taylor & Francis Group, 407–19.
Chute, Hillary. 2016. *Disaster Drawn*. Cambridge, MA: Harvard University Press.
Denzin, Norman K. 1995. *The Cinematic Society: The Voyeur's Gaze*. London and New Delhi: Sage Publications.
Ganzeer/European Culture Congress. (2011). http://www.culturecongress.eu/en/people/ganzeer (accessed December 12, 2019).
Ghaibeh, Lina. 2015. "Telling Graphic Stories of the Region: Arabic Comics After the Revolution." *Strategics Sectors Culture & Society: Panorama*: 324–9. huncwot.com. (accessed December 12, 2019).
Guyer, Jonathan. 2017. "Between Fine and Comic Art. On the Arab Page: Much Connects Art and Comics in Egypt and the Wider Middle East." *International Journal of Comic Art*, 19 (1): 334–44.
Lent, John. 2007. "Egyptian Cartooning: An Overview." *International Journal of Comic Art*, 9 (2): 140–86.

Maher, Donia. 2013. *Fī shiqqat bāb el-loq*. Illustrated by Ganzeer and Ahmed Nady. Cairo: Dar Merit.

Maher, Donia. 2017. *The Apartment in Bab el-Louk*. Trans. Elisabeth Jacquette. London: Darf Publishers.

McCloud, Scott. 1993. *Understanding Comics: The Invisible Art*. New York: William Morrow Paperbacks.

Miller, Elissa. 2018. "Egypt Leads the Pack in Internet Censorship Across the Middle East." *Atlantic Council*, August 28. http://www.atlanticcouncil.org/blogs/menasource/egypt-leads-the-pack-in-internet-censorship-across-the-middle-east/ (accessed December 12, 2019).

Mitchell, W.J.T. 2005. "There are no Visual Media." *Journal of Visual Culture*, 4 (2): 257–66.

Qualey, Marcia Lynx. 2015. "CairoComix Festival Kicks Off, Women Big Winners on Opening Night." *ArabLit Quarterly*, October 1. https://arablit.org/2015/10/01/cairocomix-festival-kicks-off-women-big-winners-on-opening-night/ (accessed December 12, 2019).

Qualey, Marcia Lynx. 2017. "Chronicling a Neighborhood. Book Review: Donia Maher's 'The Apartment in Bab El Louk.'" *Qantara*. https://en.qantara.de/content/book-review-donia-mahers-the-apartment-in-bab-el-louk-chronicling-a-neighbourhood (accessed December 12, 2019).

Reyns-Chikuma, Chris, and Houssem, Ben Lazreg. 2018. "The Discovery of Marjane Satrapi and the Translation of Works From and About the Middle East." In Baetens, Jan et al., eds. *The Cambridge History of the Graphic Novel*. Cambridge and New York: Cambridge University Press, 405–25.

Saleh, Rania. 2007. "Political Cartoons in Egypt." *International Journal of Comic Art*, 9 (2): 187–225.

Sanua, Ya'qub. 1974. *Abū Naẓẓārah Zarqah*, vol. 1: 1878–1879. Beirut: Dar Sader.

Seggerman, Alex D. 2013. "Al-Tatawwur (Evolution): An Enhanced Timeline of Egyptian Surrealism." *Dada/Surrealism*, 19 (1): 1–24.

Seggerman, Alex D. 2019. *Modernism on the Nile: Art in Egypt Between the Islamic and the Contemporary*. North Carolina: UNC Press.

4

Boys Love in Latin America: The Migration of Aesthetics in Contemporary Graphic Narrative

Camila Gutiérrez

In this section on the Latin American Graphic Novel, I would like to begin with a couple of notes to situate Latin America in the field of comics studies. First, in recognizing that while the pre-Columbian nations that inhabited the region now known as Latin America had developed rich and complex indigenous visual systems with which to paint the world around them, these systems have yet to be integrated into the inventory of contemporary Latin American graphic narratives. Therefore, when writing about the creative output of this region, it is crucial to keep in mind that the language of comics is inherently foreign to the worlds it narrates and represents. The clarification matters because oftentimes comics studies refer to "the language of comics" or "the comics medium" by grouping together the styles of European and US comics, and implicitly or explicitly treats these styles as if they described the art form itself. This misconception creates a double error, where a) the narrative styles of first-world visual cultures are seen as a universal for comics, and b) the scholarship on comics that is generated from that premise in turn hegemonizes these cultures' histories, canons, and formalisms. The point may seem self-evident, but important to keep in mind for decentering the Global North as the cultural hub of comics. The comics I read in this chapter result from a transpacific conversation between Latin America and Japan, where Latin American queer experience is imagined in the style of Japanese girls' comics in order to enter a global/glocal community of queer representation. In circumventing the validation or influence of the Global North in their reach of international readership, these comics put into evidence important faults in the lineaments that configure comics scholarship.

On the one hand, comics scholars will recognize that histories on comics often begin with the work of the Swiss Rodolphe Töpffer as a first manifestation of modern comics in the nineteenth century, and then skip ahead to early film and newspaper funnies in the USA as the one environment for modern comics' true birth. From then on, the histories of graphic narrative become the history of US comics, canonizing

---

Research for this chapter was made possible by the generous support of the Japan Foundation.

works from the Global North represented by the USA, and with some mentions of the Franco-Belgian tradition.

On the other hand, comics formalisms similarly emerge from Western European institutions and focus on the elements that dominate European graphic narratives such as the *bande desinée*. Taxonomic categories such as *logemes*, *syntactemes*, and morpho-graphemes emerged most likely because their authors were working with the distinct visual devices of the Franco-Belgian page. Its *ligne claire* and the orderliness of its layouts yield nicely to the visual structuralist, and so on. It seems that because Latin American comics (or other comics from the periphery) do not show a distinctively native style, comics studies has deemed itself functional by looking narrowly rather than widely, conversing across the two biggest regional markets of the center/Global North (again, the USA and Western Europe). This distribution of attention effectively established an institutional space for comics studies. However, it costed the field a more global perspective—as evidenced by comics' belated introduction to conversations of World Literature.

Because they are situated outside of the metropolitan centers of comics studies, Latin American studies of *historieta* and *cuadrinho*[1] are more attuned to seeing the interaction between foreign and local traditions. This volume contributes to expanding that outsider perspective in Anglophone comics studies. With respect to Latin American comics more particularly, this volume should be understood more properly as resuming regional work that critics such as Ariel Dorfman and Armand Mattelart began fifty years ago. The Chilean duet wrote their essay "How to Read Donald Duck" at a time when imported Disney titles competed in the Chilean market against local *historietas* that were rich in political and social commentary. Dorfman and Mattelart (1984) noted that the stylistic importation from Anglophone comic books to *historietas* was facilitating a sort of "capitalist indoctrination" (exemplified in Scrooge McDuck comics books that arguably promoted values of individualism and opportunity over collaboration and solidarity).[2] While the alarmist tone of their analysis belongs in the Cold War era that framed it, their work offers a fertile comparative methodology that examines the cultural politics negotiated on the page. The lineage of their critical approach was disrupted by thirteen years of right-wing dictatorship, book banning, book burnings, and life in exile. However, half a century later the basis of their comparative methodology is being picked up and resumed in studies on Latin American *historieta* and *quadrinho*, a trajectory which this chapter continues. World Literature approaches to *historieta* and *quadrinho* must begin by acknowledging that at least aesthetically speaking, these pieces are born from the global. Thus, it is crucial to unpack the relationship between what is an imported visual inventory, the cultural politics that are engrained within such sources of inspiration, and the cultural work these inspirations perform when localized. I put this worldly methodology into

---

[1] *Historieta* and *quadrinho* identify comics from Spanish- and Portuguese-speaking countries in Latin America. For comics from Spain, the term is *tebeo*.

[2] See my own *IJOCA* article for an overview and analysis of Chilean comics from the 1960s through the 1980s. In Spanish language scholarship, see Moisés Hassón's *Comics en Chile Catálogo de Revistas (1908–2000)* (2014) and Jorge Rojas' *Las Historietas en Chile 1962–1982* (2016).

practice in my reading of Latin American comics that look at Japan for inspiration in their goal to queer local histories and contemporary narrative spaces.

Elucidating a world literary methodology for reading globally born Latin American comics, this chapter analyzes the work of Pía Prado Bley, a Chilean author known for her stories about male same-sex love. She localizes the genre in scenarios such as the saltpeter mining camps in the Region of Tarapacá, or contemporary Santiago de Chile, thus visually locating her comics in a decidedly Chilean landscape. At the same time, however, her stories reference the global when she uses visual codes that are recognizable to international reading communities steeped in *manga* tropes of male–male romance fiction. In terms of content, the stories of Prado Bley are highly local: they begin with little exposition to explain the setting, and focus on the two male characters' meeting. The plot subsequently follows somewhat conventional steps for the protagonists, as they develop a romantic interest, experience mutual recognition as queer subjects, and consummate their romance. The stories do not thematize issues of globalization, multicultural encounter, or international travel—which are more conventional strategies associated with the Global Latin American Novel.[3] Instead, important plot-driving conflicts are grounded in local issues of class division and gender/sexual discrimination that are less commonly featured in mass-media representation of same-sex love in Chile. In this manner, Prado Bley's graphic narratives address representational needs within the diegetic worlds she draws, and in the local context in which the works are read. Their locality notwithstanding, I argue in this chapter that the works have a global resonance among other communities of readers. Prado Bley's circulation of the comics in both Spanish and English attests to this phenomenon. Of course, it is worth noting that existence in translation alone does not guarantee the global status of a work, as publishers and authors well know. The global reach of Prado Bley's comics is better explained by the visual style and the narrative tropes that permeate her storytelling. Prado Bley relies on her readership's capacity to identify *shōjo* and "Boys Love" elements inspired by Japanese *manga*, and utilizes that visual literacy as a refractive platform for the local. Thus, the aesthetic influence of Japan on Latin American queer narratives instates a globality that sidesteps the centripetal pull of the publishing cultures of Spain, Belgium, France, and the USA.

In *Déjame que te Llame*,[4] Prado Bley mobilizes particular *manga* tropes when the protagonists, Francisco and Sebastián, meet for the first time. Francisco's day begins

---

[3] In *Beyond Bolaño: The Global Latin American Novel*, Hector Hoyos argues that Latin American literature, unlike the literature produced in the major metropolitan centers of the world, does not "enjoy the condition of being always-already global." (6) For this reason, he reads Latin American literature as "global Latin American novel" when the works themselves "contribute to consolidating, simultaneously, both the world *and* Latin America as their chambers of resonance" (7). They do so by cultivating the tension between the local and the global (22), featuring South–South relations, and illustrating multicultural encounters or impressions generated therein, "bypassing the presumed Euro-Atlantic centers of world history, World Literature, and capitalism" (2015, 27, 66).

[4] The story can be searched under two titles: *Déjame que te Llame* in Spanish (Prado Bley 2019a), and *Let Me Call You* in English (Prado Bley 2019b). It was originally serialized as a webcomic on the *Tapas* and *Faneo* platforms. Due to the multiple re-uploads from platform to platform, the original date of publication on the Web is not available. As of December 2021, the full comic can be found in Spanish through the store of Wolu Editorial. There is only a short preview for the English version.

when he wakes up sitting at his desk, startled by the realization that he is running late to submit a report at his university. He brushes his teeth and rushes through breakfast while holding up a manuscript of the report to his face. The following scenes involve him running through his neighborhood to catch the bus, arriving at the bus stop, and boarding. This opening sequence strongly references the now clichéd first portrait of *shōjo manga* (Japanese girls' comics), where the heroine starts her day in very similar conditions (running late, forgetting an assignment, doing her commute, etc.) to show that she is an ordinary schoolgirl with ordinary problems. In these instances, authors inscribe a moment of identification with the protagonist, with whom readers share the struggles of the demanding Japanese school system. Prado Bley cites the trope, but adapts it to the Chilean university context and gender-bends the protagonist to be a young man. The depiction of urban Santiago contributes to that identification as well: local readers quickly pick up on the different social backgrounds of Francisco and Sebastián judging from their location in the city and their occupations.

When Francisco finally lays eyes on Sebastián for the first time, the usage of close-ups and extreme close-ups cites another convention of *shōjo manga*. The scene shows Francisco riding the bus when Sebastián boards and gets ready to sing. (Public transportation performers are a common sight in the city, and they are often seen with portable instruments, microphones, and amplifiers.) Francisco's reaction to Sebastián's singing is illustrated in close-ups of varying proximities (see Figures 4.1 and 4.2).

In extreme close-ups, only eyes, bangs, and the profile of the character are delineated. The rest of Francisco's head is not drawn, and the panel is filled with a greyscale color fade. In these instances, the text is neither boxed nor contained by word balloons. Rather, the text floats to represent an internal monologue. Sebastián's lyrics

Figure 4.1 Extreme close-up of Francisco when Sebastián boards the bus.

Boys Love in Latin America 79

Figure 4.2 Francisco stares at Sebastián, captivated by his voice.

float within the panel too, rendered in a different font to represent the environmental noise that is causing Francisco's response. To Thierry Groensteen, *shōjo manga*'s use of floating text is an institutionalized feature of the genre. He specifically talks about how "the words have a tendency to 'float' in balloons with expansive outlines, providing them with their own echo chamber" (2013, 58). Sebastián's singing is not depicted with the echoing balloon here described, but the foggy background of the panel, summed to the floaty lines of his listener in extreme close-up, do convey that aural quality to the transcript of his voice.

Yi-Shan Tsai has described the uses of close-ups in *manga* at length. In her survey, Tsai attributes *manga*'s frequent close-ups to the influence of cinema and the greater page count length of comics in Japan (it is a commonly held consensus that because pagination was not as restrictive in Japan as in other publishing markets of the twentieth century, *manga* narratives were less compressed, and could afford to show character reactions in detail). In time, these media influences caused Japanese comics to develop close-up variations to highlight emotion, which Tsai argues is key to *manga* culture. Tsai offers a list of close-up functions in visual media, which includes *nagare* (when a single incident is displayed across multiple panels), close-up as "lyric" (to enhance emotion focusing on the most minute details of the character's facial expression), close-up as play on physics (perceivably slower than medium shots and long shots), as gaze into blind space (using the gaze of the character in frame to direct the audience's attention beyond the visible range of the frame), and extreme close-ups as invitation into the abstract (when readers are directed towards an imaginary domain outside the panel to intensify emotion within) (Tsai 2018, 476–9). I expand on this final point to add one more effect of extreme close-up in *manga*: when the close-up gaze evokes the internal realm of the character—a realm that exists within the drawn body but cannot be captured by the traces of the drawing nor the space inside the frame. We see this in the scene when Francisco and Sebastián first meet.

This internal realm of close-up differs from the "lyric" close-up of film in that the drawn image can never capture as much detail as the camera. By contrast, *manga*'s abstract extreme close-up dissolves the character's physical features (omitting them or oversimplifying them) to simulate access to that internal world. Readers who are familiar with this language of abstraction by simplification know to interpret close-ups as a metaphor for internal emotional surges, especially in romance. For example, in the case of *Déjame que te Llame*, Francisco's depiction in Figures 1 and 2 show his own surprise regarding his attraction for Sebastián, whom he has just met. Other reactions of Francisco in close-up include frustration, bewilderment, and entrancement. However, in those occasions his face and body are fully delineated, and he is angled either facing the reader or in three-quarter view. Returning to Tsai's observations, I emphasize the importance of the character's gaze in the extreme close-up. Because Francisco's eyes see beyond our field of vision, and because his body dissolves into floating lines, readers are pulled into an abstract space inhabited by the two intangible elements that escape the frame: his psycho-emotional interiority, and the musical emanation of Sebastián's performance. The technique intensifies (in)visible emotions to charge the space of the frame.

Extreme close-ups are not exclusive to Japanese comics, of course. Nevertheless, because what I am describing is so prevalent in *manga* for girls, and because the Latin American materials in question are tapping into multiple tropes from *shōjo* and its subgenre of Boys Love (commonly abbreviated BL), it is important to understand the origin and signification of these tropes. Contemporary readers of comics in Japan and abroad have become literate enough to extract certain meanings from *shōjo* and BL images, regardless of their familiarity with the cultural background of this type of art. That is, the massification of these tropes has been such that readers completely unfamiliar with Taishō or early Shōwa Japanese print culture perceive the queer ethereality embedded in *shōjo* aesthetics without effort. Despite this legibility, I believe it is important to understand the context in which these visual-stylistic codes originate because some of their original functions find continuity in their Latin American transculturation, which is a crucial feature of World Literature (Damrosch 2003, 13). I argue that BL-inspired Latin American comics are not appropriative or derivative. Rather, in Latin America, Boys Love is employed as a visuality at the service of queer experiences in scenarios where same-sex love could not have been represented (1907 mining protests in Atacama) or where it has been deliberately censored (conservative

Chilean mass media). Prado Bley sincerely participates in a queer cultural lineage in her use of *shōjo*, especially considering that the subversive queerness of *shōjo* visuals emerged in a moment when the imposition of normative heterosexuality was in tension with Japan's pre-modern traditions of same-sex love. Therefore, with the migration and adaptation of *shōjo*'s generic features in Latin America, *shōjo* perpetuates its role in media queering. Before sketching out how *shōjo* aesthetics migrate, and the work they perform in a non-Japanese context, it is first necessary to establish the semantic range and meaning of the critical term "*shōjo*."

Delineating *Shōjo* Culture and Tropes

Studies on *shōjo* associate the term with a great deal of materials, subjects, developmental stages, diction, typescripts, and even behaviors of consumption, linking *shōjo* with micro behaviors such as high school girls' handwriting, and macro concepts such as bubble economics and the collapse of global neoliberalism.[5] The range of these associations to *shōjo* is so broad that even Japanese nationals may find it hard to gauge the reach of *shōjo* culture.[6] Outside of Japan, in global popular culture and in English-language scholarship, "*shōjo*" is mostly understood to mean "girl" or "young woman" and used to differentiate Japanese girls' comics from non-Japanese ones (*shōjo manga* versus girls' comics).[7] A more measured definition for *shōjo* delineates it as less than an economic model, but more than just comics. To study *shōjo* in Japan and in migration is in fact to study *shōjo bunka*, or "girls' culture." Deborah Shamoon (2012), responsible for one of the first comprehensive studies on this topic in English scholarship, succinctly defines *shōjo bunka* as "a discrete discourse on the social construction of girlhood" (1). Her definition contends that *shōjo* is what is said, interpreted, enacted, and projected onto *the idea* of girlhood in a context, dismantling the etymological equation of *shōjo* with "Japanese girl."[8] Therefore, as a discourse, *shōjo* is ingrained in material and visual cultures both in and out of Japan. More importantly, whereas "Japanese girlhood" cannot really travel outside of the Japanese context because it is bound to national subjects, the discursive part of this social construct does transpire into the worlds that

---

[5] See Saki Shigetomi's (2009) complete study of *shōjo-ron* in the 1980s.
[6] In their "Short Skits and Superpowers: The Evolution of the Beautiful Fighting Girl", Kathryn Hemmann (2014) responds to some misconceptions around the topic.
[7] The etymology of the word matters as well. In the Japanese language, "girl" is not a stable noun, especially during the twentieth century when the female national subject went through such rapid transformations. *Onna no ko*「女の子」, *Otome*「乙女」, *shojo*「処女」, *shōjo*「少女」, and *gyaru*「ギャル」are all translatable as "girl," but their meanings vary in context. For example, while the noun phrase *onna no ko* describes a child-woman, *shojo* is connected to maidenhood in pre-war Japan, and to virginity proper in the postwar era. Then there is the postmodern *gyaru*, evocative of cosmopolitanism and subversive sexuality. The terms destabilize the monolithic etymology of "girlhood" in their shifts of spelling and alphabet, as well as in their differentiated usage in the fields of child development, popular culture, or even fashion. For the purpose of this chapter, I am using *shōjo* to refer to Japanese girlhood broadly, especially since the Meiji period onwards.
[8] Hiromi Tsuchiya Dollase (2019) terms this separation between girl and behaviors as the "way of *shōjo*" in her recent study of *shōjo* literature since Meiji.

come in contact with its materials. This is how *shōjo* becomes global and reaches Latin America in the first place. Once abroad, the consumption of these culturally charged products—via *manga*, *anime*, music, and others—becomes a formative experience for girls, who establish affective bonds with local and foreign groups with whom they share this experience.

Studies that examine the relationship between print culture and women's affective communities have gained traction in English-language scholarship since the mid-2000s.[9] Jennifer Prough describes this phenomenon at length in her 2011 anthropological study on Japanese magazines culture. She focuses primarily on how *shōjo* magazines are gestational spaces for affective labor among young girls and women. Magazines of the early twentieth century would incentivize this relationship through readers correspondence sections and creative submission competitions. By the mid-twentieth century, calls for contributions appeared in between commercial ads, illustrated fiction, nonfiction, and poetry. Wanting to be part of the magazine themselves, readers would submit original pieces imitating the style of illustrators and writers of the magazine. In this way, they would grow up internalizing their aesthetic language. Eventually, some contributors' works could be picked up by the magazine, and a new generation of writers, drawers, and style influencers would be born. As is borne out of my own archival research at the *Jomakan* collection in Akiruno province and at the National Diet Library in Tokyo, readers' correspondence pages were instrumental in creating this culture as well. Authors could use the border of a *manga* page to talk about life events or use specific pages to address their readers. Readers would answer in published letters. In this way, the *shōjo* magazine became a communicational platform, a search for talent, and a place for aesthetic training. The platform thus strengthened the link between *shōjo* as community and *shōjo* aesthetics, securing the preservation and massification of the latter.

I do not intend to catalog the entire aesthetic apparatus of *shōjo* in this chapter (not that it can be done at all). Rather, I will focus on the origins of three sets of influential tropes (namely *jojōga*, aesthetics of sameness, and male homoromance) before returning to a discussion of their re-emergence in the Latin American transculturation of *shōjo*.x

Jojōga,[10] or "lyrical drawing" is a visual genre that appeared during the early twentieth century in Japanese girls' magazines. The word acquired its current usage around the 1980s, and nowadays it serves as an umbrella term for those styles typically described as flowery, ephemeral, emotional, and atmospheric.[11] *Jojōga* is not exactly a drawing technique, but an atmospheric emanation that participates in the narration.

---

[9] Studies on *shōjo* culture in Japanese scholarship have a much longer history. See Shigetomi (2009) or Nagasawa (1997) for Japanese-language genealogies of the field.

[10] May be found spelled as 「叙情画」 or 「抒情画」 depending on the age of the document. The latter spelling has fallen out of use. The two first kanji (「叙」 and 「抒」) mean narration or description, and are followed by the kanji for "emotion" 「情」 and "drawing" or "image" 「画」.

[11] A word search in the Yomidas Rekishikan database of newspapers shows that one of the first uses of *jojōga* to describe this type of illustration occurs in the 1980s to advertise *jojōga* artbooks that collect Taishō era art.

To exemplify, Deborah Shamoon describes the works of Takehisa Yumeji (1884–1934), an illustrator known for his lyrical drawings of girls, as follows:

> It was not so much his use of line or composition that proved influential but the atmosphere his illustrations evoked. In his sketchy style, girls appear weak, ephemeral, and nearly disembodied, reflecting the aesthetic of *chūsei*, the imaginary neutral gender idealized in girls' culture.
>
> (2012, 61)

Jojōga derived into experimental word–image combinations such as *irasuto poemu* (illustrated poems) and *fasshon ga* (fashion drawings), which in turn influenced the collaged, non-sequential layouts of *shōjo manga*. The first combines *jojōga* art and a free-floating poetic composition on the page, where the text and the image collaborate to activate a delicate, flowy atmosphere that emanates from the image. Fukiya Kōji (1898–1979), who worked on various editorial projects of the era and was influenced by Yumeji, is an illustrator known for these compositions.[12] Similarly, *fasshonga* is a type of illustration that montaged hand-drawn clothing items, architecture, flowery ornamentation, sparkles, and text to curate a style and its atmosphere. In the case of *fasshon ga*, the girl is nowhere in the image, so readers are required to decipher the montage, extract the essence of the floating composition, and embody it through self-fashioning. Together and through decades of combination and evolution, these genres cultivated in their young readers a sort of evocative visual literacy, where textual linearity or explicitness are not a mandatory principle. Thus, young readers of the *shōjo* magazine learned to infer messages from abstract montages, in turn permitting postwar *manga* artists to deal with subversive themes in a common language of suggestion and concealment. During the Meiji (1868–1912) and Taishō (1912–1926) periods, these themes of subversion manifested in the form of female homosocial/homoromantic illustrated narrative. In the late Shōwa (1926–1989), they included *manga* about male same-sex love. The broad aesthetics of *jojōga* thus converged with aesthetics of androgyny, queerness, and what I would call an aesthetics of sameness.

An "aesthetics of sameness" is how I describe the common motif of illustrations featuring two girls posed as a set pair, with nearly identical facial features, except that one is dressed in Western clothing, the other dressed in Japanese garb. These pairs could appear on magazine covers, as complement to written pieces, as ads, or as inserts.[13] The illustrated pairs convey that the Japanese girl has a responsibility to be both modern and traditional, active and contemplative, vigorous and delicate, modern and conservative, all at the same time.[14] The image, then, has an equalizing effect: the

---

[12] See Hata (2013) for a more complete analysis of *irasuto poemu* and *fasshonga*.

[13] Deborah Shamoon (2012) includes a selection of these images on pages 66–72. I found similar illustrations perusing different titles of girls' magazines of the pre-war period at the Jomakan archival collection in Akiruno, Tokyo.

[14] Keiko Ikeda (2014) has written about the emphasis on sports education in the women-oriented curriculum in modern Japan.

Figure 4.3 Juxtaposed images of a Dutch girl and a Japanese girl (right to left) in *Syōzyō* magazine.

two girls are almost the same person existing in flickering shifts. With time, and as Japan settled into its modern cosmopolitanism, page arrangements included even racial juxtapositions in a play of possibilities. For example, the August 11 issue of *Syōzyō* magazine juxtaposes an ethnically Japanese girl in a sailor school uniform on the left, on an insert, and on the right a blonde girl in *furisode kimono*, reading a scroll written in what looks like classical script 9 (see Figure 4.3).[15] Next to her, floating text reads 「雨の長崎オランダ町の今はかなしい物語」 ("A a sad story of rainy Nagasaki's now-sad Dutch Town").[16] Judging by her hair color, facial features, and the text, one can safely assume that the girl is European rather than Japanese. However, her garb and her ability to read the scroll conflate Japanese cultural staples into her ethnically white body, opening yet another flickering signification of visuality for the Japanese girl's self-imagination.[17] Given that these images of pairs and juxtaposed montages often accompanied contents in the range of homosociality and homoromance, with all likelihood they contributed to the stylization of same-sex couples in graphic narrative

[15] An alternative romanized spelling before "*shōjo*" became standardized.
[16] In March 1944 the Japanese Imperial Army occupied the East Dutch Indies (territories now known as Indonesia). The image remarks on the Netherlands' defeat.
[17] Several elements in the image connect this girl, named "Judy san" with the story of Oharu, an Italian–Japanese girl who was exiled in Jakarta during the Edo period. Her life was fictionalized in literature at the time, and in pop music by 1939. Readers would have been well aware of her story as they look at the image.

fiction of the 1970s. To be clear, I am not tracing a vector of direct influence between Taishō era same-sex relationships and postwar BL, but I am suggesting that these motifs of sameness endured through decades of transformations and adaptations in the visual ecology of the *shōjo* magazine.

Historically speaking, BL is in a complex genealogic relationship with Taishō period *dōseiai* (same-sex love broadly speaking), and traditional *nanshoku* (same-sex love between men, especially during the Edo period). Jeffrey Angles has referred more specifically to how the practice of same-sex love between men became outlawed around the end of the nineteenth century, and Michiko Suzuki has further explained how same-sex love between girls met sanction insofar as it remained platonic.[18] These differentiated reactions to same-sex love illuminate an unresolved relationship between sexuality and modernity at the turn of the twentieth century in Japan.

Girls' *dōseiai* may be best represented by the work of Nobuko Yoshiya (1896–1973), who published her *Hanamonogatari* series of short stories from 1916 to 1924 in *Girls' Graphic* magazine. As explained by Michiko Suzuki (2009) and citing Yoshiya herself, rather than abnormal, same-sex love stood as a necessary step towards the development of adult heterosexuality (36–7). Because it was expected to expire in time, the homoromantic experience of the protagonists was contained strictly within the temporality of their youth and within the homosocial space of the gender-segregated school. BL of the 1970s to 1990s tends to replicate that homosocial space in all-boys European boarding schools. This spatial and temporal containment presented same-sex love as an alternative to the mandated heteronormative roles of adulthood. The thematic subversion is also encoded in the writing mechanics of *dōseiai* stories. As exemplified in Yoshiya's prose, the stories are full of inconclusive sentences and irruptive punctuation in the form of dashes, unconventional spacing, and elongated ellipses to mark silence, stuttering, or hesitation.[19] The use of these mechanics "encod[ed] an unspeakable emotion into the silences and spaces between the actual words" (Suzuki 2009, 42). Together with the collaged visuals of the *shōjo* magazine, Yoshiya's prose furthered the aesthetic proposition of suggestion and elision in representing queer emotion.

In the case of boys' same-sex love, Inagaki Taruho's work since the 1920s is among modern precedents to BL's fascination with pairs of beautiful boys in homoromantic relationships (also called *bishōnen*, meaning "beautiful young man"). In fact, according to Angles, the flowery, beautified imagery of 1970s *shōjo manga* was heavily influenced by Taruhos' essays and short fiction (2011, 234–5). There are important ethical objections to the pedophilic connotation of Taruho's writing especially in the postwar era. However, to women artists such as Keiko Takemiya, and in the eyes of

---

[18] These changes were accompanied by heated debates on sexology and censorship, which is why the existence of non-heteronormative relationships in literatures of this time period should not be interpreted as a generalized acceptance of said relationships.
[19] Michiko Suzuki has traced these back to 1890s *shōjo* fiction (41), and Hiromi Tsuchiya Dollase (2019) has analyzed them further in the prose of various *shōjo* authors, finding a frequent motif of dreamy and steamy atmospheres to conceal the romantic and sexual interaction in a sort of disembodiment of the girls involved (39, 52).

girl readers, the beautification of young boys in romantic relationships extended an invitation to activate desire without stepping into the realm of adult heterosexuality and its responsibilities. Yoshiya's and Taruho's representations of same-sex love show important differences, but their formal, rhetoric, and thematic strategies were instrumental in introducing a fluctuating range of alterity to the sexual-affective fabric of their contemporary moment.

Although *shōjo* culture continues to welcome representations of alternative sexualities, these representations have been criticized within and without the community of *shōjo* for reproducing problematic stereotypes about homosexuality. In what follows, I consider these points, in order to determine their continuity in the migration of BL in Latin America, and discuss them in the work of Pía Prado Bley. The genre of Boys Love has had to evolve, and its consumer groups have had to reexamine their own positionality. This reflexive process has been accompanied by strong criticism of LGBTQA groups in Japan and abroad because: 1) readers and authors of BL are mostly heterosexual/cisgender women; 2) the delicate visuality of *shōjo* culture may be perceived as effeminate when applied to BL; and 3) BL can reaffirm the hetero-sexist fixity of "passive" and "active" roles (*seme* and *uke*) that queer activism has tried to denaturalize. Hitoshi Ishida refers to the debate on BL recounting that BL fandoms of the 1990s—self-denominated "rotten girls" or *fujoshi*—used an apologetic tone in public communications because they saw a negative quality in their enjoyment of *yaoi* (a more sexually explicit subgenre of BL). LGBTQA circles in Japan have taken their apologetic tone as a gesture of disdain towards homosexuality, and as a consequence BL has been pushed out of the literatures considered LGBTQA-friendly. However, although BL tropes effectively give room to problematic readings, its massive distribution permits an unprecedented circulation of the affective alterity represented on its pages.

Shōjo and the Visibility of Latin American Queer Subjecthood

To return to the story of Francisco and Sebastián, the global circulation of BL creates a communication channel for concerns that emerge from queer identities and sexualities, such as employment injustice, welfare accessibility, and historical, religious, or class inadequacies. In the case of Bley's comic *Estrellas de la Pampa*, we see that BL as a genre has been taken from the global fandom circulation and repurposed for historical critique, while in *Déjame que te Llame* we see a contemporary Latin American localization. These two works exemplify a significant evolution of BL in its transoceanic relocation in terms of problematic Japanese tropes. Among the tropes that disappear in Latin American BL are the negation of queer identification, sexual violence between the couple or coming from a third party, and the rejection of a de-closeted third party.[20] Ishida (2015) explains that this third party is often used to contrast the purity of the *seme/uke* relationship, versus the monstrosity of the threatening homosexual: "Emerging from this familiar pattern

[20] See examples in Ishida (2015) 216–21.

is the juxtaposition of 'straights who are under threat' and 'homos who threaten,'" he concludes (221). Ultimately, the conventional BL story depicts the lovers as heterosexual, except in love with another man. More recent Japanese BL *manga* put these dynamics in evidence by, for example, having a character jokingly wonder whether he should be disgusted when his partner confesses his homosexuality.[21] Such strategies criticize the internalized homophobia that pervades BL stories of the past, and counteracts the erasure of (homo)sexuality in same-sex love. Nevertheless, this recognition usually remains in the private realm of the relationship and is not thematized in terms of the public—perhaps a reflection of how sexual alterity is lived in Japan. In fact, Mark McLelland explains that up until at least the early 2000s, "the notion of 'coming out' [was] seen as undesirable by many Japanese gay men and lesbians as it necessarily involves adopting a confrontational stance against mainstream lifestyles and values, which many still wish to endorse." (McLelland 2000)

Latin American comics that align with efforts to reform genre BL feature similar scenes of recognition, with variants that signify differently in their contexts. Influenced by the independent market model of Japanese comics (*dōjinshi*), Pía Prado Bley published *Estrellas de la Pampa* as a 32-page webcomic in 2015. The English version maintains the lightweight feel of black and white *dōjinshi*, showing a correlation between the thematic migration, the formal qualities of BL, and the consumer models of the textual worlds of BL. I want to delve more extensively into this idea of textual worlds by examining the social conflict underpinning the plot of *Estrellas*: i.e., the 1907 protest for better working conditions in the saltpeter mining industry of northern Chile. As the prologue presents, the petitionary demands of the miners mobilized approximately 3,000 workers and their families and paralyzed mining operations for several days amidst demands for fair salary and fair exchange rates between token currency and real money. At the time, mining administrators (British for the most part), controlled the flow of currency by paying workers with tokens that were exchangeable only in mine-owned grocery stores. The system kept the workers trapped in the mine's monopoly. This was at the core of the social movement for justice historically known as *La Cuestión Social*. Miguel and Vicente meet in that historical context. San Lorenzo Mining Co. pays each of them the salary of a single man. This detail matters to Miguel, who is a single parent to Liliana, a little girl he has adopted. His working situation puts him at a disadvantage because his family is recognized neither by the social structure nor by his employer. We immediately access Miguel's arch from a domestic angle unfit for the capitalist modernity that he protests.

The comic introduces Miguel from the angle of a problematic masculinity. A study on Chilean masculinity explains that the beginning of the twentieth century saw a search for a "civilized" identity to contrast with the "barbaric" colonial past (Gonzalez 2004, 17). Labor and sex became interrelated for the first time in a systematic plan to achieve modernity. Facing the normative categories of capitalism that correlated subjecthood to productivity, the workers fought back to impede the loss of their existential autonomy (Illanes 1990, 90). In *Estrellas*, miners collectively organize

---

[21] See Ishida's readings of *Rats Dream of Cheese* and *Prince of Happiness* (2015).

Figure 4.4 Exchange between Miguel and an anonymous miner

as *workers*, and fight for the validation of their individual subjectivities, as seen in Figure 4.4. The panel sequence shows a frontal close-up of Miguel, followed by the interaction with an anonymous miner, and an extreme close-up of the latter's eye as he exclaims "you've seen it for yourself. If any of us dies while working, or if you make any kind of complaint … we're replaced in just a second!" The parallel transfers the condition of disposability from the collective of miners to Miguel. In this way, they become grouped in an imaginary community of expendable workers, while at the same time the presence of Liliana punctuates Miguel's familial inadequacy among the protesters. Miners' salaries would normally be higher for families, but Miguel's solo parenting of Liliana does not fulfill that condition.

Further drawing on Japanese conventions to draw attention to the nature of their developing relationship, the comic invokes *bishōnen* conventions in its opening depiction of Vicente, thereby marking the attractive youth immediately as Miguel's prospective love interest. Vicente is younger than Miguel, outgoing, fair haired, and is portrayed in a *sutairu ga* overlay (see Figure 4.5) (or "style shot" typical of *shōjo manga*[22]) that covers three rows of panels: two extreme close ups of his and Miguel's eyes, and a panoramic greyscale fade. Under conventional BL tropes, Vicente's personality would make him *uke*: the passive and less sexually aware boy who is subject to the *seme*'s advances. *Uke* usually has a lighter hair color such as bright yellow, pink,

[22] Yukari Fujimoto finds the first usage of the *sutairu ga* technique in Macoto Takahashi's *Awashi o Koete* in 1958. Macoto was also an illustrator of magazines and well acquainted with fashion illustration (Fujimoto 2012, 24). Thierry Groensteen has named this technique the "catwalk effect" (2013, 57). His term connects these images with the live performance of fashion shows, which makes more sense in the French context but not so much in Japan, where *hinagata bon* catalogs and other forms of print media played the most important role in spreading textile trends among women. I prefer to either maintain the romanized transliteration or use "style picture" as proposed by Rachel Thorn, in order to preserve the central role of print circulation.

Figure 4.5 Vicente in a *sutairu ga* image that overlaps three rows of panels

or blue.[23] In *Estrellas*, however, his personality is instrumental to the social movement of *La Cuestión Social*. Early on, Vicente reveals his involvement with a revolutionary organization, and he is the one to convince the San Lorenzo miners to journey through the desert to join others in Iquique, the region's capital. Therefore, Vicente is not a cheery *uke*, but a politically engaged subject, an activist who vocalizes and visibilizes the concerns of the oppressed. Another feature of the *uke* that is reformed in the story is the assumption that the light-haired character is sexually unaware or inactive until the approach of the *seme*. Vicente in turn is the one to identify and initiate the romantic relationship between him and Miguel. His racial difference is possibly attributed to

---

[23] There are important correspondences between the *seme/uke* binary of BL, and the *wakashu/nenja* roles in the premodern *nanshoku* relationship. Among them is the association between a particular hairstyle and a determined sexual role.

Figure 4.6 "You're just like me …"

his being born in southern Chile, where German colonies had formed since the early 1800s. The color-coding of the *seme/uke* binary is undone by the historical context of the protest and the mentioning of migratory waves in the southern cone.

Still, the visual terms of the comic clearly lay out Vicente's romantic role in visual terms, calling attention to the instantaneous intimacy that builds between him and Miguel. That intimacy is furthered by the existence of Liliana as their protegee. Later, as they struggle in their pilgrimage across the desert, Vicente gives water to Liliana, who is suffering from dehydration. The two men become Liliana's caregivers, and so the concept of family looms in the background of the labor conflict that motivates the plot. On the one hand, there are the unjust wages of the saltpeter mining world, and on the other, the broader spectrum of social injustices that they imply. In building that parallel, the narrative development of the comic insists on the impossibility that Liliana's caregivers will ever receive a family-appropriate income to support her under current conditions.

The culminating point of the protest again utilizes the visual aesthetics of BL comics to add romantic dimensions, as when the miners of various mining companies, including San Lorenzo's, convene at the Santa María de Iquique school after days of pilgrimage through the Atacama Desert. At night, Vicente and Miguel stand outside of the building alone, discussing Liliana (who at this point marks both "family" and "difference"). The greyscale fade in the background, followed by two more close-ups heighten the romantic tension of the scene. "You have a different look in your eyes, that's why I noticed. You're just like me," Vicente says, recognizing Miguel's homosexuality in an intimate scene (see Figure 4.6). The indirect recognition of same-sex love is cited in his phrasing, with the difference that Vicente mentions a "way of being," not just a desire. In this case, the localized trope of ambiguous recognition is more about an *identity* than a feeling. The scene concludes with a silent panel that shows the pair from afar, hiding behind the school building, and drinking from a flask. Multiple signs in the image hint towards the consummation of their romance.

In the final pages of the comic, Prado Bley fully integrates *shōjo*'s tropes of collaged juxtaposition, decompressed transitions, and the literacies of suggestion and concealment to portray the horrifying outcome of the protests, and the ultimate impossibility of the protagonists' existence as nonconforming subjects in their environment (see Figure 4.7). The final image of Miguel and Vicente together anticipates a kiss that never concretizes, suspended in the reader's imagination. Next, the story shifts to the narrator's account of the miners' massacre of 1907. Here, Prado Bley adapts the layout of these digital pages for vertical scrolling. As a result, the reading experience emulates a sort of "free fall and bounce" motion: first, a downward transition that simulates sinking from light grey into a pitch-black bottom. Then, a turnaround that continues downwards, but leaves readers looking upward at the starry sky. The couple's hands are at the top of the image, and blood splattered on the ground marks a bottom. The top of the fade cites the airiness in *jojōga* illustration, partly because of the fading radius of the background, and partly because the hands of the characters are not outlined to mark the edge of the gutter. Their arms look lightweight near the top of the image, and there is no panel border to hold the long image together either. The free-floating text below quotes Vicente's last thoughts: "Miguel, believe me, tomorrow everything will be all right. Tomorrow they'll hear us," he hopes. The lack of quotation marks and speech bubbles signals that his words are an internal monologue rather than dialogue. The aesthetic play of dissolving images and floating text makes us abandon the immediate space of the school and enter the abstract realm of the subjective. Much in the style of *shōjo*, this dissolution of reality into an aethereal subjectivity happens as both the romantic and the tragic reach their climaxes.

92 *Graphic Novels and Comics as World Literature*

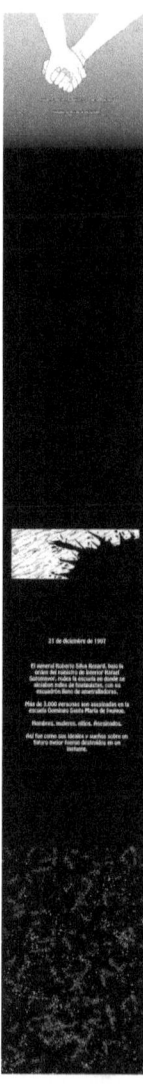

Figure 4.7 The readers scroll down this long image at the end of the story. Page numbers become unclear.

Partly thanks to the ability to scroll down the image, and mostly thanks to *shōjo*'s grammatical inventory for emotional play, the comic almost entirely dismantles the hyperframe; the page *per se* ceases to drive the narrative. Speaking of such layouts of print *shōjo manga*, Groensteen notes that "[t]he page is less a closed space that invites reading than a lower-density open-space, its emptiness allowing for the circulation of feelings, energy, dreams – a space that stirs up strong emotional involvement in the reader" (2013, 59). Here there is no page, and no white, but the effect is somewhat comparable. The aethereal grey behind the couple, rather than fading into a flowy white, fades into a hyper-dense screen/page, where the deaths of thousands of people are compressed into a dark extending mass. Reading this section is an extreme exercise in what McCloud terms closure: "a phenomenon of observing the parts but perceiving the whole" (1993, 63), or an imaginary filling of gutters. Except that the gutters are not there for us to fill. Readers extract the harrowing images and sounds of the massacre from a hyper-saturated block of black, with a splatter of blood as the only release. The comic circumvents the double victimization of the miners, avoiding the shock value of excessive violence as a narrative device, and inscribes elision in the developing romance of the protagonists, just as they are about to kiss. The invisibility of the lovers matters because the overarching theme is the twofold impossibility of gay love under turn-of-the-century Chilean mining capitalism and under *La Cuestión Social*.

Reliance on historical detail makes *Estrellas de la Pampa* a rather local work of literature. However, its overall legibility relies heavily on the reader's familiarity with the codes of *shōjo* visual culture. Prado Bley's comics may not be Japanese, but they certainly read as *manga*. Thus, Prado Bley gives a worldly resonance to her graphic narratives and succeeds as a global Latin American author thanks to a strategic management of BL generic cues. Franco Moretti has described genre as a morphological embodiment of World Literature's cycles (2010, 2452). Invested in drawing a global map of World Literature, Moretti explains that the field "cannot be understood stitching together separate bits of knowledge about individual cases, because it *isn't* a sum of individual cases: it is a collective system" (2442, emphasis in the original). Indeed, the global nature of *Déjame* and *Estrellas* is most evident to those who read them as more than individual homoromantic stories, and through the transnational lens of genre: the "middle layer of literary history where flow and form meet" (2449).

Ultimately, is it enough to find imported genre features in a work to term it World Literature? My answer leans toward no, and I draw that answer from the example of Prado Bley's stories and how they circulate. *Déjame* and *Estrellas* are localizations of BL as a genre, but they also project local concerns of queer love onto global surfaces of reception, using genre as a refractive device to that end. These works truly perform as World Literature in moving "from a national sphere into a new worldly context; [...] by being received *into* the space of a foreign culture, a space defined in many ways by the host culture's national tradition and the present needs of its own writers" (Damrosch 2003, 14). An interesting innovation in terms of circulation being that Latin American BL enacts its worldliness by circulating mostly in virtual communities that are already multicultural and global, past the national space. Thus, with the migration of BL, the mining camp or the class-segregated modern city are among the microcosms of Latin American queer visuality that enter the global multicultural exchange of same-sex love imagery, where center/periphery dynamics of consumption have less impact in what circulates where, and how. This phenomenon constitutes a bidirectional glocalism that introduces the local to the global, and captures a movement from the outside world in (Damrosch 2003, 162). In other words, aiming globally, Prado Bley exports representations of local Latin American sexual alterity and psycho-affective liminality to give them a worldly visibility—to integrate them into a queer macrocosm. In the local, she imports *shōjo*/BL aesthetics because they allow her to thematize same-sex love through a language that already exists and is particularly apt for the representation of affect and liminality. This move helps her rectify the underwhelming amount of ethical representations of queer subjects in a Latin American mass media—a space that continues to be dominated by heteronormative and conservative interests.

Analyzing the migration of Japanese BL to Latin America thus calls for a rethinking of the way that so-called genre categories of *historieta*, *manga*, and comics behave. The aesthetics of Latin American BL are removed from the Japanese market that saw them grow, but they are recognizably BL nonetheless. The transnational expansion of BL as a genre demonstrates that Latin American *historieta* is not permanently bound to the visual traditions of US comics or the *bande desinée*. Today, *historieta* and *quadrinho* are increasingly hybrid, their graphic narrative styles result from complex processes of aesthetic transculturation, which flow with little regard for the hegemonic structures of center-periphery that comics histories and scholarships have set in place.

References

Angles, Jeffrey. 2011. *Writing the Love of Boys: Origins of Bishonen Culture in Modernist Japanese Literature*. Minneapolis: University of Minnesota Press.
Damrosch, David. 2003. "What is World Literature?" *World Literature Today*, 77 (1): 9–14.
Damrosch, David. 2018. *How to Read World Literature*. Hoboken: Wiley Blackwell.
Dollase, Hiromi Tsuchiya. 2019. *Age of Shojo: The Emergence, Evolution, and Power of Japanese Girls' Magazine Fiction*. Albany: State University of New York Press.
Dorfman, Ariel, and Mattelart, Armand. 1984. *How to Read Donald Duck*. New York: International General.
Fujimoto, Yukari, and Thorn, Rachel. 2012. "Takahashi Macoto: The Origin of Shōjo Manga Style." *Mechademia*, 7: 24–55.
González, Carolina. 2004. *Entre "sodomitas" y "hombres dignos, trabajadores y honrados."* Santiago: Universidad de Chile.
Groensteen, Thierry. 2013. *Comics and Narration*. Jackson, MI: University Press of Mississippi.
Gutiérrez Fuentes, Camila. 2017. "From Socialism to Dictatorship: Editorial Ideologies in Chilean Science Fiction and Adventure Comics." *International Journal of Comic Art*, 19: 71–86.
Hassón, Moisés. 2014. *Comics en Chile, Catálogo de Revistas (1908–2000)*. Santiago: NautaColecciones Editores.
Hata, Mikako. 2013. "An Exploratory Study on the Relationship between Comics and Illustrations Appeared in Girls' Magazines." *Hanazono University Journal*, 45: 25–38.
Hemmann, Kathryn. 2014. "Short Skirts and Superpowers: The Evolution of the Beautiful Fighting Girl." *U.S.-Japan Women's Journal*, 47: 45–72.
Hoyos Ayala, Héctor. 2015. *Beyond Bolaño: The Global Latin American Novel*. New York: Columbia University Press.

Ikeda, Keiko. 2014. "From Ryosai Kenbo to Nadeshiko: Women and Sports in Japan." In Hargreaves, Jennifer, and Anderson, Eric, eds. *Routledge Handbook of Sport, Gender and Sexuality*. New York: Routledge, 97–105.

Illanes, María Angélica. 1990. "Azote, Salario y Ley. Disciplinamiento de la mano de obra en la minería de Atacama." *Proposiciones*, 19: 90–122.

Ishida, Hitoshi. 2015. "Representational Appropriation and the Autonomy of Desire in Yaoi/BL." In McLelland, Mark, Nagaike, Kazumi, Suganuma, Katsuhiko, and Welker, James, eds. *Boys Love Manga and Beyond*. Jackson: University of Mississippi Press, 210–32.

McCloud, Scott. 1993. *Understanding Comics*. New York: HarperCollins.

McLelland, Mark J. 2000. "Male homosexuality and popular culture in modern Japan." *Intersections* 1 (3). http://intersections.anu.edu.au/issue3/mclelland2.html.

Moretti, Franco. 2010. "Graphs, Maps, Trees: Abstract Models for a Literary History." In Vincent B. Leitch, ed. *The Norton Anthology of Theory and Criticism*. New York: Norton, 2441–64.

Nagasawa, Sachiko. 1997. "The Transition of Fashion Illustration in Japan." *Bulletin of the Japanese Society for the Science of Design*, 43 (5): 13–22.

Prado Bley, Pía. 2015. *Estrellas de la Pampa*. Zine. Santiago: Wolu Editorial. https://www.wolueditorial.cl/ebook-estellas-de-la-pampa

Prado Bley, Pía. 2019a. *Déjame que te Llame*. Santiago: Wolu Editorial.

Prado Bley, Pía. 2019b. *Let Me Call You*. Zine. Santiago: Wolu Editorial. https://www.wolu.cl/en-let-me-call-you.

Prough, Jennifer. 2011. *Straight from the Heart: Gender, Intimacy, and the Cultural Production of Shōjo Manga*. Honolulu: University of Hawaii Press.

Rojas, Jorge. 2016. *Las Historietas en Chile 1962–1982. Industria, ideología y prácticas sociales*. Santiago: LOM Ediciones.

Shamoon, Deborah. 2012. *Passionate Friendship: The Aesthetics of Girls' Culture in Japan*. Honolulu: University of Hawaii Press.

Shigetomi, Saki. 2009. "The Structure of 'shojo-ron': the Study of Shojo(Girls) in the 1980s." *Japan Women's University Journal*, 15 (3): 29–42.

Suzuki, Michiko. 2009. *Becoming Modern Women*. Stanford: Stanford University Press.

Tsai, Yi-Shan. 2018. "Close-ups: an emotive language in manga." *Journal of Graphic Novels and Comics*, 9 (5): 473–89.

A Sociological Approach to Francophone African Comics (1978–2016)

Sandra Federici

Although within comics studies the presence of African comics is often overlooked and ignored, some African comics have gained prominence outside the continent.[1] Barly Baruti and Pat Masioni are exemplary figures of these transnational figures, whether via black and white albums with soft cover published in Kinshasa or political cartoons appearing in local newspapers (in their case from the 1980s), and culminating in productions such as the graphic novels *Madame Livingstone* (2014) and *Rwanda 1994* (2005, 2008) released by publishers that are part of the European French-speaking comic field. Beyond these kinds of European publications, of which these are not the only ones, is it possible for an author to gain similar recognition in professional comics in Africa? What are the production, circulation, and reception conditions in Francophone African countries, and what kind of legitimization do these texts and their authors experience globally?

In order to answer these questions, I employ a sociological approach, namely Pierre Bourdieu's theory of fields, which when applied to African literatures reinvigorates this critical approach, in particular from *Les champs littéraires africains* (Fonkoua and Halen 2001). Starting from the concept of field as "a force field acting on all those who enter it, and in a different way according to the position which they hold in it … and at the same time a field of competitive struggles which tend to preserve or transform this force field" (Bourdieu 1991, 4–5), the field theory has provided tools for the study of contexts of peripheral cultural productions, especially postcolonial ones. Because it sheds light on all the productions of the cultural field in its relation to the whole of the social field, I apply it to the study of the comics sector in Africa as "one of the places of power, or a place where power is getting hierarchical" (Fonkoua and Halen 2001, 12). In this "place," several agents are active and enter into a power relationship: the authors, but also the publishers and other institutions that can allow the authors to obtain recognition in comic domain: magazines and newspapers, fanzines, author associations, festivals, local and international non-governmental

---

[1] The content of this essay comes mainly from the critical study of the comic domain of Francophone African countries and of the emergence of some authors in the European field that I carried out in my doctoral thesis, after published in Federici 2019.

organizations, and diplomacy institutions. In Bourdieu's theory, the field is established as a space of possibilities in which position taking—namely, the choices between different options more or less constituted as such—is defined by competitive and distinguishing practices. This relational web forms an autonomous microcosmos in the larger universe of society, which becomes constituted through an historical process of autonomization and differentiation from the external social space subjected to other forces. It works according to specific evaluation criteria and legitimizing institutions that are independent from "the outside" and from heteronymous values, such as religious, political, economic, and humanitarian ones.

In my view, the theory of field is also a powerful heuristic tool to keep the necessary distance from the object to question the limits of "identity predication" (Halen 2001, 15) as a condition of possibility in the path of emergence. It makes it possible to observe the authors with a gaze more aware of the mechanisms for attributing "symbolic capital" to these creators who are often considered as witnesses of more or less dramatic realities, allowing us to assess the decisive role of the institutions and agents of the field in the legitimization process. The notion of "literary institution," proposed by Jacques Dubois (1992), and taken up by Pascal Durand in his "Introduction to a sociology of symbolic fields," is particularly useful for "highlighting the devices of cultural production and dissemination, of consecration and legitimation" and to describe "the infrastructure of the system: publishing and distribution houses, reviews, newspapers" (Durand 2001, 26). In my analysis, limited to French-speaking sub-Saharan countries and focused on publishing houses, I follow his invite to "historize" (Durand 2001, 26) the analysis and to consider the field "in a given state of its evolution" (34), namely the period between the 1980s and mid 2010s.

In short, my argument is that the modalities of publication in African countries, and the scarce possibilities offered by institutions, require comic authors to adapt and improvise to advance their careers, but these less than ideal conditions also drive a number of authors to consider publication in European fields, often becoming the goal toward which they focus their efforts and strategies.

Publishing in Francophone Sub-Saharan Africa

All the African designers that I have met are heroes because they live with these difficulties every day but do not want to give up their passion. They draw for everyone: the press, NGOs, private companies, tourists, and individuals alike. They valiantly try to survive the virtual absence of worthy publishers. They dream of color albums and legitimate recognition.

(Cailleaux 2001, 9)

With these words the French cartoonist Christian Cailleaux outlines a general panorama of the professional condition of cartoonists in Africa, in his graphic essay dedicated to his experiences of comic workshops in Africa and published in an issue of *Notre Librairie* on African comics. In particular, he highlights the shortage of "authentic" publishers. European authors may complain about the growing insecurity of their profession, Cailleaux expresses the specific situation of disadvantage in which authors from most of Africa must practice their profession.

The institutions that African authors deplore the most are publishing houses that would invest in comic book collections. Comic publishing in Africa is part of a cultural sector which, although it is different country to country, is usually affected by a structural weakness that has origins in colonial times (Pinhas 2005, 39). Publishing houses are part of the cultural industries, that is, agents dedicated to transforming creativity, "change" and "new" into value in the form of commercial products, in this case books in print or digital form. They therefore remain a fundamental institution for enabling authors to assert themselves, even if the possibility of self-publishing, in particular by means of ever cheaper digital printing, has, in recent years, opened up many possibilities to authors, both European and African. The functioning of publishing in Africa has been the subject of several studies and debates supported by international institutions such as UNESCO, the European Union, and the World Bank, within the framework of development policies. If the gap between North and South is, in fact, still large, and the production is still scarce and qualitatively unequal, many researchers have nonetheless noted positive developments in the sector, particularly in the youth publishing sub-sector.

During the 1980s, 1990s, and 2000s, networks of professionals were born on purpose to compensate for the fragmented and dispersed nature of African publishing, to strengthen professionalism, to promote partnerships and North–South and South–South co-editions, to support the commercial distribution and, in general, to take measures that help to catch up with the delay affecting publishing in Africa. The most active are African Book Collective, a network of African publishers founded in Oxford in 1985 to market and distribute books published in Africa (mainly English-speaking countries are involved, but not exclusively); the Alliance of Independent Publishers, made up of eighty-five publishing houses from forty-five different countries, created in 2002 to develop solidarity-based promotion, in particular through co-publishing; the International Association of Francophone Libraries, created in Paris in 2002, which brings together around a hundred booksellers from sixty countries; Afrilivres, an association of publishers from French-speaking sub-Saharan Africa, Madagascar, and Mauritius, based in Cotonou and launched in 2001 by the Africultures portal; and APNET (African Publishers Network), a network of around thirty African book professionals, founded in 1992 in Harare and currently based in Accra. These initiatives are often part of a development assistance approach, because "publishing and book development in Africa have always been, and will continue to be, closely influenced by development in general" (Zell 2008, 188). The causes of the weakness of publishing in Africa have been analyzed by several researchers who have identified different factors: lack of policies, high illiteracy, low purchasing power, lack of reading promotion, taxes on raw materials, or even the dominance of imported schoolbooks.

In the first decades of independence, the book markets gave little opportunity for the commercial publication of albums to the few comic authors who, at the time, were the pioneers of the ninth art in their countries, and these few productions remained isolated in an unfavorable context for distribution and sales promotion. The associative world, cultural Western diplomacy and missions were almost the only agents who offered the possibilities of producing albums for authors who wanted to go beyond the publication of political cartoons or comic strips in the press.

The professional path of Mongo Sisé, one of the deans of the Congolese comic world, is paradigmatic: he had to self-finance his first album *Les Aventures de Mata Mata and Pili Pili: Le Portefeuille* (The Adventures of Mata Mata and Pili Pili: The Wallet) from Mama-Leki editions (1978), with a production company he set up, Mongoproduction ("Biographie de Mongo Sisé" 2008). Then, he continued to publish thanks to the Belgian cooperation agency AGCB, in Brussels, which promoted his famous series *Bingo* (1981–4), the adventures of a kind of African Tintin, accompanied by a small white dog and drawn in clear "Hergean" lines, who during his adventures always meets a Belgian development cooperation expert (Figure 5.1). During the same period, the other main author of the country, Barly Baruti, took the same path of collaboration with Belgian cooperation and published a first commissioned work on the African environment: *Le Temps d'agir* (Time to Act, 1982). He followed with many other works of the same type, before releasing albums unrelated to the cooperation: *Papa Wemba. Viva la musica* (Long Live the Music, 1987b) and *Mohuta & Mapeka. La voiture, c'est l'aventure* (The Car is Adventure, 1987a), the latter prefaced by Belgian cartoonist Bob de Moor who visited Kinshasa in 1985 "on the occasion of a Belgian comic event" (De Moor 1987) and then invited Baruti to the Hergé studios.

In then-Congo-Zaire, missions and international cooperation were the only institutions that offered relatively regular work for professionals and opportunities to publish for beginners. In particular, the Saint-Paul Afrique editions, founded in 1958 by three missionaries with a printing press in Limete-Kinshasa and another in Lubumbashi, hired cartoonists (Saye Lepa-Mabila, Gérard Sima Lukombo, and Pat Masioni) to produce comic book series, the illustrated magazine *Antilope*, and children's books on African legends and religious and educational subjects, many of which have been reprinted several times. Pat Masioni, from 1983, drew the series *Jesus des jeunes* (Jesus of the Young) published in three versions: French, Luba, and Swahili, between 1986 and 1996, and albums of the collection *Biographies en bandes dessinées* (Biographies in Comic) concerning the life of the saints who have lived on the African continent.

In Madagascar, the congregation of the Daughters of St. Paul, through the local label Édisiôna Md. Paoly were dedicated to publishing in the local language, and provided opportunities for Malagasy authors who could work to adapt albums released in Congo into Malagasy; for example, the biblical collection *Ny Baiboly vita tantara an-tsary* was published. The case of Madagascar stands out from the rest of French-speaking Africa because from 1979 onwards Malagasy authors enjoyed a "blessed period." This "golden age of Malagasy comics" (*Historique des BD de Madagascar* n.d.) was marked by a proliferation of professional publishing houses that produced adventure magazines and comic-books in a realistic style and in Malagasy language in imitation of Italian "fumettis." The various studies and testimonies relating to this period of Malagasy

Figure 5.1 *Bingo* (1981–1984)

comics make it possible to make the case, unique in French-speaking Africa, of a fairly developed market. It was made possible by a strong presence of publishers able to act professionally and ready to catch and experiment with formats from other national fields, such as the Italian one (read in French translations), to reinterpret them in an original way and satisfy a receptive readership which absorbed a large quantity of varied productions. This vitality and openness are confirmed by the Malagasy participation in the Angoulême Festival, at its thirteenth edition, in 1986: it was considered the first "African presence" in this annual international event. This boom ended with the economic and political crisis of 1991.

In Ivory Coast, "the country with the most titles, according to the Afrilivres census" (Pinhas 2005, 76), during the 1970s and 1980s some comic-book publishing initiatives were carried out, but were more isolated and random. For example, the famous *Dago*, an album by Maïga, a French author, published in 1973: in this case, the public's attachment to the stories of this young illiterate peasant, published regularly in *Ivoire Dimanche*, prompted a publisher to invest in an anthology. Another example is *Yao crack en math* (1985), drawn by Jess Sah Bi, newspaper cartoonist, in collaboration with Joséphine Guidy Wandja, professor of mathematics at the University of Abidjan. In Senegal, in a context where publications were also rare, emerged the first two volumes of the detective and humorous series *Les Aventures d'Aziz le reporter*, by Samba Fall, one of the forerunners of Senegalese comics, published in 1989 by Nouvelles Éditions Africaines du Sénégal.

These few examples suggest that, during the first three decades after Independence, the comic authors of French-speaking Africa were not supported very much by the book sectors of their countries. It should be remembered, however, that at the time the publishing houses were essentially based on state initiative, obviously not very interested and prepared for this type of language, and often fell into crisis at the end of the 1980s (Bgoya and Jay 2018).

Cartoonists and the Illustration of Children's Books

The 1990s were marked by a new configuration of the book market in African countries, in particular a "launch" of private initiatives that have revitalized publishing. The climate of political renewal created by the institution of multiparty systems, by the proliferation of newspapers and by the emergence of civil society has encouraged the ninth art, whose protagonists have been involved in the creation of associations, collectives, magazines, and festivals, while European cultural cooperation, particularly French and Belgian, supported this development and multiplied the opportunities for meetings with agents of European comics, through workshops and exhibitions. Many small and medium-sized publishing houses were founded during this period. For example, Bakame established itself in Rwanda after the genocide at the initiative of Agnes Gyr, who publishes in French and Kinyarwanda and who, due to its activity in children's books, is an active member of the international organization IBBY (Girard 2018, 56)[2]; Ruisseaux d'Afrique was founded in 1994 in Benin by Béatrice Lalinon Gbado and specializes in children's literature; Bibliothèque Lecture Développement was founded in Senegal as an association for the promotion of reading and education, and strengthened by a publishing component from 1996. The year 1992 saw the

---

[2] The International Board on Books for Young People (IBBY), founded in 1953 in Switzerland, is a non-profit association with official UNESCO status, which seeks to promote the meeting of children and books, through "national sections" in seventy-five countries.

establishment of several publishers: Ganndal, in Guinea, initiated by Aliou Sow; les Nouvelles Éditions Ivoiriennes, the fruit of the privatization of the Bureau Ivoirien des Nouvelles Éditions Africaines and the Éditions Livre Sud (Édilis) in Ivory Coast; Jamana, Le Figuier, Donniya, and Cauris in Mali.

While some publishing houses no longer exist, and others are not very active, many are still active and have gradually entered international book-promotion circuits and fairs. Luc Pinhas underlines this evolution: "the new African publishers, dynamic, better trained and undoubtedly more united than their elders, carry the hope of a real development of publishing on the continent." But this didn't erase their fragility and the small size of national markets "because of the low purchasing power and competition from houses in the North" (Pinhas 2006). According to Raphaël Thierry (2015, 21), "these manifestations of economic and intellectual domination" push African publishing to forms of "reaction," supported by the concept of "bibliodiversity,"[3] which has fostered, over the past twenty years, a greater presence of African productions on the international book market, and a better recognition of their diversity. The African edition is therefore part of the logic of "reaction" to persist commercially in the face of the attraction of the northern edition. Positive developments are also valued by Hans Zell, which sets out to refute negative stereotypes about book production in Africa:

> While two or three decades ago it might have been correct to describe African publishing as extremely underdeveloped, this is certainly not the picture now. It is true of course that many formidable obstacles and challenges remain, including weak technology infrastructures, high distribution costs, the lack of coherent national book policies, high tariff barriers, illiteracy, extreme poverty, and little disposable income, among them. Nevertheless, significant gains have been made, and there have been several collective efforts to build capacity.
> (Zell 2008, 191)

Viviana Quiñones (2016), editor of specialized journal *Takam Tikou*, remarks that "editorial work has evolved considerably from the situation before 2000. Editors have organized writing and illustration workshops; the work on the texts seems more in-depth. The formats have diversified, from small square books to big books. The models have become clearer, more varied, more creative." In addition, these publishers are more visible in international events (for example the Bologna Children's Bookfair or the Salon du livre de Paris), because of the principle of bibliodiversity and its application through cultural cooperation. Indeed, a certain weakness is revealed by infrequent publications, but the growing dynamism and the quality of the productions have been recognized internationally by specialized prizes reserved for publishers "from the South."[4]

---

[3] This concept is the basis of the action of the International Alliance of Independent Publishers.
[4] In 2015, the Prize for the Best Youth Publisher of the Year (BOP) for the African continent at the Bologna Children's Bookfair was awarded to Éditions Donniya, while Éditions Ruisseaux d'Afrique were nominated in 2016, with Ganndal from Guinea.

Over the past twenty years, editorial initiatives addressed to young people provide the framework within which professional opportunities are offered to comic-book authors. Picture books, novels, educational booklets in various formats, more or less illustrated, showcase an African imagination thanks to very varied themes, atmospheres, and characters: children and teenagers from all social circles, geniuses or other spirits, animals of the savannah, the forest and the farm, stories of daily life, in town or in the village, tales of adventures, and tales from the oral tradition of different cultures. This production, which has flourished especially since 2000 throughout French-speaking Africa, can be considered, in the general context of a weak and precarious African editorial production, as one of the elements that are part of the "institutional" framework of comics, because it allows designers not only to assert their competence in anonymous drawing and graphic design, and therefore to provide for their subsistence, but also to emerge as authors of albums for which illustrators sign the work with writers. Among these "duo" products, NEI hired several cartoonists: the Ivorians Benjamin Kouadio and Lassane Zohoré, the Senegalese Samba Fall, and the Beninese Hector Sonon, who illustrated a series of albums for children aged three to six, written by Beninese author O.J.R. Georges Bada and printed with the support of the Agence Internationale de la Francophonie. In Bénin, Sonon made drawings for the Éditions du Flamboyant and, above all, for Ruisseaux d'Afrique, a house about which he declared: "the big advantage, I must say, of residing in Benin is that a publishing house like Ruisseaux d'Afrique provides work regularly" (Sonon 2011).

The Central African Didier Kassaï is very active and told me in an interview that such collaborations allow him to support himself independently: "It allowed me to buy a house, buy a nice motorcycle [laughs] and I still have construction projects, so I manage to live with my job, at least in the Central African Republic" (Kassaï, forthcoming). As part of the literacy project "Educa 2000," in 2005–6, he and writer Olivier Bombasaro released, with Les Classiques Ivoiriens editions, five didactic illustrated adventure albums, forming a suite dedicated to the character of *Gipépé le pygmée*. The Beninese designer Hervé Alladayé, who sometimes uses the pen name Hodall Béo and has asserted himself as a cartoonist in several Beninese newspapers has worked frequently as an illustrator with Ruisseaux d'Afrique (series *Coco Taillé* and *Tanéka*), before releasing the "EU-subsidized" album *Faoussah: la Petite Vidomègon*, with Star éditions in 2009.

After collaborating with cartoonist and comic author Aly Zoromé for the little story of *Sitan la petite imprudente* (Bamako: Le Figuier, 1997), the writer and publisher Moussa Konaté hired him to illustrate two collections of educational albums on the historical and geographical heritage and traditional trades of Africa (*Métiers d'Afrique*) published by its publishing house Le Figuier. Balani's, founded in 2003 in Bamako by cultural animator and musician Igo Lassana Diarra, inaugurated the publications by entrusting the cartoonist Massiré Tounkara the illustration of *Les Jumeaux à la recherche de leur mère* (2004), a children's story accompanied by an audio cassette with the narration in French and Bambara. The success of the book encouraged the publication of a second episode in 2005 and, in 2006, of *La Princesse capricieuse*, by the same authors. In Senegal, the association for the promotion of reading and publishing house Bibliothèque Lecture Développement has published illustrated albums by Senegalese cartoonists Lamine Dieme and Cheikh Ba.

As part of editorial production aimed at general or youth audiences, some publishers have gradually opened their catalog to comic-book titles irregularly and with little intentionality. There are six comic-book titles listed in the 2016 catalogue of the important Ivorian NEI-CEDA house, both old and new releases: two volumes in the series "Les Nouvelles Aventures de Kimboo," a fighting youth hero: *Cap Sur Tombouctou* (1999), and *Kimboo contre la drogue* (2001); an album dedicated to the character of *John Koutoukou: Responsable, irresponsable*, by Benjamin Kouadio (pseudonym KBenjamin, 1999); *Le SIDA et les autres affaires le concernant*, an old (1985) album from the director of the magazine *Gbich!*, Lassane Zohoré. Another title is a reprint of an educational "classic" already published in 1985: *Yao crack en math*, while the last title, *Délestron*, is a comic representation of a particular problem of urban life in Ivory Coast, power cuts, proposed by the Ivorian advertising graphic designer Charles Dadié. Before being a successful comic book, Délestron grew into a Facebook page that quickly reached 5,000 likes (in April 2021 almost 7,000).

In Mali, in 1997, Le Figuier gave the Ivorian designer Yacouba Diarra the possibility of publishing two comic-book albums: *Comment le lièvre sauva les chèvres*, which is considered the first in the country (Cassiau-Haurie 2010) and *et Nassoumba et le Komo*. Diarra is a cartoonist for the *Grin-grin* newspaper (started by the Jamana cooperative and headed by President Alpha Oumar Konaré) and a star cartoonist (known as Kays) for the daily *Les Echos*. In 2008, Balani's editions launched a series of adventure comics, aimed at raising awareness of nature protection: "Issa et Wassa," with drawings by Massiré Tounkara, on script by Mahamadou Traore de Seydou. Two volumes came out: *Woroni du Bafing* and *Le Forestier du Baoulé*, but the project, which the designer said would have included four volumes, seemed to have stopped. Indeed, the founder of the publishing house, Igo Lassana Diarra, has started other projects in Bamako: the organization of the International Youth Literature Festival and the management of the Medina art space.

In Benin, publishing houses for young people have hardly published comic books, apart from two. Flamboyant editions in 1998 commissioned Jo Palmer Akligo the album *Sokrou ou les méfaits des sacs plastiques* (Sokrou or the misdeeds of plastic bags), financed by the Beninese Ministry of the Environment, Housing and Urban Planning, and distributed it free of charge to students for environmental awareness. Star editions printed in 2009 a collection of booklets, "Premises," with the European funding of the Support Program for Decentralized Cooperation in Benin, in which the comic albums *Les extraterrestres Pygamous*, by Jo Palmer Akligo, and *Koffi Azé*, by Hector Sonon are included.

In some countries, there is an almost total lack of publishing prospects. For example, the Ganndal editions (Republic of Guinea), among the eighty titles in the catalog, including several albums for young people, only have one comic book, *L'Interlocuteur* by Diane Mory, published in 1997, whose theme is family planning and contraception.

On the Cameroonian market, hope has been aroused by the Akoma Mba editions, founded in 1995 and supported by the association Auteurs et Illustrateurs du Livre pour Enfants du Cameroun. In fact, apart from the four issues of the journal *Essingan*, they produced little in the ninth art, such as the album *Kanse*, by authors Christian Ova'a, Mephisto (Edmond Mballa Elanga, designer and at the time director of Akoma Bba) and Joël Eboueme Bognomo, published in 1997 with the support of the Belgian cooperation of Yaoundé and distributed free of charge to inform readers about vaccinations; and a subpar edition of the *Shegué* collective, produced during a workshop at Fescarhy festival in 2003. Production was therefore dependent on European cooperation, and the comic book collection announced by Akoma Mba in 2003 was never published. The publishing house closed in 2005 and was reactivated in 2018.

These individual examples, which emerge almost on a case-by-case basis here and there in the catalogs of publishers and in the biographies of authors, show that the investment of generalist or children's publishers in comic books remains rare and random, often depending on international cooperation funding. It is also not framed in coherent editorial strategies, which would be identifiable by means of publishing programs or dedicated sections within the catalogues; on the contrary, in the catalogs it is often difficult to distinguish comic books from children's albums.

Aware of the consequences that the weakness of this institution, fundamental to the existence of works and the emergence of authors, has on their professional careers, authors often deplore this lack which separates them from an audience that, in their opinion, exists.

> Comic book authors find it hard to get edited. The doors of publishing houses are hermetically closed to them. To be convinced, just leaf through their catalogues.... The Ivorian public is also fond of comics. We still have to go to him with products that it could consume. Here publishers have a role to play in editing author albums. They are accused of contenting themselves most often with publishing books and keeping them warm in bookstores. Without promotion. No TV or radio spot, or participation in literary programs.
>
> (Macaire 2013)

This is what Ivorian author Benjamin Kouadio complains with journalist Etty Macaire, while Cameroonian Deubou Sikoué (2011) laments that "publishing houses are reluctant to embark on the adventure, because the financial risk is great"; as for the Senegalese T.T. Fons (2009), he declares: "what the artists deplore is this support that they do not have today, both from the authorities and from the publishers who, perhaps, are afraid to put money into comic books produced by Africans when the demand is there." Franco-Cameroonian comic writer Christophe Edimo, for his part, ironically regrets the excessive proportion of albums published to convey messages of public utility: "comics in Africa is going bad, as is the African economy .... There are few playful comic books, and a little too many themed comic books (AIDS, malaria, onchocerciasis, etc.): do you have to be sick or threatened by a disease to read a comic story in Africa?" (Giguet-Legdhen, n.d.).

The (Rare) Publishing Houses Specializing in Comics

In the hope of reaching an audience of comic-book enthusiasts, of being able to educate new readers and to mobilize networks of young people, authors and cultural operators have embarked on entrepreneurial initiatives, individually or in groups, with little financial means. Specialized publishers have thus made their appearance in the African comic landscape, publishing titles and working to make themselves effective and visible on the cultural scenes of their country and, as far as possible, internationally. If some structures have published a plurality of authors, others display the same name in their catalogue, because their authors created them only with the objective of publishing their own works. After periods of intense activity, these ephemeral houses have often ended up closing their doors, either for financial reasons or because their initiators became devoted to other activities.

Ten years before the great and brief momentum of Gabonese comics that made Libreville, with the *Journées africaines de la B.D.* (African Comic Days, 1998 and 1999), the meeting place for many authors from all over French-speaking Africa, the Dutch-Gabonese cartoonist Hans Kwaatail Achka had tried to develop the sector by creating a publishing house, to which he had given his own name. Achka editions is known as the first publishing house specializing in comics in French-speaking Africa and was based on an editorial project, in particular that of publishing the best African comic authors. It launched its catalog in 1989 with the album *Monsieur Zézé*, centered on a character conceived by the French-Ivorian designer Lacombe, who became famous in Ivory Coast (after the aforementioned *Dago*) for his stories, which had been appearing since 1978 in the weekly *Ivoire Dimanche*. The adventures of this ignorant villager arriving in Abidjan have been a notable success with readers for their staging of Ivorian urban society and the life and language of the people of the capital. Unfortunately, the life of the Achka publishing house was short, since it "ceased its production in 1992, and put an end to the dream of creating an African comic book publisher and left a great void in the country" (Cassiau-Haurie 2007).

Another attempt was initiated by the Congolese journalist (DRC) Dan Bomboko who, after completing a license in Publishing and Book Science at the Faculty Institute of Information and Communication Sciences in Kinshasa, founded Éditions Elondja in 2004, with the aim of publishing Congolese comics. Being one of the rare comic book writers from French-speaking Africa, Bomboko has written all the comics released by Éditions Elondja: three volumes in the series *Elikya, le petit orphelin* (*Elikya*, the little orphan, 2005, 2006, and 2009); two volumes from the series *Les aventures de Mamisha* (The Adventures of Mamisha, 2005 and 2007), for which he entrusted the Congolese designers Alain Kojele and Dick Esale; and other occasional publications, some of them financed by foreign development cooperation. But dissemination was difficult and turnover low. Since 2009, Elondja has also been active in the sale of schoolbooks, children's literature, and stationery. Afterwards, *Elikya*'s sales figures appear to have improved: the publisher says in his blog that he sold 12,000 copies because the Ministry of Education has classified *Elikya* as a didactic book ("Elikya, le petit orphelin bientôt de retour!" 2012). However, the precariousness of this cultural enterprise remains constant over time. For example, in September 2012, Elondja claimed to be in great difficulty, following the decision of the sponsoring bank to no longer support its publications. From what is currently published on the Facebook page and its blog, Elondja is still active, between re-editions of past series, cultural animation activities, and the publication of new titles from time to time.

In Ivory Coast, the 2000s saw the emergence of editions linked to the successful satirical magazine *Gbich!* (onomatopoeia which means "punch"), launched in 1999 by cartoonists Lassane Zohoré and Simplice Hillary, and soon become very well known, even internationally. The Gbich! Éditions Group launched in 2004 the women's magazine *Go Magazine*—subsequently becoming the country's leading weekly with more than 20,000 sales per issue—and *Allo Police*, specializing in news, launched in 2009. Very active, Gbich! Group has diversified into a wide range of cultural fields, such as a website, comedy shows, and a 2D and 3D cartoon production structure (Afrikatoon). However, concerning comics, it has published only a few collections produced by authors who were already part of the weekly journal team. These are the *Proverbes sérieusement illustrés* (Seriously Illustrated Proverbs, 2003) of Mendozza, and the album *L'Amour est Roi* (Love is King, 2009), featuring the stories of the "seducer" Jo Bleck, and *Gbassman* (2006), a character with supernatural powers and able to handle magic conceived by Kan Souffle. This author has also published with Go Média ("sister" of Gbich!) in the series *Les sorcières*, telling the daily adventures of three beautiful girls in three episodes in 2009, 2011, and 2012. At the same time, *Les Sorcières* have spawned a five-minute TV series adaptation. The authors of *Gbich!* sometimes collaborate with the "Olvis Dabley Agency," a company specializing in events created by Olvis Dabley, director of the Ivorian Cocobulles comic festival, which was held in 2001, 2003, and 2007 in Grand Bassam and which was suspended for ten years and then reactivated in 2017. Dabley is an entrepreneur also active on the "market" of foreign development cooperation, and designed editorial projects intended to convey messages, notably to urge unity in the face of rising tribalism and xenophobia. He brought together cartoonists, mainly from *Gbich!*, and released collective albums: *Cultivons l'amour*, published with the financial assistance of the US government to be distributed free of charge as part of a campaign for national unity, and *On va où là? 1993–2006. 13 ans de crise politique en dessins de presse* (Where are we going? 1993–2006. 13 years of political crisis in press cartoons, 2007), which, according to the publisher, had some commercial success. After five years, thanks to the support of the City of Geneva, a Volume 2 followed with the title *On va où là? 2007–2011. Des accords de Ouaga à une incroyable élection!* (From the Ouaga accords to an incredible election!, 2012).

At present, Ago Media, a small company in Lomé headed by the writer Paulin Koffivi Mawuto Assem, is particularly active, often present at the Bologna Children's Book Fair. Assem wrote books in the field of children's literature, such as the novel *Rose-fleur— Blanche-Neige (version actualisée)* (Pink flower—Snow White—updated version, 2003). Then, this young writer started publishing comics when he created Ago editions, in 2011, with the illustrator KanAd. The albums are often co-signed by the two authors, like *Haiti mon amour* (Haiti My Love, 2012), *Le bon, la bourse et le corrompu* (The

Figure 5.2 *Chroniques de Lomé*

Good, the Purse and the Corrupt, 2012) and *Monfay chez les magiciens du fer* (Monfay Among the Iron Magicians, 2016), or produced collectively, like *Chroniques de Lomé*, an album published in 2013 after a workshop that brought together nine cartoonists, led by the French writer Alain Brezault and financed by the Intergovernmental Agency for the French-Speaking Community (Figure 5.2). Before structuring themselves into an editorial company, the creatives of Ago Media had already demonstrated their vitality in 2006, when they started producing comic book magazines in small format: *Ago feuilleton* and *Ago fiction*. The short comic tales "to be continued" contained in these magazines tell the problems and the daily life of the young people, or the adventures of superheroes inspired by US comics but located in Africa, while short articles deal with scientific subjects to attract young people from Togo and elsewhere to read for pleasure. In the same format and in the same spirit Ago printed in 2012 *Flore à tout prix*, a love story and rivalry among the young people of a district of Lomé. This group continues its activity, despite the difficulties of managing a publishing house specializing in comics in Togo, where for a long time, due to an economic embargo of several years (1993–2005), children had difficulty getting comics, and where "a large part of a whole generation … grew up without comics … To overcome this problem, in addition to publishing comics, the publishing house organizes comic strip courses in schools and libraries, and organizes festivals" (KanAd 2014).

In the rather varied typology of structures devoted to the publication of comics, we can still register the initiative of a French designer and architect living in N'Djamena, Gérard Leclaire, who, through his Graphi-Culture Foundation, has brought together a group of Chadian designers to produce collective albums and exhibitions, with the support of institutions or private sponsors. Adji Moussa, Samy Daina, and Abou Abakar Issaka thus produced *La grande épopée du Tchad* (The great epic of Chad, 2005), a historical comic book inspired by the colonization of Chad in 1898, printed in 5,000 copies, presented at the Angoulême Festival in 2006, and then sold for years in N'Djamena in bookstores, hotels, and restaurants (Figure 5.3).

Self-publishing

The economic and cultural dimension of the micro-environments represented by the small editorial structures that we have described becomes even more uncertain in the case of self-publishing, either individually or collectively. Indeed, authors often start their professional careers by producing booklets in an informal way, by directly addressing a printing company which functions as a service provider, or by publishing "à compte d'auteur" (i.e. with a non-specialized publisher who, for his part, has not borne the costs and risks of publication and has not included the work in a cultural project), or even by establishing a production structure dedicated to the promotion of its own works. Alleging the same goals as a small specialized publishing house, these latter cases are difficult to distinguish from those examined in the previous paragraph: we have therefore included in self-production the companies that have limited their activity to publication of works by the author–publisher.

In general, self-publishing represents an alternative adopted by novice cartoonists to be able to print their creations, using "on-line" on-demand printing services or established printing houses, and then sell them. In Europe, this kind of production sometimes responds to a need for autonomy felt by an author, who can thus get rid of "the constraint of having to please a publisher, of having to fit into an editorial line" (Lesage 2014, 138), but it is often also due to the hyper-competition of a market that forces authors to produce themselves in an attempt to exist in bookstores or in more informal markets. In African countries, self-publishing is first and foremost a practical solution put in place by authors to cope with the dearth of publishers. The

Figure 5.3 *La grande épopée du Tchad*

product can be of the same quality as the traditional edition, or be much more modest, even artisanal. Distribution takes place through various distribution channels: sale at festivals, distribution in restaurants, on the street or in front of schools, purchases by donors, direct sales by authors. Remaining on the margins of the editorial system, these publications manage to reach readers who do not access either bookstores or libraries.

Benin is a good example of these difficult contexts that force comic-book authors to take the initiative to self-publish to start their professional careers (Tessy 2015). The *Zinsou et Sagbo* album, which has symbolic value because it is the country's first comic-book album, was only possible thanks to the initiative of Hector Sonon, the currently most internationally recognized cartoonist in the country, who self-published 300 copies in 1989.[5]

Before starting his close collaboration with Ruisseaux d'Afrique, Hervé Alladayé made a name for himself by publishing *Chiottes et cacahuètes* in 1999 and, the following year, the booklet *Les Zemidjans protestent*, a short humorous report devoted to "kékénos" (mototaxis). Well received by the public, it had a sequel: *Les Zemidjans persistent*, published in 2006.

The Congolese duo (RDC) Tshibanda-Kibwanga published *Alerte à Kamoto* (1989) and *Les refoulés du Katanga* (1994) (Figure 5.4), examples of the rare non-religious albums published in the Congo after independence, notably in the city of Lubumbashi. These two albums with political content were published thanks to small editorial initiatives by authors, Lanterne and IMPALA, to "convey to the public the messages and information that the press ignored (for example, ethnic cleansing in Kasai which claimed the lives of more than 100,000 people in the early 1990s)" (Riva 2006, 241). Pie Tshibanda confirmed the goals and conditions of these comics in an interview:

> *Alerte à Kamoto* is an album published by me (sort of self-publishing). I could have expanded to other writers if the war hadn't stopped me. Even though it's not a commissioned album, a mining company, other than the one mentioned in the adventure, still bought us a big package. The story told is true.
>
> *Les refoulés du Katanga* is an album published by Éditions IMPALA by Max Pierre (now deceased)... Here I am telling the story on behalf of those who lost their lives. The perpetrators of these events have never been tried. They thought they were erasing the traces of their misdeeds and I, through this album, left the proof.
>
> ... "IMPALA"... is an abbreviation of *Imprimé Par L'Auteur* (Printed By Author) ..."Lantern" is also part of the desire to self-publish, first, and to publish others. The idea is that if not being a sun shining in the sky, the lantern can modestly light up a corner.
>
> (Tshibanda, forthcoming)

From December 2006 to March 2007, the Cameroonian Almo The Best published at Éditions Fluide Thermal (founded by himself) four issues of the magazine *Fluide Thermal*. Very active in communication, in 2010 he created Almo Productions, a label dedicated to the publication of comic-book albums.

Another example of an author's initiative that aspires to expand to the publication of other authors is the Éditions du Crayon Noir, established in Kinshasa in 2013 by the

---

[5] "Self-published in 1989 in 300 copies by the young Hector Sonon, Zinsou and Sagbo recounts in a series of gags in one sheet the comic misadventures of twins. This is the first comic book album released in Benin." This information about the self-published album by Sonon in 1989 can be found in the presentation sheet of an album published with the same title by Ruisseaux d'Afrique in 2003, illustrated by children's drawings, where the name of Sonon does not appear (Zinsou et Sagbo, 2003).

Figure 5.4 *Les refoulés du Katanga*

cartoonist and writer Asimba Bathy, already an organizer of associations and of journals. The singularity of Bathy lies in its good ability to unite local authors around subsidized collective projects, as much as to manage a personal network of international relations, in particular with the Belgian cultural cooperation, which allows him to obtain invitations to festivals in Europe and Africa. Anyway, for many years his publishing house released only one album, from the same Bathy: *Panique à Kinshasa*, at the end of 2013.

Senegalese author Alphonse Mendy, creator of Goorgoorlou, one of the best-known African heroes, is one example of the success of self-publishing in Africa.

Mendy, whose pseudonym is T.T. Fons, in other words "uncle Alphonse," published, at the end of the 1980s, in the satirical Dakar newspaper *Le Cafard libéré*, stories centered on the character of Goorgoorlou, whose Wolof name means "to fight like a man." Representing "the average Senegalese," unemployed since the first Structural Adjustment Plan, Goorgoorlou is still setting up small informal businesses to collect "the daily expense" that he must give to his wife Diek to ensure the needs of the family. The success of this narration, which shows and records "from below" the changes in Senegalese society and politics, prompted its author, in 1991 and 1992, to bring together the one-page stories in two albums at the Sogedit editor. In 1994, T.T. Fons released his third album: *1993, L'année Goorgoorlou* (*1993, The Year Goorgoorlou*), with his own company, Atelier Fons, specializing in graphics, publishing, advertising, and visual communication, which allowed him to work in advertising for companies and in social communication for international organizations. A fourth album, *Goorgoorlou survivant de la Dévaluation* (Goorgoorlou survivor of Devaluation), was released in 1995. These albums contain color advertising pages (while the rest of the album is in black and white), the "testimonial" of which is the same Goorgoorlou who promotes drinks, phone companies, or detergent. Due to their success, some of these stories became episodes of a Wolof-language "sitcom" produced and broadcast by Radio Télévision Sénégalaise. At the end of 2002, the author–publisher launched a comic and cultural information magazine, *Goor mag*, which published nine issues before disappearing.

Another category of self-publication relates to so-called popular comics, distributed at low prices in city markets or in restaurants. The booklets produced and distributed in Kinshasa by the author Mfumu'eto are emblematic both for their content strictly linked to the Congolese urban context and for the success achieved with the public. From 1990, Mfumu'eto began to self-publish "magazines" printed on an offset press, on poor-quality paper, in A5 size and monochrome. His publications were immediately popular, so much so that he claimed to have sold 100,000 copies of the first story (Hunt 2015, 266). Historian Nancy Rose Hunt is currently studying the archives of this author and, on the occasion of the *Beauté Congo* exhibition, presented in Paris in 2015, she inventoried his prolific production and collected his testimony: "in 1990 I was very productive. I was not working alone; four people were assisting me. I had trained young people... It was a real comic book studio... At least one or two impressions per week" (Hunt 2015, 267).

Having proclaimed himself "His Majesty the Emperor Papa Mfumu'eto I," he produced, from 1990 to the beginning of the 2000s, a large number of stories, almost all in Lingala, the most widely used language in Kinshasa; they were devoted to everyday life, relationships between men and women, popular beliefs, and the supernatural. As Repetti (2007b) noted, the vernacular lexicon and the handling of irony, used to denounce the abuses of power at the top of the state and in his entourage, had a strong resonance with the public. This fruitful production lasted until the 2000s, when the artist turned to painting, especially the so-called "popular" genre. Despite the success of its sales, Mfumu'eto has remained quite far from the international field of comics, being outside collectives, transnational, French-speaking, and global circuits as well as projects linked to commissioned comics, he has instead chosen to address directly to its readership, focused on Kinshasa. He was further integrated into the field of international contemporary art, which began in the late 1980s to focus on authors from the peripheries. The *Beauté Congo—1926-2015—Congo Kitoko* exhibition in Paris, where his comics were exhibited and where he gave "performances" by producing stories that were published as they went along on the website of the exhibition, represented a consecration for the author, rather in the field of contemporary art, however, than in that of comics.

This analysis of the book sector in French-speaking Africa in relation to possibilities of publishing albums shows the scarcity and weakness of institutions essential to professional and artistic legitimation. Faced with comics that they have written that do appeal to narrow publishing norms, authors themselves act as publishers: the production, distribution, and communication phases are very often managed, with great difficulty, by the artists themselves, to give visibility and existence to their works, and thus gain artistic recognition within the system. Indeed, these productions serve more to ensure economic income through direct sales and, ultimately, to *exist*, to allow the manuscripts to be taken out of the drawer and transformed into an object to be presented in a festival, communicated to the media and bought by readers. Asked about the importance of his self-published albums, Pie Tshibanda told me: "An important role, yes .... Something realized is always a business card, a certain credibility. When you show up somewhere and show what you have already achieved, some doors open" (Tshibanda, forthcoming).

The authors are in any case aware of the institutive role of publishing, because it may condition the following stages in their trajectory. We can say that the investment of an initial endowment of economic capital to self-publish provides the author with a material base that can allow him or her to initiate or strengthen exchanges, and to structure networks which can increase his or her influence as an artist.

Other Institutions

Other institutions have an important role in defining an autonomization of the comic field, but we have space here only to shortly outline it. Firstly, the written press (the general press, satirical magazines as well as comic magazines) played an important role for the emergence of authors, especially in the 1990s and 2000s, as shown in the sociological and historical analysis by scholars such as Massimo Repetti (2002, 2007a) and Hillary Mbiye Lumbala (2009). In several African nations, freedom of opinion and expression, in a context of media effervescence encouraged by the adoption of a multiparty system, fostered the phenomenon of satirical reviews and promoted the presence of satirical cartoons in newspapers. The criticism has resulted in caricatured and derisive forms of corruption and politicians, often represented through the evocation of physical defects, in a continuous and complicated negotiation with censorship. Some of the authors were forced to emigrate to Europe, facing difficult times but also acquired the symbolic capital of exiled artists.

Another important element—almost always present as a lever for action or, at least, as a tool of emergence—are the associations of authors. This socialization form mixes artistic, professional, and political approaches: the authors meet to draw together, participate in training, organize one-off cultural activities such as workshops and exhibitions or more structured programs in the form of festivals, set up activities in schools to promote a culture of comics, and publish magazines or collective albums. Particularly during the 1990s and 2000s, the authors commonly used associative forms to dialogue with the institutions supposed to support them and to benefit from a stronger impact with public opinion and the press. Independent countries have witnessed and are still witnessing the birth and death of comic associations and collectives, most often in capitals but also in other major cities. These associations borrow their names from local languages (this is the case with the Congolese association Lamuka which means "wake up"), or acronyms that indicate the composition and the geographical location, such as BDB, Bande des Dessinateurs de Bamako (Bamako Cartoonists Band), or metaphors linked to the semantic universe of comics: Tache d'Encre (Ink spot) in Ivory Coast, Trait Noir (Black Line) in Cameroon.

As an important institutional entity for the artists' itinerary, cultural events must be mentioned, in particular large and small festivals, fairs, workshops, and conferences relating to comics. They are part of a wave of events aimed at cultural promotion, with the claimed objective of allowing artists—also writers, musicians, actors, or dancers—to present themselves to the public, to meet creators from other countries and to distinguish themselves through competitions. Often organized or sponsored by European nations' cultural diplomacy, in collaboration with local authors' associations, they generally define the programs around the invitation of authors from the metropolis, for workshops and meetings with local artists. The circulation of authors has gradually enabled them to have some networking and professional and cultural training, but these events do not benefit from the stable investment of established associations or public bodies that could ensure them continuity and perpetuate them as permanent institutions of a local comic field (Cassiau-Haurie 2008). Authors recognize that festivals, workshops, and other promotional initiatives are often the only way to promote publications and meet an audience; they are thus encouraged to become actively involved in the process of marketing and promoting their works by participating in signing sessions. The success obtained during one-off events is, moreover, quite relative: it is often superficial and only media-oriented, because it is not based on continuous work and professional organization.

Authors and associations give priority to the search for partnerships with Western institutions, such as the French, Belgian, Swiss, German, Portuguese cultural centers or Embassies, as well as other international institutions involved in development cooperation (such as Belgian Red-Cross, Belgian federal association Africalia, Communauté Wallonie-Bruxelles, The French aid agency Coopération Française), and non-governmental associations such as the Italian Africa e Mediterraneo.[6] They offer international funding, logistical or political support to the authors and the creation of

---

[6] Africa e Mediterraneo collected a large number of original comics, drawings, and publications from almost all African sub-Saharan countries. The catalog consists of more than 2,500 items and represents one of the richest collections of African comics in the world, available online at http://www.africacomics.net.

contacts and opportunities for collaboration with recognized European authors, giving a profound influence. In reality, local NGOs and national governments also provide the opportunity to work in social, educational, and humanitarian projects.

Another important factor to consider with regard to authors' career paths is the gradual diffusion of the Internet. From the end of the 1990s it has played a triple role in the professional careers of African authors: it first technically transformed the production cycle (e-mail correspondence and file exchange, possibility to scan the drawings, techniques of digital coloring); it then offered them opportunities to make themselves visible (in personal blogs) and be hired; finally, to a lesser extent, it had consequences for the publication of their works (crowdfunding and online platforms for publishing). Indeed, from 2007, when the technology of Web 2.0 was imposed, blogs were gradually supplanted by Facebook and, later, Instagram pages, where the communication, content sharing and networking are much easier to access. The social media success is also due to the diffusion of the mobile phone, which allows easy connection to them.

To conclude this institutional panorama of the conditions of possibility of comics in French-speaking Africa, I mention the theme of criticism, saying that the production of these authors, in Europe or in Africa, has received very few critical articles and reviews published in comic specialized journals. Rarely do we find judgments that are based on a language and critical tools consistent with the subject of "modern comics" and that are not influenced by a focus on African issues and by the spirit of *a priori* approval which shapes what Halen (2008, 42) calls "positions of dominance, at least relative, ... masked by constant calls for 'dominated' positions, the moral benefit of which also reflects on the critic who promotes them."

Conclusion

I have quickly described the space of possibilities in which African artists implement their artistic and professional strategies. They undergo artistic training in an educational institution or as a self-taught person, then they aspire to enter into competition with other beginners, or even with those who already occupy dominant positions, to become professionals of the ninth art. The institutional analysis of the conditions of production, circulation, and reception of comics makes it clear that despite the emergence of several generations of authors, with leading figures whose reputations have transcended national and continental borders, it is quite difficult to apply the concept of literary field to these cultural environments, as defined by Pierre Bourdieu, both nationally and, more broadly, in relation to all African countries where French is the language of culture.

As we have already observed, the theory of field emphasizes that, in local contexts, several actors and institutions are at work and maintain power relations. I recall that power is here to be understood as the ability to obtain and keep capital in one of its forms: economic, cultural, social, and symbolic (Sapiro 2019). In this sense, if it is difficult to discern a literary field in the case concerning us, and a fortiori a relatively autonomous literary field, on the other hand we can say that there is indeed *a logic of field* that is at work. First, because there are competing forces there, then because the structures of a field within which the struggles for recognition take place are more or less established (there are institutions, authors, modes, and rules of legitimation). These agents play a role at one point or another in the authors' professional career: emergence (workshop, publication in review or in collective albums), legitimation (personal album, award, visibility in the media, participation in a festival as a guest), consecration (publication in northern houses, participation in a northern festival). The authors show that they are quite capable to move within a field in which the institutions offer more or less substantial opportunities and present a certain openness according to variable and fluctuating principles. Under the conditions of possibility that are offered to them, taking into account their social and cultural capital, the authors implement what Bourdieu calls "strategy"—publications, invitations, interviews in the media, membership of an association, relations with a European or African writer—thanks to their "habitus," that is to say their practical sense, their patterns of perception, action, and evaluation of the world (Dewerpe 1996). They are aware of having to make their way in a context subject to instances that are heteronomous in relation to the specific values of the comic field, and that these are the forms of recognition available locally. However, in concrete professional situations, criteria are applied, in fact, to define the success of an author. Publish an album with a local publisher, receive an award by a European Embassy, become the official author of a satirical newspaper, regularly obtain orders from the associative world: notable facts which constitute tangible indicators of the success achieved by an author, because they are forms of a judgment, at a given moment, of the complexity of the balance of power in the environment concerned.

Beside the economic weakness of the comic book market, we must consider the cultural weight of the prestigious Franco-Belgian "bande dessinée," as well as the great consideration enjoyed by European authors, known occasionally during workshops organized in African cities by the diplomatic services. To all these factors, we must add the example of the first African authors who moved to Europe during a period (the 1980s and 1990s) of relative permeability of European borders. All this explains the tendency of many African authors to aspire to pass their career through the European field, either by emigrating or by staying physically in their country.

From a historical point of view, it should be noted that from the beginning of the 2000s, several factors raised the expectations of African authors. Their work, as an underprivileged cultural production worthy of promotion, aroused a certain interest from the European associative world, an interest which was manifested by the use of different creative languages in cooperation initiatives. Development education projects carried out in Europe have made it possible to organize exhibitions and publications in which some authors have been involved, mainly in the form of collectives. In hindsight, this period during which a structural change was hoped for seems to have constituted a kind of parenthesis in the history of African comic strip; only a few authors, in fact, managed to materialize the expected improvement and follow a path of success in Europe, so that hope finally fell. Along with these paths characterized by extraversion (Bayart 1999), opportunities have continued to open up to authors, despite the difficulties, in African cities. New avenues have opened up in what the authors call "the comm": communication service companies (media animation, digital games, advertisements, etc.) have flourished, while the authors continue to obtain funds to organize cultural events (workshops, bookfairs, festivals). In this context, it would be fairer to speak, rather than a resignation of the authors, of a correction of their strategies of professional affirmation. The possibilities of publication in Europe currently accessible to authors are no longer seen as the doors of a sure success nor as obligatory passages, even if the edition in a prestigious Franco-Belgian house undoubtedly remains a dream cherished by any cartoonist on the planet. The authors know that building a solid career and maintaining won positions in the field are not goals that can be considered achieved once the first doors are opened. With a certain realism, they are more and more committed to local circles and have learned through experience that when it comes to publishing with a European publisher, even if it is small or medium, even if it is linked to the associative world, this is useful, above all to strengthen their reputation and, in this way, obtain communication and creative work in their country.

References

Baruti, B., Arys, A., and Colyn, M. 1982. *Le Temps d'agir*. Bruxelles: AGCD.
Baruti, B. 1987a. *Mohuta & Mapeka. La Voiture, c'est l'aventure!* Kinshasa: Afrique Éditions.
Baruti, B. 1987b. *Papa Wemba, Viva la musica*. Kinshasa: Afrique Éditions.
Baruti, B., Cassiau-Haurie, Ch. and Appollo. 2014. *Madame Livingstone. Congo, la Grande Guerre*. Grenoble: Glénat.
Bayart, F. 1999. "L'Afrique dans le monde: une histoire d'extraversion." *Critique Internationale*, 5: 97–120.
Bgoya, W., and Jay, M. 2018. "L'édition en Afrique, de l'indépendance à nos jours." *Africa e Mediterraneo*, 2: 7–18.
"Biographie de Mongo Sisé" 2008. *Blog de Mongo Sisé*, November 6. http://mongosise.skyrock.com/2120306319-Biographie-de-MONGO-Sise.html (accessed March 18, 2021).
Bourdieu, P. 1991. "Le champ littéraire." *Actes de la recherche en sciences sociales*, 89, Sept: 3–46.
Cailleaux, C. 2001. "En Afrique." *Notre Librairie. Revue des littératures du Sud*, 145, dossier "La bande dessinée", July–Sept: 5–10.
Cassiau-Haurie, C. 2007. "Bande dessinée gabonaise: le grand sommeil." *Africultures*, October 18. http://www.africultures.com/php/?nav=article&no=6998 (accessed March 18, 2021).
Cassiau-Haurie, Ch. 2008. "Festivals de BD d'Afrique: comment sortir de l'événementiel?" *Africultures*, 2 (73): 125–30.
Cassiau-Haurie, Ch. 2010. "Brève histoire de la bande dessinée au Mali." *Africultures*, November 21. http://www.africultures.com/php/?nav=article&no=9821 (accessed March 18, 2021).
De Moor, B. 1987. "Préface." In Baruti, B., ed. *Mohuta & Mapeka. La Voiture, c'est l'aventure!* Kinshasa: Afrique Éditions.

Deubou Sikoué, Y. 2011. "Le collectif A3 et le magazine Bitchakala (Cameroun)." *Takam Tikou*. http://takamtikou.bnf.fr/dossiers/dossier-2011-la-bande-dessinee/le-collectif-a3-et-le-magazine-bitchakala-cameroun (accessed March 20, 2021).

Dewerpe, A. 1996. "La 'stratégie' chez Pierre Bourdieu." *Enquête*, published online 11 July 2013. http://enquete.revues.org/533 (accessed March 20, 2021).

Dubois, J. 1992. "L'institution du texte." In Neefs, J. and Repars, M.-C. eds. *La politique du texte. Enjeux sociocritiques. Pour Claude Duchet*. Lille: Presses universitaires de Lille, 125–44.

Durand, P. 2001. "Introduction à une sociologie des champs symboliques." In Fonkoua, R., and Halen, P., eds., *Les Champs littéraires africains, Les Champs littéraires africains*. Paris: Karthala, 19–55.

"Elikya, le petit orphelin bientôt de retour!" 2012. *Blog des éditions Elondja*, March 30. http://elondja.blogspot.it/2012/03/elikya-le-petit-oprhelin-bientot-de.html (accessed March 18, 2021).

Federici, S. 2019. *L'entrance des auteurs africains dans le champ de la bande dessinée européenne de langue française (1978–2016)*. Paris: L'Harmattan.

Fonkoua, R., and Halen, P., eds. 2001. *Les champs littéraires africains*. Paris: Karthala.

Giguet-Legdhen, E. (n.d.). "L'Afrique dessinée. Entretien avec Christophe Ngalle Edimo, Président de l'association L'Afrique dessinée." *La Boîte à outils pédagogiques*, n.d. https://bop.fipf.org/lafrique-dessinee/ (accessed March 20, 2021).

Girard, A. 2018. "Les éditions Bakame, pionnières de la littérature jeunesse au Rwanda." *Africa e Mediterraneo*, 2: 52–8.

KanAd 2014. "Afrique et Caraïbes en création. […] Rapport de résidence." [August] http://ifmapp.institutfrancais.com/fichier/i_dwl/538/dwl_fichier_fr_rapport.residence.adrien.folly.notsron.afrique.caraibes.creation.pdf (accessed March 28, 2021).

"Kinshasa – bandes dessinées: les Editions Elondja en Danger." 2012. *CongoForum*, September 7. http://www.congoforum.be/fr/nieuwsdetail.asp?subitem=3&newsid=188865&Actualiteit=selected (accessed March 28, 2021).

Halen, P. 2001. "Constructions identitaires et stratégies d'émergence: notes pour une analyse institutionnelle du système littéraire francophone." *Études françaises*, 37 (2): 13–31.

Halen, P. 2008. "À propos des modalités d'insertion des littératures issues de l'immigration dans le système littéraire francophone." In Dumontet, D. and Ziffel, F. eds. *Écriture migrante / Migrant Writing*. Hildesheim Zurich New York: Georg Olms Verlag, 37–48.

"Historique des BD de Madagascar" [n.d.]. *Pensée-Chrétienne*. http://www.pensee-chretienne.org/madagascar_ravo_txt/BD.htm (accessed March 18, 2021).

Hunt, N.R. 2015. "Papa Mfumu'eto 1er, star de la bande dessinée congolaise." In Magnin, André, ed. *Beauté Congo—1926–2015—Congo Kitoko*. Paris: Fondation Cartier pour l'art contemporain, 266–9.

Kassaï, D. (forthcoming). "Entretien recueilli par S. Federici, Alger, 9 octobre 2015." In Federici, S., *"Je ne voulais pas d'histoires-calebasses". Entretiens avec les bédéistes africains*. Paris, Sépia.

Lesage, S. 2014. "L'édition sans éditeurs? La bande dessinée franco-belge au prisme de l'auto-édition, années 1970–1980", in Dony, C., Habrand, T., Meesters, G., eds. In *La bande dessinée en dissidence/Comics in Dissent*. Liège: Presses Universitaires de Liège, 137–50.

Macaire, E. 2013. "Dossier: La bande dessinée ivoirienne en question. Des spécialistes se prononcent." *100pour100culture.com*, October 21. http://100pour100culture.com/2013/10/dossier-la-bande-dessinee-ivoirienne-en-question-des-specialistes-se-prononcent/ (accessed March 19, 2021).

Masioni, P., Grénier, C., and Ralph. 2005. *Rwanda 1994. T. 1: Descente en enfer*. Paris: Albin Michel.

Masioni, P., Grénier, C., and Ralph. 2008. *Rwanda 1994. T. 2: Le camp de la vie*. Paris: Vent des Savanes.

Mbiye Lumbala, H. 2009. *Cases et bulles africaines. Introduction à la bande dessinée africaine francophone*. Alger: Dalimen.

Mongo Sisé. 1978. *Les Aventures de Mata Mata and Pili Pili: Le Portefeuille*. Kinshasa: Mama-Leki editions.

Pinhas, L. 2005. *Éditer dans l'espace francophone: législation, diffusion, distribution et commercialisation du livre*. Paris: Alliance des éditeurs indépendants.

Pinhas, L. 2006. "L'édition africaine à la croisée des chemins", *Africultures*, 4. http://www.africultures.com/php/index.php?nav=article&no=5808/ (accessed March 30, 2021).

Quiñones, V. 2016. "La littérature de jeunesse, un art africain: Panorama 2000-2015." *Takam Tikou, Dossier 2016: La belle histoire de la littérature africaine pour la jeunesse: 2000-2015*, 16 March. http://takamtikou.bnf.fr/dossiers/la-litt-rature-de-jeunesse-un-art-africain-0#note16 (accessed March 15, 2021).

Repetti, M. 2002. "Gulp! Un fumetto *africano*?" In Federici, S., Marchesini Reggiani, A., and Repetti, M. eds. *Matite africane, fumetti e vignette dall'Africa*. Sasso Marconi: Lai-momo: 23–34.

Repetti, M. 2007a. "African 'Ligne Claire': the Comics of Francophone Africa." *International Journal of Comic Art*, Philadelphia, 9 (1): 515–41.

Repetti, M. 2007b. "African Wave: Specificity and Cosmopolitanism in African Comics." *African Arts*, Los Angeles: UCLA/MIT, 40 (2): 16–35.

Riva, S. (2006). *Nouvelle histoire de la littérature du Congo-Kinshasa*. Paris: L'Harmattan.

Sapiro, G. 2019. "A Field", *Politika*, Aug. 8. https://www.politika.io/en/notice/a-field (accessed March 18, 2021).

Sonon, H. 2011. "Hector Sonon: Les caricaturistes ont joué un rôle important dans la transition démocratique au Bénin. Entretien recueilli par Ch. Cassiau-Haurie." *Africultures.com*, June 7. africultures.com/hector-sonon-les-caricaturistes-ont-joue-un-role-important-dans-la-transition-democratique-au-benin-10232/ (accessed March 18, 2021).

Tessy, D.R. 2015. *Édition de la bande dessinée au Bénin: état des lieux et perspectives pour une augmentation de la production*, Université Senghor, El Mancheya, Alexandrie, Egypte. HAL Id: mem 01346467. http://memsic.ccsd.cnrs.fr/mem_01346467/document (accessed March 18, 2021).

Thierry, R. 2015. *Le Marché du livre africain et ses dynamiques littéraires. Le cas du Cameroun*. Pessac: Presses Universitaires de Bordeaux.

Tounkara, M. (forthcoming). "Entretien recueilli par S. Federici, Alger, 8 octobre 2015." In Federici, S., "*Je ne voulais pas d'histoires-calebasses*". *Entretiens avec les bédéistes africains*

Tshibanda, P. (forthcoming), "Entretien recueilli via courriel par S. Federici, 13 mai 2016." In Federici, S., "*Je ne voulais pas d'histoires-calebasses*". *Entretiens avec les bédéistes africains*

T.T. Fons. 2009. "T.T. Fons, auteur de bandes dessinées: 'Les bédéistes africains ont besoin d'être édités', propos recueillis par El Hadji Massiga Faye." All Africa, Aug 7. http://fr.allafrica.com/stories/200908070582.html (accessed March 20, 2021).

Zell, H.M. 2008. "Publishing in Africa: where are we now? Part One: Some spurious claims debunked." *LOGOS* 19/4: 187–95.

Zinsou et Sagbo. Le Club des conteurs de Possotomè (Collectif). 2003. Cotonou: Ruisseaux d'Afrique. http://www.africultures.com/php/index.php?nav=livre&no=6766# (accessed March 18, 2021).

6

Born in the "World": Leila Abdelrazaq's Writing and Art as World Literature

Allison Blecker

In 2016, Palestinian–American artist and author Leila Abdelrazaq painted an 8x10-foot mural, *Map of Palestine*, to anchor her solo exhibition at the Arab American National Museum in Dearborn, Michigan (Figure 6.1). *Map of Palestine* is, in fact, a map of the entire world in black and white, which Abdelrazaq has overlaid with *tatreez* (traditional Palestinian embroidery) patterns, marking in red the vast geography of the Palestinian diaspora. In the foreground, beneath the map and facing it as if it is his own canvas, stands the figure of Handala, an unmistakable icon of Palestinian identity. Created over five decades ago in 1969 by Palestinian political cartoonist Naji al-Ali, Handala is a barefoot and ragged-looking boy of ten, the same age al-Ali was when he and his family were expelled from Palestine to a refugee camp in Lebanon. Traditionally depicted with his back turned against the viewer and his hands clasped behind him, Handala symbolizes the steadfastness of Palestinian resistance and witnessing. In Abdelrazaq's painting, he holds the embroidery needle aloft in his right hand, the red thread pulled taut as it runs across the map, tying the dispersed communities to each other and back to Palestine. In his left hand, Handala grips a large key behind his back, evoking the homes hastily left behind by Palestinians when they were forced into diaspora. Significantly, by rendering young Handala with active hands, Abdelrazaq signals a creative shift away from witnessing the undoing of the Palestinian homeland to assemblage and homemaking.

With significant populations of Palestinians now making their homes on every continent save Antarctica, the narration of Palestine in art and literature is a microcosm of the world, as well as of the diverse and complex identities of the Palestinians who live in it. But how, or where, can the narration of Palestine belong to *World Literature*, a corpus that has been famously understood to encompass those texts that transcend the fixed national and linguistic borders from which they originate? Similarly, how does one begin to define or understand Palestinian literature, the literature of a lost homeland bound by its connection to a homeland that has lost (great numbers of) its people? Do such categorizations even matter? In this chapter, I argue that Abdelrazaq, as a graphic artist and illustrator whose approaches to identity and storytelling are intentionally layered and hybridized, belongs to both world and Palestinian literatures.

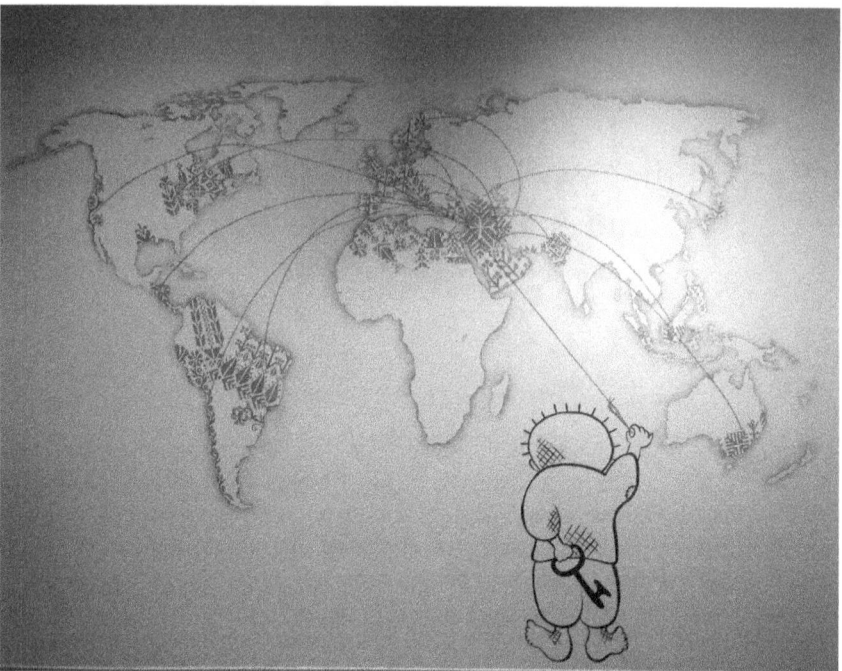

Figure 6.1 *Map of Palestine*

But, as she expands, shapes, and redraws their boundaries in her art, writing, and life, she also reveals their multiplicity, taking ownership of both categorizations as she dismantles and rebuilds the narratives of inclusion and exclusion that make up their foundations.

Belonging to Palestine, Belonging to the World

It is difficult to estimate the total number of Palestinians living outside of Palestine and Israel. As of December 2019, there were over three-million registered Palestinian refugees residing in Jordan, Lebanon, and Syria, according to the United Nations Relief and Works Agency for Palestine Refugees in the Near East (UNRWA) ("UNRWA" 2020). In 2018, the USA alone was home to a Palestinian community of anywhere between 2.04 and 3.67 million people ("Demographics" 2018). Abdelrazaq belongs to this community. Born in Chicago, the daughter of a Palestinian refugee, and raised between Chicago and Seoul, South Korea, the author/artist now lives in Detroit. Both her interviews and her work reflect the centrality of her identity as a Palestinian–American. Abdelrazaq's debut graphic novel, *Baddawi* (2015a), her shorter comics—including *The Opening* (2017a), *The Fig Tree* (2018e), and *Smuggling Books Across the Border: An Illustrated Diary* (2015d)—and standalone pieces such as *Map of Palestine* are unified by their focus on the experiences of Palestinians as refugees and in diaspora. Beyond her own creative output, the author/artist also cofounded Maamoul Press with the goal of "uplifting" the work of other creators, especially women and nonbinary individuals, from historically marginalized communities. A multi-disciplinary small press and collective, Maamoul Press seeks to tell stories "for us, by us." The intersection of Abdelrazaq's work with her activism and her identity will be explored at greater length below.

Abdelrazaq's creative work has ethnographic elements, documenting Palestinian society and traditions as they existed at home in Palestine and in the generation following expulsion, and as they persist and evolve in diaspora. Her illustrated storytelling also has a political dimension, as it shifts the erasure of Palestine and the creation of Israel from the realm of distant history to the author/artist's everyday present, giving the trauma of displacement an immediacy that may be uncomfortable, or at least unfamiliar, to non-Palestinians and even some Palestinian Americans and other English-reading Palestinians. Abdelrazaq's work asserts the rightful presence of Palestinian culture and history within the broader narrative of the USA.

As a Palestinian American, Abdelrazaq is located outside of Palestine, never having made a physical home there, even as she creates from within and speaks to the Palestinian diaspora.

Her work unquestionably qualifies as Arab-American literature.[1] Abdelrazaq's positionality, however, exacerbated by the lack of an internationally recognized Palestinian state, highlights the challenge of articulating what it is, exactly, that makes Palestinian literature Palestinian (if not national borders and language) and whether Abdelrazaq's work "counts." Recalling her *Map of Palestine*, Abdelrazaq's inclusion within the body of World Literature might seem clearer, but the author/artist and her work complicate and/or force an expansion of some common (albeit already contested) definitions of this categorization as well.

For example, in *What is World Literature?*, David Damrosch locates "all literary works that circulate beyond their culture of origin, either in translation or in their original language" under the expansive umbrella of "World Literature" (Damrosch 2003, 4). This definition, deceptive in its simplicity and conciseness, has served as the starting point for countless qualifications and complications by later scholars. Damrosch's conception of World Literature is seductive in its apparent simplicity: on the surface, a text either meets the conditions he lays out for inclusion or does not. Abdelrazaq's graphic novel *Baddawi* checks the right boxes: written in English, the text has been translated into Korean, Arabic, and French. However, in reality, Abdelrazaq's work does not need to cross boundaries of culture and country to come into the "world": her writing and art are born at these borders, in a constant state of in-betweenness and movement, created *in* the world by virtue of Abdelrazaq's own transnational identity.

Damrosch goes on to clarify that the purpose of his definition is not to delimit a canon, but rather to characterize "a mode of circulation and reading" that is neither

---

[1] For more on Arab-American literature, see Salaita (2011) and Hassan (2011).

fixed nor universal across space and time (Damrosch 2003, 5). Palestinian literary and artistic production (including that of Abdelrazaq) certainly embodies this "mode of circulation." Indeed, Palestinian literature post-1948 comes into being not as the result of its boundedness by linguistic, geographic, or ideological borders, but precisely through the movement of texts, art, and people across them. On the surface, this movement can be seen among the North African and Iraqi diasporas, and perhaps among people of all ethnicities, races, and religions as they disperse from their "homelands" over time. But the lack of a recognized Palestinian homeland makes Palestinian literature unique: no matter where else it may intersect, it is always in the world.

In the absence of an independent nation state, scholars have variously drawn the boundaries of the Palestinian "national canon" according to theme, language, and author self-identification, encompassing texts written by Palestinians in the Palestinian territories and Israel as well as work written mostly in Arabic by Palestinians in diaspora. The effort to clarify and contain these boundaries has become problematic in many cases, however, leading to increasingly complicated systems ranking the authenticity and authority of different authors and texts—often without explicit articulation. As an example, a scholar might envision Palestinian literature as a series of concentric circles, with texts produced in the West Bank and Gaza at the center. Outside of that is writing from Palestinians within Israel. Then comes the work of Palestinians living in countries of the Arab World, such as Jordan, Lebanon, and Syria (although allowances might be made for periods of exile in European capitals—Paris in particular). In the outer ring lies literature written by Palestinians who have resettled permanently outside of the Arab world and write in the language of their new home country. Language presents an additional litmus test, with Arabic works being privileged, while those written in Hebrew, English, and other languages sometimes require some sort of justification for their inclusion within the "canon."

One problem with this ranking system is that it excludes (or otherwise delegitimizes) "outside" texts that reflect the diversity and complexity of the Palestinian experience at the outer reaches (geographically, linguistically, and otherwise) of diaspora, thereby reinforcing a reductive and static understanding of what it means to be Palestinian. Seeking to address this limitation, Maurice Ebileeni proposes broadening the parameters of Palestinian literature to include a "polylingual literary category" that captures "the increasing production of Palestinian writings in languages other than Arabic," thereby incorporating the experiences and memories they contain into the narration of Palestine and understandings of Palestinian identities (Ebileeni 2017, 259). Such a move has the potential to "challenge the fundamental idea of an immutable Palestinian identity that lies at the core of the national script" by making room for writings in languages other than Arabic, produced in diverse geographies and cultural contexts (Ebileeni 2017, 261–2). Incorporating these works into the Palestinian national canon "may entail the acknowledgement that these authors have carried their Palestinian stories in different directions, severely unsettling the dominant national narrative" (Ebileeni 2017, 263). However, alongside this expansion of the canon, Ebileeni argues that connecting these diverse iterations of Palestinian literature to each other "triggers a process of intertextuality that produces a single narrative of intercommunal solidarity among Palestinians with distinct experiences of displacement" (Ebileeni 2017, 277). Furthermore, while Arabic may be an important marker of Palestinian identity and literature, the *loss* of Arabic (and the gain of a different language) is of equal significance in the forging of a diasporic identity for a community several generations removed from its homeland and with no internationally recognized national identity (Ebileeni 2017, 263–4). And, in many cases, the Arabic that is lost is not the language in its entirety but rather the local dialect of Arabic, to be replaced by a different Arabic—or Arabics—as future generations are born into the linguistic rhythms of new environs and adopt new dialects, forge new hybrids, or sometimes renew an inherited linguistic connection by seeking out Arabic learning in the classroom.

Ebileeni's polylingual category represents one path to locating Abdelrazaq's work within Palestinian literature, but, to be clear, it is one path among many. Similarly, different arguments can be made for including Abdelrazaq and her work within the corpus of World Literature, and it is this classification that will be the focus of the following sections. The graphic novel and other hybrid creations combining narrative words with visual art, through their own generic boundary-crossing and facilitation of radical modes of reading, provide the ideal lens for interrogating Abdelrazaq's place in the world of literature.

But, again, why does it matter? It is possible that Abdelrazaq creates with little concern for where critics may place her work. However, categorizations and canons can influence which authors are included in syllabi, are invited to events, and are the recipients of scholarly attention. It is with this in mind that Emily Apter praises World Literature's role in the "deprovincialization of the canon" even as she notes that she feels "uneasy in the face of the entrepreneurial, bulimic drive to anthologize and curricularize the world's cultural resources"—a critique of what she views as the project of World Literature (Apter 2013, 18). Outside of the academy, a work's classification may impact who buys it, reads/views it, and reviews it, affecting everything from the size of an author's royalty check to larger cultural conversations about history, politics, marginalized groups, relationships, and any other topic. For example, Abdelrazaq's work is positioned to play a role in shaping the conversation about Palestine among English-reading audiences. This point will be explored at greater length below.

Between Universalism and Particularity: Translating Comics

Many of the challenges—and criticisms—of World Literature have been connected to language and the barriers it creates to accessing a truly global canon. Franco Moretti suggested "distant reading" as a solution for a broader computational study of the diffusion of literature while Gayatri Spivak has advocated for intensive language training that would preserve "the skill of reading closely in the original" and "disclose the irreducible hybridity of all languages" as part of an overhaul of the discipline of comparative literature (Spivak 2003, 6, 9). Apter critiques the flattening effect of World Literature by exploring the inevitable mistranslations that students and scholars must navigate as they work with texts in translation. She calls these words and phrases the "untranslatable": "an incorruptible or intransigent nub of meaning that triggers endless translating in response to its resistant singularity," leading to misreadings and misinterpretations (Apter 2013, 235). Damrosch acknowledges these linguistic minefields, but nevertheless embraces translation as a vital tool for more far-reaching and comparative study. He thus emphasizes the necessary fluidity of texts that pass into World Literature, as well as that of World Literature itself. He writes that works must "take on a new life" as they change and shift through translation and encounters with different cultures, times, and geographies, meaning that World Literature, as a mode of reading rather than a body of texts, "resolves always into a *variety* of worlds" (Damrosch 2003, 24, 12).

Abdelrazaq's creative activity occurs in these spaces of encounter, or contact zones, even though she writes mostly in English and only her graphic novel *Baddawi* has appeared in multiple languages. Her English-language writing and art are also acts of translation in themselves. They represent the translation of a history and story well-told in Arabic into English and the nonlinguistic translation of words into the images of a graphic novel. This is especially noteworthy given that, as Jan Baetens writes, "World Literature" has generally been taken to mean "'word' literature"—not the first field to overlook or exclude comics in the pursuit of the study of "serious" literature (Baetens 2012, 338). *Baddawi* is an ideal lens for thinking through what stories told in comic form might add to broader conversations. As Hiyem Cheurfa notes, Abdelrazaq's references to Handala, "the seeing child," frames *Baddawi* as a "witness narrative," highlighting "the intersection between visual culture and the politics of resistance" (Cheurfa 2020, 366). In other words, the comic form brings the act of witnessing to the fore in a way that oral narratives and written accounts cannot.

Furthermore, Abdelrazaq's dynamic and rich visual storytelling, so clearly situated within the narration of Palestine and the experiences of the Palestinian diaspora, provides an example of the kinds of underrepresented voices and perspectives that, while not silenced, may not be amplified when other texts represent a more conventional, less challenging "fit" with traditional understandings of literature. In World Literature, a field of study at least superficially dedicated to bringing diverse voices into transnational conversation, such rigidity represents a barrier to that goal, as if suggesting that while differences in language and culture may be overcome, variations in form may not. For Abdelrazaq, it is the two acts of translation together—adaptations of content as well as form at the moment of creation—that provide for the widest circulation of her art and writing across cultures.

After all, as a form, comics inherently muddle the significance of language and linguistic translation. How much do the images rely on the written text to communicate meaning? What gaps exist for the reader that would not in a narrative of only words? What spaces of the imagination are filled by images?

Comics have the potential to overcome some of the challenges of translation, across cultures as well as languages, by facilitating the reader's visualization of unfamiliar objects and places. It can be argued that representation in art provides clarity without the need for "pyramids of footnotes" (Damrosch 2003, 158). The graphic element of graphic novels can suggest a natural universality or worldliness, independent of translation, that rests on unmediated communication in visual language. However, even, or especially, the most powerful images do not always contain the kinds of cultural and historical information that makes them meaningful to an audience without that context and require some kind of textual gloss or translation to communicate their significance.

When comics do contain language, the mediating role of linguistic translation can be significant. Comics may rely heavily on their visual elements for storytelling, but when text is present, it renders the work as a whole vulnerable to reinterpretation via its translation into another language and culture. In its essence, according to David M. Ball, the graphic novel/comic is "caught between universalism and radical particularity," as it "remain[s] radically open to the vagaries of context, reception, and hermeneutic instability, never more so than in [its] internationalization, threatening misunderstanding amid the seeming interpretive clarity of [its] visual impact" (Ball 2018, 594). Moreover, the threat of misunderstanding is only heightened when the comic strives to communicate geographies and political realities to an audience removed from them in space and time, as in *Baddawi*.

Baddawi as an Act of Remembering

In *Baddawi*, Abdelrazaq retells pivotal events in Palestinian history that are canonical in the literature of the Arab world, including the 1948 expulsion of Palestinians during the *nakba* (catastrophe); the 1967 *naksa* (setback), also known as the Six Day War, which led to the Israeli occupation of the West Bank and Gaza Strip; and the Lebanese Civil War (1975–90). Although *Baddawi* is commonly referred to as a graphic novel, Abdelrazaq's narrative is not fiction, but a mix of reportage and biography based on the childhood experiences of her father, Ahmad. Born to refugees from the Palestinian village of Safsaf, Ahmad grew up between Baddawi Refugee Camp in northern Lebanon and the capital city of Beirut. In an overt reference to Naji al-Ali's Handala, Abdelrazaq draws Ahmad on the cover of *Baddawi* as a child with his back to the reader and his hands clasped behind him. With this gesture, the author/artist positions her central character as not just a protagonist but also a witness-bearer, on whom her reader must rely to gain access to the past. As Abdelrazaq writes in her preface:

The story you are about to read isn't about only my father.
This story is about Handala. It is about my cousins and aunts and uncles. It is about those displaced multiple times, first from Palestine, then from countries like Kuwait and Syria. It is about five million people, born into a life of exile and persecution, indefinitely suspended in statelessness.

(Abdelrazaq 2015a, 12)

Born in the Galilee in 1936, Naji al-Ali was a child when he and his family were displaced to Lebanon during the *nakba*. He became one of the most recognized—and controversial—cartoonists in the Arabic-speaking world and was assassinated in London in 1987. Al-Ali began drawing Handala in 1969. Almost always depicted with his back turned to the viewer, Handala witnesses al-Ali's scathing cartoon critiques of Israel and Palestinian and Arab leadership, shutting out those who choose to look away. He is barefoot and usually small in size in comparison to the rest of the cartoon. Handala is an eternal child, a reference to al-Ali's own childhood: "He was the age I was when I had left Palestine and, in a sense, I am still that age today" (al-Ali 2009, 2). As imagined by al-Ali, Handala would only grow up when Palestinians were able to return home.

With her reference to Handala on the cover of *Baddawi,* Abdelrazaq also calls attention to her own presence in the text: as a second-hand witness, the author/artist relies on her father's memories and reports to understand the past and shape it into a story. "Even though I don't write myself into the story," Abdelrazaq explained in a 2018 interview, "I see the graphic novelist as a character in the story" (Abdelrazaq 2018a). And while her reconstruction of Ahmad's youth is a fictionalization, Abdelrazaq insists that "there's nothing that's made up," emphasizing the biographical element of *Baddawi* by including family photos at the close of the text. Well aware that the struggle against the erasure of the past is a key tenet of Palestinian resistance, Abdelrazaq affirms in her preface: "This book is a testament to the fact that we have not forgotten" (Abdelrazaq 2015a, 12). With *Baddawi*, Abdelrazaq refuses to forget the experiences of her family and the Palestinian people not only through the act of communal and historical record keeping, but also by translating that record into English (Abdelrazaq 2018a).

In *Baddawi* and other works, Abdelrazaq sometimes takes on the role of ethnographer, using the comic form to introduce American and other English-language readers to some of the most recognizable markers of Palestinian identity. In Palestinian art and literature, especially that which is written in Arabic and created in the Arab world, many of these markers have become a kind of shorthand for Palestine and its loss. She translates this catalog into English, bringing it to new audiences through the mediums of comics and the graphic novel. These markers include pastoral and nature scenes linked to village life, the preparation of certain foods and beverages, and the continuation of traditional activities such as embroidery. In *Baddawi*, these ethnographic sections emphasize the normalcy of everyday life, as well as the trauma of the violence that interrupts its rhythms and almost sacred routines. For example, Abdelrazaq juxtaposes panels depicting a Palestinian woman preparing bread against images of the refugee camp being destroyed by an Israeli cluster bomb. The life-sustaining act of nourishment of the former contrasts with the deadly impact of the latter. The woman, the wife of Ahmad's cousin, is killed when she is thrown into the oven while baking the bread during the bombing. While the village of Safsaf and its former residents' livelihoods as farmers and shepherds are tied to the physical space of Palestine, culinary and craft traditions are nearly as portable as memories and stories themselves. Sometimes they are the only things that refugees can carry with them when they are forced from their homes. They function as tools for the construction of a sense of collective memory and community.

Culinary Tradition as a Link to Belonging

Throughout the Palestinian diaspora, traditional dishes and foods local to the village or city of origin represent a way, in literature as well as in everyday life, to maintain a connection to Palestine.[2] A four-page chapter of *Baddawi* is devoted to *za'atar*, a mixture of spices, herbs, and sesame seeds, from the gathering of thyme for its preparation to the roasting of sesame seeds and the baking of *manaqish*, a kind of flatbread topped with ingredients like *za'atar* or ground meat. Text explaining the significance of *za'atar* and the ways it is consumed is accompanied by drawings of the community working together to make it. Regional and family differences in its preparation connect *za'atar*, and its consumption, to the past and personal familial geographies. Gathering thyme from the hills surrounding the refugee camp in Lebanon and mixing and eating it here tie the present to that past. "Palestinian history," Abdelrazaq reminds us, "just like Palestinian people, is now dispersed all over the world" (Abdelrazaq 2015b). For Ahmad's mother, making *za'atar* is also an act of hope for the future. She tells Ahmad: "Next time you gather thyme for the *za'atar* it will be in Palestine" (Abdelrazaq 2015a, 34). Ahmad's imagined Safsaf, identified by its idyllic willow, the village's namesake, and rolling hills, is juxtaposed with the cement walls and racing cars and people of the refugee camp. Although Safsaf is beautiful with its empty landscape, the positioning of the two panels is a reminder that the present is here.

Food has been repeatedly mobilized in the conflict over the right to own and dwell on the land in Palestine and Israel. The olive tree is the most well-known symbol of these struggles: it speaks to the past and present through its embodiment of a history of Palestinian habitation and cultivation and to the future in the promise of nourishment that it offers through the provision of olive oil, a dietary staple. Locally rooted cultures of food set up a cycle that affirms belonging as individual and communal processes of production and consumption repeatedly re-forge relationships to the land. This is especially true in a pastoral setting where the balance of sowing and harvesting, for example, is experienced most directly, or, perhaps more accurately, where poets, artists, and writers most often imagine such an idyllic balance to exist. These literary and artistic imaginings become urgent in the face of displacement or in its aftermath, as in the Palestinian case. Although seemingly minor in comparison to the explosive violence that accompanied the establishment of Israel and has been its legacy, the Israeli

---

[2] In Palestinian–American poet Naomi Shihab Nye's picture book *Sitti's Secrets* (1997), for children ages five to eight, Mona travels from her home in the USA to Palestine to visit her grandmother in her small village. While there, Mona sees men and women performing the labor that brings food to their table. Drawings of men picking lentils and her grandmother baking bread each fill a double-page spread. Mona eats produce grown on the land—lemons, zucchini, almonds, and apricots. An illustration shows her gathering mint in the house's courtyard for the lemonade made with fresh lemons from her grandmother's tree.

appropriation of Palestinian foods and food culture further undermines Palestinian claims to the land.[3]

The construction of Israeli food culture, as an element of the construction of Israeli national identity, was part of a "mixture of romanticization, admiration and imitation of the local Arab-Palestinian, together with a desire (overt or covert) to become a political *replacement* to this people" (Ranta and Mendel 2014, 424). While the origin of a dish may seem insignificant, its importance comes into focus when considered as a step in the larger campaign that began before the *nakba* to substitute one history with another and one memory with another, while incorporating or erasing all traces—archeological, linguistic, or, yes, even culinary—of what had come before. What is now known as Israeli food largely represents a reassemblage of the cuisine of the Levant and Palestine prior to the establishment of Israel. Its continued preparation by Palestinians in Palestine and in diaspora, as well as its depiction in art and literature, resists this appropriation and recreates some of the spaces that have been lost.

Pastoral Identity and Loss

Palestine provides the anchor for Abdelrazaq's re-narration, but the town of Safsaf itself is reduced to little more than the image of a weeping willow[4] when accessed from the USA by way of Ahmad's memories of his childhood in Lebanon. Other refugees rely on pastoralism to recreate Palestine in Lebanon as well. But while cuisine may be carried across national borders with relative ease, it is more challenging to transport pastoral practices like farming and shepherding to new environments, especially urban ones, as these practices are so directly connected to rural spaces, village life, and the inheritance of land, trees, seeds, and stock over generations. In *Baddawi*, Ahmad's maternal grandfather continues to tend sheep in the hills around the refugee camp, but his flock of three is always overshadowed by what is missing—the large flock that spread across the countryside in Palestine that he remembers when he closes his eyes. Every day, before he takes his small flock to graze, Ahmad's grandfather eats a raw egg and drinks a little bit of olive oil to maintain his "perfect eyesight." These rituals represent a tradition that keeps him connected to the past and helps ensure clear sight of Palestine and the former rhythms of his daily life in his mind.

Ahmad himself wears these markers of Palestinian pastoral provincial identity lightly. The map of Palestine, Syria, and Lebanon that Abdelrazaq includes at the opening of *Baddawi* centers Lebanon, decentering Palestine and Safsaf. Ahmad was born a refugee in Lebanon and he inherited the loss of Palestine, rather than experiencing it firsthand. Safsaf lives in the everyday practices of his parents and

---

[3] See Bardenstein (1998) and *The Wanted 18* (2014) for more on the relationship between food, food production, and narratives of belonging.

[4] This is reminiscent of A.'s lemon tree in Anton Shammas' "Autocartography": "that authentic, irreproducible tree in Yafa" (Shammas 1995, 8). A. is the granddaughter of a Palestinian refugee and lives in Michigan. For her grandmother, Palestine becomes "no more than a lemon tree in the backyard of the house she left in Jafa" (Shammas 1985, 7).

grandparents in Lebanon while it is reduced to no more than a willow tree, beautiful but abstract, in his imagined Palestine.

Palestine, and Safsaf in particular, come into clearest focus for Ahmad when he listens to his grandfather's stories. As his grandfather speaks, the roots of the lonely willow tree in the countryside stretch between the stones of a village street, where a woman in traditional dress stands, surrounded by well-kept homes. When Ahmad later falls asleep to the sound of the sea at his grandparents' house, he is pictured afloat on the ocean, his head resting on a pillow like a raft. The black water looks like his grandfather's pupil, with the two shores that curve at each side forming the iris. It is only in dreams that he can access what his grandfather still sees with his perfect vision of the past. For Abdelrazaq, Safsaf is even hazier and more distant; though she may travel to Palestine in the present, she no longer even has family there to visit, and Safsaf itself no longer exists. On October 29, 1948, Israeli forces executed seventy of the village's men. The remaining inhabitants were ordered to leave, displacing the population, including Ahmad's parents, to Lebanon (Pappe 2006, 184). Today, the Israeli moshav of Kfar Hoshen stands in Safsaf's place, part of the widespread effort to "Hebraize" the geography, undertaken with the help of archaeologists and biblical scholars, as well as the Israeli Defense Forces of course (Pappe 2006, 226).

The Specter of Violence

Baddawi's ethnographic interludes are repeatedly interrupted by violence. Tanks, guns, and soldiers intrude upon the text, pressing in from the margins. The imagery helps the reader to feel the constant threat they represent and their looming presence in the background, whether or not they explode into the scene. These images are faceless and somewhat shapeless, hardly even silhouettes at times. The lack of detail and nuance in their depiction is intentional. Abdelrazaq explains in an interview that she felt a responsibility for her father's story and her portrayal of Ahmad, but was "not responsible for keeping balance." The Israeli soldiers in particular, with the full strength of Israel and its allies behind them, "can speak for themselves" given their relative power on the ground in the refugee camp as well as in the shaping of the historical narrative (Abdelrazaq 2018a).

In "Critique, Caricature and Compulsion in Joe Sacco's Comics Journalism," Adam Rosenblatt and Andrea A. Lunsford look at Sacco's graphic war reporting alongside Francisco Goya's *Disasters of War* (1810–20) and Pablo Picasso's *Guernica* (1937). *Baddawi* invites similar comparisons. All of these works "thrust the viewer into the scene" while the artists "aim to present truths about war by moving beyond realism into the hallucinatory, fragmented, and speechless horrors that war always entails" (Rosenblatt and Lunsford 2010, 71). The imagery in *Baddawi*, accompanying Abdelrazaq's text, represents what is unwritable in words. Given that Ahmad is a child at the beginning of the narrative, as was Handala, Abdelrazaq's art also communicates the nightmarish horror that remains even when individual memories grow hazy and blur.

Violence and death are as much a part of Ahmad's childhood as is the preparation of *za'atar* and the celebration of Ramadan and Eid al-Fitr, but Abdelrazaq neither normalizes nor exoticizes them. Following a night raid of the refugee camp by the Israeli and Lebanese armies, Ahmad and his friends play in the streets alongside the shadowy ghosts of the soldiers and the dead that had been there only hours before. As Ahmad enters young adulthood, he realizes that "nowhere [is] safe for Palestinians" and makes the decision to leave his life in Lebanon, including marriage to his friend Manal, and emigrate to the USA (Abdelrazaq 2015a, 101). He contemplates the two paths before him, one leading through the USA and the other through Lebanon. Both paths continue on over the horizon to Palestine. For Ahmad, neither the USA nor Lebanon is a destination at this juncture, but rather a waypoint on a journey that leads always to Palestine.

Abdelrazaq and Her Audience

Abdelrazaq is clear that her chosen audience is almost always other Palestinian Americans, dedicating *Baddawi* to "all of those children of immigrants who have not forgotten their parents' stories." The author/artist describes her creative work as being "unapologetically political" and committed to "sparking necessary critical conversations in the Palestinian community" (Abdelrazaq 2018b). She openly pushes back against shouldering the work of challenging stereotypes and misinformation about Palestinian identity and experience as they exist in the wider population, declining to "[defend] [her] humanity or [act] as a token spokesperson to non-Palestinian audiences" (Abdelrazaq 2018c). In *Smuggling Books across the Border*, a response to Abdelrazaq's trip to Palestine to participate in the annual Palestine Festival of Literature in 2015, she quotes Mahmoud Darwish's poem, "Passport": "They put my wound on show / For tourists who love collecting pictures" (Al-Udhari 1986, 125). In *Baddawi* and even more so in some of her later work, Abdelrazaq resists voyeurism by limiting the accommodations she makes to "outside" readers and viewers, careful that her didacticism does not veer into spectacle. For example, *Baddawi* contains a glossary, with entries marked with an asterisk in the text, to convey the historical and cultural information that she is unable to capture on the page.

Although Abdelrazaq may not write for a non-Palestinian audience, her chosen medium and approach to storytelling do make her work accessible to readers from a range of backgrounds, regardless of the depth of their prior historical, cultural, or political knowledge. Her focus on the rich, complex lives of Palestinian refugees in her storytelling, portraying them at play and in sorrow and humanizing the traumatic loss of Palestine in a way that does not dwell in it, puts narratives into circulation that, as Abdelrazaq notes, have been "left out of dominant Palestine discourse in the United States" (Abdelrazaq 2018c). In *Baddawi*, Abdelrazaq captures pieces of the oral history that has been passed on to her by her father—stories that may be common within the Palestinian community but largely unknown outside of it. She explains her motivation for drawing the Web comic series that would become *Baddawi*, revealing cautious consideration for her non-Palestinian readers: "I really was interested in telling the stories, the kind of anecdotes that my dad had always told my brother and I from an early age, like over and over again. Because a lot of those stories seem very normal within the Palestinian community but were not as widely heard outside of that community" (Abdelrazaq 2015c). As a medium, the comic invites the stranger into this intimate circle of storytelling, welcoming people "who might otherwise not be so interested in the subject matter" (Abdelrazaq 2015c). The illustrated form also allows for the simplification of complicated issues, facilitating wider understanding without being "pretentious" (Abdelrazaq 2018a).

In the above discussion, I have explored how *Baddawi*—by re-narrating in English the communal history of Palestinian displacement and dispersal across the world through the personal stories of a refugee family, and by adapting this narrative to the comic form—constitutes an act of cultural, linguistic, and formal translation. Through this process of translation, as Abdelrazaq unsettles the current Palestinian canon and incorporates another strand into its fabric, the story of Palestine and its peoples gains additional nuance and depth. It also gains new audiences, who encounter the Palestinian experience in English, in images, and as part of a growing disruption of the English-language American canon. If we accept Damrosch's premise that "works become World Literature when they gain on balance in translation," then we must recognize *Baddawi* in this realm (Damrosch 2003, 289).

At the same time, *Baddawi*'s inclusion within Damrosch's World Literature *without* linguistic translation is possible because of the language of its text: English. Aamir Mufti, in his exploration of the interconnectedness of World Literature with Orientalism, argues that "*World Literature has functioned from the very beginning as a border regime*, a system for the regulation of movement, rather than as a set of literary relations beyond or without borders" (Mufti 2016, 9). English provides a global language for the field while "the assimilation of vastly dispersed and heterogenous writing practices and traditions into the space of 'literature'" flattens out difference—a process also critiqued by Apter above (Mufti 2016, 57). However, *Baddawi* does not need to move into English, because it is already at home there, and the graphic novel, especially when considered as part of Abdelrazaq's larger corpus of comic work, offers a formal hybridity that invites creativity and experimentation, resisting assimilation. Abdelrazaq, as a Palestinian American and inheritor of multiple colonial histories, challenges and erodes the borders of World Literature that Mufti maps out even as her creations are born within them.

Other Works, Smaller Histories

If *Baddawi* is a story about the past, much of Abdelrazaq's subsequent work shows how that past is still a part of the present, even in the USA. While "Still Born" (a 4-minute animated comic) and *The Opening* (a 27-page comic) center the experiences of an American refugee family, *The Fig Tree* (a 14-page comic) tightens its view to the level of the individual. All three feel more personal and intimate than *Baddawi*. By privileging what might be thought of as small histories, Abdelrazaq relinquishes the didactic responsibility she assumed with *Baddawi's* narration of the sweeping stories of the conflict over Palestine and the Lebanese Civil War. There is no intimation of Handala's presence as a witness to the stories in "Still Born," *The Opening*, or *The Fig Tree*, despite his occasional appearance, or that these characters' experiences represent or belong to a larger community. Instead, the Palestinian–American experience resolves, like World Literature itself, "into a *variety* of worlds," connected always by a Palestine that is often in the background.

Both "Still Born" and *The Opening* are reflections on loss centered around grief for a stillborn child. "Still Born" is inspired by and based on a 2002 essay by Abdelrazaq's mother, Sandra Young, called "How to Be the Mother of a Stillborn Baby." *The Opening* is about a Palestinian–American family in Chicago coping with a stillborn child, narrated by her sister, Leila.

For Abdelrazaq, the only grief great enough to encompass the death of an unborn child and sibling is the loss of an entire nation. In "Still Born," she illustrates the silent birth through panels that contain glimpses of Palestine—metal decorative doors, a hot glass of tea, a barbed wire fence, and finally an entire village. She distills the memory of the baby, like that of Palestine, into a handful of objects described as "something rare": pebbles from the baby's grave, a photograph of her quiet face, and a piece of paper with her footprints on it for one, and a key to a door, a Handala keychain, and a kuffiya for the other (Abdelrazaq 2018d, 2:15). Keys to homes that no longer stand or are now occupied by Jewish Israeli families are a particularly poignant symbol of the haste of departure, the loss of Palestine, and the unwillingness to surrender the right of return. In *The Opening*, Leila's mother swaddles her dead child, Hana, in a blanket like that used by Leila's grandmother to hold the few belongings she took with her when she was expelled from Palestine (Figure 6.2). On the following page, Leila's mother holds a picture of her baby. Leila's grandmother holds open her empty wrinkled hands.

In "Still Born," Abdelrazaq illustrates the evolution of a young woman's grief alongside these words from Young's essay:

> You will have steeped yourself in briny grief for so long, it will have soaked into your pores and become a part of you. Eventually, you will wash up on shore. You'll make a new life in a new land.
>
> (quoted in Abdelrazaq 2018d, 3:08–3:42).

The woman visits a pier where, only the frame before, a child—the stillborn baby—is led out of the bordered panel and into the surrounding darkness by Handala. Similarly, as the narrator of *The Opening* mourns Hana, her lost sister leads her to the lost village of Safsaf. In both works, Palestine becomes an imaginal site where loss is centered and stored even as life continues in the present in the USA.

The Opening ends with an image of the narrator, Leila, holding hands with a small child, their backs turned to the viewer. But the child here is Hana, not Handala. The accompanying text, in Arabic, reads: "We belong to her and to her we will return" (*The Opening*, final page). The line is a reference to verse 2:156 in the Qur'an: "Indeed

Figure 6.2 *The Opening*

we belong to Allah and to Him we will return." The "her" is both Hana and Palestine, bound together by their loss, and yearned for with an almost religious fervency.

If *Baddawi* is Abdelrazaq's father's story, "Still Born" is her mother's story, and *The Opening* is her family's story, then *The Fig Tree* is the author/artist's own story. Her dedication addresses a narrow audience: "for all palestinian womxn, with or without pussies." The central question she asks is the same that seems to frame much of her work: "How do you keep alive the spirit of a place you never knew & can't go to?" The answer that Abdelrazaq explores through the text suggests that the carrying on of traditions, and the preservation of the stories that accompany them, across generations and regardless of geography, sustains that memory and the hope of homecoming, even when it is inherited. As Abdelrazaq writes in her preface to *Baddawi*: "We stir the tales into our coffee with cardamom, and read our return in the grounds" (Abdelrazaq 2015a, 12).

The Fig Tree opens with the narrator boiling water to make a different beverage as it was and is traditionally prepared in Palestine: tea. After it has steeped in the kettle, she strains it into a small curved glass with a handle like a tiny ear. She adds sugar. The following spread shows the narrator carrying her single glass in her hand alongside an image of her grandmother bearing a tray with three glasses on it, signaling the passing down of this ritual and its transformation from a social and communal activity to a solitary one. These traditions that are carried through time and across oceans, the narrator explains, "are often the ones we need most to survive... traditions that hold us together while everything else is falling apart" (Abdelrazaq 2018e, third spread). By adopting the traditions she learned from her grandmother, not out of duty nor obligation but out of desire, and by doing so in a private space, alone, the performative element of the narrator's actions is removed, and, along with it, any negative cultural baggage or exotification that may attach to them.

Figure 6.3 *The Fig Tree*

The circular motion of stirring sugar into the tea—inherited muscle memory—transforms into masturbation (Figure 6.3). The pleasure of the shared act of drinking tea becomes the pleasure of an intimate personal act. The narrator muses: "Often, it's assumed that these rituals are continued out of a sense of duty, obligation, for utilitarian purposes, or for the benefit of others" (Abdelrazaq 2018e, fourth spread). "But what if," she asks, "… we did them for ourselves? For our own personal pleasure?" (Abdelrazaq 2018e, fifth spread). Abdelrazaq creates not with World Literature, nor Palestinian literature, nor even Palestinian–American literature in mind, though she may indeed belong to these corpuses. She creates instead for herself and for a community of other women that she herself is working to build.

Above, I have traced Abdelrazaq's movement from the large-scale collective, where her father's story becomes the story of a community of refugees, to the intimately individual, personal, and private—a place of bodily and intellectual pleasure. By speaking about sexuality through masturbation, the author/artist universalizes her experience as the daughter of a Palestinian refugee, opening up her individuality for identification by other women. In the following section, I will discuss Abdelrazaq's connection, at the human microlevel, to other communities—especially women or nonbinary people of color—and their artistic productions, bringing her creations in particular, and Palestine more broadly, back into the world in which it was born.

Networks of Local and Transnational Crisis

Although Abdelrazaq may shy away from overt activism in the works discussed above, her engagement with current political and social issues both elsewhere in her art and outside of it connects *Baddawi*, "Still Born," *The Opening*, and *The Fig Tree* to transnational movements and crises with epicenters mostly in the USA, geographically distant from Palestine, despite their global tremors. By adding her voice to the protest of police violence and brutality against black people, the detainment of immigrants at America's southern border, and the Trump presidency, among other issues, the author/artist forges new cross-border networks for the circulation of her work and ideas. Furthermore, by co-founding Maamoul Press to print art, comics, and graphic novels "for us, by us," "uplifting" creators from marginalized groups and bringing them into conversation with each other, Abdelrazaq tangibly participates in the production of a new World Literature. She facilitates the circulation and reading of their work, and her work alongside it. Abdelrazaq's activism as discussed in this section is practical and personal—seemingly always informed by her own identity and experiences as a Palestinian American.

Political commentators and activists have drawn comparisons between the "uprising" for racial justice in the USA and the Palestinian resistance movement, pointing to the similar oppressions and mechanisms that lie at the heart of both as well as the training that some American law enforcement officials have received from

Israeli security services.[5] Most visibly, the brutal treatment of black Americans at the hands of police parallels the violence inflicted upon Palestinians by Israeli authorities. Similar expressions of solidarity erupted in the aftermath of the shooting of Michael Brown and the protests and unrest that followed in Ferguson, Missouri. More recently, the murder of George Floyd in Minneapolis, Minnesota, has been likened to that of Eyad al-Hallaq, a Palestinian man with autism shot dead in Jerusalem less than one week later.

Some Palestinian cartoonists and artists, like Mohammad Sabaaneh and Taqi Spateen, have produced images, or "texts," that speak concisely and persuasively to the Black Lives Matter movement as a global moment in time ("Palestinian Artist" and @Sabaaneh). In contrast, Abdelrazaq has directed her outrage over the oppression and killing of black people in the USA to an intentionally local audience—attempting change at the level of the community. Between 2016 and 2019, Abdelrazaq screen printed "Palestinians for Black Power" and "Arabs for Black Power" t-shirts by hand. She conceived of the project as a way "to spark conversations and solidarity in the Palestinian community with the Movement for Black Lives," with profits going to "community initiatives for Black Power" (Abdelrazaq 2016–19). A secondary motivation was to "more proactively challenge anti-Black racism in Arab communities" (Abdelrazaq 2020). For a brief period beginning at the end of May 2020, Abdelrazaq reopened orders for the t-shirts with the promise that "100% of all proceeds [would] go to a local grassroots, Detroit, Black-led org doing community organizing work on the ground" (Abdelrazaq 2020). Abdelrazaq's participation at what she called a "micro level" sought to influence behavior and shape the conversation in the Palestinian community while providing support to the Detroit community—both communities to which she herself belongs (Abdelrazaq 2020).

Unlike the t-shirt sales, much of Abdelrazaq's public activism tends to take the form of storytelling that raises the voices of Palestinians, rather than directing her message primarily to them. She translates narratives and experiences that she feels connected to but that do not belong to her into a form that travels easily and is accessible to readers from a range of backgrounds, as she did with *Baddawi*. For example, "Mariposa" (2016) (a fifteen-page comic) gives a factual account of two Palestinian refugees, Hisham and Mounis, who escaped Gaza only to be detained by US Immigration and Customs Enforcement (ICE) at the Nogales-Mariposa Arizona Port of Entry into the USA. Abdelrazaq created it to bring attention to their case and also designed a "Free Hisham & Mounis" logo for the campaign for their release. They were let free in 2016 and granted asylum the following year. Similarly, in "Same Old, Same Old" (2017b), a comic published in *Harper's Magazine*, Abdelrazaq asks a cross-section of Palestinian Americans to "reflect" on what Trump's presidency "means for us," illustrating them alongside their responses. In her brief introduction to the piece, she calls out "Trump's talk of travel restrictions, refugee and Muslim bans, and wall-building," as well as "his stated intention to move the embassy from Tel Aviv to Jerusalem" (a promise he made

---

[5] See Shank (2020).

good on in May 2018) (Abdelrazaq 2017b). In both "Mariposa" and "Same Old, Same Old," Abdelrazaq uses her art to bring attention to the injustices experienced by others, as described in their own words. This is an approach that aligns with the mission of Maamoul Press.

Abdelrazaq founded Maamoul Press with two other artists, Aya Krisht and Zainab Saab. Its ethos centers on three guiding mandates: 1. "Storytelling for us, by us"; 2. "Forging the arts spaces we need"; and 3. "Generating knowledge through community" ("Maamoul Press"). Together, these three principles assert the right to a history, an independent space, and a community—in essence, the foundational elements of a nation consistently denied Palestinians since the creation of Israel. For Abdelrazaq in particular, Maamoul Press contributes to the creation of a space and community that enable her writing and art to circulate in fuller complexity by diversifying and expanding the corpus of texts and art within which it is read, viewed, and understood.

Since its publication, *Baddawi*, Abdelrazaq's most well-known work, has been held up alongside other graphic works about the Middle East written in diaspora or by outsiders, including Marjane Satrapi's autobiographical *Persepolis* series (2000–4), Sarah Glidden's *How to Understand Israel in 60 Days or Less* (2011), and Joe Sacco's *Palestine* (1993–5) and *Footnotes in Gaza* (2009). Abdelrazaq's art and comics have also been compared to the work of American women cartoonists such as Alison Bechdel and Phoebe Gloeckner. These two distinct sets of texts mark Abdelrazaq and her work as Palestinian or American, consistently privileging one half of her hyphenated identity over the other, rather than making the space for her hybridity that Maamoul Press is designed to hold.

Part of Maamoul Press' purpose is "positioning the work of diaspora artists alongside the work of artists living in [their] home countries" to "break down barriers that fragment [these] communities" ("Maamoul Press"). Narrating personal, family, and communal histories together facilitates a better understanding of the diversity of experiences that form the individual and make up a community, as in the multilingual, multiple-geography Palestinian literature described by Ebileeni above. Maamoul Press rejects the role played by "outside 'experts'" (like the author of this chapter, presumably) in crafting these narratives, seeking out insider voices, with all of their contradictions and complexity, which may be silenced or smoothed over in other contexts ("Maamoul Press").

When it comes to space, Maamoul Press strives to "create opportunities for [its creators'] work and the work of others like [them] to enter spaces that [they] are often (both implicitly and explicitly) barred from," resisting "forces of oppression that seek to keep [them] silenced and marginalized" ("Maamoul Press"). These may be physical spaces, such as museums and universities, and Palestine itself, or intellectual, artistic, and literary spaces, such as Palestinian literature, American literature, and World Literature. Abdelrazaq asserts her belonging in all three and, through Maamoul Press, builds a network of circulation and multiple affiliation for herself and other creators from historically marginalized groups.

Conclusion

Literature and art by Palestinians like Abdelrazaq are indeed born into the world, as argued above. But, in a concrete sense, it is a world of nations and passports and checkpoints that is designed to accommodate neither them nor their creative productions. In *Border Diary*, Abdelrazaq writes: "In the eyes of the state, we without countries are the most terrifying people in the world" (Abdelrazaq 2018f, 10). Being born at the borders, in the space in-between the spaces internationally recognized by the world, can be dressed up as a kind of freedom but can be a prison in practice.

In *Baddawi*, Ahmad's childhood exists in objects: marbles, the school supplies he is given as a first grader at the UNRWA school (four notebooks, two pencils, two crayons, and one eraser), a cluster bomb (Abdelrazaq 2015a, 22). These small things that can be held in the hand play a central role in *The Fig Tree* and "Still Born" as well. This is where you anchor a story when it does not fit in the house or city or nation where you are.

It is the world that Abdelrazaq creates through her art, her activism, and her work at Maamoul Press, rather than the one she is born into, that makes up the "world" in her World Literature. There is no flattening of difference here, beyond what is wrought universally, and unevenly, by globalization. It is instead a mode of reading and circulation, of art, words, and ideas, of translation and conversation, dependent on the shared and porous borders of countless diverse individual communities that change and form and reform and constantly renew—a living thing that sustains and is sustained by the colonies of smaller organisms that compose it.

References

Abdelrazaq, Leila. 2015a. *Baddawi*. Charlottesville: Just World Books.

Abdelrazaq, Leila. 2015b. "New Graphic Novel Explores What It's Really Like To Be a Palestinian Refugee." Review by Beenish Ahmed of *Baddawi* by Leila Abdelrazaq. *Think Progress*, April 24. https://archive.thinkprogress.org/new-graphic-novel-explores-what-its-really-like-to-be-a-palestinian-refugee-845c0bebe728/ (accessed February 2, 2022).

Abdelrazaq, Leila. 2015c. "Interview with Leila Abdelrazaq, author of Baddawi." Interview with Khelil Bouarrouj. *Institute for Palestine Studies*. https://www.youtube.com/watch?v=-gY-UhGhmbA (accessed June 25, 2020).

Abdelrazaq, Leila. 2015d. "Smuggling Books Across the Border: PalFest 2015." *Electronic Intifada*, June 10. https://electronicintifada.net/blogs/leila-abdelrazaq/smuggling-books-across-border-palfest-2015 (accessed June 5, 2020).

Abdelrazaq, Leila. 2016. "Mariposa." *Electronic Intifada*. February 9. https://electronicintifada.net/blogs/leila-abdelrazaq/hisham-and-mounis-besieged-gaza-us-immigration-jail (accessed July 11, 2020).

Abdelrazaq, Leila. 2016–19. "Palestinians for Black Power Tees." Leila Abdelrazaq's website. https://lalaleila.com/Palestinians-for-Black-Power-Tees (accessed June 25, 2020).

Abdelrazaq, Leila. 2017a. *The Opening*. Beirut: Tosh Fesh.

Abdelrazaq, Leila. 2017b. "Same Old, Same Old." *Harper's Magazine*. April 18. https://harpers.org/2017/04/same-old-same-old (accessed July 1, 2020).

Abdelrazaq, Leila. 2018a. "Leila Abdelrazaq Interview." Interview with Quest Sawyer. May 18. *Asian American Art Oral History Project*. https://via.library.depaul.edu/cgi/viewcontent.cgi?article=1110&context=oral_his_series (accessed June 5, 2020).

Abdelrazaq, Leila. 2018b. "Artist Statement." *Art Matters*. https://artmattersfoundation.org/grantees/a0M0Z00000IgGx9UAF (accessed July 1, 2020).

Abdelrazaq, Leila. 2018c. "Interview with Palestinian Artist and Author Leila Abdelrazaq." *follow the halo*, https://www.followthehalo.com/features/2018/7/15/interview-with-palestinian-artist-and-author-leila-abdelrazaq (accessed June 25, 2020).

Abdelrazaq, Leila. 2018d. "Still Born." https://lalaleila.com/Still-Born (accessed July 1, 2020).

Abdelrazaq, Leila. 2018e. *The Fig Tree*. Self-published.

Abdelrazaq, Leila. 2018f. "Border Diary." *The Believer*. August 1. https://believermag.com/border-diary (accessed July 1, 2020).

Abdelrazaq, Leila. 2020. "Palestinians for Black Power." Instagram, May 31. https://www.instagram.com/p/CA3WanLAGFm (accessed August 16, 2020).

al-Ali, Naji. 2009. *A Child in Palestine: The Cartoons of Naji al-Ali*. New York: Verso Books.

Al-Udhari, Abdullah. 1986. "The Passport." In *Modern Poetry of the Arab World*. New York: Penguin.

Apter, Emily. 2013. *Against World Literature: On the Politics of Untranslatability*. London: Verso Books.

Baetens, Jan. 2012. "World Literature and Popular Literature: Toward a Wordless Literature?" In D'haen, Theo, Damrosch, David, and Kadir, Djelal, eds. *The Routledge Companion to World Literature*. New York: Routledge, 336–44.

Ball, David M. 2018. "World Literature." In Baetens, Jan, Frey, Hugo, and Tabachnick, Stephen E., eds. *The Cambridge History of the Graphic Novel*. Cambridge: Cambridge University Press, 591–608.

Bardenstein, Carol. 1998. "Threads of Memory and Discourses of Rootedness: Of Trees, Oranges and the Prickly-Pear Cactus in Israel/Palestine." *Edebiyat*, 8: 1–36.

Cheurfa, Hiyem. 2020. "Testifying Graphically: Bearing Witness to a Palestinian Childhood in Leila Abdelrazaq's *Baddawi*." *Auto/Biography Studies*, 35 (2): 359–82.

Damrosch, David. 2003. *What is World Literature?* Princeton: Princeton University Press.

"Demographics." 2018. *Arab American Institute Foundation*. https://censuscounts.org/wp-content/uploads/2019/03/National_Demographics_SubAncestries-2018.pdf (accessed August 17, 2020).

Ebileeni, Maurice. 2017. "Palestinian Writings in the World: A Polylingual Literary Category Between Local and Transnational Realms." *Interventions*. 19 (2): 258–91.

Hassan, Waïl S. 2011. *Immigrant Narratives: Orientalism and Cultural Translation in Arab American and Arab British Literature*. Oxford: Oxford University Press.

"Maamoul Press – About." *Maamoul Press*, https://maamoulpress.com/About (accessed June 28, 2020).

Mufti, Aamir. 2016. *Forget English!: Orientalisms and World Literatures*. Cambridge, MA: Harvard University Press.

Nye, Naomi Shihab. 1997. *Sitti's Secrets*. New York: Aladdin Picture Books.

"Palestinian Artist Taqi Spateen Painting George Floyd on the Separation Wall." *Mondoweiss*, June 11, 2020. https://www.youtube.com/watch?v=Y7DThxjVZ28 (accessed August 17, 2020).

Pappe, Ilan. 2006. *The Ethnic Cleansing of Palestine*. Oxford: Oneworld.
The Qur'an. Sahih International Translation, https://www.quran.com/2/156 (accessed January 15, 2022).
Ranta, Ronald, and Mendel, Yonatan. 2014. "Consuming Palestine: Palestine and Palestinians in Israeli Food Culture." *Ethnicities*, 14 (3): 412–35.
Rosenblatt, Adam, and Lunsford, Yonatan. 2010. "Critique, Caricature, and Compulsion in Joe Sacco's Comics Journalism." In Williams, Paul, and Lyons, James, eds. *The Rise of the American Comics Artist*. Jackson: University Press of Mississippi, 68–89.
@Sabaaneh, Mohammad. 2020. "The #rasism and the #apartheid is the same. #Israeli occupation and the #American #rasism is the same #BlackLivesMatter." Twitter, May 28, 5:02pm. http://www.twitter.com/Sabaaneh/status/1266112717322162176.
Salaita, Steven. 2011. *Modern American Fiction: A Reader's Guide*. Syracuse: Syracuse University Press.
Shammas, Anton. 1995. "Autocartography." *The Threepenny Review*, 63: 7–9.
Shank, Michael. 2020. "How Police Became Paramilitaries." *The New York Review of Books*, June 3. https://www.nybooks.com/daily/2020/06/03/how-police-became-paramilitaries/ (accessed August 17, 2020).
Spivak, Gayatri. 2003. *Death of a Discipline*. New York: Columbia University Press.
"UNWRA in Figures." 2020. *UNWRA*, June. https://www.unrwa.org/sites/default/files/content/resources/unrwa_in_figures_2020_eng_v2_final.pdf (accessed July 26, 2020).
The Wanted 18. 2014. Directed by Amer Shomali and Paul Cowan. Kino Lorber.

7

Utopias Gone Wrong: Representing the Dystopic Urban in the Indian Graphic Narrative

Debadrita Chakraborty

Introduction

The comic narrative genre in India is synonymous with childhood nostalgia. Despite enjoying a fan base within the Indian urban middle class, comic books and comic strips (like their American counterpart) have been essentially perceived as "low brow" in the literary world. The Indian comic cultural phenomenon that gained popularity with the likes of *Amar Chitra Katha*, *Mandrake*, and *Phantom* have been regarded as disposable, low-rent visual medium packed with easily digestible, fantastical, superficial content concerning Hindu mythology, superhero adventures, hero worship, fables, and light humor (Varughese 2018, 6). With the turn of the millennium, it was the graphic novel form that overhauled the comic cultural scene in India. Although at times viewed as a case of aesthetic gentrification wherein the classic comic-book form has been transformed into a "glossier product marked by high prices and middle-class values" (Dunst 2019), graphic novels in India have merited serious critical analysis in the recent years due to their ability to tackle nuanced sociopolitical discourses and voice public-sphere issues otherwise under-reported in conventional news media. The transition of this genre from adolescent fantasies to a cultural mode of artistic expression and communication have encouraged serious writers and artists in India whose thematic complexities have traditionally been expressed in literary narratives, films, and photo essays to choose graphic narrative as an expression of their sociopolitical arguments through illustrations and prose.

Among the first graphic narratives in India, it was Orijit Sen's *The River of Stories* (1994) that resonated with the cultural and political aesthetics of its Euro–American counterpart. Known for its thematic and narrative maturity, Sen's graphic novel eschewed history in favor of "fantasy, horror and adventure" (Varughese 2018, 9) engaging with the sociopolitical and environmental discourses around the controversial Narmada Project in western India and the activism movement around it. Influenced by Sen's revolutionary work, Indian graphic-narrative writers have since created a niche for themselves in the new millennium, vernacularizing the graphic-narrative medium as they debate social and historical constructs such as casteism, classism, child abuse, gender homogeneity, homophobia, Islamophobia, and the existential malaise in urban India using a distinctively "Indian idiom" of the graphic-narrative form. As Nayar observes, "the graphic narrative in English Language in India, is thus constitutive like Indian literature, of Indian urban imaginaries among the English-speaking classes, to which it offers alternative readings of history, draws attention to the lacunae and follies of our cultural practices and makes visible hitherto taboo subjects" (Nayar 2016, 7). Indian graphic narratives encode postcolonial modernity in new styles, grammar, and modes of visuality that are different from the Western ideas of graphic-narrative production. Through its rhetorical and representational strategies, the graphic narrative is able to offer a deeper immersion into everyday forms of structural inequalities, public histories, gender hierarchies, social taboos, and political prejudices. In doing so, the verbal–visual narrative is able to guide readers toward a "critical literacy" that enables them to evaluate the position they choose to take vis-à-vis the issues represented in the text.

One of the ways in which the Indian graphic narrative aims to convey the "loopholes, storylines, black holes, dead ends and labyrinths" (Nayar 2016, 14) of both the past and the present is through the dystopian aesthetic. However, the dystopian imaginary employed within the graphic novels is not a teleological narrative of degeneration that foreshadows the world's end in apocalypse neither does it encapsulate in its negative form a "utopian wish." Instead, dystopia in graphic narratives is always presentist. By placing its readers in a dark and depressing reality, they serve as a "warning, conjuring the present as a continuous with the future if its symptoms are not treated in the here and now" (Harvey 1973, 14). It is through the critique of the present that the dystopia in graphic novels enables readers to rethink the future in terms of new sociocultural, political and economic imaginaries including cultural identity, social injustices, national belonging, political systems, justice, and equity.

Given this dystopian phenomenon of examining the present via the past in graphic narratives, this chapter draws from two Indian graphic novels, *Corridor* (2004) by Sarnath Banerjee and *Delhi Calm* (2010) by Vishwajyoti Ghosh to argue on the ways in which the dystopic aesthetic traces the cultural and political histories of India including sociopolitical discourses and voices that have thus far been under-reported in conventional news media and largely missing from public-sphere deliberations. Stripping away the veneer of "India Rising," both *Corridor* and *Delhi Calm* manifest the myriad ways in which the nation-state has been constantly falling apart in the face of neoliberal and nationalist ideologies—be they political crises such as "The Emergency" of 1975–7, when India's president declared a state of emergency and suspended civil rights across the country, or the ensuing existential anxiety, insecurity, dystopic and disintegrating realities of both individual and collective lives emanating from complex economic realities of late capitalism, laws, neoliberal norms or institutions.

This politics is played out most of all in urban spaces given the large number of postcolonial texts that situate their stories in metropolitan India. In Indian graphic narratives, the urban space is presented as the only environment susceptible to support modern and postmodern communication, the only place where real action can take place. It is also a display-case for the infinite and dangerous possibilities of the future and their corresponding effects, both positive and negative, upon readers' perception of reality. In both Banerjee and Ghosh's narratives, the "urban" not only signifies the encompassing physical spaces that comprise metropolitan areas, but also the complex relationships that are forged among living spaces, work spaces, and leisure spaces and the people who inhabit them, which the writers portray using both textual and visual dimensions. In this chapter I connect the term "dystopia" with the term "urban" since both Banerjee and Ghosh employ the urban paradigm as dystopian agents in their graphic narratives. The purpose behind representing the city as a dystopian, dysfunctional space is two-fold here. Both Banerjee and Ghosh not only aim to associate the urban dystopia with notions of chaos, crime, daily antagonism, and subhuman living but also make attempts at re-imagining and revitalizing urban environments through vocal and vital grassroots to keep dystopian realities at bay. The urban dystopia aesthetic thus makes an intervention in the constitution of the urban imaginary by emphasizing what the authors see as problematic to those living within the urban space. Simultaneously, it also helps readers realize that the metropolitan city is also a vibrant setting for the collision of ideas and creativity, a symbol of sociocultural modernity and economic opportunity. In order to analyze the representation of the urban Indian space and its dystopic realities that influence and invisibilize subaltern lives, in this chapter I aim to employ the dual framework of biopolitics and necropolitics. The framework of biopolitics and necropolitics manifests how sovereign power proliferates those conditions in which individuals marginalized by race, class, and gender configurations are "stripped of political significance and exposed to murderous violence" (Ziarek 2008, 90). In other words, both the theoretical paradigms aim towards understanding how state and societal mechanisms of power that ideally should administer and foster life, guaranteeing health and productivity of populations pushes them into precarious living situations and confers upon them the status of "living-dead" (Mbembe, 2019). Employing the two theoretical frameworks this paper will showcase how both state and the society following The Emergency of 1975–7 in Ghosh's *Delhi Calm* and the deepening economic and existential crisis generated by the neoliberal state in Banerjee's *Corridor*, systematically exploit, injure, and even eliminate the section of the population who are shown to reside at the bottommost of the biopolitical/necropolitical[1] hierarchy. In addition, this article will also respond to questions that emerge from the graphic novel in India: How do graphic-narrative forms destabilize origins? Do they formulate a new ethics in a new heterogeneous world? How do they forge new languages and create new forms of representation?

---

[1] Achille Mbembe merges Foucault's right to take life and let live and Agamben's discussion of homo-sacer resulting in an account of a new and different dimension to contemporary biopower that is necropower. Extending and intensifying Foucault's arguably incomplete meditations on biopolitics and racism, Mbembe directs the reader's attention to the way in which necropower functions to destroy persons by creating the rigidly striated spaces he calls "death-worlds."

The City as a "Necropolis" in *Delhi Calm*

The "state of emergency" that India witnessed on June 25, 1975 is not a postcolonial phenomenon[2] but is a legislative practice framed and employed by colonial governments to control the territories and populations they govern, especially during periods of anti-colonial resistance and struggle, thereby consolidating the power of the colonial state. The state of emergency implies an emergency legislation wherein an executive power of a country is used to suspend the normal rule of law. The power is transferred to the police and the military who are instructed to use necessary force to "put down breaches of the peace, such as riots and other disturbances" (Morton 2013, 2). While emergency legislation is often associated with totalitarian government, liberal democracies have made use of this law in times of political and social crisis, often branding (democratic) resistance movements as terrorism and insurgence. Ghosh's *Delhi Calm* documents this normalization of lawful state violence painfully experienced by the city's urban poor and the pro-democratic subversive forces guided by their socialist leader, the Prophet (modelled after the socialist Jayprakash Narayan) who advocated for Total Revolution. Using visual archives from the Emergency including verbal allusions to original newspaper headlines and literal quotes from official political spaces (Ghosh 2010, 4), Ghosh further emphasizes the "state of exception" where the nation state in a sovereign-like manner has the right over the life and death of their subjects.

Conflating the visual and verbal form, Vishwajyoti Ghosh in his graphic novel *Delhi Calm* published in 2010 attempts to answer the larger question as to how the counter history of the Emergency can be presented. Ghosh fills the gaps within history through the visual dimension in *Delhi Calm*. By representing "in pictures and in writing, spoken memories," (Syposz, 2016) *Delhi Calm* acts as an oral history narrating the persecution of oppressed groups. As Nayar notes, "In many cases the speaker-narrator is telling us a story he or she has heard from a member of the family or community." In such a case *Delhi Calm* is both a literary and visual retelling of (hi)story (Nayar 2016). Besides, the visual narrative aims to humanize history by highlighting the expressions of the characters and their location in the panels in an attempt to indicate how individuals perceive and receive events as these happen. In so doing, Ghosh attempts to interrupt the public history of the Emergency by shifting the focus on the impact of national trauma on common lives and subjectivities.

The narrative opens with the announcement of the Emergency on the morning of June 26, 1975 by the Indian prime minister and the ensuing dystopic forms of oppression already perceived by the protagonist Vibhuti Prasad (VP). A junior writer in a newspaper, VP is shown to be lamenting the impending job loss and the financial crisis that he will suffer as a result of this political upheaval. Before Ghosh begins to unravel sovereignty's onslaughts on everyday life beginning with the sudden withdrawal of every civil right of the people, the loss of jobs and material security, through his protagonist Vibhuti Prasad (VP), he familiarizes

---

[2] Contemporary states of emergency owe much to colonial forms of sovereignty.

his readers to a pre-dystopian Delhi which was a "powerpolis"—the capital of the "world's largest democracy." For young men like VP, the city was synonymous with "connections, clubs, circles, [and] opportunities" (Ghosh 2010, 10), for the middle classes the city represented enterprises whilst for the working class it was symbolic of the cash they earned from their twelve-hour shift every day. Juxtaposing such verbal panels with visual ones as depicted in the sketch in Figure 7.1, with quotes such as "Keep distance, keep quiet," "do not think," "do not guess," "work more, talk less" (Ghosh, 2010, 5), Ghosh aims to highlight and document the public trauma

Figure 7.1 Vishwajyoti Ghosh, *Delhi Calm*

generated from the state's betrayal of the expectation or promise of the Nehruvian idea of India and democracy. In doing so, Ghosh not only aims to unsettle authority and their standard narratives that entail a form of forgetting, but also attempts to produce models of witnessing by reintegrating "an ethics of attention" into the reader regarding the pain of others (Chute 2016, 50). The result is not an accusatory or disciplinary invocation upon the reader, but the cultivation of an "intimate" witnessing, one that produces a shared affective agency between readers and victims of political crisis.

In his lectures, "Society Must Be Defended" Foucault observes that the modern State can scarcely function without becoming involved with racism at some point, within certain limits and subject to certain conditions (2013, 74). In *Delhi Calm* Ghosh investigates this thought by providing his readers a graphic (which is visual and textual) overview of Prime Minister Indira Gandhi's ascension to power and governance that undid the "fine balance between state power and democracy" (Prakash 2019, 41) in 1975 with the declaration of the Emergency. Although Ghosh does not engage in historical discourses that reflect the causes behind the Prime Minister's call for the Emergency, he employs the bildungsroman mode using both visual and textual dimensions to help readers identify with her "coming of age story" which is one of "storm and trouble." Using a black and white tint (in the panels dedicated to Indira Gandhi)—a visual metaphor that evokes Gandhi's past life—her growing up years, Ghosh portrays the young Moon (Ghosh chooses to address her as "moon" since the name "Indira" translates into "moon") in a frock, ambitious, alone, and full of insecurities. While her association with the stars at once symbolizes her star status, her lonesomeness, and her aspirations, Moon's coldness and her insecurities are attributed to her growing up in a family that was constantly in the national spotlight. While her father was mostly away on political work or in prison for dissenting against British imperialists, Moon found emotional proximity with her mother, which was short-lived due to the latter's ailments. Ghosh allows his readers to deduce from the graphic bildungsroman that it is these strains of family dynamics that made Moon solitary and insecure and negotiating them also forced her to be self-reliant, stubborn, and adamant. It is this persistence and obstinacy in the face of familial and political hurdles that empowered her at first to marry a Parsi despite her father's disapproval and later to alter the course of India's history by suspending the constitutional rights of Indian citizens.

According to Italian philosopher, Giorgio Agamben, the "state of exception" is a modern institution with roots in the French Revolution and is a condition wherein governments have the right to legally justify limits on personal and constitutional freedoms. Within a "state of exception" juridical law is suspended due to an emergency or a serious crisis threatening the state. Agamben posits that "the state of exception" is not a "state of law" but a space without law" (2005, 18). It is not equivalent to a dictatorship, where laws continue to be made and applied (albeit non-democratically), but one in which law is rather entirely emptied of content. Agamben concludes that the state of exception is therefore "a fictio iuris (legal fiction) par excellence which claims to maintain the law in its very suspension," but produces instead a violence that has shed every relation to law (2005, 59). In *Delhi Calm*, Ghosh mirrors the dystopic reality of Delhi confronted by police brutalities and military violence when Mother Moon creates a state-of-exception condition for the citizens with the declaration of the Emergency. In a bid to establish the "state of exception" that would keep oppositional forces at bay, Gandhi not only used Article 35 that laid the legal foundations for an Emergency so that the Executive power can become the state and exercise power directly and unrestrictedly, she also ensured the physical elimination not only of political adversaries but of entire categories of citizens who could be integrated into the political system (Agamben 2005, 2). The state-controlled narrative portrayed Jayprakash Narayan (the seventy-two-year-old Gandhian socialist and a former freedom fighter against British rule, who had come out of political retirement to lead a youth upsurge against Indira Gandhi's state racism and politically malicious governance) as the national enemy.

In order to symbolize the extent to which Mother Moon's state of exception dissolved the boundaries of society, government, and law, Ghosh uses digitally tinted sepia to reproduce the memory of Delhi's dystopic past. The urban space as represented in his graphic panels, are populated by masked men known as Smiling Saviours (Moon's supporters) as depicted in Figures 7.2 and 7.3. They are shown to exhort citizen's to abide by Emergency rules to cope with social disorder and economic crisis—vocabularies of war that the Indira regime maintains to "justify recourse to extensive government powers" (Agamben 2005, 5). What is interesting about Ghosh's representation of the masked men in these panels is the semblance of their smile to that of Mother Moon's, which is not only symbolic of state manipulation of people's thought processes but also an attempt by this section of the population to protect themselves from being subject to death or a "death-in-life" condition imposed on those who were anti-establishment. From a historical lens, these visual images of the Indira Gandhi's supporters and their vocal enthusiasm, "The greatest and our best leader, Mother Moon is always right" (Ghosh 2010, 130), are reminiscent of those who stood behind the Emergency regime, chanting "Indira is India, India is Indira" thus further authentifying Ghosh's narrative of the Emergency cultural memory. The all-pervading necropolitical force of Moon's state of exception can be witnessed through censorship and suspension of press rights in the city. In *Delhi Calm*, the protagonist VP and his friend Parvez come across a giant TV and are asked by a group of Smiling Saviours to help them install a poster that carries the dominant discourse on the Emergency declared for the larger biopolitical good of the nation.

Within the state of exception that functions on violence and anomie, the biopolitical body is stripped of its political and legal attributes, culminating in what Agamben calls a "bare life"—"a legally unnamable and unclassifiable being" (Agamben 2013, 134). Extending Foucault's notion of biopolitics (a practice by liberal governments that employs mechanisms and technologies of power to

Figures 7.2 and 7.3 Vishwajyoti Ghosh, *Delhi Calm*

regulate, nourish, and preserve the life of the population), Agamben argues that the defense of life often takes place in a zone of indistinction between violence and the law; that is, in the camp where one group's life is violently secured through the demise of the other. Ghosh envisions this dystopia of "bare life" through his portrayal of coerced sterilization in the city's make-shift "camps" in *Delhi Calm*. The sterilization drive was a part of the Indira government's renewed commitment to the Family Planning Program, initiated five days after the imposition of Emergency. The goal was to limit population growth through mass male sterilization. As per the data collected by Brown, civil servants were one of the targets of this program who were deterred from producing a fourth child after September 1977 or risk losing their jobs. Incentives such as cash payments of up to several hundred rupees were given to men who submitted to sterilization. While the sterilization drive to achieve birth control was geared toward the entire population, it was the Muslim and the working-class section of the population who were humiliated and tortured into adopting sterilization by the Emergency regime. The panel depicting a mosaic of blades and smiling masks is symbolic of the murderous violence that residents had been subjected to by the sovereign (Indira regime) within sterilization camps that bore semblance with Agamben's definition of concentration camps. Here, the Emergency regime does not exclude one life to reinforce another, instead in a dystopic way, Indira governance aims to expose the entire population to violation through sterilization for the sake of the nation's biopolitical welfare in terms of controlled population growth and "urban beautification."

The urban population's extreme degradation and subjection to disciplinary power becomes all the more intense with the slum-clearance drive under the Slum Areas (Improvement and Clearance) Act, 1956 for beautification purposes executed in the heart of Delhi by Indira Gandhi's younger son, Sanjay Gandhi. While the official narrative legitimized the loss of homes due to the slum-demolition drive as a biopolitical move and the counter-narrative led by the Shah Commission that condemned the crimes committed by the Emergency regime, Ghosh presents to his readers a version of the slum inhabitant's (the *homosacer* in Agamben's words) protest against public- and private-sphere violations. Employing the literary device of satire, Ghosh portrays the biopolitical divide where upper- and middle-class elites are shown to support the slum-clearance drive in the Walled city in Delhi, which appeared unaesthetic and an eyesore of the capital as they dreamt of a globalized, beautified, cosmopolitan Delhi, resembling the city of Paris (Ghosh, 2010, 193). On the other hand, some sections of the population are still oblivious of the loss of homes and lives generated by this movement. Instead they have glued themselves to their transistors listening to the cricket commentary of an international match played by India (2010, 194). The state of exception not only violated the rights of the socially marginalized despite state-speak of development and efficiency, it also employed necropower to torture and ultimately kill those who opposed the regime. Throughout the narrative, Ghosh creates a sense of foreboding and oppressive silence in panels peopled with Smiling Saviours mouthing both subtle and alarming intimidations like "Keep smiling, keep disciplined," "if you don't fear then death is near" and policemen on the lookout for miscreants and anti-establishment activists (Ghosh 2010, 58, 183). This unsettling undercurrent of violence culminates when readers are confronted with VP's arrest. Ghosh manifests the necropower employed by the Indira government by not only portraying the humiliation VP is forced to go through in the hands of the policemen, including relentless beatings and forced consumption of urine, he also superimposes the panel with newspaper clippings of innocent individuals detained by the police on the pretext of supposed misconducts (which in a lawful state would not be considered a crime) such as a certain Bala aged 27 who was arrested since he refused to pay a bribe to the policemen, or the arrest of a poet who refused to read poetry on the Police Annual Day. Such arbitrary detentions thus portray the myriad ways in which the Emergency used the state of exception to strip human life to bare life so that the latter can be easily exposed to death and the city transformed into a "necropolis."[3]

Can a city that has transitioned into a "camp" where the state of exception is the rule show signs of emancipatory possibilities? According to Lefebvre, possibilities of collective action and revolutionary trajectories are possible when people long for the restoration of the traditional centrality of the city. However, what is also

---

[3] Although the term "necropolis" connotes a large cemetery of an ancient city, I use this term to define the city of Delhi during the Emergency to emphasize the necropolitics of the state that created death-like situations for its citizens subjecting them to state racism and reducing them to a "bare life."

important to note is how long until such protest movements fall and whether the revolutionary potential of such struggles have a staying power. Ghosh focuses on this very aspect through his representation of the ambivalent aspects of the JP Movement, his calls for "Total Revolution"—and the half-committedness of JP's followers (Holmberg, 2013). While on one side, Ghosh attempts to mockingly portray the pervading force of the totalitarian nature of Indira's regime, he also realistically manifests the trajectory of India's educated young population through the character of VP, who even though he believed in creating a different legacy of postcolonial modernity for India, ultimately succumbed to the city's capitalist dynamic and the allure of neoliberal consumption as evident in both VP and Parvez's reference of Delhi as a "Powerpolis," more than once in the novel. VP's move from political activism to compromise and cynicism can be witnessed at various points in the novel when he says, "my only involvement [in the movement] is emotional, I just write about it" or later in the narrative when post his police brutalization, VP grows both resentful and fearful of the system and decides that he "doesn't want more trouble" (Ghosh, 2010, 20, 175). So what went wrong with the movement and why couldn't such a campaign mobilize citizens reduced to a bare life to emancipate themselves from the government's necropolitical tactics? One of the reasons is that the nature of the political, social, and technical battles that have to be fought and won and the organizational principles and practices were mismatched (Harvey, 2012, 145). Ghosh deftly portrays this paradox in his narrative wherein the panel early in the novel represents JP's charisma as a socialist leader whose objective is "Total Revolution," which is to both overthrow the corrupt government and bring about "change in the society and the individual" (Ghosh, 2010, 102). In a contrasting panel toward the end of the narrative, Ghosh captures the futility and bitterness rendered by JP's promise as manifested by the character of Masterji—the leader of a faction of the JP movement who doubts his political affiliation and his existential position throughout the movement when he inquires, "Am I a character of any significance or a conductor of the chorus in the wings?"(Ghosh, 2010, 235). As JP's biographers have stated, an otherwise selfless, democratic socialist's contemplation for a united opposition to challenge Gandhi's regime led to the movement's ultimate downfall. JP had joined hands with the Rashtriya Swayamsevak Sangh (RSS) known to engage in communal politics, which did not bode well for many of his supporters. That the movement did little to awaken the residents of Delhi (reduced to bare life) for political intervention demanding a transformation of power relations and a redress for injustice can be evinced in the final few panels of the novel when post Emergency, Mother Moon's dissemination of the official narrative, which emphasized the Emergency as the only potent solution to overcome internal (oppositional) threats, was accepted by the public. An entire panel dedicated to Moon's public speech and a huge gathering of supporters ready to listen to her justified actions including the socio-economic opportunities that the Emergency generated for the class and caste subalterns captures Ghosh's satirical attempt at portraying dystopia and a sense of foreboding that continue to persist in Delhi city despite the culmination of Emergency. The next section will explore whether the state of exception reveals itself in contemporary India which is governed by neoliberal capital and consumption and the ways in which biopower and necropower play out against the sociopolitical milieu of Delhi.

Between Neoliberal and Biopolitical Rationalities: The City and the *Flâneur* in *Corridor*

Like Ghosh's *Delhi Calm,* Banerjee's *Corridor* portrays the metropolis of Delhi as the prototypical site of dreams and hopes that allows newcomers to make a living and possibly find spatial as well as social freedom (Sarma 2017). However, unlike in *Delhi Calm* where the protagonist VP's aspirations of belonging and inclusivity in the city gets briefly deterred by the dystopia of Emergency, *Corridor* represents a city permanently marked by twenty-first-century neoliberal segregationism that caters to the political and cosmopolitan elites who shape the city after their own desires whilst leaving the marginal communities dangling in a world of anomie and alienation, anger and frustration. In contrast to the characters in *Delhi Calm* who claimed their "right to the city" by resisting the necropolitical forces that aimed to wipe out the unwanted poverty-ridden sections of the city and its population, Banerjee using a mixed medium of photographs, sketches, and texts captures tropes of identity and belonging of his protagonists who suffer from emotional and existential insecurity even as they defend their personal and territorial space from neoliberal hegemony. In order to overcome individualistic isolation, discontents, and anxiety borne off the dystopic malaise of individualistic neoliberal ethic, the characters in *Corridor* attempt to reshape the city and the ideals of urban identity, citizenship, and belonging by inhabiting fragmented urban landscapes such as the "bylanes," "underworlds," "overworlds," and "corridors" that are excluded from globalization and neoliberal growth. These liminal spaces of exception to use Agamben's expression are "other global cities"; that is, interstitial territories that are literally neither here nor there, both included and excluded, inside and outside the fabric of the global city and the neoliberal growth it supports. These exceptional, extraterritorial spaces operate as a counter to the capitalist, globalized city even as they are integral to the functioning of the city's cosmopolitan spaces. By making such "spaces of exception" visible through visual images, Banerjee manifests the demand made by Delhi's displaced and disenfranchised population for a "renewed right to urban life" that constitutes an insistence for the need to rebuild and recreate the city in a completely different image. In so doing, Banerjee through *Corridor* aims to respond to the question: Is there an urban alternative and where might it come from?

The narrative begins with this utopic search for an alternative vision of the city, in its outer circles comprising corridors, lanes, and bylanes. In the outset, Banerjee focuses on one such outer, marginal space where the central characters caught between the urban dimensions of security (biopolitics) and insecurity (necropolitics) engendered by neoliberal urbanism and its enforcement of the regulatory regime, attempt to reinvent the city with the kinds of social relations they seek, the style of life they desire and the aesthetic values they hold. Like VP, Parvez and the members of the anti-establishment movement who resist the state politics of necropower within Delhi's interstitial spaces in times of the Emergency, Banerjee too creates a "citizen's agora"[4] organized around a second-hand bookstore in the "outer circle" of Delhi's Connaught Place. The outer, marginal space is a metaphor for a socially heterogeneous space associated with struggles against consumerism, and the economy of the spectacle that creates segregated enclaves of poverty and wealth. The bookstore at Connaught Place becomes the "centre of the Universe" not just for the bookseller, Jehangir Rangoonwalla but also for the central characters for whom the space is a common, central point where the characters and their stories interact albeit as a result of what Brighu calls a "cosmic accident" (Banerjee 2004, 14, 108). At the outset, Banerjee mobilizes a subversive urban politics by contrasting the signage of a globalized India installed on the historical pillars of Connaught Place to that of the open, democratic, egalitarian space comprising the stacks of books of Rangoonwalla's second-hand book store where each character in the novel wanders in, wanders out, sharing a fragment of a personal quest before wandering away. Using the devices of irony, exaggeration, and humor throughout *Corridor*, Banerjee through multiple story sequences reveals "the poly-semantic urban realities and hidden undercurrents [of] the 'new' metropolis" (Sandten 2011, 514).

Like VP and his friend Parvez in *Delhi Calm* whose navigation through the urban spaces in Delhi capturing the "camp" life forced upon the class, caste, and religious minorities by the government during Emergency, the protagonist in *Corridor*, Brighu, too traverses through the city's urban spaces whose act of perception becomes the subject of representation. Banerjee models Brighu as a *flâneur*-like figure, a popular archetype of the nineteenth century that figured in literature, describing the metropolitan experience. The word "*flâneur*" evokes the idea of a man of leisure observing and exploring the streets of Paris and the activity of strolling and looking is known as *flânerie*. The original *flâneur* was modeled on and for a specific landscape, which according to the likes of Walter Benjamin were the Parisian arcades—a site where the nineteenth-century Paris made its debut. Against the characterization of the *flâneur* in popular culture as "a lazybones, a loafer, a man of insufferable idleness, who doesn't know where to carry his trouble and his boredom" (D'Hautel [1808] quoted in Ferguson 1994)—as something of a deviant in emerging bourgeois society—writers redefined the figure defending his idle and lounger-like nature which was counterbalanced by his intense intellectual activity. The primary traits of the *flâneur* are namely, detachment from the ordinary social world, attachment to Paris, and the real if indirect association to art (Ferguson 1994, 26). The *flâneur's* field of action is encompassed by his field of vision, in the Paris of the arcades, the city of restaurants and boulevards and gardens, of crowds jostling in public places (Ferguson 1994, 27).

---

[4] An alternate space that exists beyond the public sphere and institutions.

Like the *flâneur* that originated in Baudelaire's poetry and can be traced in Benjamin's theory, Brighu is portrayed as a postmodern *flâneur*—a spectator of the streets of a postmodern Delhi whose subjective gaze facilitates readers to experience bordering, exclusions, and necropolitics within the city of Delhi. Loitering in the arcades of Delhi's business and financial hub, Connaught Place, Brighu remains anonymous, devoid of personality, unremarkable in the crowd studying the city from a distance. Brighu at the outset documents the everyday life of the Delhi cityscape that although free of the structures of surveillance employed during Emergency as witnessed in *Delhi Calm*, is entrapped within the dystopic structures of state-enforced dual forces of biopolitical and neoliberal rationalities. The Delhi documented by Brighu is shown to crumble under the pressure of neoliberal politics (which promotes inequality, competition, and individual responsibility) that forces the state (which is given to care for the population) to undertake biopolitical racism, dividing human beings into competing species/races and normalizing the view that the death of "the inferior race ... will make life in general healthier" (Foucault 2003, 255). Caught between the oppressive politics of state-induced biopolitical racism and neoliberal consumption, Brighu's Delhi is shown to "slowly stretch itself awake" to existential "contemplate[ion]" and is "reluctant" to engage with the neoliberal order, instead of "jumpstart[ing] the day" as is expected from a human capital (Banerjee 2004, 13). Banerjee's portrayal of a sluggish, unenterprising Delhi (through Brighu) is symbolic of the ontological insecurities and existential anxieties that are suffered by the main characters (including him) in the novel. The uneven infrastructures of citizenship whereby infrastructural services and citizenship rights are seized by the neoliberal urban elite at the expense of the less privileged and oppressed is hinted in the beginning by Brighu through the visual of a DNA structure as shown in Figure 7.4, supported by Brighu's remark, "the streets are empty save for a few hardcore urban warriors" (Banerjee, 2004, 3). Against the urban elites, the section of population favored within the neoliberal and biopolitical order, Brighu suggests that it is the other half of the population, subject to biopolitical racism, who need to have a special DNA to survive the dystopic divisive structures of the city symbolized by the scorching heat of Delhi's weather in June (Banerjee, 2004, 3).

As he saunters down the corridors, in the outer circle of Delhi's Connaught Place, Brighu introduces to the readers the life stories of some of those urban warriors who visit Rangoonwalla's second-hand bookshop, thus enabling readers to orient themselves within both the city and the narrative. Brighu's interaction with Rangoonwalla at his bookstore introduces us to the latter's *flâneur*-esque life in Bombay that challenged the neoliberal mechanisms of competition and the logics of biopolitical racism that permits life to those who participate within the capitalist hierarchical order and leaves to die those who resist the neoliberal mechanisms of exploitation. Like the *flâneur* who observes, studies, and analyses his surroundings, Rangoonwalla, too, provides a critical understanding of Bombay of the 1970s, capturing the dystopia of "urban angst"—a consequence of joblessness and the growing number of "dead-heads and dropouts" in the city (Banerjee 2004, 15). Unlike these sections of the population who sought to escape from their existential anxieties and ontological insecurities with

158 Graphic Novels and Comics as World Literature

Figure 7.4 Sarnath Banerjee, *Corridor*

alternative means of survival such as the "vipassana" or taking refuge by consuming drugs such as the "kerala grass"(15), Rangoonwalla after having "changed some forty jobs" despite possessing a university degree elects a *flâneur's* life, selling books, observing, accumulating knowledge, and disseminating them in the city through his customers. By juxtaposing Rangoonwalla's choices with that of Angrez Bosch, a regular customer at Rangoonwalla's bookstore, Banerjee satirizes the cosmocratic *flâneur* Bosch who, instead of observing the city from a distance engages in cultural consumption of commodities and in the process expands the realm of capitalism as much as a shopper in the arcade. As an Englishman in India, Bosch represents the quintessential cosmopolitan consumer of the globalization era who accumulates "cosmopolitan capital" by commodifying and consuming Indian cuisine, fashion, and lifestyle that gives him a global consciousness and identity and positions him within the category of a cosmocrat. Even though his cultural disposition involves a "stance of openness towards divergent experiences" (Urry 1995, 167) from India, in effect he never genuinely interacts with cultural differences. This can be witnessed through his engagement with Indian spiritual practices through "vipassana," which is nothing more than a consumer tourist trip where Bosch accumulates knowledge for shallow self-gratification.

Not all are able to remain disinterested and disinvolved from neoliberalism and its mechanisms of production and consumption that marks Delhi's urbanscape. Banerjee's homodiegetic character–narrator, Brighu, unlike *flâneurs* like Rangoonwalla is "disabled" and overwhelmed by the city as he surrenders to the "extravagant, conspicuous, displays of merchandise" (Ferguson 1994, 34). From the corridors, the outer circle of Delhi, Banerjee relocates Brighu within the city's cafeterias and pubs to consume an exotic array of food, fashion and other cultural products that globalization makes available in Delhi's upper-class neighborhoods. However, even as he partakes in the cultural ritual of consumption with his girlfriend, Kali, Brighu resuscitates the traits of the original *flâneur* when he critically observes the section of Delhi's urban population privileged by the dual structures of neoliberal[5] and biopolitical mechanisms, name-calling them "Delhi superbabies" who are "taller than the tall, richer than the rich and less and less like normal human beings" (Banerjee 2004, 80). Banerjee uses visual exaggeration, as depicted in Figure. 7.5, to capture Brighu's impression of Delhi's neoliberal culture by presenting grotesque caricatures of the "smiles" of attendees at a funding agency party, which is symbolic of their frivolity and their ever-ready nature to serve neoliberal capitalism that according to both Banerjee and Brighu are the pathologies of Delhi's urban culture (Banerjee 2004, 24).

Brighu's ability to uphold the original *flâneur's* traits of disengagement, dispassion, and disinterestedness from Delhi's capitalist culture is due to his imagined affiliation with Ibn Batuta a Sufi Muslim scholar who like Baudelaire's artiste-*flâneur* sought to understand and analyze human sensibilities as he traveled through South and South-East Asia in the fourteenth century. Brighu's haplessness due to his estrangement from the city that demands economic productivity and affiliation with state-favored neoliberal rationalities from its citizens can be witnessed in the characters Digital Dutta and Dr. DVD Murthy who frequent Rangoonwalla's book shop. In different ways both these characters are overwhelmed by the city's oppressive, over-enterprising nature instead of being fascinated by it. Both Dutta and Murthy are portrayed as victims of the neoliberal regime of governance whose primary goal has shifted from the biopolitical endeavor to administer and optimize the population to "incit[ing], reinforce[ing], monitor[ing], optimis[ing] and organis[ing] forces under it" in

---

[5] Neoliberalism is a configuration of discursive and material practices globalizing extreme individualism in order to transform the world into a market.

Figure 7.5 Sarnath Banerjee, *Corridor*

order to integrate the population into neoliberal "systems of efficient and economic controls" thus producing entrepreneurial and strategizing subjects (Foucault 1978, 139). Both Dutta, a software engineer by profession, and Dr. Murthy, a forensic and autopsy specialist, are forced to subjectify themselves as entrepreneurial/enterprising subjects or the *homo-oeconomicus* in order to withstand a dystopic neoliberal life loaded with uncertainty and risk and deprived of social protections. However, while Dr. Murthy is able to seek respite from the stench of the dead that symbolize a necropolitical "living-dead" situation for him through "poisons, reggae and John Keats" (31) and later discovers a solution to his problem in the form of a Marks & Spencer perfume (109) thus ultimately submerging himself within the realm of urban consumption, Dutta is temporarily able to escape from the urban neoliberal order in his dreams where his socialist idol, Marx, tells him "to go to the villages where his programming skills can be optimally utilized in land distribution" (110). Unlike Brighu and Rangoonwala both Dutta (in his dreams) and Murthy (in his poetry) are lost in the labyrinth of their own mind that render both incapable of interacting with and apprehending the bustling city. Like Ghosh who in *Delhi Calm* represents India's rural areas as spaces of liberation that "reside beyond the oppressive censorship infrastructure of the capital" (Dominic 2018, 420) where VP and his resistance group are able to gather momentum through politicized interactions and discussions on the notion of a subcultural protest, Banerjee, too, gives import to the rural space as a medium of man's redemption from the urban dystopia of neoliberal, biopolitical hierarchies and rationalities.

Banerjee not only critiques the oppressive, dystopic effects of neoliberal order but also the state's biopolitical production of homogeneous, dutiful citizenry as the embodiment of the modern state. A case in point is the state-driven "Ideal Boy" poster series by Indian Book Depot introduced in the 1980s that aimed to cultivate the model child-citizen through repeated invocation of personal and domestic hygiene in "an attempt to constitute a 'hygienic' public sphere full of 'appropriately' domesticated bodies" (Doron 2016, 719). From a biopolitical sense, the regimen of habits and hygiene also implies a technology of control with its calculated management of human populations aimed at achieving the subjugation of bodies and improving the quality of citizenry. The "Ideal Boy" poster campaign also points toward a causal connection between cleanliness and model masculinity. Failure to abide by personal and domestic hygiene within the public and private spheres culminated in emasculation and crisis in the construction and performance of masculinities. Banerjee, like Ghosh, captures the state's biopolitical governance that aims to discard those unable to meet the standards of masculine virility and hygiene through the character of Shintu in *Corridor*. Unlike *flâneurs* Brighu and Rangoonwalla, Shintu ambles through the streets of Delhi in his quest for an antidote to his sexual dysfunction that has emasculated him. A victim of neoliberal capitalism, Shintu is shown to engage in the urban practice of consumption through relentless shopping—from consuming "sande ka tel," "a pale yellow extract from the bile of lizards" to the book-defining ways of inducing one's masculine virility at Rangoonwalla's shop. Banerjee captures Shintu's symbolic consumption of antidotes through his life-size sketch of the Indian virile man in a "langot" who is a product of "good habits" and hygiene which Banerjee exemplifies as shown in Figure 7.6 through his visual reference of the Ideal Boy poster.

Through Shintu's emasculation, Banerjee not only critiques and contests the image of the ideal masculinity that is constantly invoked through campaigns and discourses within the public sphere, but also questions the postcolonial foundations of the metropolis that is caught between the brahmanical hegemony of the past and excesses

Figure 7.6 Sarnath Banerjee, *Corridor*

of neoliberal consumption and globalization of the present. At the end, even though all the characters in *Corridor* are able to transcend their existential crisis by disconnecting themselves from the city's capitalist, consumption-centric nature in their own limited ways, the question still remains whether the possibility of an urban alternative can help overcome the urban malaise of class hierarchies and the oppressive order of neoliberal governance that engages in segregationist developments.

Conclusion

According to Nayar, the Indian urban space as portrayed in graphic narratives are often spaces of traumatic pasts and uncertain presents, of "alternative desires, doubling, of secrets and secrecy and of violent undercurrents" (2016, 50). Nayar's definition holds true for India's capital city Delhi, a setting used by both Banerjee and Ghosh in their narratives: A city full of paradoxes, one that continues to hold to memory remnants of colonial knowledge whilst restructuring the cityscape according to the tenets of neoliberal capitalism. Whilst the inherited legacies of caste, race, religion, and nation from the colonial encounter continue to shape the sociopolitical fabric of the city, institutional and cultural hierarchies, neoliberalism's draconian policies have further deepened inequalities undermining those forces and public-sphere institutions that are designed to provide a modicum of protection for workers, the poor, diseased, and vulnerable section of the population. The complex systems of division and segregation and discriminatory infrastructural development are further deepened by governmentality that combines biopolitical and necropolitical logics to establish social, political, and physical borders that classify and stratify populations using symbolic and material markers such as nationality, gender, ethnicity, race, sexuality, social class, and/or disability. Living within the city's unevenly developed and increasingly segregated infrastructural space, what happens to those sections of the population who do not fit the "look" of the modern city? Through their exploration of biopolitical and necropolitical techniques of governmentality during the Emergency years in *Delhi Calm* and in the age of neoliberal consumption in contemporary Delhi in *Corridor*, both Ghosh and Banerjee portray how spaces of desire transform into dystopic spaces of vulnerability for the urban youth and *flâneurs* of Delhi. Even as the likes of VP and Parvez in *Delhi Calm* and Brighu and Rangoonwalla in *Corridor* attempt to resist the segregationist developments, biopolitical hierarchies, and class divides by conceiving alternative models of urban habitation and socialization within the dilapidated side streets and underdeveloped alleyways, which in turn undercut the state's planned infrastructural edifices, such attempts at reclaiming their "right to the city" are often limited. By capturing this urban dystopia through visual and textual techniques, both Ghosh and Banerjee aim to generate a critical literacy about the discriminatory reality of urban landscapes in their attempt to help urban readers realize the need for progressive and participatory forms of democratic politics and social activism as a way out of state hegemony and neoliberal rationalities.

References

Agamben, G. 2005. *State of Exception*, translated by Kevin Attell. Chicago: The University of Chicago Press.

Agamben, G. 2013. "Introduction to Homo Sacer: Sovereign Power and Bare Life." In Campbell, Timothy and Sitze, Adam eds. *Biopolitics: A Reader*. Durham, NC: Duke University Press, 134–44.

Banerjee, S. 2004. *Corridor*. London: Penguin Books.
Chute, H.L. 2016. "Histories of visual witness." *Disaster Drawn Visual Witness, Comics, and Documentary Form*. Cambridge, MA/London: Harvard University Press, 39–68.
Dominic, D. 2018. "Urban Comix: Subcultures, Infrastructures and 'the Right to the City' in Delhi". *Journal of Postcolonial Writing*, 54 (3), 411–30.
Doron, A. 2016. "Unclean, Unseen: Social Media, Civic Action and Urban Hygiene in India." *South Asia: Journal of South Asian Studies*, 39(4): 715–39.
Dunst, A. 2019. "Graphic Novels Are Comic Books, But Gentrified." *Jacobin*, 31 December. https://jacobinmag.com/2019/12/graphic-novels-comic-books-gentrification (accessed July 30, 2020).
Ferguson, P. 1994. "The *flâneur* on and off the streets of Paris." In Tester, Keith, ed. *The Flaneur*. London/New York: Routledge, 22–42.
Foucault, M. 1978. *The History of Sexuality*. New York: Pantheon Books.
Foucault, M. 2003. *Society Must be Defended: Lectures at the Collège de France, 1975–76*, translated by D. Macey. New York: Picador.
Foucault, M. 2013. "Society Must Be Defended," Lecture at the Collège de France, March 17, 1976." In Campbell, Timothy, and Sitze, Adam, eds. *Biopolitics: A Reader*. London/Durham, NC: Duke University Press, 61–81.
Ghosh, V. 2010. *Delhi Calm*. New Delhi: HarperCollins Publishers.
Harvey, D. 1973. "Introduction." *Social Justice and the City*. Oxford: Blackwell Publishers, 9–22.
Harvey, D. 2012. "Reclaiming the City for Anti-Capitalist Struggle." *Rebel Cities: From the Right to the City to the Urban Revolution*. London/New York: Verso, 115–54.
Holmberg, R. 2013. "Inverted Calm: An Interview with Vishwajyoti Ghosh." *The Comics Journal*, 23 October. http://www.tcj.com/inverted-calm-an-interview-with-vishwajyoti-ghosh/ (accessed April 9, 2020).
Mbembe, A. 2003. "Necropolitics." *Public Culture*, 15(1): 11–40.
Mbembe, A. 2019. *Necropolitics*. Durham, NC: Duke University Press.
Morton, S. 2013. *States of Emergency: Colonialism, Literature and Law*. Liverpool: Liverpool University Press, 1–35.
Nayar, P.K. 2016. "Introduction: The Graphic Turn in Indian Writing in English." *The Indian Graphic Novel: Nation, History and Critique*. London/New York: Routledge, 3–13.
Prakash, G. 2019. "A Fine Balance." *Emergency Chronicles: Indira Gandhi and Democracy's Turning Point*. Princeton, NJ/Oxford: Princeton University Press, 38–74.
Sandten, C. 2011. "Intermedial Fictions of the 'New Metropolis': Calcutta, Delhi and Cairo in the Graphic Novels of Sarnath Banerjee and G. Willow Wilson." *Journal of Postcolonial Writing*, 47 (5): 510–22.
Sarma, I. 2017. "Negotiations of Home and Belonging in the Indian Graphic Novels Corridor by Sarnath Banerjee and Kari by Amruta Patil." *South Asia Multidisciplinary Academic Journal*. http://journals.openedition.org/samaj/4384.
Syposz, J. 2016. "Exploring the Potential for Historical Graphic Narratives to Challenge Hegemony and Empower the Afflicted: Subaltern Affliction in Maus and Delhi Calm." *Porrridge Magazine*, July 20. https://porridgemagazine.com/2016/07/20/exploring-the-potential-for-historical-graphic-narratives-to-challenge-hegemony-and-empower-the-afflicted-subaltern-affliction-in-maus-and-delhi-calm-jessica-syposz/ (accessed 17 January, 2022).

Urry, J. 1995. *Consuming Places*. London: Routledge.
Varughese, E.D. 2018. "Publishing Indian Graphic Narratives Post Millenium." *Visuality and Identity in Post-millenial Indian Graphic Narratives*. London: Palgrave Macmillan, 1–13.
Ziarek, E.P. 2008. "Bare Life on Strike: Notes on the Biopolitics of Race and Gender." *South Atlantic Quarterly*, 107 (1): 90.

8

Opening Up a World and the Temporal–Normative Dimension: Keum Suk Gendry-Kim's *Grass* as World Literature

Jin Lee

Keum Suk Gendry-Kim's graphic narrative *Grass* portrays the true story of Ok-sun Lee, a Korean "comfort woman," a victim of Japanese military sexual slavery. Ok-sun was kidnapped and forced to service Japanese soldiers during World War II. Although the term "comfort women" problematically privileges the Japanese imperialist perspective, Gendry-Kim decides to use it for her book. Her rationale for choosing the term—it's commonly used within Korea—reflects the victims' subalternity even in her home country. I use the word "subaltern" for Ok-sun to highlight how comfort women like her have been marginalized by their class, nationality, and gender. The feudal system in Korea under Japanese occupation led Ok-sun's poor parents to send her out for adoption, which eventually contributed to Ok-sun's kidnapping and subsequent sex-slavery.

By portraying Ok-sun's victimhood and her activism, *Grass* opens up a new world for comfort women like Ok-sun whose world was destroyed by Japanese colonialism. This "new world" counters Japanese neocolonial discourses that repress histories of comfort women. To tell Ok-sun's story, Gendry-Kim uses the black and white images of "grass" and other kinds of vegetation.[1] Specifically, the figures of "grass," which includes various kinds of vegetation in the Korean language, suggest the temporal dimension of Ok-sun's world: both its brevity and longevity. On the one hand, the vegetation reflects the repercussions of Japan's colonial temporality that destroy Ok-sun's pre-slavery world. On the other, at the end of the narrative, the lush vegetation in Yanji, China highlights nature's vitality, an analogy of Ok-sun's persistence in that the vegetation outlived the Japanese military buildings demolished nearby. This vitality of the vegetation refers, in Pheng Cheah's terms, to "inhuman temporalization as a force of worlding" (2016, 240) that can open up a world against Japan's (neo)colonial "temporality" that tries to erase the comfort women's stories.

---

[1] While "grass" is an inclusive term in Korean, it does not include trees. Thus, to discuss Gendry-Kim's unique figures of trees, as well as "grass," I will use the word, "vegetation," in this essay to collectively refer to grass, trees, and other kinds of plants. At times, I will also use "grass" to include vegetation other than grass to relate its meaning to the title or the theme of the graphic narrative.

Unlike the dominant view of the world as a space of global circulation, Pheng Cheah's view emphasizes the need to consider a temporal-normative dimension of "worldhood." Drawing on Goethe's *Weltliteratur*, Cheah claims that the theories of World Literature including those of David Damrosch, Franco Moretti, and Pascale Casanova emphasize "Goethe's use of metaphors of mercantile activity and commercial exchange" (2014, 317–18), so much so that they overlook the normative dimension of World Literature. Yet, for Goethe, "the world as a normative phenomenon" is "a higher intellectual community concerned with 'the truth and progress of humanity'" (2014, 318).[2] In this vein, the ideal of World Literature is to show universal humanity and bring about "mutual understanding and tolerance among cultures and nations" (2014, 318). Cheah highlights the world as a temporal category, not just a spatial one, which most World Literature theories are predicated upon, so that he could critique the modern capitalist world-system. Cheah's conceptualization of the world in temporal terms theorizes the role of World Literature as "an active power" in the (re)making of the world, in contrast to the existing scholarship's reactive view of World Literature as shaped by social forces (2016, 2, 18).

In terms of the temporal-normative dimension of World Literature, Cheah focuses on four criteria that are fruitful to discuss *Grass* as World Literature. First, he suggests literature "must take the existing world created by globalization as one of its main themes in order to cognitively map (in Fredric Jameson's sense) how a given society is situated in the world-system" (2016, 210). Second, he addresses "activist literature" which portrays a "world being destroyed by globalization" and the relations between national collectivity and disadvantaged minority groups affected by "various global flows" (2016, 210). Third, he points out the need to "reinvent the dynamic aspect of worldhood in Goethe, Hegel, and Marx without its teleology" (2016, 210). Fourth, he claims that "World Literature must also exemplify the process of worlding" (2016, 210).

Grass engages with these criteria both implicitly and explicitly. Gendry-Kim intentionally contextualizes Ok-sun's experiences against the backdrop of Japanese colonial efforts to restructure the world-system to become "the core country" and peripheralize other countries, including Korea and China. When narrating how Ok-sun faints on the street because of malnutrition, Gendry-Kim depicts her father saying, "The landlords may have taken all our crops, but the Japanese bastards are way worse" (36). During the Japanese occupation in the early twentieth century, Koreans were oppressed by the Japanese Empire, in addition to Korean feudalism. Also, the author–artist introduces Japan's imperial invasion into China between the pages portraying Ok-sun's failed attempt to steal persimmons from a neighbor's tree. She further limns Ok-sun's world being destroyed by Japan's colonization, which caused her forced migration to China, a ramification of a "global flow." Near the end of the graphic narrative, she shows how South Korea's national collectivity, "in cooperation

---

[2] Cheah quotes Goethe, "Aus dem Faszikel zu Carlyles *Leben Schillers*," in *Sämtliche Werke*, I. Abteilung, vol. 22.

with" Japan's neocolonial effort "disadvantages" comfort women like Ok-sun.[3] Better yet, *Grass* presents the vitality of vegetation as "inhuman temporalization as a force of worlding" that cannot be appropriated by Japan's and Korea's "dislocated" nationalism (2016, 240, and 210).

Grass foregrounds the inhuman temporalization by connecting Ok-sun's survival to the vitality of vegetation. Cheah addresses the inhuman force that gives time and opens up a world for *postcolonial* narrative fiction's participation in "worlding" processes (2016, 213). He discusses how the novel "gestures toward inhuman temporalization as a force of worlding" (2016, 240). Cheah highlights the persistence of time, which points to "what holds the world together" which is "the force that gives time" (2016, 245). He states, "this force is inhuman, escapes calculation, and cannot be appropriated by teleological time" (2016, 245). While it is unclear whether Ok-sun's activism to bring more awareness to the unresolved comfort-women issue between Korea and Japan will be successful, the vitality of vegetation highlights that the inhuman force that sustains and gives time to the vegetation can also open up a new world for people like Ok-sun. Although *Grass* does not mention it explicitly, South Korea made an agreement with Japan in 2015 over the comfort women issue, as well as in 1965 over colonial issues because the former recognized the latter as an inevitable partner with which to cooperate for their politico-economic wellbeing under the current world-system. Such a gesture for détente between South Korea and Japan hints at the former's subordination to global capital although it has played as a relatively more independent agent in the world-system after liberation from Japan. While illuminating South Korea's "postcolonial" state, which implies repression of histories of comfort women, *Grass* points to the inhuman force that gives time and hope that Ok-sun's activism will continue through the publication and dissemination of the graphic narrative.

The graphic narrative continues Ok-sun's activism through Gendry-Kim presenting what Cheah might call World Literature. In *What Is A World?* Cheah explains how "postcolonial narrative fiction... has become World Literature by virtue of its participation in worlding processes" (2016, 213). "Worlding," originally coined by Heidegger, "refers to how a world is held together and given unity by the force of time" (2016, 8).[4] Engaging with what Cheah calls "temporal-normative dimension of world," *Grass* participates in "worlding processes" and becomes World Literature. If we approach world as "a normative temporal category and understand World Literature in a normative sense," then *Grass* can be, as Cheah might put it, "an exemplary case of World Literature in its most robust meaning precisely because it seeks to change the unequal power relations of the existing world" (2020, 91). In addition, *Grass*

---

[3] As aforementioned, the 2015 agreement between South Korea and Japan remains still controversial. While keeping in mind the view that it was the best possible diplomatic achievement for the Korean government, I also acknowledge here that the voice of the subaltern cannot be fully represented or heard. Thus, I use the words "in cooperation with Japan's neocolonial effort" by echoing Ok-sun's words, "How could our government be *in cahoots with the Japanese government*, instead of speaking on our behalf?" (470, emphasis added).

[4] Cheah notes, "Gayatri Spivak introduced the term to postcolonial theory... to describe how European imperialist cultural representations constructed the geography of colonies" (2016, 8). She "drew an analogy between worlding and imperialist cartography" (2016, 8).

presents an alternative model to postcolonial World Literature in that it does not automatically factor in (and center) the West as a significant player in the world system it depicts. Since Edward Said's critical responses to colonial classics (D'haen 2017, 436), postcolonialism has engaged mostly in criticizing Eurocentrism. Even in the field of World Literature, "east-west cross cultural dialogues have been at the root of Weltliteratur [World Literature] debates since coining of the term" (Lopez-Calvo 2018, 16), which is often predicated upon the "rivalry between the Asian and Euro-American world systems vying for literary hegemony" (Lopez-Calvo 2018, 17). In this vein, countering Euro–American (imperial) visions can come across as Western-centric in that it orients the fields to be reactive to them, thereby ironically privileging these very perspectives in their attempts to counter them. However, *Grass* presents different worlding processes from those often found in postcolonial World Literature by "ignoring" the West and positing Asia as a world. By focusing on a text depicting Japan's imperial efforts and their victims during World War II, this essay contributes to "deoccidentalize" postcolonial studies and World Literature, too.[5]

The Comfort Women Controversy

The issue of comfort women remains controversial between Korea and Japan, as the latter does not fully acknowledge the victimhood of comfort women. For instance, "[i]n 2018 Japan officially replaced the terms 'wartime forced laborers' and 'sexual slaves' by 'wartime laborers' and 'women who worked in wartime brothels, including those who did so against their will, to provide sex to Japanese soldiers" (Mandaville 2020, 94). Also, a 2014 *New York Times* opinion essay reports, "Mr. Abe's administration denies that imperial Japan ran a system of human trafficking and coerced prostitution, implying that comfort women were simply camp-following prostitutes" (Kotler 2014). The NYT essay further claims that Japan's reframing of comfort women as "camp-following prostitutes... cast[s] the Japanese people—rather than the comfort women of the Asia-Pacific theater—as the victims of this story" (Kotler 2014).

Even within South Korea, comfort women have been marginalized. First, comfort women were silenced by the patriarchal value system. It is sobering to remember that it was not until 1991, almost half a century after World War II, that a comfort woman spoke up for victims for the first time in South Korea (Kiaer and Yates-Lu 2019, 106). Many comfort women in East Asian countries were not welcomed by their families upon returning home. Instead, they faced ostracism "as premarital chastity was traditionally considered more important even than one's life—choosing to survive the ordeal and come home was considered to be bringing shame on one's family" (Kiaer and Yates-Lu 2019, 106). Thus, as *Grass* reveals, Ok-sun's family members, whom she finally met after fifty-four years of separation, were alienated from her upon learning

---

[5] In a 2020 MLA Conference panel, panelists Robert Tierney, Edyta M. Bojanowska, and Arif Camoglu emphasized that the field of postcolonial studies needs to be "deoccidentalized" in that it centers on global Anglophone areas, which is Western centric, and often excludes other colonial practices and legacies, such as those of Russia, Japan, and Turkey. As a result, the field ignores their imperial histories and status.

that she was a comfort woman. Her question, "what kind of family likes hearing you used to be a comfort woman?" (433), reflects the history of the comfort women not being welcomed by their patriarchal societies after the war. Second, comfort women were not properly compensated when the Japanese government provided the Korean government with $800 million in economic aid and loans for their colonial past in 1965, which was used instead to develop Korean economy. Considering that none of the comfort women spoke up about their victimhood until 1991, it was impossible for them to be compensated in 1965. Furthermore, more recently in 2015, "Japanese Prime Minister Shinzo Abe made an agreement with South Korea to endow [one] billion yen foundation to compensate" the comfort women (Cheung 2019), but this agreement has been criticized for not including the victims' voice. Ok-sun questions, "How can an agreement be made without the consent of the victims? How could our government be in cahoots with the Japanese government, instead of speaking on our behalf?" (470).[6] In 2020, a year after the publication of *Grass*, it was revealed that a Korean NGO, which has supposedly advocated for the comfort women, allegedly embezzled donations made to the victims (Shin and Smith 2020). The NGO encouraged comfort women to participate in fundraising movements, but misappropriated the money intended to aid the comfort women themselves. All in all, such circumstances highlight the subalternity of the comfort women. Yet, near the end of the graphic narrative, Ok-sun attempts in her activism to speak in the midst of and against her subalternity.

Grass as Resistance

"Min Cho [民草]" in Korean is often used to mean people resilient in the face of oppression. They are compared to weeds because of the plants' persistent vitality. In a similar vein, a literary work well-known to Koreans, Kim Suyong's "P'ul" (Grasses), is often interpreted as a "participatory poem" against the oppressive social structure. As Young-Jun Lee (2012) notes, the poem depicts how the grass resists and confronts the wind through its movement of "lie, rise, cry, laugh, and lie" while the laugh signifies "a hopeful future for the Korean people" (116). In particular, "the school of 'literature of the people' (*minjung munhak*) read 'grasses' [in the poem] as signifying the 'oppressed people'" (101).[7] Gendry-Kim seems to use this interpretation when she connects the

---

[6] Some view the 2015 agreement as the best the Korean government could achieve for the comfort women, especially when many of them had already passed away and the surviving ones could be financially compensated while they were still alive. Others argue that the agreement is unacceptable because it does not reflect the victims' voice. They also note that Japan neither fully accepts the comfort women's victimhood by denying their forced relocation and sexual slavery, nor acknowledges their war crime during World War II in their history textbooks.

[7] Lee notes the scholarly discussions on the meaning of "grasses" and introduces the opposing view too: "[t]he controversy invariably centers on the metaphorical meaning of the title, 'Grasses.' In fact, the reading of this word was employed as a litmus test for classifying literary positions in the 1970s and 1980s: the school of 'literature of the people' (*minjung munhak*) read 'grasses' as signifying the 'oppressed people,' whereas modernist critics like Kim Hyŏn, Hwang Tonggyu, and Chŏng Kwari read it simply as a representation of the natural world" (Lee 2012, 101). Many Korean people remember the poem's "grasses" as "oppressed people" because, as Jung-seop Shin points out, Korean high-school literature textbook privileges and only introduces such interpretation.

vitality of "grass" to Ok-sun's survival and her activism. Near the end of the graphic narrative, she presents Ok-sun as an activist, who with other comfort women fights against Japanese (neo)colonialism. The graphic narrative introduces the 2015 agreement over the unresolved issue of comfort women between South Korea and Japan. After portraying Ok-sun's weekly protest "in front of the Japanese embassy in Seoul, demanding justice from Japan for its past treatment of comfort women" (470), Gendry-Kim compares Ok-sun's activism to grass resisting external oppressive forces: "[g]rass springs up again, though knocked down by the wind, trampled and crushed under foot. Maybe it will brush against our legs and whisper a shy greeting" (475). The graphic narrative "is an effort by the author to present comfort women not just as victims, but as human beings, whose *tenacity* to not just survive, but live, is like *grass*, which stands up again no matter how many times you step on it" (Kiaer and Yates-Lu 2019, 106, emphasis added).

Ok-sun's World and Unworlding

As the story unfolds, Ok-sun turns out to be triply marginalized by feudalism and Japanese colonialism, in addition to patriarchy. Because of their landlords and the Japanese colonizers taking away their crops, her family in Korea had hardly anything to eat although her parents worked hard as peasants. Her father took additional jobs to support the family, which only made things worse: he got injured and her mother became the sole provider. Although her mother "did anything and everything" (45), they often ate watery porridge made of roots (and bean sprouts if lucky), and on other days, they did not eat at all. Because they were too poor to afford education for a girl, her parents would only send their sons to school. Ok-sun wanted to go to school so much that she agreed to be adopted by a stranger who promised to provide an education for her. Her parents finally decided to send her to this stranger for adoption, who owned a Udon shop, thinking that, at the very least, she would not starve. However, Ok-sun's dream of going to school was not only stunted, but also completely destroyed. The Udon shop owner and his wife never sent her to school, but only enslaved her at the shop. Ok-sun demanded that the owner send her home, but he sold her to a tavern owner instead. One day, while she was back from an errand for the tavern owner, she was kidnapped and sold at the comfort stations in Yanji, China. She was only fifteen.

Mapping Ok-sun's forced relocation from Busan, Korea to Yanji, China, *Grass* shows Japan's horrific cartography of colonizing the comfort women's bodies. The Japanese soldiers inscribed an identity of no more than "a public toilet" on the comfort women's bodies (259).[8] Furthermore, their inhumane treatment led the women to see themselves as animals (200). For the Japanese soldiers, the comfort women were available whenever and however they wanted. These women were not only unpaid (the

---

[8] Cf. Cheah notes, "Imperialism inscribed worlds that were inhabited prior to European conquest as the uninhabited space of *terra nullius*" (2016, 8). Ok-sun states, "A comfort station is just like a public toilet. That's what the general *said*" (259, emphasis added).

Figure 8.1 One of the identical bleed pages depicting Ok-sun's hometown in a realistic style (80).

Japanese comfort station managers intercepted their pay), but also forced to constantly service the Japanese soldiers, even during menstruation or pregnancy. According to Ok-sun's story, during the weekends, each comfort woman received thirty to forty soldiers per night. To the managers, the comfort women's bodies were just a means to a profit. When Ok-sun got venereal disease without improvement for about two months, the Japanese managers became "desperate," as they were unable to capitalize on Ok-sun's body, so they had her "expose [her] genitals to the vapor" of boiling mercury to heal her (263). The treatment worked, but caused her infertility. For the Japanese, the colonized women's bodies were, as the word "*comfort* women" suggests, merely a means to cope with the war's horror to keep up their colonial expansion.

To represent Ok-sun's lost world before she became a comfort woman, Gendry-Kim draws vegetation in a dreamy, yet more realistic and detailed style, as seen in Figure 8.1, in contrast to the abstract and cartoonish one in preceding pages. Following the agreement of Ok-sun to be adopted, Gendry-Kim draws two, almost identical "bleed" pages of Ok-sun's hometown with trees and mountains. In a "bleed" page, "a panel runs off the edge of the page" and "[t]ime is no longer contained by the familiar icon of the *closed panel*, but instead *hemorrhages* and escapes into *timeless space*" (McCloud 1993, 103, emphasis in original). In these bleed pages, snow is covering the village, and the large snowflakes in the dark night make it beautiful and dreamy. These pages are drawn in a style different from the cartoonish one used for previous pages. This scene's dreaminess is heightened with Ok-sun's words in white letters in the middle of the dark sky without speech balloons or captions, like a voiceover, a style used throughout the graphic narrative to signal that the scene is Ok-sun's flashback: "I shouldn't have said yes. I had no idea I wouldn't be coming back. Never in my wildest dreams did I think I'd be saying goodbye forever" (80–1). Literally, there is no boundary between Ok-sun's words from the present time and space, and the time and space of Ok-sun's childhood represented in the bleed pages. While the "voiceover" indicates the time difference between Ok-sun's decision to leave her family and her regret in hindsight, the beautiful landscape signifies Ok-sun's relatively "safe" world prior to adoption. After this scene, we hardly find landscapes like this peaceful one. Considering how bleed pages can communicate timelessness, the beautiful landscape in Figure 8.1 can mean Ok-sun's lost world that only exists in her memory. This *timeless space* represents the hometown that she could revisit only in her mind over and over again.

The vegetation in Figure 8.1 contrasts with the trees drawn in a more abstract style, especially when they appear ominous later in the same chapter, foreshadowing Ok-sun's unfortunate future. In contrast to the peaceful scenery in Figure 8.1, a tree begins to change into a threatening form. This tree appears in the panels about the night before Ok-sun leaves for her new home. In the panels, while Gendry-Kim places Ok-sun's words—"I couldn't sleep that night. I was leaving in the morning. I didn't have to go hungry anymore" (86)—without speech balloons or captions to indicate that this is Ok-sun's reflection, she presents only parts of a tree. They are smudged and blackened, including a big thorn-looking twig that is eerily sharp, foreshadowing the horrific future waiting for Ok-sun. Two pages later, Gendry-Kim draws a big, black tree with white background in another pair of bleed pages. This black tree almost covers the two pages in the foreground while mountains and Ok-sun's village are small in the background. This black tree's form changes as some of its twigs are smudged with black ink. The following bleed pages have more abstract forms of trees. In white letters without a speech balloon or a caption on the black background (like a voiceover), her words state, "I'd been so happy at the thought of attending school, but when reality sank in, that I was going to a place where I didn't know a single soul, I started to feel scared" (91). The smudged background with trees in ominous forms foretells that Ok-sun's adoption was not an auspicious occasion. She will lose this relatively "safe" world of her home forever.

Figure 8.2 Ok-sun on her errand for the madam of the tavern is about to meet her abductors (160).

Figure 8.3 Being Abducted (164).

Figure 8.4 Reflection in old age (167).

By blurring the boundaries between vegetation and the abductors, Gendry-Kim shows how Ok-sun's pre-abduction-world is destroyed by Japanese colonial temporality. In the first two panels, Ok-sun's soon-to-be-lost world is represented in the form of harmless vegetation while the abductors in the form of black figures suggest Japanese colonial temporality invading Ok-sun's world. This happened while she was returning from an errand for the tavern, to which the Udon shop owners sold her. Right before Ok-sun is kidnapped, the vegetation in the landscape is turning into more abstract, mysterious black figures. At first, it is unclear whether the black figures are the shade of

Keum Suk Gendry-Kim's Grass 177

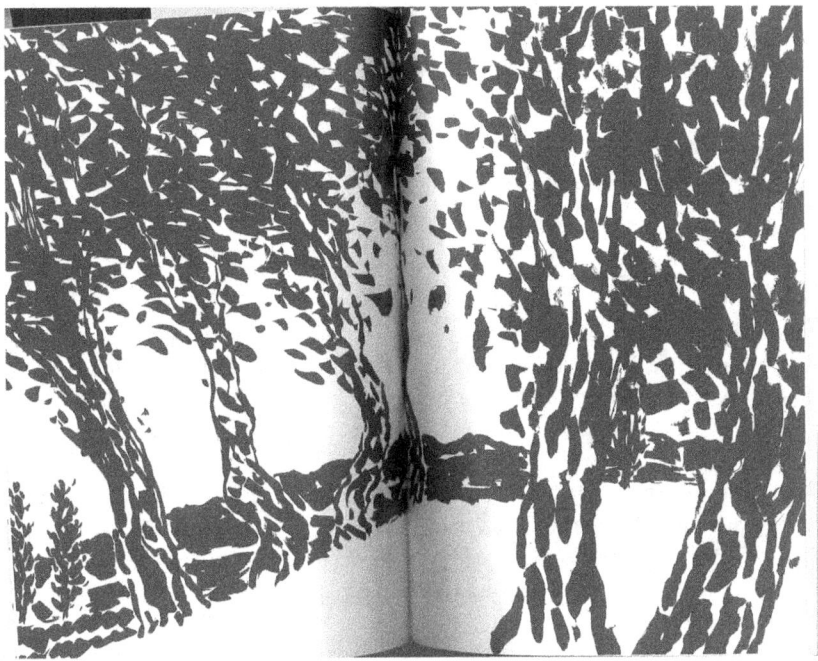

Figure 8.5 The bleed pages after Ok-sun's abduction (166–7).

the vegetation or that of the abductors until the next page, where the abductors appear in more human-like forms, colored in black, and the vegetation is no longer visible. Portrayed like part of the trees, or overlaying their shade, Japan's colonial temporality in the forms of the abductors overshadows and deceitfully invades Ok-sun's world. Here, Gendry-Kim not only overlays multiple worlds, but also shows how Ok-sun's world is replaced, and destroyed by another (Japanese colonial temporality). Thus, when the men are taking her away, the trees seem shattered as depicted with rough strokes in Figure 8.5. The "shattered" trees reflect Ok-sun's world, destroyed by Japan's colonial temporality, as well as foreshadow Ok-sun's devastated future.

It is important that vegetation does not always seem harmless even in Ok-sun's world prior to her adoption. Shortly after she fainted on the street because of her extreme hunger, she attempted to pick persimmons from a neighbor's tree. However, she fell from the tree without even a bite. Gendry-Kim draws this scene in rough strokes, contrasting the craggy, spiraling tree and its jutting branches to the soft round face of the girl to induce foreboding, quickly realized when Ok-sun falls out of the tree. In fact, the story of the persimmon tree shows Ok-sun's world was not really "pre-colonial," free from Japan's colonial force, which had already permeated through the fabric of the society. Between the pages on the story of the persimmon tree, Gendry-Kim briefly inserts the history—the Second Sino-Japanese War and the Nanjing Massacre: Japan took over Chinese cities and massacred about 300,000 people in Nanjing. Thus, she makes the connection between the persimmon tree and Japan's colonial history, meaning Japan's colonial history contributed to Ok-sun's poverty, which prompted her to climb the tree. This attempt foreshadows and parallels Ok-sun's later attempt to acquire education through adoption, which only puts her into slavery at the Udon shop, the tavern, and the comfort station. These attempts all stem from Japanese colonialist actions.

The Persistence of Time

Gendry-Kim atemporalizes figures of vegetation to open up a new, postcolonial world for Ok-sun where the longevity of the vegetation signifies Ok-sun's resistance against Japanese colonialism. Specifically, the vegetation in the three bleed pages between the chapter page titled, "Busan Udon Shop," and the panels of Ok-sun's current place, blurs the time difference, thereby creating an effect that the vegetation might have endured the entire time—more than half a century—between now and Ok-sun's childhood. This chapter picks up Ok-sun's adoption story from the end of the previous chapter where she leaves her family, and the chapter page shows the fourteen-year-old Ok-sun and the Udon shop. Thus, the vegetation in the following bleed pages can represent her way to a new home, the Udon shop. Like a voiceover, Gendry-Kim places Ok-sun's words without speech balloons or captions: "I was fourteen years old. Sometimes I blamed my Mom. If she had sent me to school, I would have never left" (100–1). With her words in the background, the leaves, trees, and grass portray the landscape she might have seen on her way to the Udon shop. At the same time, the vegetation seems to belong to the current time and space, as the very next page depicts the House of Sharing, where Ok-sun lives with other comfort women at the moment of narration.[9] Because it is uncertain whether it belongs to the past or the present, the vegetation connects the two worlds: Ok-sun's lost world and her current one. By connecting the two worlds, the atemporal vegetation opens up a new world, a liminal time–space that reflects Ok-sun's endurance of or resistance against Japanese colonialism. That is, like Ok-sun, the vegetation might have survived and outlived Japanese colonial temporality, which was terminated in the 1940s. In this vein, the atemporality of the vegetation signifies its longevity; the vegetation represents Ok-sun, whose very survival not only resists but also defies the murderous Japanese colonial temporality.

In addition to memorializing Ok-sun's survival and resistance, figures of atemporal vegetation function to continue Ok-sun's activism by creating a world where Ok-sun fights the Japanese colonial temporality as a persistent witness. In Figure 8.6, when Ok-sun starts telling the story of another comfort woman, Mija, the panel makes transitions from the present to past, from Ok-sun's room in the House of Sharing through landscapes to Mija's childhood stories. The first panel depicts grasses in the

---

[9] Gendry-Kim notes, "The House of Sharing in Gwangju, Gyeonggi Province, is a nursing home for surviving comfort women. Located on the grounds is a memorial hall and museum" (41).

Figure 8.6 Ok-sun tells Mija's story (274).

middle ground, seen through the window of Ok-sun's room. The subsequent panel of a landscape in Figure 8.6 can be a close-up of the scenery outside Ok-sun's room, or the wilderness around the comfort station in Ok-sun's flashback. Transitioning to Mija's hometown, Figure 8.6 blurs the time difference between the panels and thus atemporalizes their vegetation. Meanwhile, the blurring of the time difference signals opening up of a new world, where Ok-sun's witnessing voice takes readers to Mija's childhood, passing through atemporalized landscapes. In these landscapes, the atemporal vegetation once again gestures to a possibility that the vegetation survived

180 Graphic Novels and Comics as World Literature

difficult times like Ok-sun and Mija. Specifically, among the three bleed pages following Figure 8.6, the third bleed page depicts Mija's face as part of the cloud in the sky. This bleed page represents multiple temporalities, thereby blurring the difference between the past and present. If Mija's face points to the present time when Ok-sun tells her friend's story, the landscape may belong to both the past and present: while this landscape seems to be part of Ok-sun's memory and thus belong to the past, Ok-sun's words, "Seo Mija…, " signifies the present time, like a voice-over integrated in the landscape without speech balloons or captions. At the same time, the landscape, especially the vegetation, seems similar to those in the following panels dedicated to Mija's childhood stories. Here, Gendry-Kim blurs the time difference between the bleed pages and the following panels. In so doing, she highlights the vitality and longevity of the vegetation, which is connected to those of Ok-sun's witnessing. In this liminal time–space, both the vegetation and Ok-sun survived the horrific Japanese colonial forces and now witness Mija's victimhood even decades later. Thus, the blurred time

Figure 8.7 Mija gives birth to a girl at the comfort station (292).

Figure 8.8 ... and later a boy (303).

in atemporalized vegetation takes the meaning of Ok-sun's survival to another level: from "outliving" to "witnessing." Or, outlasting witnessing: the witnessing voice in the atemporalized vegetation can mean the persistence of Ok-sun's testimony. In this vein, Ok-sun's perseverance includes her witnessing, as well as surviving Japanese colonialism.

While linking the longevity of the vegetation to the vitality of Ok-sun and her persistent witnessing, figures of vegetation signify the persistence of life. Gendry-Kim achieves this effect by drawing vegetation in the panels for Mija's babies, who survived despite challenging circumstances. When Mija was pregnant for the first time in the comfort station, Mija attempted abortion and her managers mistreated her. As Ok-sun says, "The managers were brutal. They forced her to service soldiers until she was eight months along. Then they made her work in the kitchen until the day she gave birth" (291). Mija tried hard to abort the baby. However, "the baby clung to life" (290). Portraying Mija's giving birth to a girl, Gendry-Kim literally connects the baby's life to vegetation by conflating the bodies of Mija and her baby with grasses (see Figure 8.7). Considering how certain vegetation becomes atemporal and suggests Ok-sun's vitality, the vegetation in Figure 8.7 can also emphasize both its own longevity (as we cannot be sure how long it has lived there) and the baby's survival. Thus, Gendry-Kim relates the vitality of the baby to that of the vegetation: the baby survives because she is like grass that resists and endures hardships. If the author–artist conflates the vegetation and the baby in Figure 8.7 to connect the vitality of the vegetation to that of the baby, she portrays a big, old tree in Figure 8.8 to communicate the survival of another baby of Mija's as if the tree is a metonym for the baby. After being liberated from the comfort station, Mija was raped by lumberjacks while she lived and worked for them in the mountains. Ok-sun narrates, Mija "couldn't bear the thought of having another kid with no father" (302). In a panel for Mija's delivery, Gendry-Kim places a big tree and Ok-sun's voice without speech balloons or captions: "Mija eonni rolled down a hill and did all sorts of things to lose the baby, but nothing worked. In the end, she had a boy" (303; see Figure 8.8). Without the baby in the scene, the old, big tree functions to explain the baby's birth despite Mija's constant attempts to abort him. In the following panel, Gendry-Kim portrays a tree with blossoming flowers and puts Ok-sun's voice in the background, "That boy grew up and got married" (304). Once again, the vitality of the tree is connected to that of the boy who not only survived but also has grown to start his own family. Further, by portraying the vitality of the vegetation to narrate the story of survival of Mija's babies, Gendry-Kim illustrates the persistence of life: Mija's babies miraculously survived and her son continues the family line through his marriage.

The persistence of life portrayed in the atemporal vegetation ultimately points us to an inhuman force, external to the time–space of the human experience, that gives time and enables the persistence of time. Whereas the atemporal vegetation in the aforementioned scenes appears as backdrops of the stories Ok-sun tells—Ok-sun's current place, the comfort station, or the places where Mija gave birth—the vegetation in Figure 8.9 seems to re-emerge "here and now" from Ok-sun's past as she flashes back to her memories of her family. Up until this point, Gendry-Kim portrays the tragedies of Ok-sun's story, including the adoption and the series of human trafficking, rapes and abuses, poverty and homelessness, and failed marriages and infertility. Finally, readers might expect some sort of happy ending when learning about Ok-sun's return to South Korea to be back with her family over a half a century later, but her family is eventually alienated from her. First, they deny her victimhood: they do not believe that her mother sent her for adoption. Even worse, "they wanted nothing to do with [her]" (436) upon learning that she was a comfort woman. Then, the grass starts to fill up the panels in Figure 8.9 when her readers witness Ok-sun's never-ending traumatic stories and might wonder whether she could ever cope with the loss of her family, who seem to be the last thing she could hold onto. The grass shows up while Ok-sun tells her story in the first panel, but in the third it covers the entire panel even without Ok-sun. On the one hand, this "invasion" of the grass represents her past overwhelming, overshadowing her present—her family rejects her because of what happened to her. That is, her past

Figure 8.9 Ok-sun tells her story after she came to South Korea (434).

determines her present, so much so that the grass from her past dominates the panel about her current situation in Korea. On the other hand, considering how the atemporal vegetation means the vitality and persistence of Ok-sun in Figures 8.6, 8.7 and 8.8, the atemporal vegetation in Figure 8.9 communicates what sustains her in the midst of the devastating circumstances. That is, the atemporal vegetation appears when Ok-sun might need it because she has nothing to rely on or hope for. Here, the vegetation gestures to something deeper than the vitality and persistence of Ok-sun. While the contrast between light and shade in Figure 8.9 shows that Ok-sun's heart is broken so much so that she almost "fades out," the vegetation that might have witnessed and endured the difficult times with her *stands in* to testify on Ok-sun's behalf when even her family does not believe her words. Significantly, it is the vegetation's persistence of life that speaks a volume. Its testimony is powerful because the persistence of life in the vegetation points us to the persistence of time, or the inhuman force that gives time, that sustains the vitality of the vegetation.

The themes of the persistence of life, persistent witnessing, and the persistence of time becomes amalgamated through the vegetation symbolism at the end of *Grass*. Gendry-Kim uses vegetation to connect the persistence of life to the persistence of time in the last chapter. Gendry-Kim visits Yanji in China where Ok-sun might have serviced the Japanese soldiers. While showing the figure of vegetation flourishing there, she narrates how the Japanese army's buildings (will) have disappeared. As she notes, "[a Japanese military office building] was going to be pulled down to make room for a new building. Construction was set to begin soon" (465). To show a place where "the [comfort] women used to bathe" (465), Gendry-Kim uses two bleed pages in which vegetation—flowers and leaves—dominates the place, covering the wall and the land. These pages show not only how long the place has been abandoned, but also how long the vegetation has survived vis-à-vis the demolition of the buildings, i.e. the end of the Japanese colonial temporality. Here, Gendry-Kim contrasts the impermanence of the Japanese Empire with the persistence of life shown in the vegetation. After this scene of the lush vegetation, she places panels of a winter tree, Gendry-Kim on the phone discussing her manuscript for *Grass*, and Ok-sun's protest against the 2015 agreement between Japan and South Korea. Thus, she associates the vitality of the lush vegetation with that of the winter tree, which may seem at first lifeless but will revive again in spring. Then, she relates the persistence of life in the winter tree to the persistent witnessing in Ok-sun's protest, which will continue through *Grass*. Gendry-Kim notes after the scene of Ok-sun's activism, "When this harsh winter passes, a sun-kissed letter will surely come from the south, bearing news of spring. Delicate sprigs are trembling at the end of a long winter. New life is struggling to emerge from within" (472). Readers know by now that the survival of the winter trees means that of Ok-sun, and Gendry-Kim highlights something that undergirds and sustains their lives: if the winter trees with no leaves mean what seems to be dead during the time of the devastating, traumatic events, the fresh green sprouts in the spring signify the persistence of life, given by the inhuman force, which points to a world other than the present time and space, i.e. the persistence of time. As she writes, "The ground that had been slumbering wakes, and the young grass pokes out from between the dead withered leaves. Grass springs up again, though knocked down by the wind, trampled and crushed under foot. Maybe it will brush against your legs and whisper a shy greeting" (475). Gendry-Kim highlights the hope that the inhuman force implies while pointing out the transient and everlasting nature of vegetation: "Hello! The winter is over, and the cold that seemed to last forever is thawing. Spring has finally come" (476). The persistence of life in vegetation is embedded in the very transience of winter itself—the winter does not last forever and spring follows, which gestures to the persistence of time that enables the unending cycle of the seasons. Likewise, Ok-sun's protest may not seem successful now, but Gendry-Kim speaks hope. *Grass* may survive and continue Ok-sun's protest, portraying the persistence of life, the persistence of witnessing, and the persistence of time.

Thus, *Grass* enacts the opening up of a new world and becomes World Literature. The graphic narrative not only *represents* Ok-sun's lost world but also seeks to *(re)make the world* to counter Japan's (neo)colonial temporality that tries to erase the comfort women's stories. For such purposes, Gendry-Kim uses figures of vegetation to communicate Ok-sun's unspeakable, untranslatable wounds that reveal larger repressed histories.[10] Furthermore, these figures ultimately point to the persistence of life, the persistence of witnessing, and the persistence of time found in both Ok-sun and the vegetation. In so doing, *Grass* speaks hope that the graphic narrative will continue Ok-sun's activism and "world" a new world against the unequal, hegemonic socio-politico-economic power relations of the existing world. Thus, *Grass* in Cheah's words "opens up the existing world to politically committed literature that seeks to change the world" (2016, 186).

References

Cheah, Pheng. 2014. "World Against Globe: Toward a Normative Conception of World Literature." *New Literary History*, 45 (3): 303–29.

Cheah, Pheng. 2016. *What Is a World? On Postcolonial Literature as World Literature*. Durham, NC: Duke University Press.

Cheah, Pheng. 2020. "Global Literature, World Literature and Worlding Literature: Some Conceptual Differences." In Stefan Helgesson, Birgit Neumann, and Gabriele Rippl, eds. *Handbook of Anglophone World Literature*. Berlin: De Gruyter, 85–101.

Cheung, Ysabelle. 2019. "Graphic Novel Biography of Korean Wartime Sex Slave of Japanese Army, Grass, Doesn't Pull Its Punches." *South China Morning Post*, October 9. https://www.scmp.com/lifestyle/arts-culture/article/3032118/graphic-novel-biography-korean-wartime-sex-slave-japanese (accessed March 14, 2020).

D'haen, Theo. 2017. "Worlding Comparative Literature: Beyond Postcolonialism." *Canadian Review of Comparative Literature*, 44 (3): 436–48.

Gendry-Kim, Keum Suk. 2019. *Grass*. Tran. Janet Hong. Montreal: Drawn and Quarterly.

Kiaer, Jieun and Yates-Lu, Anna. 2019. *Korean Literature Through the Korean Wave*. London: Routledge.

Kotler, Mindy. 2014. "The Comfort Women and Japan's War on Truth." *The New York Times*, November 14. https://www.nytimes.com/2014/11/15/opinion/comfort-women-and-japans-war-on-truth.html (accessed March 23, 2020).

Lee, Young-Jun. 2012. "Howling Plants and Animals: Kim Suyŏng's Sovereign Language and Rereading 'Grasses.'" *Harvard Journal of Asiatic Studies*, 72 (1): 101–39. *Project MUSE*. https://doi.org/10.1353/jas.2012.0000.

López-Calvo, Ignacio. 2018. "Worlding and Decolonizing the Literary World-system: Asian-Latin American Literature as an Alternative Type of Weltliteratur." In Gesine Müller, Jorge J. Locane, and Benjamin Loy, eds. *Re-mapping World Literature: Writing, Book Markets and Epistemologies between Latin America and the Global South / Escrituras, mercados y epistemologías entre América Latina y el Sur Global*. Berlin, Boston: De Gruyter, 15–32. https://doi.org/10.1515/9783110549577-002.

---

[10] Citing Jean-Luc Nancy's *The Creation of the World of Globalization* (2007), Birgit Neumann argues that "Anglophone World Literature configures a world that 'preserves something untranslatable' (Nuemann 2018, 28), a potentiality that conjures up alternative meanings and repressed histories" (245).

Mandaville, Alison. 2020. "Grass." *World Literature Today*, 91 (1): 93–4.
McCloud, Scott. 1993. *Understanding Comics: The Invisible Art*. New York: HarperCollins Publishers.
Neumann, Birgit. 2018. "Verrnacular Cosmopolitanism in Anglophone World Literatures: Comparative Histories of Literary Worlding." *Arcadia*, 53 (2): 239–57.
Shin, Hyonhee, and Smith, Josh. 2020. "South Korea Charges Former 'Comfort Women' Activist With Fraud, Embezzlement." *U.S. News*, September 14. https://www.usnews.com/news/world/articles/2020-09-14/south-korea-charges-former-comfort-women-activist-with-fraud-embezzlement (accessed December 30, 2020).
Shin, Jung-seop. 2016. "How was Kim Suyong's 'P'ul' disguised as the people?" *Mediapen*, June 2. http://www.mediapen.com/news/view/155053 (accessed December 12, 2021).

9

Between the Saltwater and the Desert: Indigenous Australian Tales from the Margins

Catherine Sly

As early as 1983, in his introduction to Frederik L. Schodt's influential publication *Manga! Manga! The World of Japanese Comics*, the esteemed Japanese mangaka, Osamu Tezuka, wrote:

> My experience convinces me that comics, regardless of what language they are printed in, are an important form of expression that crosses all national and cultural boundaries.
>
> (Schodt 1983, 11)

In the twenty-first century the burgeoning interest in graphic narratives across the globe is testament to the comics medium being apposite for the transmission of stories that traverse national, cultural, and even linguistic borders.

In addition, the recent proliferation of cross-cultural graphic narratives indicates that creators, publishers, readers, and scholars are becoming increasingly aware of the significance of the medium as a forum for expressing voices, viewpoints, and ideas from less-dominant cultures as well as from other socially marginalized groups. Publications such as *Persepolis* (2003) by Marjane Satrapi, *The Arrival* (2006) by Shaun Tan, *Louis Riel* (2006) by Chester Brown, *Pyongyang* (2007) by Guy Delisle, *Aya* (2007) by Marguerite Abouet and Clément Oubrerie, *American Born Chinese* (2008) by Gene Luen Yang, and others in this vein, utilize the *language of comics* to "cue, trigger, and move reader–viewers to engage with complex schemas of race and ethnicity" (Rifas 2010, 20). Such publications, along with lesser-known examples, have a significant role to play in the sphere of texts considered for inclusion in studies on "World Literature."

In this chapter, I wish to examine three graphic novels, which constitute the *Ubby's Underdogs* trilogy, a substantial work by Australia's first published Indigenous graphic novelist, Brenton E. McKenna, a descendent of the Yawuru people of First Nations Australians from the north of Western Australia. McKenna utilizes the codes and conventions of comics to express cultural, intercultural, and cross-cultural interchanges within a Global South community. His books are published by Magabala Books, a publishing house dedicated to works by Aboriginal and Torres Strait Islander authors, artists and illustrators. Released between 2011 and 2019 the *Ubby's Underdogs* tales comprise three sizable episodes: *The Legend of the Phoenix Dragon* (2011); *Heroes Beginnings* (2013); and *Return of the Dragons* (2019) (see Figures 9.1, 9.2, and 9.3).

Figure 9.1 *The Legend of the Phoenix Dragon* (2011)

Figure 9.2 *Heroes Beginnings* (2013)

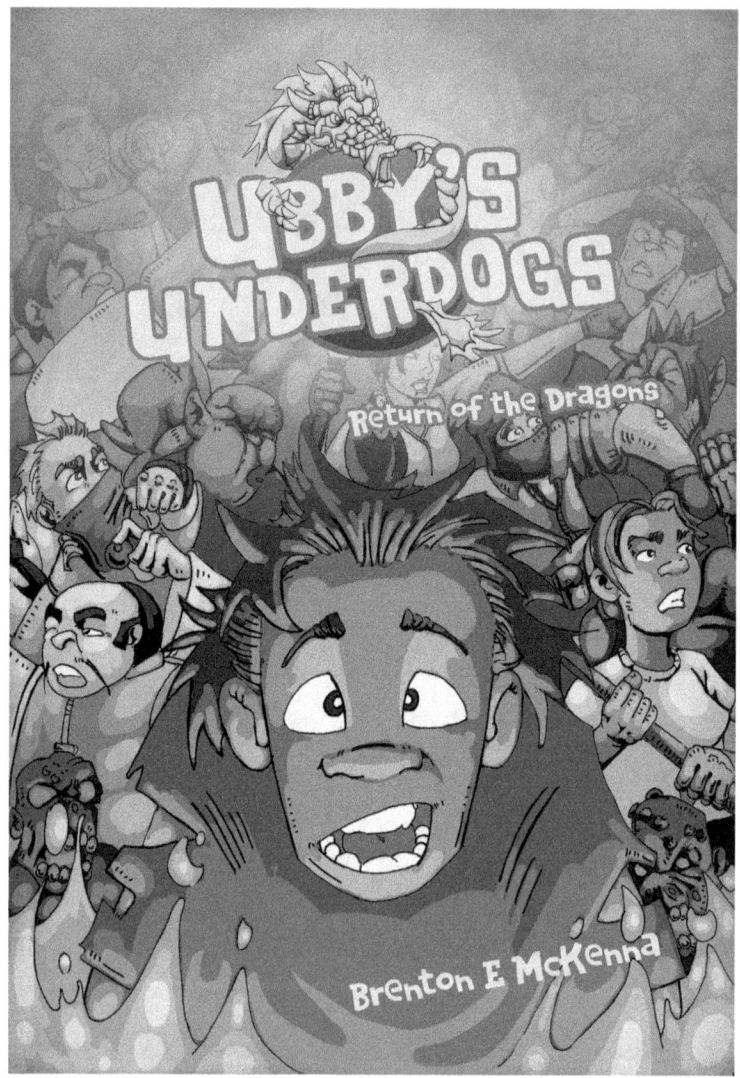

Figure 9.3 *Return of the Dragons* (2019)

Investigating World and Worldliness

Whilst debates on defining "World Literature" and establishing criteria for "selecting" works as examples is ongoing and understandably elusive, I wish to draw upon ideas put forward by Pheng Cheah in his book *What Is a World?* (2016). Cheah offers a "rethinking of World Literature as literature that is an active power in the making of worlds" (2016, 2). He investigates notions of World Literature expressed by earlier theorists and proceeding from ideas originally posed by Johann Wolfgang von Goethe and Erich Auerbach, along with more contemporary theorists, he argues that, in understanding the notion of World Literature

> we should conceive of the world not only as a spatio-geographical entity but also as an ongoing dynamic process of becoming, something that possesses a historical-temporal dimension and hence is continually being made and remade.
> (2016, 42)

This understanding of World Literature, as being mutable and potentially displaying "other worlds to come" (Cheah 2016, 189), enables more recent literary formats, such as graphic novels (and more specifically those from the Global South) to be investigated in terms of their cultural value and contribution to an understanding of "world" in World Literature, and as valued publications that can be appreciated as literature *of* the world.

In conjunction with Cheah's theory, three concepts outlined by Monika Schmitz-Emans in a chapter titled "Graphic Novels as World Literature" (2015) offer guidelines for assessing the potential "worldliness" of particular graphic novels. In brief, Schmitz-Emans' notions include "aesthetic achievements, broad distribution and reception, or multi-faceted stylistic influences from culturally different sources" (2015, 369). Since the *Ubby's Underdogs* trilogy utilizes the graphic-novel format, propositions suggested by Cheah and Schmitz-Emans provide a useful framework for exploring these texts and investigating the extent to which they adopt and portray aspects of "worldliness."

McKenna's trilogy comprises an epic narrative that captures many facets of a multicultural community of "Indigenous people as well as... a cocktail of nationalities from ancient lands and exotic cultures" (McKenna 2011) and their complex struggle for "decolonial freedom." This vibrant saga melds history, legend, fantasy, magic, multiculturalism, and general mayhem in its delivery of a local tale for a global audience. The *Ubby's Underdogs* trilogy embraces a number of genres, including the hero's journey, coming-of-age narrative (bildungsroman), historical adventure, and magical realism. This melding of venturesome genres, with a focus on the fellowship, mutual respect, and collaboration of a group of mixed-race youngsters, generates high appeal for indigenous and non-indigenous readers alike. These tales from the Global South generate "reworlding" in the sense outlined by Cheah (2016) whereby they operate to "subvert European colonial worlding and open other worlds where new collective subjects can emerge and change the world-political stage" (2016).

Indigenous Australia through Graphic Narrative

For over sixty-thousand years Indigenous Australian storytelling has relied on the oral tradition, often supported by art, music, and dance, to convey cultural experiences, knowledge, and beliefs. Narrative delivered in the graphic medium appears to accommodate the traditional performative nature of orality that involves the "telling" and "showing" of stories. As with the storyteller in the oral tradition, a graphic novel as a mode of storytelling relies on the reader to interpret and infer information delivered through dialogue, facial expressions, and gestures, albeit that these are delivered in a printed format.

Apart from their contribution to the "worlding process," the literary merit of the *Ubby's Underdogs* books will be considered in the light of contemporary narratological theory. By utilizing a narratological lens to explore aspects such as the function of the narrator(s), characterization, setting, atmosphere, voice, dialogue, point-of-view, themes, and discourses, I will draw attention to medium-specific codes and conventions of comics. The overall intention is to provide an analysis of the focus texts as literary works, to reveal the sophistication, richness, and depth that can be found in these vibrant multimodal publications, and to assess what they have to offer World Literature.

For centuries, stories from all parts of the world have been told and retold in different ways and through a variety of media. The evolution of narrative theory to its postclassical iteration has paved the way for the analysis of works from diverse media including visual and visu–verbal stories such as graphic novels. The work of scholars such as Monika Fludernik (2009), Jan Alber (2010), Jared Gardner and David Herman (2011), and others have breached the boundaries of classical narratology to embrace the study of narratives presented in media beyond the written word. Theorists such as Thierry Groensteen (2013), Jan Baetens and Hugo Frey (2014), and Kai Mikkonen (2017) have demonstrated that the application of narratology to comics is particularly useful. As Mikkonen argues,

> narratology is... a heuristic tool that helps to arrive at a clearer understanding of narrative literature, art, and communication... it enriches the interpretation and understanding of particular narrative works.
>
> (2017, 9)

With this in mind, the following close reading of McKenna's trilogy aspires to argue for the notable contribution these texts can make as examples of World Literature. Studies of such sequential art narratives are essential because as Charlotta Salmi points out in her chapter titled "The Worldliness of Graphic Narrative," "The graphic narrative as World Literature... offers a route for marginal arts as well as marginal voices to receive recognition" (2018, Kindle location 7431).

Tales in the *Ubby's Underdogs* trilogy focus on the zany activities of a "streetwise" Aboriginal girl, Ubby, and her "rag-tag" gang of "multicultural misfits" (McKenna

2011, 5), known as the Underdogs. The trilogy is situated in the late 1940s in Broome, a town in far northwestern Australia. At this time the remote, marginal township, nestled between the vast Indian Ocean and an equally expansive desert region, is the hub of a lucrative pearling industry and home to a multicultural mix of people. It operates metaphorically as a microcosm of "world" and "worldliness" and the stories acknowledge these notions thematically.

In the first episode, *The Legend of the Phoenix Dragon,* Ubby and the gang befriend Sai Fong, a Chinese girl who, with her uncle, has just disembarked in Broome. This friendship with Sai Fong unleashes unexpected adventures and challenges, steeped in myth, magic, and a maelstrom of frantic activity for the Underdogs. The first volume introduces many significant characters and sets the scene for the two subsequent volumes of a complex adventure tale that melds the inhabitants of a multicultural township, cross-cultural legends, magic and supernatural forces in a quest to repel evil and restore harmony.

The second book, *Heroes Beginnings,* centers on the search for Sai Fong who disappears at the end of the first instalment. Her uncle, Yupman Poe, has great fears for her safety as Sai Fong is not only being sought by her friends but is also being pursued by other groups with sinister intentions. High action adventure is punctuated with backstory cameos, such as that of Ubby's mother, Maryanne, as a young pearl diver.

In *Return of the Dragons,* the disparate factions tracking Sai Fong are drawn into conflict in the Forbidden Zone. Hunters, employed by pearling entrepreneur, Paul Donappleton; the ruthless Uning, from China, who has infiltrated the Black Guard warriors; the Magic Council of Broome; an array of other weird and wonderful beings; and Ubby and the Underdogs are all seeking the whereabouts of the dragon-summoning Chinese girl. The action of these clashing forces conveys a thrilling spectacle that leads to a dramatic conclusion of the epic tale.

While McKenna's colorful publications are entertaining and accessible to a wide readership, serious discourses on race, ethnicity, cultural diversity, and gender are not far below the glossy surface. By adopting this visu–verbal medium, McKenna imparts thought-provoking ideas on the significance of ancestral stories, culture, customs, interpersonal and intercultural relations, individual talents, respect, and cooperation. An understanding and appreciation of difference and diversity emanates from his tales. As with many comics-style narratives, their apparent simplicity belies a complex web of socio-cultural concerns.

A number of ethnic groups exist within the storyworld, some of which are represented in the Gangs of Broome. These gangs encompass a group of Chinese known as the Dragonflys; the Numunburrs or Aboriginal Broome brothers; the Japanese Tanto Cubs; the Balisongs who are of Malay origin; the Thracians of mixed European backgrounds; the belligerent and unscrupulous Pearl Juniors who are sons of the wealthy entrepreneurs of the pearling industry; and the titular Underdogs. Led by Ubby, a courageous Aboriginal girl, the Underdogs include Sel, a large friendly Malay boy; Gabe who is a descendent of Maori warriors; and Fin, a calm Irish boy who has defected from the Pearl Juniors and currently has a penchant to spit at the mere mention of "the British" (2011, 42–3).

Within this remote, multiethnic domain, tensions arising between gangs are usually settled by farcical competitive sporting events such as the game of Gruff (2011, 49–79) and the Dolby Dance (2011, 118–31). These bizarre tournaments involve quirky physical activities often leading to slapstick comedy and scatological humor. However, as the saga unfolds, the courage, tenacity, and cooperation displayed in these challenges is required to repel the sinister external forces that threaten the isolated community.

On returning to the appraisal of these books as examples of World Literature, while being mindful of continuing "struggles over criteria that govern the production and recognition of literary value as cultural capital" (Cheah 2016, 37), I suggest that the *Ubby's Underdogs* books display the characteristics of World Literature detailed by Schmitz-Emans. Thus, the ensuing content of this chapter will pay close attention to these criteria—that is, the aesthetic value of the publications and the way they display a skillful and astute use of the comics medium; their publication and marketing by an independent Indigenous publishing house, with their production in English making them accessible to a wide audience; and their obvious demonstration of being "shaped by multicultural influences, sometimes as culturally hybrid phenomena"(Schmitz-Emans 2015, 368).

Although McKenna adopts the medium of comics for his narratives, he also adapts this mode of expression by including elements of other literary genres. For instance, as a means of framing and contextualizing the tales, each of the *Ubby's Underdogs* episodes incorporates a detailed preamble that includes a *dramatis personae*-style cast of characters, with brief notes and visual images of the characters appearing in the episode. This is followed by a sequential art prologue and a section titled "Setting the scene" in Volume 1, and commensurately with "The story so far…" in Volumes 2 and 3. Apart from providing important background information, the combination of prose, visual images, maps, and character sketches at the beginning of each book display a hybridity of literary forms that reflects the hybridity of the world they present.

The opening pages also exhibit a key narratorial concept, that of an extradiegetic narrator (or storyteller), who furnishes the reader with detailed information about the characters and context before the main story begins. This occurs through both visual and written coding and functions as a *fundamental narrator* (Groensteen 2013, 86), who is not a character in the narrative but an entity that is also responsible for the numerous caption boxes providing ongoing details about time, place, and background throughout the narratives.

In relation to the visual track, recent advancements in technology have made quality color printing an affordable option and the *Ubby's Underdogs* series makes judicious use of this superior printing facility with color schemes that are atmospheric, symbolic, and highly affective. Color or tone convey a wealth of information in the visual track of graphic narratives. For example, the "Prologue" in Volume 1 is depicted in sepia-colored panels with fine, black line images implying that the tale being recounted is from the distant past.

On closer attention the sepia-wash minimalistic backgrounds and sketchy, black fine line characters of the prologue create a dreamlike quality. Irregular-sized panels and ragged-edged frames reinforce the somnolent state of the "viewer," through whose eyes the reader is perceiving the legend. The narrator of this segment, who differs from the previously mentioned "fundamental narrator," tells of the destruction of a peaceful mountain village in China. In the tale, a barbaric tribe, known as the Hede, attack a peaceful mountain village. When the Phoenix Dragon of the North hears the cries of the mountain people, it comes to their rescue, driving the Hede from the village. As a consequence, the brave but still immature, Phoenix Dragon suffers injuries that can only be cured by the mighty Sandpaper Dragon and Warrior Woman in a far-off southern land. However, not until the end of this introductory story does the reader become aware of who is telling the tale and its audience. The final panel on page 23, depicts the face of a Chinese girl emerging from the sepia mist of the visualized legend into the richer colors of the present time (Figure 9.4).

In the immediately ensuing panels it becomes apparent that the girl is Sai Fong and the narrator of this "orally" delivered tale is her uncle, Yupman Poe. The girl is unwell, and she and her uncle are on a ship sailing south to a land where Yupman hopes to find a cure for his niece. Their destination is Broome, and it is here in a marginal space between the saltwater shores of the Indian Ocean and the vast red Great Sandy Desert that the central story begins.

Visually, the story transitions from the sepia color of the prologue into rich, somber colors that create an air of anxiety contrasted with hope as Yupman Poe stands on the bow of a boat gazing toward a distant horizon where an orange sunset meets the indigo sea and the enveloping darkness terminates the connection with his homeland (24–5, see Figure 9.5). Use of a legendary tale as a prologue operates as a "worlding" device in that it links an ancient Chinese village with Indigenous Australians of the northwestern desert region. It creates an enduring historical context uniting two venerable cultures.

The introductory section is followed by a significant color change at the beginning of the central narrative. A rich blue, cloudless tropical sky is juxtaposed with vibrant ochre and ruddy hues of the landscape and the clothing of the inhabitants, who are said to be "as rugged and rough as the red-dirt country that surrounds them" (2011, 4). While the choice of color palettes and interpretation of the symbolic meaning of colors are undoubtedly open to different cultural interpretations, the alteration between monochromic and full-color renderings express shifts between past and present and are employed throughout the graphic novels.

Another visual technique employed throughout is the utilization of minimal backgrounds. Transformations in surroundings, such as, outdoors to indoors; day to night; or land to ocean are depicted through salient color changes. Scenes involving magical powers generally include vivid purple, yellow, orange, and green hues. In the context of these graphic novels, inferring meaning relating to the minimalist backgrounds is open to several possible interpretations. For instance, they may be seen to depict the vastness of the desert setting in which the action takes place; they may suggest the cosmic void beyond the human world; and/or they may recollect the style of indigenous Australian rock art with strong foregrounded images set against monoliths of the natural environment.

Figure 9.4 Final panel on page 23 of *Ubby's Underdogs: The Legend of the Phoenix Dragon*

Sepia or grey tone sequences, employed on occasions, designate legendary tales, historical events, flashbacks, or memories. Black, page and gutter framing, used throughout the novels, operate to intensify the color within the panels and create a theatrical or cinematic impression of the action occurring within the paneled confines of the storyworld. This artistic choice once again engenders a performative element to the saga and evokes the oral tradition.

Figure 9.5 Yupman Poe and his ailing niece on a boat sailing south in *Ubby's Underdogs: The Legend of the Phoenix Dragon*.

If, as Schmitz-Emans postulates, the graphic novel as "World Literature" involves "artists from various countries and different cultures creat[ing] generically similar works of graphic storytelling" that display "an exchange of ideas and strategies of representation" (2015, 370) then the *Ubby's Underdogs* trilogy encapsulates this notion. McKenna draws upon many cross-cultural narrative devices while imbuing them with a uniquely indigenous Australian flavor. For instance, the opening pages of the main narrative in *The Legend of the Phoenix Dragon* images orientate the reader through the

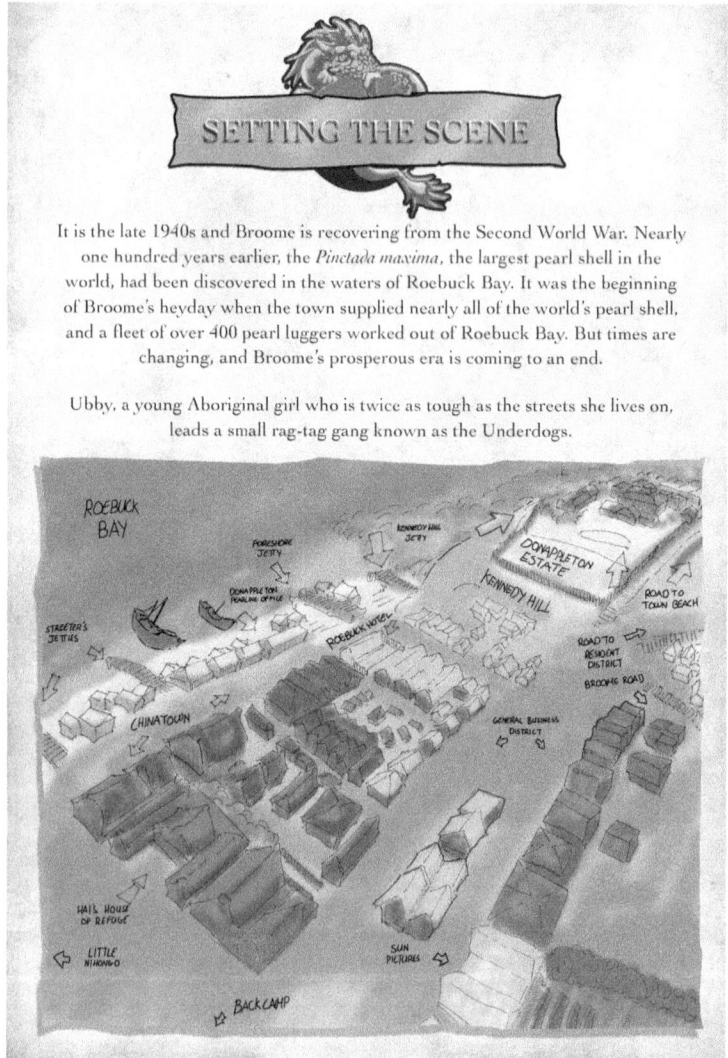

Figure 9.6 Map of the township of Broome in *Ubby's Underdogs: The Legend of the Phoenix Dragon*.

inclusion of a colorful illustrated map of the township. Drawn from a bird's-eye-view angle, it indicates the town's marginal situation between the saltwater inlet of Roebuck Bay and the encroaching vast red desert. Labeling indicates the various settlements and public places (Figure 9.6). On subsequent pages grids of panels provide mid and close-up shots depicting aspects of the town and its inhabitants. These operate in the manner of establishment shots creating a sense of place and atmosphere.

In addition to framing the action of the narrative, the size, shape, and orientation of sequential panels also create the rhythm and pace of the story. Given the myriad of high-action incidents occurring throughout the *Ubby's Underdogs* books, most page grids comprise several panels of varying size and shape. These multiple panels depict a flurry of lively moments punctuated occasionally by a large panel or splash page. Segments frequently shift in time and place, using scene-to-scene transitions, which are like "jump-cuts" used in film. This rapid pacing generates an atmosphere of adventure, excitement, and uncertainty experienced by the focal characters.

Establishing Cross-Cultural Empathy

As with most literary works, a significant feature in the comprehension of graphic narratives is characterization. When investigating narratological elements in a postcolonial context, Gerald Prince notes that

> narratology would aim to account for the kind of characters inhabiting these spatial and temporal settings and ... supply instruments for the exploration and description of their significance, their complexity, the stability of their designation and identity.
>
> (2005, 375)

Characterization, as most narratologists agree, is paramount in the construction of compelling stories. According to Mieke Bal, "Narrative ... thrives on the affective appeal of characters" (2009, Kindle location 2932). She goes on to argue that "As readers, we 'see' characters, feel with them and like or dislike them" (2009). Karin Kukkonen develops this idea with specific reference to graphic characters. She notes that

> when you read a panel ... your mind begins taking in all kinds of information from the images and the written text—the facial expressions, gestures, and postures of the CHARACTERS, their speech, the layout of the image, and many other features.
>
> (Kukkonen, 2013, Kindle location 292).

Characters entice readers to share their story. McKenna renders a multiplicity of characters and voices that engage the reader in a multicultural, polyphonic storyscape. His characters enable readers from a variety of cultural backgrounds to identify with characters who are both similar to and different from themselves. The Underdogs and their allies evoke empathy, while antagonists like the ruthless British entrepreneur, Paul Donappleton along with his sycophantic right-hand man, Clancy Bankler, and the archvillain Uning with his zombie-like warriors, generate antipathy and position a reader to recognize the story's conventional good versus evil dichotomy.

McKenna's visual images evidence a range of influences and thereby attest to one of the attributes of World Literature put forward by Schmitz-Emans, that is a *"mutual literary influence between different countries and cultures*" (2015, 365). In a recent interview aired on the regional ABC Kimberley radio station, McKenna recounts his introduction to the "magic of comics." He recollects the impact of American comics:

> "One day I picked up a Ghost Rider comic book and flicked it open, and the words I couldn't read, but the action… I thought this was awesome," he said.
>
> …
>
> But as a Broome kid in the 1990s, being Aboriginal meant opportunities in life were limited and it was hard to identify with mainstream superheroes.
> "We knew no-one here in Broome who looked like Clark Kent," he said.
> "Whereas Ghost Rider, his alter-ego was stuntman Johnny Blaze who was riddled with all kinds of problems."
>
> (Collins 2019)

The influence of Anglo-American superhero comics and Japanese manga is readily discernible in McKenna's graphic novels. Panels of wild activity that prompt page turning; cycles of rising tension counterpointed by bathos; and the cliff-hanger endings of Volume 1 and Volume 2 are typical of American and British serial comics. The influence of Japanese manga style is especially evident in the expressive, prominent eyes and mouths of the characters; in the visually enhanced onomatopoeic exclamations and sounds; in the overt comics "runes" (symbols) depicting bodily emissions such as blood, sweat, and tears; and in the exaggerated action lines. While McKenna's characters are rendered in a unique, individual style, his blend of codes and conventions from different traditions reflects the fusion of cultures in the society he is portraying and subscribes to Schmitz-Emans' suggestion that a feature of World Literature involves

> an exchange of ideas and strategies of representation that, at the same time, illustrates and fosters complex processes of cultural and economic transfer and interaction.
>
> (2015, 369)

The Underdogs' saga encompasses a wide assortment of personae including those from different ethnic backgrounds; mystical, magical, or fiendish beings; animals and other strange creatures that shape the course and outcome of the tales. McKenna entreats his readers to delight in the diversity of this "carnivalesque" storyworld in which he "addresses serious and weighty concerns—intercultural relations, colonialism, race-based discrimination—through a carnivalesque orientation which enables satire, humor and comical excess" (Bradford, Sly, and Xu, 2016, 216).

While the graphic novel adheres to literary concepts put forward by postclassical narratologists, it is also a form which as Charlotta Salmi notes "challenges the established parameters and definitions of World Literature" (2018, Kindle location 7054). Graphic novels from the Global South offer an avenue by way of popular culture to express marginalized voices in an accessible mode of communication. Drawn characters and diverse voices readily engross readers in cross-cultural exchange and furnish "new collective subjects" who, as Cheah suggests, "can emerge and change the world-political stage" (2016, 194).

In considering comics-style characters, an area of concern worth noting is that expressed by some theorists, including Leonard Rifas (2010) and Derek Parker-Royal (2007), about the tendency of comics to stereotype characters in a way that denigrates ethnic minorities or other marginalized peoples. Derek Parker-Royal argues that,

> In comics and graphic art there is always the all-too-real danger of negative stereotype and caricature, which strips others of any unique identity and dehumanizes by means of reductive iconography.
>
> (2007, 8)

However, I would argue that McKenna employs two salient techniques to safeguard all his characters from the oversimplification associated with "reductive iconography."

First, he creates highly distinctive iconic characters, whether human, animal, or supernatural. While the characters are cartoonish in style, their identities derive from assiduously honed facial expressions, posture, and presence. Even in crowd scenes, such as the multitude witnessing the shame of the Pearl Juniors' defeat in the game of Gruff in Volume 1 (79) or the scene in *Heroes Beginnings*, in which people with different interests are trying to recapture Medinga, the chess-playing baboon (102–3, see Figure 9.7), each character regardless of gender, ethnicity, or occupation is presented as a unique individual. Through his attention to detail, McKenna dispels the notion that iconographic characters representing different races necessarily devalue their subjects. On the contrary, he creates unique, memorable characters that engage a reader effectively and affectively. As Suzanne Keen observes, in graphic narratives

> illustrations of faces and bodily postures may capitalize on the availability of visual coding for human emotions, eliciting readers' feelings before they even read the accompanying text.
>
> (2011, 135)

McKenna's characters are both engaging and endearing. Each exudes her/his individual attributes and foibles thereby enabling readers to identify with their fundamental "humanity" and attesting to Cheah's argument that "the world's different literary cultures can help us compose a universal history of the human spirit that underlies these literatures" (2016, 25).

Secondly, McKenna gives several of his characters distinctive vocal features. Most graphic novels rely on dialogue to supplement the visual track so as to convey character, propel the action, and express discourses and ideologies. Apart from the actual words used, various stylistic permutations inflect narration and dialogue. These include the particular representation of caption boxes, speech balloons, thought bubbles, typography, "pictorial runes" (Kennedy, 1982), and other comics codes and conventions. For the most part conventional comics balloonics and font are used throughout the *Ubby's Underdogs* series (although the lettering does change from the

Figure 9.7 Panels showing the pursuit of Medinga in *Ubby's Underdogs: Heroes Beginnings*

traditional comics-style upper case in Volume 1 to the more contemporary mixed or sentence case in the following two volumes). Much of the verbal track of the *Ubby's Underdogs* episodes is presented in Standard English. However, strategically placed variation in register, dialect, or accent operates to specify particular characters and provide a sense of the polyphonic nature of the township and its residents.

Referencing the work of Monika Fludernik and Marion Gymnich, Gerald Prince points out, languages used by the narrator and characters constitute a fruitful area of narratorial inquiry. They may be quite similar or very different, standard or nonstandard, positively or negatively marked, and so forth.

(2005, 374)

Conventions such as typography, punctuation, spelling, grammar, syntax, culturally specific words and phrases, and other recognizable symbols are employed in the delivery of a variety of voices, non-verbal utterances, and diegetic sounds.

In graphic novels the visual operates to inflect lexical symbols and to evoke a synesthetic manifestation of aurality. The Standard English of the majority of characters acts as a foil against which to contrast distinctive accents and dialects. Generated through non-standard orthographies, the idiosyncratic voices function as a means to create what Monika Fludernik refers to as "pseudo-aurality," or the "evocation of characters' mode of utterance," as it is "heard" by the "inner voice" of the reader (2013, 95–6). For instance, Gabe, the Maori member of the Underdogs, has a prominent lisp because he is missing his upper front teeth. Gabe's distinctive speech is conveyed through substituting "th" for sibilant sounds such as "s," "sh," "z," and "zh." An example can be seen in Gabe's response to the distasteful medicinal elixir offered to him by Safa. With his hand over his mouth, Gabe says, "Oooh, dithguthing. What ith that thtuff? It thmelth putrid!" (2013, 14).

These vocal variations add individuality and authenticity. They give specific characters their own language and voice, and within the context of these graphic narratives, rather than functioning as a means of *othering*, the non-standard voices augment the texture, vibrancy, and heteroglossia of the multicultural community. As Marjorie C. Allison (2014) argues "the graphic text is a valuable vehicle for understanding ways readers can re-envision the world." She suggests that, "What has been marginalized is brought to the centre and given a privileged place in these stories" (2014, 74). This is especially evident in the portrayal of the character, Ubby.

Ubby's indigeneity is reflected in her Aboriginal English dialect which is achieved through minimal use of "allegro speech" (or fused words), alternative grammar and syntax, and the inclusion of words and phrases pertaining to her cultural group. For example, in response to Scotty Donappleton's taunts, Ubby responds, "The name's Ubby! And this is my gang! Get it right or I'll belt you blackfella style" (V.1, 34). Later, when Sai Fong has transferred some of her own blood to Ubby to neutralize the poison from a snakebite, Ubby exclaims, "I got bad feeling. They in danger. I can feel something, and its moving proper fast" (V.1, 124). Other characters like the Caribbean vagabond, Safa; Gahn Stryper, the head groundsman on the Donappleton estate; and Bone Iron Jonas, Gahn Stryper's eccentric younger brother, who appears as a disembodied voice in Volume 3, have specific accents achieved through elements of *allegro speech* which involves the elision of words such as "watcha" for "what are you"; *dialect spelling* which attempts to capture features of pronounciation; and *eye-dialect* or phonetic spelling such as "sez" for "says" or "wuz" for "was" (Hodson 2014).

Through his inclusion of different voices, McKenna affirms the multicultural nature of the community. The accents and dialects create a unique orality and are not delivered in a sarcastic or derisive manner. They operate more as a means of demystifying alterity and exhibit a storyworld rich with a plurality of nuanced vocalizations. McKenna uses language to foreground heterogeneity in an affirmative manner. The different voices encode variation in cultures and support the conveyance of underlying themes relating to the understanding and appreciation of difference in the world at large.

Beyond the Oral Tradition

Another device employed to great effect in the *Ubby's Underdogs* books is the inclusion of "nested narratives," or stories within the story. Since these are presented as if being delivered orally, the visu–verbal medium resonates with the tradition at the heart of Indigenous storytelling. In *The Legend of the Phoenix Dragon*, apart from Yupman Poe's prologue about the defeat of the mountain people by the Hede, Fin tells Sai Fong about how tensions between the cultural groups in Broome led to "the last riot" (93–4) in which Ubby's father lost his life. In *Heroes Beginnings* there are several recounted tales including that of Samuel Donappleton's pearl divers, the Ocean Maids, of whom Ubby's mother was one (27–8). Later Maryanne tells her story about rescuing the young Sylvania Neocrati from harassment at the hands of the adolescent Paul Donappleton and his ruthless friends, which provides the backstory for Sylvania's indebtedness to Ubby's mother (143–5). Finally, in *Return of the Dragons*, the most significant backstory is that told by Yupman Poe about how he became the sole guardian and protector of Sai Fong and how they were relentlessly pursued throughout China by the Hede (84–95, 98–103).

The nested or frame stories in the graphic medium utilize techniques that distinguish them from the main narrative. In *Ubby's Underdogs*, tales from the past are often presented in sepia tones or greyscale, which serve to distance them from the present time. They often include colored text boxes to convey the verbal track of the story and inverted commas suggesting that the teller is outside the visual story track in terms of time and space. By adopting these medium-specific techniques, McKenna is able to demonstrate an aspect of graphic narrative whereby "the pedagogy of oral stories... is being made relevant to a younger generation through the images in these novels" (Langston 2018, 117).

Like other well-crafted graphic novels, the *Ubby's Underdogs* trilogy is open to a multiplicity of readings and interpretations. The overarching theme of reconciliation, or peaceful concord between Australia's First Nations peoples, settler groups, and immigrants, is delivered through a visu–verbal tale that incorporates history, adventure, fantasy, and a generous serving of madcap humor. McKenna's graphic trilogy not only recognizes but also applauds the so-called "underdog" in ways that position a reader to sympathize with his antiheroes as they attempt to overcome seemingly unsurmountable challenges.

McKenna's protagonists are endearing because they are unpretentious. Initially, their mission is to find and free Safa's baboon, Madinga, who has been stolen by Paul Donappleton and is imprisoned in his estate. It is a sense of fairness, justice, and care for a fellow citizen that leads the Underdogs to take on this challenge, but it lures them into a situation that is far more complex than they could have imagined. When Sai Fong disappears at the end of *The Legend of the Phoenix Dragon*, it becomes apparent that there is something malevolent afoot in the land and that such a threat can only be overcome and defeated by a concerted and collaborative effort from the tenacious Underdogs and their supporters.

Humor and Subversion

Another strategic device employed in "the reworlding of the world" (Cheah 2016) in these graphic narratives is the inclusion of humor. Through his use of the comics medium and a good deal of zany humor, McKenna creates a carnivalistic world in the Bakhtinian sense. That is "a world of topsy-turvy, of hetroglot exhuberance,... where all is mixed, hybrid, ritually degraded and defiled" (Stallybrass and White 1986, 8). Russian philosopher and literary theorist Mikhail Bakhtin (1895–1975) perceived the great carnivals of Medieval Europe as a metaphor for literary tendencies, especially in the emerging format known as "the novel." He saw carnival times as periods of liberation when the authority of church and state were inverted, and when rules and beliefs became the subject of ridicule thereby questioning the status quo and allowing new ideas to enter into public discourse. In the world of Ubby's Underdogs the established power group is undermined both by its own corruption and by the actions of the youthful Underdogs as they seek social justice. In this sense a new generation of individuals from mixed racial and ethnic backgrounds challenge the status quo and affirm the value of transcultural respect and cooperation.

According to Bakhtin, a significant aspect of the carnivalesque is laughter, which he argues, is "the laughter of all people... it is universal in scope; it is directed at all and everyone, including the carnival's participants... It asserts and denies, it buries and revives" (Bakhtin and Iswolsky 1984, 12). Throughout the *Ubby's Underdogs* books, McKenna employs various facets of the visual and verbal to generate laughter. Following the panels that establish the setting of the story in Volume 1, *The Legend of the Phoenix Dragon*, there is a panel depicting an overtly buck-toothed lizard and a voice off saying, "Look, you mob. I gonna get 'em." In the following panels Ubby and her friends burst upon the scene, evidently chasing, but missing, the illusive Gunada, a Gilbert's Dragon lizard that is believed by Gabe to have stolen his front teeth. The pursuit of this creature becomes a motif that recurs throughout the saga. The taunting lizard appears, often at inopportune times, and provides a diversion through the slapstick comic relief of a fruitless chase.

Adam Shoemaker explains,

> Aboriginal people... have managed to retain a distinctive sense of humor which acts to combat depression and to promote the cohesion of the Black Australian group... The mimicry and mockery of whites and the humorous celebration of their

own lifestyle has been one way in which blacks have opposed the encroachments of European society.

(2004, 233)

The animosity between Ubby's group and the Pearl Juniors, the sons of the British businessmen who run the pearling industry, is evident in their mutual taunting, name-calling, and competitive game challenges. Although there is antagonism from each group toward the other, the reader is positioned to have sympathy for the Underdogs and to feel their aversion toward the ruthless, cheating Pearl Juniors. For example, Sai Fong witnesses Fin and the other members of the Underdogs spitting at the mention of the British. When Sai Fong asks why they are doing this, the Irish boy Fin explains, "It's something you do when you mention the British. My Dad does it all the time" (V.1, 32–3).

Sai Fong's misunderstanding of this "ritual" leads to an ironic interchange later. When Sergeant MacIntyre introduces himself to Sai Fong, she spits into his hand (V.1, 72). Greatly embarrassed by his niece's unusual greeting, Yupman tries to save face by telling MacIntyre that the spitting is "a Chinese gesture ... for formal introductions" (V.1, 73). The joke runs into Volume 2 *Heroes Beginnings* because when Sergeant MacIntyre meets Uncle Lolo, the Sergeant spits into his own hand before offering his hand to this Chinese visitor (V.2, 99). In addition, there is dramatic irony in this interchange. The reader is aware that the so-called Uncle Lolo is actually the baboon, Medinga, sitting on Gabe's shoulders disguised in a coolie hat and long cloak as Sel steers them through the busy township. These spitting segments employ manga-style iconography with large droplets of spittle being depicted, thereby exaggerating the humor and producing a tactile sensation through the amplified runes in the visual image.

Humor in various guises abounds in this trilogy and is used both as a means of entertainment and of resistance. As Sezen Turkmen (2014) notes,

> transforming the stereotypical racial and cultural representations in comics and graphic novels remains to be a necessary step towards opening up a critical space for generating healthy discussions about the issues of racial inclusion/exclusion between different members of a globalized community and for producing fruitful strategies to overcome delineating prejudices towards minorities in public spaces.
>
> (2014, 2–3)

McKenna's use of humor, which ranges from epigrammatic humor through bipartisan name calling to outright slapstick, operates to demystify and defuse elements of prejudice and racism in a positive way. Some subtle and less subtle instances of humor are evident in the following examples. In *Heroes Beginnings* Yupman is coerced into attending an important dinner at Donappleton's estate. Yupman and Ubby discuss a plan to infiltrate Donappleton's property and rescue Madinga, the baboon. Yupman says, "I suggest we make a plan. One that gives them what they think they want, but takes what they think they have" (V.2, 13). Ubby's offhand epigrammatic response to

Yupman's enigmatic suggestion is, "Get something. Lose something. Now that's proper black" (V.2, 13). This witty interchange captures a shared philosophical understanding between the Chinese man and the Aboriginal girl.

Name calling between the opposing factions is another mode of humor. Presented in the manner of childish banter, these name-calling interchanges function more as a means of dispelling tensions rather than any serious vilification. Fin refers to Scotty Donappleton as "You mongrel" (V.1, 87); "Silverspooner"; and "Tryhard" (V.2, 11). Ubby, Sel, and his brother, Quick, label Paul Donappleton as a "monkey-brain"; "Dirty rotten..."; "Crooked mangy..."; and "Stomach Maggot!" (V.2, 12–13). Scotty Donappleton shows his animosity toward Ubby by sarcastically addressing her formally and then following up with a snide reference to her gang when he says, "Greetings, Alberta. How is your playgroup today?" (V.1, 34). However, name calling becomes particularly sardonic when the fiendish ancient leader of the Hede, Uning, refers to Ubby as a "little street rat" (V.2, 130).

An additional device used to create humor, and often operating as "comic relief," is irony. Towards the end of *The Legend of the Phoenix Dragon*, a tourist couple, oblivious to the wild activity around them, complain to one another about how uneventful Broome is. Facial features of both husband and wife convey their boredom and disapproval, confirmed by comments such as, "There's nothing here, no excitement, no adventure, but hey what else would you expect from the desert?" (V.1, 150) (Figure 9.8).

At this point Ubby bursts into the cab of the tourists' vehicle in her frantic attempt to lure an aggressive, spitting War Crown Spider from the township and ironically indicating that things are not always as they seem. Such moments of humor alleviate the rising tension and this incident suggests outsiders rarely understand and appreciate the background and complexities of an unfamiliar place.

In this topsy-turvy story world, another subversive aspect is that of defying traditional authority figures. Youngsters and novices see the world from a different perspective and McKenna positions the reader to sympathize with these views that challenge conventional authority. Examples of this insubordination include Sai Fong furtively vacating the safety of Hai's house of refuge and leaving a note for her uncle on her pillow (V.1, 107). Similarly, at the end of *Heroes Beginnings*, Ubby disregards her mother's wishes about keeping her distance from dangerous activities. Like Sai Fong, Ubby leaves a note on her hammock. It reads, "<u>DEAR MUM</u> UNDERDOGS 4 LIFE!" (V.2, 155), which is supposed to justify her defiance.

Other examples of challenging authority are evidenced in unexpected interchanges. The young Nanren novice, Snow, is concerned about the appropriateness of his master's judgment in relation to Yupman Poe being a fugitive. However, in deference to his master, Snow follows Hai's orders. On the other hand, when Scotty Donappleton sees problems arising from his father's controlling nature, Scotty takes his own decision to defy his father by finding and helping Sai Fong. Power shifts, such as these, support the notion that the younger generation has a growing understanding of social circumstances and can contribute in a positive manner to bring about necessary change.

McKenna's compelling trilogy on the escapades of a gang of "multicultural misfits" foregrounds strong female characters. According to McKenna, Ubby was inspired by

Figure 9.8 Humor in this segment derives from the tourists' comments about the lack of events in Broome while Ubby and others frantically try to protect the township from the War Crown Spider in *Ubby's Underdogs: The Legend of the Phoenix Dragon*.

his grandmother, Alberta Dolby. In a biography, he explains that his tales are based on family stories

> about Nan and her sisters getting into fights and causing trouble when she was young… I took my knowledge of my grandmother, placed the character in a

situation, then I tried to imagine what I think my nan would have done to hopefully project the character's (Ubby's) attitude and actions.

(Fisher 2009)

Apart from Ubby, the respected leader or "boss" of the Underdogs, other female characters are highly significant. Sai Fong exhibits powerful retaliation against the deceitful Pearl Juniors in the game of Gruff (V.1, 49–79). By making use of a number of silent panels, reminiscent of the high-action sequences in manga comics, McKenna presents Sai Fong, eyes ablaze, performing a series of acrobatic stunts that keep the ball out of the hands of the unscrupulous Pearl Juniors and enable the Underdogs to win the game.

Other assertive female characters include Sylvania Neocrati, Maryanne, and Lady Mudang. First appearing in the second volume, *Heroes Beginnings*, Sylvania is the owner of Neo-krate pearls, the only pearling fleet operating in opposition to Paul Donappleton's near-monopoly of the industry. Her admiration and gratitude toward Ubby's mother, Maryanne, leads Sylvania to aid the Underdogs in their pursuits. Maryanne, the straight-talking, broom-wielding mother of Ubby is reluctantly drawn into the battle and yet displays her skills when she attacks and defeats Uning's ghoulish warrior with ease (V.3, 37). At the request of Mulli and the Council of Magic, a Korean shaman with exceptional abilities, Lady Mudang is also drawn into the fray and demonstrates her accomplishments by leaping into an abyss to locate the Sandpaper Dragon (V.3, 113–14). The prominence of such forthright female characters is yet another example of the subversive elements embraced by these narratives.

By focusing on theories pertaining to World Literature and narratological aspects connected to the process of storytelling in the graphic format, it is possible to understand how the Ubby's Underdogs tales present a world in which a number of Western ideologies are alternatively envisaged. As Cheah suggests, such narratives

> play a part in the making of worlds ... because worlding destabilizes any existing world and opens up reality to interpretation.
>
> (2016, 311)

The power of these narratives can be found in their use of the comics mode, a popular and yet previously marginalized medium that is beginning to speak more convincingly to contemporary readers.

By employing theories pertaining to World Literature and salient aspects of postclassical narratology, this chapter has considered ways in which graphic novels from the Global South can challenge and change both these theoretical realms. As Salmi suggests, graphic narratives can provide,

> cultural, as well as social, commentary: they both satirize literary texts and establishments, and provide a counter to dominant historical and cultural narratives around the globe. The graphic narrative as World Literature thus offers a route for marginal arts as well as marginal voices to receive recognition.
>
> (Salmi 2018, Kindle locations 7429–7430).

McKenna's graphic narratives examine aspects of decolonization and offer reflections on reconciliation. He is an author who, like others, can be seen to be doing what Langston describes as "adopting and adapting the colonizer's tradition for their own purposes" (Langston 2018, 122). In recent decades Indigenous Australian plays, novels, poetry, and picture books have played an important role in revealing the voices of Aboriginal and Torres Strait Islander Peoples for a world audience. Shoemaker claims that these literary works display a means of asserting "identity—with that complex of attitudes, beliefs and mores which constitute Aboriginality" (277). If, as Shoemaker argues, "Aboriginal literature is centrally involved with the maintenance and extension of Aboriginal confidence and the feeling of self-worth" (2004, 278), I would argue that McKenna's work goes above and beyond this to present a multicultural society in which mutual respect, collaboration, and cooperation are fundamental to the survival of mixed race and multiethnic communities. His graphic narratives participate in the worlding process envisaged by Cheah, whereby "literature opens a world because it magically gives a world or makes one 'appear' in the imagination in a manner similar to evocation or conjuration" (2016, 311). With such notions in mind, it can be asserted that, as an indigenous Australian, McKenna has taken the lead in creating a trilogy of high-quality graphic novels that deserve to be acknowledged, enjoyed, studied, and appreciated as fine examples of multimodal World Literature.

References

Abouet, M., and Oubrerie, C. 2007. *Aya*. Montreal, Canada: Drawn and Quarterly.
Alber, J., and Fludernik, M. eds. 2010. *Postclassical Narratology: Approaches and Analyses*. Columbus, OH: Ohio State University Press.
Allison, M.C. 2014. "(Not) Lost in the Margins: Gender and Identity in Graphic Texts." *Mosaic: An Interdisciplinary Critical Journal*, 47(4): 73–97.
Baetens, J., and Frey, H. 2014. *The Graphic Novel: An Introduction*. Cambridge, UK: Cambridge University Press.
Bakhtin, M., and Iswolsky, H. 1984. *Rabelais and His World*. Bloomington, IN: Indiana University Press.
Bal, M. 2009. *Narratology: Introduction to the Theory of Narrative*. 3rd ed. Toronto, Canada: University of Toronto Press. Kindle Edition.
Bradford, C., Sly, C., and Xu, D. 2016. "Ubby's Underdogs: A Transformative Vision of Australian Community." *Papers: Explorations into Children's Literature*, 24: 101–31, University of Canberra.
Brown, C. 2006. *Louis Riel*. Montreal, Canada: Drawn and Quarterly.
Cheah, P. 2016. *What Is a World?* Durham, NC: Duke University Press.
Collins, B. 2019. *Indigenous Broome Author Brenton E McKenna's Epic Journey Behind his Graphic-Novel Success*, ABC Kimberley. https://www.abc.net.au/news/2019-08-24/story-behind-brenton-e-mckennas-graphic-novel-success/11239202 (accessed September 20, 2020).
Delisle, G. 2007. *Pyongyang: A Journey in North Korea*. Montreal, Canada: Drawn and Quarterly.

Fisher, L. 2009. *Brenton E. McKenna—Biography, Design & Art Australia Online*. https://www.daao.org.au/bio/brenton-mckenna/biography/ (accessed September 21, 2020).

Fludernik, M. 2009. *An Introduction to Narratology*. Oxford, UK: Routledge.

Fludernik, M. 2013. "Conversational Narration – Oral Narration." In Hühn, P. et al., eds. *The Living Handbook of Narratology*. Germany: Hamburg University. https://www.lhn.uni-hamburg.de/node/34.html (accessed January 17, 2022).

Gardner, J., and Herman, D. 2011. Graphic Narratives and Narrative Theory: Introduction. *SubStance*. Baltimore, MA: The Johns Hopkins University Press.

Groensteen, T. 2013. *Comics and Narration*. Jackson: University Press of Mississippi.

Hodson, J. 2014. *Dialect in Film and Literature*. London: Red Globe Press.

Keen, S. 2011. "Fast Tracks to Narrative Empathy: Anthropomorphism and Dehumanization in Graphic Narratives." *SubStance*, 40(1): 135–55. https://doi.org/10.1353/sub.2011.0003 (accessed December 5, 2021).

Kennedy, J.M. 1982. "Metaphor in Pictures." *Perception*, 589–605.

Kukkonen, K. 2013. *Studying Comics and Graphic Novels*. Chichester, UK: Wiley. Kindle Edition.

Langston, J. (2018) "'Once Upon a Time This Was a True Story': Indigenous Peoples Graphic Novels and Orature." In Grace, D., and Hoffman, E., eds. *The Canadian Alternative: Cartoonists, Comics, and Graphic Novels*. Jackson: University Press of Mississippi, 113–26.

McKenna, B.E. 2011. *Ubby's Underdogs: The Legend of the Phoenix Dragon*. Broome, Western Australia: Magabala Books.

McKenna, B.E. 2013. *Ubby's Underdogs: Heroes Beginnings*. Broome, Western Australia: Magabala Books.

McKenna, B.E. 2019. *Ubby's Underdogs: Return of the Dragons*. Broome, Western Australia: Magabala Books.

Mikkonen, K. 2017. *The Narratology of Comic Art*. New York: Routledge.

Prince, G. 2005. "On a Postclassical Narratology." In Phelan, J., and Rabinowitz, P.J., eds. *A Companion to Narrative Theory*. Malden, MA/Oxford, UK: Blackwell Publishing Ltd, 372–81.

Rifas, L. 2010. "Race and Comix." In Aldama, F.L., ed. *Multicultural Comics*. Austin, TX: University of Texas Press, 27–38.

Royal, D.P. 2007. "Introduction: Coloring America: Multi-Ethnic Engagements with Graphic Narrative." *MELUS*, 32(3): 7–22.

Salmi, C. 2018. "The Worldliness of Graphic Narrative." In Etherington, B., and Zimbler, J., eds. *The Cambridge Companion to World Literature*. Cambridge, UK: Cambridge University Press. Kindle Edition.

Satrapi, M. 2003. *Persepolis: The Story of a Childhood*. 1st ed. New York: Pantheon.

Schmitz-Emans, M. 2015. "Graphic Novels as World Literature." In Stein, D., and Thon, J.-N., eds. *From Comic Strips to Graphic Novels*. 2nd ed. Berlin: De Gruyter, 367–87.

Schodt, F.L.1983. *Manga! Manga! The World of Japanese Comics*. New York: Kodansha International.

Shoemaker, A. 2004. *Black Words White Page*. Canberra: ANU Press.

Stallybrass, P., and White, A. 1986. *The Politics and Poetics of Transgression*. London: Methuen.

Tan, S. 2006. *The Arrival*. Sydney: Lothian Books.

Turkmen, S. 2014. *American Born Chinese" and Identity Construction in the Global Age*, *Academia*. https://www.academia.edu/27635760/_American_Born_Chinese_and_Identity_Construction_in_the_Global_Age (accessed December 5, 2021).

Yang, G.L. 2008. *American Born Chinese*. New York: Square Fish.

10

A Case Study of *Sita's Ramayana*, Diasporic Negotiations, COVID-19, and the Television Serial *Ramayana*

Shilpa Daithota Bhat

Introduction

This essay examines the narrative power of the Ramayana plot and how the story has been adapted and represented in *Sita's Ramayana*. The universal appeal of the story to South Asians scattered around the globe highlights how the story's retelling continues to intrigue human imagination. In the graphic novel format, the retold Ramayana story in *Sita's Ramayana*, happens to centralize the woman protagonist. While looking at the discourse and narrative power of the plot, it is notable that media discourse around the plot also highlights how the story continues to resonate not only in India but also among the South Asian diaspora. A comparison of *Sita's Ramayana* discourse in the graphic narrative format and media discourse surrounding the Ramayana story can meaningfully contribute the idea of how the patriarchal voice in the original plot has been palpably shifted in the graphic novel to underline the woman protagonist's thoughts and reflections. Hence, the perception of such a plot in the graphic novel, in the framework of global or World Literature deserves analysis and conceptual interpretation because the work raises significant questions emphasizing the position of women. It is interesting, for the purpose of contextualizing, to look at the implications of the "graphic narrative." Mazur and Danner (2017) underline that the graphic novel "has largely always been, an international form, boasting rich international cross-pollination" (58). The idea that the genre is "an international form" invokes the critical question of what might make it "international" and I contend in this essay that certain populations have frequently turned to the *Ramayana* epic from time to time, in times of crisis for a variety of reasons. To look at this, I cite instances to suggest the idea of universality, narrative power and media discourses being emphatic reasons for the choice of *Ramayana* for cultural and social expression. While conceptualizing the significance of narrative power and universality, I tie the understanding of the *Ramayana* performances in history as vantage points that offered opportunities for international dissemination of the plot, thereby allowing universality to operate, not only in the various contexts but also in its choice as a narrative for different formats such as *Ramleela* performance or its choice for the graphic novel *Sita's Ramayana*. The epic is popular in South Asia and people who migrated from the region to different parts of the world, that is, the members of the South Asian diasporic community. The *Ramayana* plot has evoked questions of the unjust treatment meted out to Sita and how this portrays the marginalization of women. Also, the pain and anguish Sita had to go through are remembered and cited whenever women of the South Asian region go through domestic abuse. Of course, the fact that the South Asians are familiar with the story allows them the chance to quote Sita's pain—they can empathize with her and ponder over how women are frequently subjected to emotional and physical abuse. In such a context, Arni and Chitrakar's *Sita's Ramayana* (2011) suggests an attempt to question patriarchal societies and what it means to relate the plot from Sita's point of view. Hence, this graphic narrative is extremely crucial since it suggests an effort to address the discourse of women's marginalization.

Through conceptualizing and deploying the notion of "universality" and narrative power, this study looks at how the graphic format creatively operates in *Sita's Ramayana*, rendered in a graphic format. To critically comprehend the thematic implications of the plot, a comparative framework of the same story, represented in different media would be useful. By "universality" and narrative power, the implication is that the epic has always had universal appeal. To put this in perspective in this chapter, what is interesting to note is the manner in which the pandemic lockdown awakened renewed interest in the story. In the moment of crisis, the South Asians turned to the *Ramayana* again—this time, however, to a serial produced decades ago. There are several remakes of the epic—cartoons, serials, and books. How does the work generate universal appeal? And how does universality and narrative power interrelate with World Literature? To critically explore these questions, I bring into a comparative ambit, the re-telecasting of the 1990's Ramanand Sagar's popular television serial, *Ramayana*,[1] on Delhi Doordarshan channel (owned by the Government of India and Ministry of Information and Broadcasting); and how this development has been generally represented across online news media. Intriguingly, the serial was re-telecast on "public demand," to keep them entertained during the COVID-19 crisis and lockdown in India.[2] Online news media hailed the viewership ratings as surprising and even shocking because the Doordarshan, in comparison with other television channels has never had high ratings. However, the re-telecasting of the *Ramayan* serial made the general public nostalgic, who urged the younger generation to watch the serial and learn the timeless story. This was considered no mean feat by the Doordarshan in terms of ratings because the Indian masses have been generally seen enjoying *saas-bahu*[3] serials of late that are being telecast by other channels.

---

[1] There have been several serialized versions of the Ramayana epic in India. However, for the purpose of this essay, I look at the serial made by Ramanand Sagar that was telecast on Delhi Doordarshan in 1987 first and the second time during the COVID-19 lockdown in India.
[2] The Doordarshan brought back not only the Ramayan serial but also the other old serials and even advertisements.
[3] *Saas-Bahu*, meaning mother-in-law/daughter-in-law, to suggest serials that are daily soaps and considered "typical," addictive, and less meaningful in comparison with serials like the Ramayana.

The perception that a television serial can entertain audiences, facilitate social distancing, and help prevent the spread of the disease highlights the importance accorded to the epic. Of course, the other serials and programs have also been favorites among the audience but the *Ramayan* is being considered respectfully for the significance it holds in the framework of socio-cultural values, its epic status in the domain of narratives, and its implications concerning religion and spiritual ideas. However, the purpose of this essay is to explore the notion of "universality," narrative power, and World Literature in *Sita's Ramayana* graphic narrative in a comparative frame through the analysis of the same story rendered in different formats. For this purpose, I will look at: (i) the notion of "universality" and narrative power in the *Ramayana* epic; (ii) the re-telecasting of Ramanand Sagar's *Ramayan* on Delhi Doordarshan, which was viewed not only in India but also abroad, that is, among the diaspora; and (iii) Arni and Chitrakar's *Sita's Ramayana*, the use of the Patua art form in the graphic novel to articulate female suppression and marginalization—a subject that is relevant in feminist studies across cultures and history.

Thematic Structure in *Sita's Ramayana*

Sita's Ramayana is a re-rendering of the *Ramayana* epic but from the point of view of Sita. The original story is seen glorifying Rama and his actions, his regal status in his kingdom and therefore his prerogative of using power at his discretion. His functioning and decision-making have been seen as being operative in the religious frame of *dharma*—righteousness and duty. Whatever he did was because of his kingdom and the interests of the citizens. His wife Sita, meanwhile, is not a citizen; and as a wife, she is suspected, abandoned—in other words, discarded at will. This has been seen as a tragedy befalling Sita, whose identity is obliterated and whose chastity is repeatedly questioned—all in the name of "dharma." This questioning of Sita has been questioned in *Sita's Ramayana*, through making her the central voice, unlike the original Ramayana story where Sita has no voice. It is only at the end of the story that *she* decides to leave Rama and go back to her mother, Earth. So, how does she feel throughout the duration in which she accompanies her husband to the forest; what trauma and feelings does she go through when she is abducted by Ravana to his kingdom Lanka; how does she feel in the *Ashoka Vatika*—the royal garden of Ravana; how does she feel when she is asked to go through the fire-test to prove her chastity to Rama; and how does she feel when she is left in the forest during her pregnancy. *Sita's Ramayana*, is an attempt to address these sidelined questions—making the graphic novel relevant in the context of women's and feminist studies and World Literature.

To explore these questions and layers that characterize *Sita's Ramayana* plot, it is necessary to first look at the story that has been popular in the world in various formats. In the *Ramayana* epic, Rama, Bharata, Lakshmana, and Shatrughna are brothers, whose father is King Dasharatha. Rama marries Sita (who is the daughter of King Janaka) in a grand *swayamvara* (an event where Sita can choose the man of her

Figure 10.1 Sita's Abduction

choice as her life-partner/husband) where he breaks a bow—a condition to be able to marry Sita.

Of the four princes, Rama is the eldest and Dasharatha wishes that he become the king of Ayodhya. However, this is not acceptable to Queen Kaikeyi, the second wife of the king. She desires that her son succeeds her husband and this drives her to make two demands from the king—an opportunity that he had given Kaikeyi when she had helped him in a battle. At that time, she suggested that she had nothing to ask but might do so later in life if need be. This postponed chance emerges at an opportune moment for the second queen during the decision-making of the succeeding prince. In addition to wanting her son to accede the throne, she wants Rama exiled from the kingdom for fourteen years (Figure 10.1).

This development becomes a vantage point where life becomes tragic for the protagonists with Sita becoming a victim (Figure 10.2). In the forest, she is abducted by Ravana, the King of Lanka. She is kept at *Ashokavana*, the royal garden of Ravana (Figure 10.3).

In due course, Rama along with Lakshmana, Hanuman, and the monkey army invade Lanka and kill Ravana. The shocking episode here is when Rama suspects Sita's fidelity before taking her back, making her go through *agnipariksha* (fire test) (Figure 10.4). So Sita passes through fire and remains unburned suggesting that she was pure and chaste.

After going back to Ayodhya, for a brief period, life seems to be peaceful. However, after Sita becomes pregnant, Rama arranges for leaving her in a forest because one of his subjects points a finger at her chastity. The acme of the tragedy

A Case Study of Sita's Ramayana

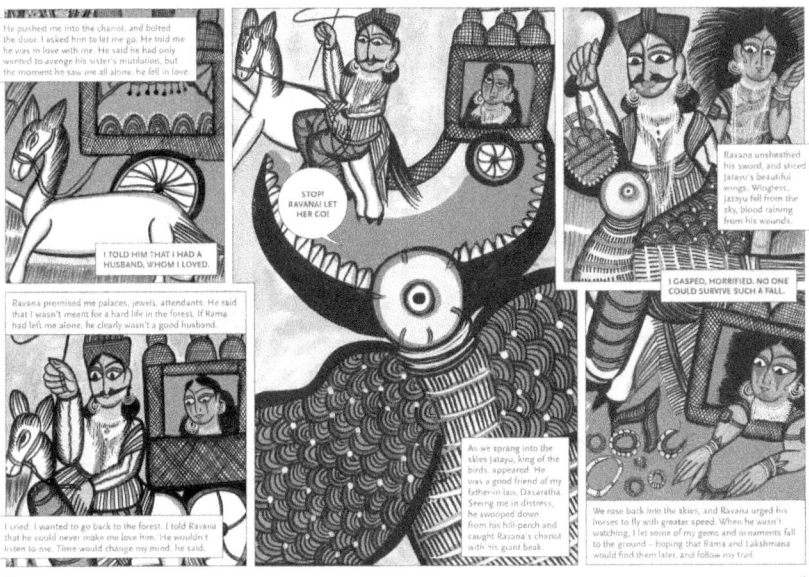

Figure 10.2 Sita's reflections

Figure 10.3 Waiting

Figure 10.4 War

for Sita is expressed in *Sita's Ramayana* in the words of Rama, when he says: "Sita you are free. I have freed you. You can do whatever you want. Go wherever you want" (115). The sense of complete abandonment of the woman who followed her husband throughout the exile, her complete marginalization and eventually her rejection, has evoked questions of femininity, patriarchal dominance and suppression of the female voice. *Sita's Ramayana*'s standpoint of the woman protagonist narrating her story and the authors' use of the Patua painting is significant in defining the role and choice of such art forms in the graphic narrative. Scholars have underlined the significance of art in the representation of stories (Sen Gupta 1973; Bhattacharjee 1980; McCutchion and Bhaumika 1999; Hauser 2002; Ghosh 2003; Korom 2006; Bertocci 2007; Eaton 2013; Newman 2013; Ponte 2015; Chandra 2017). Chatterji (2012) quotes Gamberi (2014) to note "The patuas' patriarchal representation of women has begun to be criticized with the increased presence of female patuas since the 1970s and, in particular, with the workshops sponsored by the Handcrafts Board of West Bengal from 1986 to1991" (Chatterji 2012, 27). This information is extremely important here because we see Chitrakar—a woman Patua artist, in the terrain of the so-called patriarchal art form Patua, and portraying the plight of Sita, to articulate her suppression in the Ramayana plot. This experimentation through the use of the Patua art form gestures at feminist reply to patriarchal domination—both through narration and through the graphic art form, making the text an interesting case in the study of World Literature.

The episodes in the *Ramayana* plot, in a patriarchal framework, are justified in the context of "dharma" or righteousness and duty. However, what is conspicuous is the injustice to Sita whose gender happens to be instrumental in determining her marginalized situation. While this seems to be the primary objective in *Sita's Ramayana*, the story seems to be a rendering of the original story with the narrator being Sita. It is left to the reader to deduce her sense of unfairness meted out to her. She doesn't become a formidable "voice" to explicate her condition. One palpable difference in the story is she is seen describing the battle as something that she had been hearing about from the *rakshashis* (the demonic women) at Ashokavana.

The plot of *Sita's Ramayana*, it is to be noted, happens to be based on the original *Ramayana* by Valmiki. Therefore, while the original story has been retained in Arni and Chitrakar's work, what is different is the female narration in the plot, to highlight Sita's travails, which is observable in the original story too. Another obvious element is the creative deployment of Patua painting format that represents Indian fine arts culture, highlighting ideas and emotions that are identifiable universally, making the work relevant and meaningful globally.

Thematically, several layers in the *Ramayana* plot have universal appeal. The idea of universality can be frequently identified in a variety of contexts. Take, for instance, the members of the diasporic community. In her incisive study, Singh (2013) notes:

> In the global context of the Indian diaspora, the Ramayana tradition has both commented on and contributed to the transformation of Indian culture in "alien" lands. The Southall Black Sisters' production of Ramleela (also Ram Lila, the play or dramatic form of the Ramayana) in the United Kingdom in 1979 reflects their particular circumstances of migration, reworking the Ramayana story through the concepts of race, class, gender, and colonialism. Although this production was performed with a celebratory spirit, it provides a vivid example of the recent effort to combat both sexism and racism by satirically questioning patriarchal attitude within Indian culture while using Ravana, the villain of the story, as a symbol of the British stage.
>
> (749)

Noteworthy is the idea of how the Ramayana epic operates through multifarious conceptual and theoretical interests, raising questions relevant to "race, class, gender and colonialism," underlining that the plot has a narrative power transcending spatio-temporality. *Sita's Ramayana* is able to achieve this sense of universality through its gesturing at female confinement, physical and emotional violence and suppression; and the general portrayal that a woman is weak, can be physically harassed and vulnerable, that she can and should be existing within the limits of patriarchy. This representation of Sita in *Sita's Ramayana* is comparable to what Singh (2013) suggests while referring to the indentured women laborers in the Carribean islands in her article. Further, Singh's allusion to the Ramleela production in the UK and the "reworking" of the Ramayana story shows how the plot has been repurposed to articulate specific ideas—again underlining the universal value of the story, despite alterations, like changes in the narrator or identifying the oppressor Ravana with oppressors in other contexts, such as the British Raj during colonialism etc. The intensity of the character in the original as well as the reinvented story remains unchanged—the implications being the same. We find the same interpretive and representative strategy in the graphic narrative *Sita's Ramayana* where the earlier main story of the centralized male character of Lord Rama is repurposed to articulate the centrality of Sita and how she understood her circumstances, injustice, her position in the patriarchal society, and whether and how long she could withstand patriarchal domination. This component in the plot—of the centrality of the woman character, her relation to the society and her marginalization, raises questions of women's subjugation across generations and attempts at emancipation. The subject is as much related to religion (since the epic is considered a sacred book by the Hindus) as it is to society and is, therefore, an emotional one because it voices concerns regarding the societal pressures that women have to endure. The universal appeal of the story is palpable and the choice of such a subject in a graphic narrative highlights its significance and why and how it becomes a part of global discourses on specific/selected literary narratives.

Ramayana Media Representation and COVID-19

Harsha Bhat (May 2, 2020) in his article "What The Success Of Ramayan's Re-Telecast Tells About The Changes In Lifestyle In The Times Of Coronavirus" states

> one of the key reasons is that this is a tale that is a household one, one that is part of popular psyche and folklore, and one whose characters are not just religious entities but also cultural icons that through oral transmission were conceived of only in imagination for generations together, until for the first time this televised version personified them and brought them into people's personal spaces.
>
> (Bhat, *Swarajya Magazine* online)

Bhat gestures at the idea of universality via underscoring a variety of layers in the re-telecasting of the serial—nostalgia, culture, folklore, religion, oral transmission, generational understanding, and reception of the Ramayana.

The epic is canonical in terms of its themes. The story that Arni and Chitrakar adapt in *Sita's Ramayana* highlights the fact that the work has universal appeal in terms of its portrayal of Sita and the subsequent questions of women's representation in literature, culture, and so on. The *Telegraph India* mentions "*Sita's Ramayana* won rave reviews and made it to the *New York Times* bestseller list for graphic novels. It hit the 7th spot on the list and stayed there for two weeks" (*Telegraph India* online, June 14, 2020).

Arni's response to the stupendous success of her graphic narrative was "I think there's a lot of interest in India, plus the traditional artwork with a contemporary presentation worked for the book" (*Telegraph India* online, June 14, 2020). The article further states about Arni, "She is quick to give credit to Moyna Chitrakar, the Patua artist from Bengal on whose scroll paintings the graphic novel is based. Tara Books, a Chennai-based publishing house, invited Patua artist Moyna Chitrakar to Chennai and came up with the idea of a graphic novel after seeing her work" (*Telegraph India* online, June 14, 2020). The selection of the Ramayana story for *Sita's Ramayana*, was, therefore, a careful one and not an arbitrary choice. Its popularity among the masses, its appeal as one representing Indian culture, mythology, and religion and the plots' questions on social and cultural values make it ideal for graphic narration.

There have been innumerable representations of the *Ramayana* narrative. However, for the purpose of this essay's central premise, I look at the re-telecasting of the Ramayana serial on the Indian Doordarshan channel during the COVID-19 lockdown in India and how the reception of the serial suggests the narrative power of the plot and its stronghold on South Asian imagination (Figure 10.5).[4] Arni's and Chitrakar's graphic narrative also reiterate the power of the discourse in terms of its gesturing at the original plot but with a twist. While the original story suggested in the serial underlines "dharma" (righteousness) as paramount, *Sita's Ramayana* is a clear questioning of the patriarchal discourse that continues in such portrayals (not only in the serial but also in various others' representations of the plot). The representations of the original plot in the serial and its astounding reception gestures at how the discourse of male domination is accepted, even revered—highlighting that the "woman" is fated to go through pain. It is a necessary "sacrifice" deemed by destiny, family, society—something that the

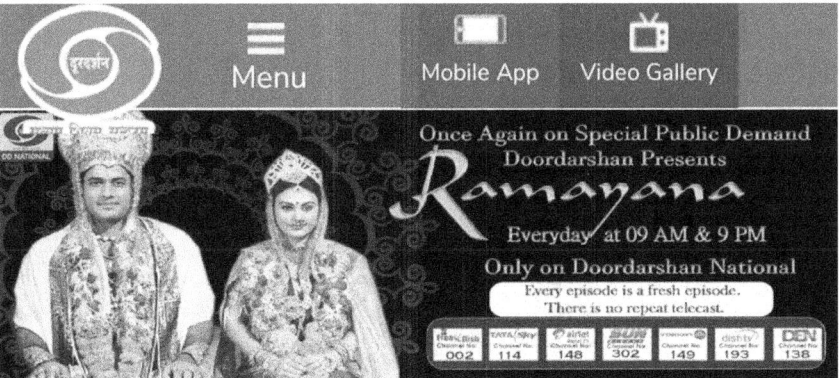

Figure 10.5 Image of the Ramayana serial from the Indian Doordarshan website (https://doordarshan.gov.in/).

---

[4] This image is for the scholarly purpose of understanding the serial's representation for the Indian masses.

woman is born to endure. It is unavoidable. A comparison of the plot lines in the *Ramayana* and *Sita's Ramayana* is critically significant—while one upholds "dharma," also patriarchy; the other questions that "dharma" and patriarchy. The serial reiterates Rama's heroism; *Sita's Ramayana* questions that heroism. This serial gained viewership the world over because people are familiar with the story and due to its mythological significance are aware of its story that is believed to be emblematic of Indian culture. K.R. Srinivas Iyegar in 1986 published *Sītāyaṇam*, where the objective is to draw attention to the fact that Sita decides to go back to her mother who happens to be Mother Earth.[5] This argument of mistreatment of Sita has resonated with the Indian society because the condition of women has been compared and likened to that of Sita in terms of injustice, marginalization, patriarchal control, lack of individuality, "sacrificing" for the sake of family name/honor/prestige, fear of what the society might think about the woman who raises her voice against her husband, and so on. This idea persists even today since the emancipation of women despite raising educational standards hasn't happened significantly and therefore Sita's plight becomes a question that reverberates as a universal situation when it comes to women's treatment.

The popularity of the Ramayana story in India is understandable. The *Business Insider* online (a business news website) stated,

> [t]his isn't the time Ramayan made a world record. From 1987 to 1988, 'Ramayan' became the most watched serial in the world. After India shut itself down to contain the COVID-19 outbreak, Doordarshan brought back all its classics from the eighties to entertain people. Ramayan gained 174 million viewers within four days of re-telecast. Whereas, it received more than 500 million views between 28 March and 4 April. The re-telecast of three-decades-old mythological series Ramayan made DD national the most-watched channel. Its viewership grew 22% within a week (April 4–10), according to rating agency BARC.
>
> (*Business Insider India*; May 1, 2020)

Several newspapers and magazines noted and wrote extensively about this record-breaking viewership of the television serial. *The Print* e-paper stated, "With much of India locked indoors on account of the COVID-19 pandemic, Doordarshan brought back its mythological classic Ramayan to keep people entertained" (Dutta 2020). The e-paper went on to describe the serial's early telecast on the Doordarshan channel and its popularity owing to the re-telecast:

> Ramanand Sagar's *Ramayan* originally went on air on Doordarshan from 25 January 1987. It was aired for over a year-and-a-half, spread over 75 episodes of 35 minutes each. The series garnered such popularity that it was rerun years later by private channels such as *Zee TV* and *NDTV Imagine*.

---

[5] It is to be noted that Sita was found by Lord Janaka while ploughing a barren land in his kingdom. Such rituals of ploughing lands are believed to have been followed to ensure fertility of agricultural lands.

Beginning 28 March, three days into the lockdown, the show made a comeback on Doordarshan and two fresh episodes of the show began to be aired in as many time slots—morning and evening.

The return of the show helped Doordarshan beat private general entertainment channels (GECs)—left without original content amid the lockdown—and emerge as India's most-watched channel.

In the first weekend of *Ramayan*'s return, Doordarshan registered a record-breaking viewership of 17 crore [one crore = 10 million], with its YouTube numbers doubling too. DD National has since consistently topped viewership charts across genres.

(Dutta, The Print online)

The popularity of *Ramayana* story is apparent through the fact that it garnered viewership not only the first time when it was telecast in 1987 but also during COVID-19 when it was aired upon popular demand. While this was perceived to be a good idea to entertain people during the lockdown in India, the fact that it was viewed abroad suggests how the Indian diaspora looks at Ramayana.[6] As already suggested, the story exists in folklore, oral transmission, literature, and the cultural psyche of the Indians.

During the colonial forced displacement of Indians to British colonies, the *Ramayana* story became a source of solace for the indentured migrants. Consider the fact that, like Rama, Sita and Lakshmana were banished from the kingdom, and therefore had to migrate away from Ayodhya, their homeland; the indentured laborers too had to migrate away from their homeland, India. However, there was hope that like Rama, Sita and Lakshmana who returned to Ayodhya, their homeland, after their long exile; and an intense struggle with Ravana (for the indentured laborers, the British symbolized Ravana, the evil one), the Indians forced to go abroad would also be able to return to their homeland.

In his 1992, Nobel Lecture "The Antilles: Fragments of Epic Memory," Derek Walcott described the performance of Ramleela in Trinidad. He began the lecture with this introduction:

Felicity is a village in Trinidad on the edge of the Caroni plain, the wide central plain that still grows sugar and to which indentured cane cutters were brought after emancipation, so the small population of Felicity is East Indian, and on the afternoon that I visited it with friends from America, all the faces along its road were Indian, which, as I hope to show, was a moving, beautiful thing, because this Saturday afternoon *Ramleela,* the epic dramatization of the Hindu epic the *Ramayana* […]

(from the Nobel Prize website)

---

[6] While the Ramayana serial might have been watched by people of other nationalities too, in this essay the focus is the Indians living abroad.

The suggestion, while reminiscing the enactment of the *Ramayana* through the performance of *Ramleela*,[7] is the perennial remembrance and universality value that the epic carries with it, globally. It has had and continues to have enduring significance in terms of it being deployed as an element in culture and society among the South Asians around the world. The choice of the plot for performance by the indentured laborers (from India) in Trinidad (Caribbean islands) and also watched by Walcott's "friends from America," gestures at the importance that the epic has in the context of Indian culture. Walcott goes on to say:

> What an unfortunate confession! "Gods, I suppose" is the shrug that embodies our African and Asian diasporas. I had often thought of but never seen *Ramleela*, and had never seen this theatre, an open field, with village children as warriors, princes, and gods.
>
> (from the Nobel Prize website)

The idea of not knowing the *Ramayana* epic, yet watching it shows how narratives can migrate, be produced away from the point of origin, yet make a mark through its reception, its plot, and cultural values. At the same time, when Walcott remarks that "Gods embody African and Asian diasporas," there is an attempt to draw parallels in culture. It is this possibility of comparison and adaptation that allows narratives belonging to different cultures to be diffused amongst people located in different geographical regions. In the context of Walcott's lecture, it is also noteworthy that for the indentured laborers, their displacement from India to Trinidad was a crisis. Enacting *Ramayana*, through *Ramleela* was a means to recreate Indian culture in a different country. People "apart from the Indians" partaking the experience was an instance of sharing and understanding a different culture. However, the suggestion of Rama as the "hero" while Sita (although a great woman) had to and did succumb to patriarchal pressure persists in these representations. *Sita's Ramayana* questions that. Compare the international representations that highlighted Rama and the oppression of Sita and *Sita's Ramayana* that presents the story via the Patua art and questioning patriarchy through the images and the title. We find two different perspectives emerging out of the different discourses around the same story.

Describing the Ramleela performance[8] in Southall, Greater London, Richman (1999) expressed, "The play reveals a great deal about how a religious text can migrate

---

[7] Ramleela is the dramatic performance of the Ramayana story.

[8] The context of this performance of the Ramayana story was the funding of the costs for the arrested neo-Nazi National Front members. Richman (1999) mentions: On 19 October 1979, Southall Black Sisters [henceforth SBS], a feminist group of South Asian and African Caribbean women from Southall, Greater London, mounted a performance of the Ramlila. SBS contributed ticket sales to a fund for legal costs of community members arrested in a recent demonstration against the neo-Nazi National Front. Suppression of the protest was marked by notable police brutality. SBS framed and periodically interrupted their rendition of the Ramlila with humorous commentary that gave a topical slant to the story's events, relating them to racism, socio-economic conditions in their area, local and national politics, and sexism. The character playing Ravana, king of the demons, wore a huge mask on which each of his ten heads had been drawn to represent an aspect of the racism that Black groups in Britain encounter (34–5).

from South Asia to Britain, retain its formal contours, and express diverse aspects of the diaspora experience" (34). The context of this performance of the *Ramayana* story was the funding of the costs for the arrested neo-Nazi National Front members. Richman (1999) mentions: "On 19 October 1979, Southall Black Sisters [...] a feminist group of South Asian and African Caribbean women from Southall, Greater London, mounted a performance of the Ramlila. SBS contributed ticket sales to a fund for legal costs of community members arrested in a recent demonstration against the neo-Nazi National Front" (33). Like Walcott's Nobel Lecture concerning the Indian indentured laborers for whom migratory movement from India to Trinidad was a crisis, in Richman's study too, we find that it is a crisis (funding required for helping arrested members of the neo-Nazi National Front) that triggers the performance of the *Ramayana*. This gestures at how the *Ramayana* story has been able to adapt to diverse situations: the notion of a return to the homeland as in the case of the indentured laborers or the neo-Nazi members' arrests and so on.

The Ramayana story therefore has had universal appeal and attraction in times of crisis due to the possibility of being able to liken certain situations, particularly the fact that women's freedom has been compromised in various contexts in the Indian society. *Sita's Ramayana* gestures at this lack of freedom to live with dignity. Therefore, Sita's portrayal in Arni and Chitrakar's graphic narrative can be contextualized within the larger picture of the global discursive construction of a work with universal appeal and implications. Consider here, Mazur's and Danner's (2017) idea of "international cross pollination" (58) in graphic novels that I cited at the beginning of this chapter. Cross-pollination suggests enrichment and even within *Sita's Ramayana*, the fact that the plot has been represented with a specialized/niche Patua art form goes on to show the nature of automatic cross-pollination in the genre's format itself. It is cross-pollination both in terms of the format as well as in terms of its implications and global understanding. The argument of Western dominance when it comes to looking at the graphic novel genre is clearly and palpably refuted when we look at the scale of influence of the Ramayana epic. Also consider how the serial *Ramayana* that valorizes Rama as opposed to the centralization of Sita in the graphic narrative are in stark contrast to each other. Several formats have used the basic plot of the Ramayana story, highlighting its impact. The fact that it was performed in the Western world shows its effect, acceptance, and relevance in a variety of contexts. The comparisons of the various discourses around the Ramayana plot, and the different kinds of questions they endorse allow the plot to be contextualized in a variety of contexts. *Sita's Ramayana* becomes a significant work because it underlines the rights of women and the compulsion on them to prove their righteousness, virtue, and loyalty over and over again. At the same time, the graphic narrative, due to its powerfully evocative and bright images highlights how the plot emerges as a strong symbol of cultural representation.

Conclusion

Sita's Ramayana—its choice of the Ramayana plot structure but rendered through the eyes of Sita—gestures at the attempt to explore the story through swapped narration.

The fact that the basic plot is derived from Valmiki's *Ramayana* but experimented with through deploying Patua paintings, suggests how graphic narratives can be positioned in the domain of World Literature via using cultural elements that are globally popular. In that sense, *Sita's Ramayana* transcends spatio-temporality. The Patua art form that was traditionally considered men's dominion has been intervened through the use of the artistic creation of Chitrakar. A look at the basic plot of *Sita's Ramayana* shows how an ancient story can be adapted to articulate a woman's voice graphically. Further, the fact that the plot has been used to describe various historical episodes in the world goes on to show how a narrative can be globally relevant. The epic's story has been adapted to diverse situations—in the colonial, postcolonial, and diasporic frames—and in the new global COVID-19 pandemic, in India has been seen as critical in entertaining citizens under lockdown and thus contributing to the objective of "protecting" citizens from the deadly disease's spread and flattening the curve. These various instances go on to provide evidence with regard to how the "universality" of the epic can affect the perception and categorization of the epic in terms of its discursive construction and narrativity. *Sita's Ramayana*, therefore, comes across as a graphic representation that is globally relevant and theoretically readable through the lens of World Literature.

References

Arni, Samhita, Chitrakar, Moyna, and Vālmīki. 2011. *Sita's Ramayana*. Chennai, India: Tara Books.

Bertocci, Peter J. 2007. "Lives of the Bengali Painters." *Visual Anthropology*, 20 (4): 305–7. https://doi.org/10.1080/08949460701424270.

Bhat, Harsha. 2020. "What The Success Of Ramayan's Re-Telecast Tells About The Changes In Lifestyle In The Times Of Coronavirus." *Swarajya Magazine*, May 2. https://swarajyamag.com/culture/coronavirus-has-forced-changes-in-our-lifestyle-and-some-are-for-good (accessed 12 September, 2020).

Bhattacharjee, Binoy. 1980. *Cultural Oscillation: A Study on Patua Culture*. Calcutta: Naya Prokash.

BI Indian Bureau. 2020. "Ramayan is the most-watched entertainment show in the world, says Doordarshan." May 1. https://www.businessinsider.in/entertainment/news/.ramayan-is-the-most-watch-entertainment-show-in-the-world-says-doordarshan/articleshow/75483891.cms.

Chandra, Sharmila. 2017. *The Patuas of West Bengal and Odisha: An Evaluative Analysis*. Mumbai, India: Himalaya Publishing House.

Chatterji, Roma. 2012. *Speaking with Pictures: Folk Art and the Narrative Tradition in India*. New Delhi, India: Routledge.

Dutta, Amrita Nayak. 2020. "DD viewership down by nearly 50% after Ramayan ends, plans afoot to bring back Vishnu Puran." *The Print*, April 30. https://theprint.in/india/dd-viewership-down-by-nearly-50-after-ramayan-ends-plans-afoot-to-bring-back-vishnu-puran/412175/.

Eaton, Natasha. 2013. "Swadeshi Color: Artistic Production and Indian Nationalism, Ca. 1905–ca. 1947." *The Art Bulletin*, 95 (4): 623–708.

Gamberi, Valentina. 2014. "Escaping from Rama: Portraits of Indian Women." *Culture and Religion*, 15 (3): 354–72. https://doi.org/10.1080/14755610.2014.945469.

Ghosh, Pika. 2003. "Unrolling a Narrative Scroll: Artistic Practice and Identity in Late-Nineteenth-Century Bengal." *The Journal of Asian Studies*, 62 (3): 835–71. https://doi:10.2307/3591862.

Hauser, Beatrix. 2002. "From Oral Tradition to 'Folk Art': Reevaluating Bengali Scroll Paintings." *Asian Folklore Studies* 61 (1): 105–22. https://doi:10.2307/1178679.

Iyengar, K.R., Srinivasa [Vālmīki]. 1987 [1987]. *Sitayana: Epic of the Earth-born: Sītāyaṇam*. Pondicherry, India: All India Press.

Korom, Frank J. 2006. *Village of Painters: Narrative Scrolls from West Bengal*. Santa Fe: Museum of New Mexico Press.

Mazur, Dan, and Danner, Alexander. 2017. "The International Graphic Novel." In Tabachnick, Stephen E., ed. *The Cambridge Companion to the Graphic Novel, Cambridge Companions to Literature*. Cambridge, UK: Cambridge University Press, 58–79.

McCutchion, David., and Suhrdkumara. 1999. *Patuas and Patua Art in Bengal*. Calcutta: Firma KLM.

Newman, John. 2013. "The Enduring Ark." *The School Librarian*, 61 (3):150. https://search.proquest.com/docview/1461371402?accountid=13042.

Ponte, Ines. 2015. "Cosmopolitan Impressions from a Contemporary Bengali Patachitra Painting Museum Collection in Portugal." *Ateliers Du LESC*, 41 (41): Ateliers Du LESC, DOI: 10.4000/ateliers.9771

Richman, P. 1999. "A Diaspora Ramayana in Southall, Greater London." *Journal of the American Academy of Religion*, 67(1): 33–58.

Sagar, Ramanand. 1987. *Ramayan*, Television Serial. Mumbai: Sagar Group.

Sen Gupta, Sankar. 1973. *The Patas and the Patuas of Bengal*. Calcutta, India: Indian Publications.

Singh, Sherry-Ann. 2013. "Ramayana." In Taylor, Patrick, Case Frederick I., Meighoo Sean, and Leung, Joyce, eds. *The Encyclopedia of Caribbean Religions: Volume 1: A–L; Volume 2: M–Z*, University of Illinois Press, 749–57. https://www.jstor.org/stable/10.5406/j.ctt2tt9kw.92 (accessed April 10, 2020).

The Telegraph. 2020. "A Graphic Edge." June 14. https://www.telegraphindia.com/culture/a-graphic-edge/cid/481142

Walcott, Derek. 1992. "The Antilles: Fragments of Epic Memory." Nobel Lecture. Stockholm, December 7. https://www.nobelprize.org/prizes/literature/1992/walcott/lecture/.

11

Wakanda as a Sustainable Smart Society: Africanfuturism in Marvel's *Black Panther*

Jana Fedtke

For a brief period of time in 2019, the online tariff tracker of the US Department of Agriculture listed "Wakanda" as one of the free-trade partners of the USA (BBC 2019). While it was not entirely clear whether listing Wakanda was a test, a prank, or a misconception, the mistake has since been rectified. This incident shows how Wakanda has recently entered popular discourses and the social imaginary. Despite Wakanda's popularity over the past few years, the country remains a fictional setting on the African continent as represented in Marvel's *Black Panther* comic book series. In this chapter, I analyze representations of the fictional African country of Wakanda in *Black Panther*. The character of the Black Panther has appeared in Marvel comics since 1966, but I am specifically interested in some of its most recent iterations: *A Nation Under Our Feet* (2016–17), *Avengers of the New World* (2017), and *The Intergalactic Empire of Wakanda* (2018–21), all written by Ta-Nehisi Coates, as well as *Long Live the King* (2017), written by Nnedi Okorafor and André Araújo. In contrast to earlier versions of Wakanda, which remained rather rudimentary with generic places such as forest, mountain, farm land, and central Wakanda, the more recent texts have engaged in rewriting and expanding the fictional empire. Their success has also been complemented by the immense popularity of the *Black Panther* movie (Marvel Studios, 2018). While it remains a predominantly American creation, *Black Panther* is an Africancentric text that functions as an Afropolitan graphic narrative in the context of contemporary World Literature. I analyze Wakanda through the lens of Africanfuturism to argue that *Black Panther* represents the reimagined nation of Wakanda as an Africanfuturist space in its portrayal of technology. The comics showcase the country as a technologically advanced monarchy built on oppression among the Wakandan people. This central contradiction remains at the heart of the texts. While Ta-Nehisi Coates and Nnedi Okorafor have created a sustainable Africanfuturist society, the comics ultimately show Wakanda's inability to confront its heritage.

Wakanda as a Sustainable Smart Society

The *Black Panther* comics by Ta-Nehisi Coates and Nnedi Okorafor present the kingdom of Wakanda as a technologically advanced society. In contrast to earlier versions of Wakanda, the country is developed in much more detail in the writing and the drawings. The capital Birnin Zana and the Learned City of Birnin Azzaria function as the two focal points of Wakanda's smart society which relies on vibranium-based technology and Wakandan traditions.

In an interview in *A Nation Under Our Feet* (2016), artist Brian Stelfreeze addresses the importance of Wakanda in the *Black Panther* comics: "Wakanda is one of the biggest characters ... I want the country to have a duality of old world and city of the future" (Issue 1). Stelfreeze contributes to personifying Wakanda as its newly created version unites both elements from the traditions of the past and the technology-driven future. While previous appearances of the Black Panther were invested in propagating stereotypical images of Africa, Ta-Nehisi Coates and Brian Stelfreeze move beyond such outdated images to represent Wakanda as a character in its own right. Part of this rewriting process was the recreation of the map of Wakanda as a fictional nation on the African continent. Kwame Opam has pointed out that, "Wakanda, as originally imagined by Lee, Kirby, and later Don McGregor, was a collection of characterless and problematic locations, with names like Piranha Cove, Primitive Peaks, and Serpent Valley that traded on Western stereotypes and ignorance" (Opam 2017, Slide 21). In the newly imagined Wakanda, these stereotypically named locations have given way to places that are considered more authentic such as Birnin Zana, Birnin Azzaria, the Crystal Forest, the Alkama Fields, the Girma Delta, Birnin Tsauni, the Jabari-Lands, Birnin Benzahin, and Birnin T'Chaka—to name but a few. The revised map reflects Wakanda's history. It also locates the country in a unique position that is "protected by hills, mountains, and the sprawling Lake Nyanza" (Issue 4). Wakanda's detailed geography gives the place an identity of its own. In this sense, it allows Wakanda to speak for itself in a voice that is, however, mediated from an American perspective. Even though several of the writers, artists, and publishers highlight their African heritage, *Black Panther* remains a US-based enterprise.

Birnin Zana—the Golden City and capital of Wakanda—and Birnin Azzaria—the Learned City—are represented as smart cities that rely on science, technology, and teaching knowledge to create a vision of Wakanda as the most advanced country on the African continent. The cities portray a forward-looking image of Wakanda. Outside the cities, the *Black Panther* comics present an idealized version of a rural Wakanda, for example in the Alkama Fields that showcase "African sun, African wind, African rain" (Issue 3). These idyllic images are contrasted with the urban spaces of Birnin Zana. As Wakanda's capital, the city is also known as the Golden City. It is presented as a modern miracle of shining skyscrapers in the background of virtually any image of the city. It also features the gleaming palace as the home and work space of the royal family of the Black Panther (Issue 1). The city is spacious, clean, modern, and shiny—an image that conforms to its name of the Golden City.

Also known by its old name of Birnin Zanariya as used by the eighteenth Mansa of the old kingdom, the capital of Wakanda has existed for over 4,000 years (Issue 11). *A Nation Under Our Feet* challenges the city's might by staging a revolution that questions the Black Panther's power and legitimacy (Issue 11). As Birnin Zana seems about to fall, the Black Panther T'Challa aims to resurrect its power and that of the family's ancestors: "the fortress was an emblem of their power, not the power itself… Wakanda is but a word. One which names all who have toiled here" (Issue 11). T'Challa wants to reunite the population behind the royal family for the sake of Wakanda. He envisions the country as a nation in which everyone's contribution matters. To him, Birnin Zana functions as a *pars pro toto*: "The Golden City belies its own name… it is a symbol of our mettle… that symbol will be our ultimate defense" (Issue 10). T'Challa's pride in the city reflects his appreciation for all of Wakanda, which he is willing to defend against any enemy to the very end. This vision of Wakanda imagines the country as the oxymoron of a "democratic monarchy." The *Black Panther* comics may question the institution of the absolute monarchy, but they ultimately endorse its existence by presenting the revolution as a failure. Even more so than the comic books, the 2018 movie version of the *Black Panther* focuses on the power of royalty, which the acclaimed novelist Teju Cole (2018) bemoans in his essay, "On the Blackness of the Panther." Speculating on future fictional narratives from Africa, Cole asks: "Why are monarchies the narrative default? Can we dream beyond royalty?" (para. 8). Describing his personal antipathy to monarchies, Cole proposes to leave them behind in a move toward a democratic future: "The societies I dream organize themselves around knowledgeable democratic choice. The dream extends past even the nation state. No kings, no queens. No royal presidents" (para.14). Such an abolition of the monarchy could entail a focus on merit and knowledge. African narratives without royalty could present a future free from enslavement and neo-colonial reliance on hierarchical power relationships.

Technology is of paramount importance in these efforts of defending the city and the nation. From the very beginning of *A Nation Under Our Feet*, Wakanda is announced as "the most technologically advanced society on the globe" (Issue 1). Many issues of the series feature technological inventions that are unique to Wakanda. These include the Black Panther's vibranium suit which functions as a protective shield and equips the Panther with superhuman strength (Issue 6), the soul-stalker power that allows the Panther special vision (Issue 5), the mystical spear that provides him with energy (Issue 11), the interface of 3D images that display strategic plans, grids, imagined places and visualize projections of the mind (Issue 2). In addition to these features, the kimoyo net facilitates communication among the Wakandans (Issue 11 and Issue 18), which also provides secure kimoyo messaging channels as they use the kimoyo beads on the kimoyo bracelets for communication (Issue 168). Wakanda's secret police, the Hatut Zeraze, have psionic defenses that allow them to use telepathy (Issue 17). The Engineering Lab is a central part of Birnin Zana (Issue 8). While T'Challa acknowledges his position as the rightful king, he also sees himself as a scientist at heart (Issue 6). He is proud of his achievements and those of Wakanda: "Upon the land of the Originators … we built the most advanced society ever known" (Issue 167). This pride in society's advanced development is also evident when discussing the bombing technology used as biotechnology connected to people's hearts: "it was obvious that the bombing tech did not come out of anything Wakandan in origin" (Issue 6). T'Challa is convinced that Wakandan technology is made for the improvement of society instead of hurting people by bombing them. He perceives this technology as foreign to Wakanda as he places its origin outside the country.

Most places in Birnin Zana speak of technological progress for Wakanda, whereas Birnin Azzaria or the Learned City is shown as promoting knowledge, predominantly from a philosophical perspective. In this sense, Birnin Azzaria complements Birnin Zana. Birnin Azzaria's focal point is an academy called Hekima Shule, where Changamire teaches (Issue 2). Old, well-read, and wise, with a gray beard and dreadlocks, Changamire stands for the quest for knowledge in this male-dominated environment. He used to be T'Challa's handpicked tutor, but is now considered a dissident philosopher (Issue 4). Changamire encourages his students to think actively, discussing and debating issues rather than following traditions blindly: "How should the weak marshal justice against the powerful?... The questions are the point" (Issue 4). In contrast to Birnin Zana's skyscrapers that represent phallic symbols, Birnin Azzaria's buildings in the background are dome-shaped with golden roofs like honeycombs.

At first, Changamire is presented in opposition to T'Challa and the institution of the monarchy as he joins the fight against the royal family. While he is a dissident, he also follows established traditions when he bows to Queen Ramonda, T'Challa's mother, and touches her feet as a gesture of reverence (Issue 11). One fundamental difference is how T'Challa and Changamire see Wakanda's role in the world. With regard to the 2018 movie version of *Black Panther*, Derilene Marco has called Wakanda's representation "a kind of spectacularization of blackness, a kind of exceptionalism both celebrated and desired in ways that have seemingly never been experienced in relation to blackness" (2018, 6). This concept of Wakanda's exceptionalism is central to the nation's understanding of its role on the African continent and in the world at large. T'Challa wants to defend Wakanda at all cost, but is opposed to assigning the country and its citizens a special status: "Wakandans think themselves a race all of their own—it is... foolish" (Issue 8). T'Challa ridicules this understanding of a Wakandan exceptionalism, while Changamire uses this concept to his advantage to convince people of Wakanda's special powers: "Liberators turned slave-holders... we were supposed to be better... Wakanda the unconquered, Wakanda the advanced, Wakanda the exceptional" (Issue 8). Ultimately convinced that war and fighting are not the answer to sustain Wakanda, he shifts his position to support T'Challa. Using the kimoyo band, his speech is broadcast to everyone across the country: "Come back to the house of your ancestors... let us show them that we are exceptional" (Issue 11). Changamire believes in the power of Wakanda as a place that is different from other countries in Africa and worldwide. His vision is to inspire people through his words to see this exceptionalism as well.

Just as the *Black Panther* comics contrast different approaches to Wakanda's role in the world, they also juxtapose the country's present with its past in the Plane of Ancestral Memory, also known as the Djalia. The Plane of Ancestral Memory is another way of introducing balance and sustainability into Wakanda's representation as an advanced nation that is rooted in its traditions of the past. When Shuri, the Black Panther's sister, is presumed dead, her spirit travels the Djalia (Issue 2). The Djalia is another idyllic space that is "memory incarnate" (Issue 167). The Plane of Ancestral Memory represents "Wakanda's collective past, present, and future" (Issue 5). It helps Wakandans foresee and plan the future. It also functions as a bridge between the current inhabitants of the country and their ancestors.

Wakanda is represented as a sustainable society in *Black Panther* through its depiction of Birnin Zana and Birnin Azzaria as two smart cities, its status as an exceptional and advanced society that is rooted in its past through communication with its ancestors in the Plane of Wakandan Memory, and its use of technology. This technology depends on the country's use of vibranium, which is the raw material that forms the basis for all of Wakanda's technological inventions.

Vibranium: "The Blood of This Wakanda"

Vibranium as a raw material that is only found in Wakanda cements the country's special status as an exceptional nation among its neighbors in Africa and also worldwide. It sustains Wakanda and provides an important lifeline. The *Black Panther* comics describe the material as "the blood of this Wakanda" (Issue 166), implying that it is the single most significant resource on which the country runs.

Virtually all of Wakanda relies on vibranium. The artist Brian Stelfreeze describes how he positioned Birnin Zana in relation to vibranium: "I've set the Golden City as a ring surrounding a giant crater lake to suggest that it's possibly the result of an ancient vibranium meteor strike" (Issue 1). This shows how Wakanda was a coincidental recipient of this precious resource, which allowed the country to build its society on this wealth based on "a large deposit of an extremely rare natural resource" (Issue 1). T'Challa is aware of the special nature of this raw material and the people who mine it when he describes them as "the heart of my country, the vibranium miners of the Great Mound" (Issue 1). Also known as Mena Ngai, the Great Mound is the location of vibranium near Birnin Zana. Wakanda depends on its natural resource in the invention and production of its technological gadgets such as the panther suit and the kimoyo net and beads.

Brian Stelfreeze details the unique properties of vibranium, which "absorbs sound and kinetic energy, but that energy stays locked within the vibranium itself. Wakandan scientists can... use vibranium as a limitless power source... All the military spears and even the personal bracelets network into this power source" (Issue 1). The artist also explains Wakanda's exceptionalism when he shows that this technology cannot be exported to other places: "It would be the equivalent of having the world's greatest laptop but with no battery. Perhaps this is a metaphor of the Wakandan people. They believe a part of their very soul exists within the country itself" (Issue 1). Stelfreeze envisions an intimate connection between vibranium and the people of Wakanda.

As a fictional raw material, vibranium has inspired critical engagement with the elements and their arrangement in the periodic table. Sibrina Collins and LaVetta Appleby explore where current students of chemistry would place vibranium based on their understanding of the "amazing chemical and physical properties" of vibranium (2018, 1243). The authors also argue that the *Black Panther* movie offers a "unique opportunity" to highlight the role of women and people of color in STEM fields (2018, 1244). They interpret Shuri as a shining example of such a future. This is particularly evident in the movie version. Compared to the comics in which T'Challa occupies the role of lead scientist, Shuri is cast as running the Engineering Lab in Wakanda, designing new technology on a daily basis. As James Hodapp has shown, Shuri's role in the comics increases in the eponymous series, which provides the character with a "rounded backstory" (Okorafor 2019, 10). Similarly, Nathan Holbert, Michael Dando, and Isabel Correa argue that the *Black Panther* movie allows for "reflection on the present that situates critical design... as future-making that centers the histories, perspectives, and values of people of color to critique structural inequalities that pervade our current social and political systems" and to "disrupt dominant notions of what counts as STEM as well as who belongs in these fields" (2020, 329). The vibranium in Wakanda is a potential catalyst to discuss its role in society as well as Wakanda's dependence on this raw material.

Nnedi Okorafor has added another feature to the versatile nature of vibranium. In *Long Live the King* (2017), Okorafor personifies the raw material to make it seem alive. The lead researcher uses a quantum computer "to model the interactions between subatomic components of vibranium molecules" (Issue 5). Endowing vibranium with special properties, it becomes a "weapon that no one would need to wield" (Issue 5) since this version of vibranium would be "sentient," i.e., a conscious material that is alive. Personifying vibranium raises the issue of agency in the context of colonialism in Africa. Since Wakanda heavily relies on vibranium to produce all its technology and inventions in society, the country is presented as dependent on this raw material. This echoes colonial dependencies of the exploitation of resources in Africa, but also of the exploitation of labor. The choice of vibranium as a raw material on which a country's fortune depends negates other abilities that lie outside a resource that is found in the ground. It shows Wakanda's reliance on nature, but it neglects original intellectual abilities. Read this way, *Black Panther* presents a stereotypical image of Africa as dependent on raw materials and lacking ingenuity. While Wakanda is presented as a scientifically advanced society under the leadership of the mighty Black Panther, the texts show that this advancement depends on some uncomfortable parallels between resource extraction and comparing Africans to animals that echo colonialist mindsets. This indicates that futurist spaces are not viable without reference to their colonial heritage.

A similar stereotype is at work in the representation of the protagonist, the Black Panther himself. While he is represented as a well-rounded character with superhuman strength and intelligence, his representation also depends on dehumanization and animalistic features. Black Panther is the ceremonial title of T'Challa as the King of Wakanda. Throughout the comic, he is shown as a muscular body in his panther suit made of vibranium. T'Challa cherishes the combination of his title with his animalistic features: "My name is my nature. I can track a body through wind and rain. For I track not the body, but the soul within" (Issue 1). He highlights the features that allow him to smell and track people similar to an animal. His mother, Queen Ramonda, warns him to use his strength wisely: "it is not enough to be the sword—you must be the intelligence behind it" (Issue 1). She reminds him to use his body as a weapon, but at the same time, not neglect his intellectual prowess. The artist Brian Stelfreeze explains his attitude towards his creation: "I have always liked the simplicity of the Black Panther costume... 'Black Panther' suggests a sleek efficiency... I am adding small touches to make him feel more aggressive and catlike" (Issue 1). Stelfreeze also emphasizes the animalistic nature of the Black Panther by calling him "catlike." The Black Panther himself sees being an animal as his "essence," which he embraces (Issue 13). Similar to Wakanda's reliance on vibranium, the Black Panther relies on his identity as a panther, an animal guided by instincts and nature rather than by rational decisions. Teju Cole also emphasizes the catlike nature of the panther in Rainer Maria Rilke's poem, "Der Panther." Pacing in its cage, the panther is constantly being observed in a zoo-like environment. Cole interprets the panther as "a racialized subject" (Cole 2018), which becomes even more evident in the context of exhibitions which featured African people on display in zoos and circuses around the end of the nineteenth century and the beginning of the twentieth century (Cole 2018).

Both vibranium and the Black Panther are presented as forces of nature that determine Wakanda's future. Their representation is reminiscent of colonial stereotypes of raw materials and the following exploitation of the African continent as well as the animalistic nature of people on that continent, which is problematic in the *Black Panther* comics. The reimagination of Wakanda as a fictional country in *Black Panther* can be seen as a push-back against portrayals of Africa as poor, war torn, and diseased. Wakanda is presented as a scientifically advanced nation that is not afflicted by any of the problems that are often represented in fictional texts set on the African continent.

Africanfuturism in *Black Panther*

With a renewed focus on the "Africanness" of the characters and the environment, Wakanda in the *Black Panther* comics is an example of Africanfuturism.

Afrofuturism and Africanfuturism are two related terms that attempt to explain an engagement with "Africanness" and Blackness in fiction. Ytasha L. Womack defines Afrofuturism as an "intersection of imagination, technology, the future, and liberation" (2013, 9). The focus is on fictional accounts that imagine a bright future based on technological advancement. This future signifies freedom from oppression or slavery. Imagining Afrofuturist projects happens across various disciplines: in literature, the arts, and music. According to Womack, "Afrofuturists redefine culture and notions of blackness for today and the future. Both an artistic aesthetic and a framework for critical theory, Afrofuturism combines elements of science fiction, historical fiction, speculative fiction, fantasy, Afrocentricity, and magic realism with non-Western beliefs" (2013, 9). Womack specifically points out the critical nature of some Afroturist projects: "In some cases, it's a total reenvisioning of the past and speculation about the future rife with cultural critiques" (2013, 9). Such a critique is also evident in the *Black Panther* comics.

In *Afrofuturism 2.0: The Rise of Astro-Blackness*, Reynaldo Anderson and Charles E. Jones address a further development of Afrofuturism which they call Astro-Blackness. Anderson and Jones see Astro-Blackness as "the emergence of a black identity framework within emerging global technocultural assemblages, migration, human reproduction, algorithms, digital networks, software platforms, bio-technical augmentation" (2016, vii). This contemporary shift is concerned with "blackness transitioning through a digitized era toward and in tension with post-digital perspectives as a global response to the planetary and near planetary challenges facing black life in the early twenty-first century" (2016, viii). This definition emphasizes the changing nature of futurisms with a focus on technology. Alex Zamalin also delineates the development of Afrofuturism via Black Nationalism and ideas of black utopias. According to Zamalin, black utopia "insists that combining black utopia's unseen transformative possibilities with an awareness of its limitations can invigorate contemporary political thinking" (2019, 2). In all of these approaches, the term "Afro" refers to "Africanness" in the US context.

Contrary to these hopeful reimaginations of Afrofutures, Frank B. Wilderson III introduces the notion of Afropessimism as a metatheoretical framework (2020, 14). He argues that "*Blacks are not Human subjects, but are instead structurally inert props, implements for the execution of White and non-Black fantasies and sadomasochistic pleasures*" (2020, 15, emphasis in the original). The *Black Panther* movie with its powerful affirmation of Wakanda as a futuristic society on the African continent embraces Afrofuturism since it also refers to various places in the USA as connected to the future of Wakanda. The movie does not represent Afropessimism. The *Black Panther* comics, on the other hand, can be interpreted as yet a third possibility of reading "Africanness" in the texts: Africanfuturism as opposed to Afrofuturism.

Nnedi Okorafor claims the term Africanfuturism as her own in her blog post in October 2019. She clarifies it with regard to the term Afrofuturism and her own work as a writer of what she proceeds to call Africanfuturism. Okorafor addresses the similarities between the two terms: "Africanfuturism is similar to 'Afrofuturism' in the way that blacks on the continent and in the Black Diaspora are all connected by blood, spirit, history and future" (Okorafor 2019). Okorafor explains the differences: "Africanfuturism is specifically and more directly rooted in African culture, history, mythology and point-of-view as it then branches into the Black Diaspora, and it does not privilege or center the West" (Okorafor 2019). Okorafor emphasizes the optimistic future of Africanfuturism: "Africanfuturism is concerned with visions of the future, is interested in technology, leaves the earth, skews optimistic, is centered on and predominantly written by people of African descent (black people) and it is rooted first and foremost in Africa" (Okorafor 2019). The author specifically mentions the differences between the *Black Panther* comics and the *Black Panther* movie: "Afrofuturism: Wakanda builds its first outpost in Oakland, CA, USA.

Africanfuturism: Wakanda builds its first outpost in a neighboring African country" (Okorafor 2019). Following this definition, the *Black Panther* movie would be an example of Afrofuturism, emphasizing the effects on the Black diaspora, while the *Black Panther* comics would be an example of Africanfuturism, more clearly rooted in the African continent.

This definition and understanding of Africanfuturism has been gaining more ground. Jenna Hanchey has examined desire and the politics of Africanfuturism in Okorafor's own writing. Hanchey sees Okorafor's texts as part of "a rising tide of Africanfuturist work" (2020, 119). Along these lines, Nnedi Okorafor's blogpost was also published as the introduction to Wole Talabi's (2020) anthology on Africanfuturism, which features Okorafor's writing as well as additional stories by other Africanfuturists. James Hodapp explores the *Shuri* comics in the *Black Panther* series as an example of Africanfuturism since "Okorafor was given license to (re)create the character and its publication coincides with Okorafor's development of Africanfuturism" (2021, 4).

Reading the *Black Panther* comics as examples of Africanfuturism, the most obvious element under this umbrella would be the exclusively African locations. The comics mention a few places in the USA, but unlike the movie version, they do so in passing. These foreign locations do not move the plot forward. Instead, the narrative mentions a few African locations outside Wakanda, but mostly focuses on Wakanda itself with Birnin Zana, Birnin Azzaria, the Jabari-Lands, the Crystal Forest, and other locations. Equally important are the references to the technological inventions that point to the developed nature of the country and that help orient Wakanda towards a prosperous future. The futuristic design of the technology as well as the "coolness" of the smart cities complement the notion of Africanfuturism in the texts. Artist Brian Stelfreeze has also addressed the "African feel" as evident in the customs, clothes, and food: "Ta-Nehisi's script feels very African, so I wanted the art to reflect this. I'm pulling from cultures all over the continent to establish the look: Masi tribesmen, Ancient Zulu warriors, and even modern Kalashnikov-wielding rebels will all influence the look of Wakanda" (Issue 1). Stelfreeze credits writer Ta-Nehisi Coates with this Panafrican collection of contexts to create a Wakandan Africanfuturist nation.

A Nation Under Our Feet exhibits the same features as the *Shuri* comics, for which James Hodapp has identified the use of "metonymic gaps" (Hodapp 2021, 11). The comics are predominantly written in English, but they feature a few terms in Wakandan. As an African language, Wakandan is made up, but also includes some references to Swahili and other Bantu languages. In the movie version, some characters also speak in Xhosa. Examples of these linguistic features include "haramu fal," meaning "the orphan king," which is meant to mock the Black Panther (Issue 1) as Wakandans are shown to be prejudiced against orphans (Issue 12). On the other hand, his name and title are presented as "damisa sarki," which stands for "the Black Panther" (Issue 1). He also uses "taifa ngao—the Shield of the Nation" (Issue 2). Outsiders are shown as ignorant with regard to the language and terms as seen when Ezekiel Stane asks: "Is that, like some Wakandan voodoo-speak? Some Swahili jive-talk?" (Issue 7). For Wakandans themselves, some terms also signify power and alliances with other cultural contexts such as Shuri's use of "amandla," meaning "power" in several Bantu languages in Africa and implying a struggle against oppression (Issue 7). Over the course of the comic series, the linguistic features become less and less evident, giving way to English more and more often.

Black Panther constitutes an example of Africanfuturism as defined by Nnedi Okorafor. The comics reimagine a future of Wakanda as technologically advanced. They propose a viable futuristic version of Wakanda that is invested in promoting "African" traditions and values. Despite these efforts of presenting Wakanda as an Africanfuturist space, *Black Panther* remains an American creation by artists who partly identify as "African" but are, at the same time, "rooted" in the US-American context from which they write and create and where the works are published.

Power Struggles and Colonial Echoes

On the one hand, the *Black Panther* comics appear scientifically advanced in their portrayal of Africanfuturism including technology and elements of sustainability. On the other hand, Wakanda as a reimagined country also faces struggles of equality within its borders. The comics represent these power struggles as colonial echoes in an Africanfuturist context.

In "Redefining the Colonial: An Afrofuturist Analysis of Wakanda and Speculative Fiction," Ricardo Guthrie asks, "*What does a modern African nation look like, if it has not been created though colonialism?*" (2019, 15, emphasis in the original). Elisabeth Abena Osei attests the movie a "de-colonial agenda" (2020, 378), while Shenid Bhayroo interprets the film as a Disney commodity that presents a Wakanda "untouched by the ravages of colonialism and ruled by benevolent leaders endowed with superpowers" (2019, 1). The author shows that the film "sustains the system that produced it" (Bhayroo 2019, 1). I argue that this holds true for the comics as well, as they represent a society that is technologically advanced, yet built on oppression among its own ranks.

The *Black Panther* comics present Wakanda as the "perfect kingdom" with one strong leader, the Black Panther himself (Issue 1). What seems to be working on the surface soon raises some doubt as part of the Wakandan population challenges the king's rule with the slogan: "Death to tyrants, a throne for Wakandans" (Issue 1). This call aims for a fair and just democracy where governance is shared instead of dominated by one person.

More criticism comes from the Djalia as well where Queen Ramonda talks to Shuri in the form of an ancient griot or storyteller. She is critical of the technological development that Wakanda has recently taken. In Birnin Azzaria, Changamire offers a similar critique of Wakanda's supposed advancement: "Wakanda is science and wonder, all of it achieved by ensuring your subjects do not ask too many questions. Wakanda has all the intelligence any advanced society would want, and none of the wisdom that any free society needs" (Issue 4). Changamire believes that Wakanda needs more philosophy, wisdom, and morality to advance instead of more and more technology. Later on, it is also Changamire who questions the rationale of Wakanda's current way of achieving its advancement: "Who, in full sanity, would try to hold a nation under their feet?" (Issue 10). This allusion to the title of the series may be a reference to Steve Hahn's 2003 Pulitzer Prize-winning book on American slavery and freedom. Changamire's call for more freedom is opposed by the royal family. Queen Ramonda appeals to T'Challa's sense of tradition: "the throne is still the glue of Wakanda, for the throne is the will of Bast herself" (Issue 6). She warns T'Challa not to question the will of Bast, who protects all Panthers and Wakanda itself. Shuri also asks the Black Panther to believe in his own power: "You are a king, the king of the most advanced country in the world... if you want new traditions and new morality, then create them..." (Issue 12). She is in favor of the monarchy, but she is also open to changes.

After much deliberation, Wakanda forms the Wakandan Constitutional Council. This move toward elections and a government is ridiculed by Dr. Faustus in Azania, one of Wakanda's enemies: "Now they bend to the pieties of the West—democracy, 'a throne for the people'" (Issue 14).

The theme of corruption and a self-serving leadership is also carried into Nnedi Okorafor's *Long Live the King* (2017). This version of Wakanda indicates in its title that T'Challa retains his power. The revolution against him is lead by M'baku of the White Gorilla Cult: "The time has come to lead Wakanda back to greatness. The current leadership is corrupted by the West and other influences... restore Wakanda's pride. We will be able to rightfully expand our empire" (Issue 4). The idea of outside influence having corrupted Wakanda is used as a selling point to convince people of T'Challa's inability to lead the country. This vision of expanding Wakanda's sphere of influence is taken to new levels in the following series titled *The Intergalactic Empire of Wakanda*, written by Ta-Nehisi Coates (2018–21).

Wakanda's space mission in *The Intergalactic Empire of Wakanda* reveals an unknown part of the fictional nation. T'Challa had originally sent the mission to discover the origins of vibranium, but it accidentally landed about 2,000 years back in time. The space mission uncovers an entire empire that spans five galaxies (Issue 1). As the term empire suggests, some territories were taken from other people by force. Aptly described as "mules," the people living in those regions were turned into slaves and had to work in the vibranium mines (Issue 1). These miners remain nameless, they are "orphans of the cosmos" (Issue 1). They do not know their history since they have been mind-wiped (Issue 1). In contrast to this lack of history, the highest cast of Wakandans in the empire is called Imperials. The rebels are intent on destroying the empire, again leading to power struggles.

The Intergalactic Empire faces the same issue as Prime Wakanda on Earth: while it seems forward-looking in its inventions and achievements in space, it is also built on slavery and enslaved labor: "Like all empires, the Empire of Wakanda is counterfeit... empires do not enlighten, they plunder... all of it plundered from the millions they've enslaved" (Issue 7). Talking to Bast, T'Challa slowly realizes the problematic nature of the empire: "across the vastness of space, I saw the very name of Wakanda expand. And what I found in this expansion was not merely the faithful, but the fanatic" (Issue 6). Understanding its fanatic and destructive power, he exclaims: "All our wisdom, science, ethics... it was Wakanda unbound... Wakanda amplified, augmented and evolved... I should have seen the empire for what it was... This empire must fall" (Issue 18). This realization is accompanied by a map of the African continent on the globe with T'Challa represented as falling off that map (Issue 18).

Several scholars have analyzed the *Black Panther* comics and the movie version in a postcolonial context. Tim Posada and Todd Steven Burroughs explore the changing character of the *Black Panther* over the years. Posada sees this change from Blaxploitation to "modern power" in the most recent versions of *Black Panther* (Posada 2019, 626), while Burroughs (2018) details the previous struggle to create an Afrocentric character knowing that the majority of the audience would be white. Similarly, Adélékè Adéèkó offers a "postcolonial critique" of the movie (2020, 136). Godfried A. Asante and Gloria Nziba Pindi have identified transnational Blackness as a unifying feature: "*Black Panther* draws on the shared histories among African Americans, diasporic Africans, and continental Africans of the Middle Passage by imagining a transnational Blackness that resists the cultural dislocation, estrangement, and alienation experienced by Black bodies everywhere" (2020, 221). This idea of a transnational belonging is also echoed in Richard Thompson Ford's reading of *Black Panther* as "stylized pan-Africanism" (2018, para. 12). Finally, Bibi Burger and Laura Engels suggest reading Ta-Nehisi Coates' comics as "a space in which black culture is created in the shadow of collective traumas and memories. We argue that in *a nation under our feet* the fictional African country of Wakanda functions as a metaphorical Mecca," using Coates' term from his non-fiction (2019, 1). The authors explore how "this representation of Wakanda questions the idea of a unified black people and how Wakanda, like the real world Meccas described by Coates, display internal ideological and political struggles among its people" (2019, 1).

The *Black Panther* comics represent the power struggle in Wakanda and its Intergalactic Empire. They situate T'Challa as the King of Wakanda at the forefront of examining his own attitudes towards colonialism, the responsibility for a people, corruption, and possible futures for Wakanda. The comics do not provide definitive answers as to what Wakanda should be, but they present various open-ended options.

Conclusion

Recent re-writings of the fictional country of Wakanda by Ta-Nehisi Coates and Nnedi Okorafor have contributed to the increasing popularity of the *Black Panther* comics. In this paper, I focused on the aspect of providing more detail to Wakandan characters as well as to Wakanda itself as a character. I showed how Wakanda's reliance on vibranium in its technological advancement can be problematic. Using the examples of Birnin Zana as Wakanda's tech capital and Birnin Azzaria as the Learned City, I proposed to read the *Black Panther* comics as establishing a continuous power struggle. Several scholars have linked this power struggle to the postcolonial context in which Wakanda operates. While Wakanda is, on the one hand, presented as a smart society that is able to sustain itself due to its wealth in vibranium, the country, on the other hand, engages in questionable practices that reinforce colonial attitudes. This is particularly evident in *The Intergalactic Empire of Wakanda*, but even in *A Nation Under Our Feet*. The texts showcase a constant struggle between those in power as part of the royal family and those "serving" the monarchy. I situated this struggle in the Africanfuturist settings of Prime Wakanda on Earth, specifically the smart cities of Birnin Zana and Birnin Azzaria, and the Intergalactic Empire of Wakanda in space. In this paper, I argued for a reading of Wakanda in these particular texts as an Africanfuturist space, following Nnedi Okorafor's definition of the term Africanfuturism as opposed to Afrofuturism. This lens allows us to read Wakanda as a fictional space that combines futurism with technology, yet at the same time enables a critique of societal practices with regard to oppression. Coates and Okorafor have created a Wakandan world of power in an African context, but they have also shown how this power can be abused.

References

Adéẹ̀kọ́, Adélékè. 2020. "Postcolonial Critique in Ryan Coogler's *Black Panther*." *Cambridge Journal of Postcolonial Literary Inquiry*, 7 (2): 136–46. https://www.cambridge.org/core/journals/cambridge-journal-of-postcolonial-literary-inquiry/article/postcolonial-critique-in-ryan-cooglers-black-panther/99FF1C725CE370B68E4A9A355F084660.

Anderson, Reynaldo, and Jones, Charles E., eds. 2016. *Afrofuturism 2.0: The Rise of Astro-Blackness*. Lanham, MD: Lexington Books.

Asante, Godfried A., and Nziba Pindi, Gloria. 2020. "(Re)imagining African Futures: Wakanda and the Politics of Transnational Blackness." *Review of Communication*, 20 3: 220–8. https://www.tandfonline.com/doi/full/10.1080/15358593.2020.1778072.

Bhayroo, Shenid. 2019. "Wakanda Rising: Black Panther and Commodity Production in the Disney Universe." *Image and Text*, 33: 1–20. http://www.scielo.org.za/scielo.php?script=sci_arttext&pid=S1021-14972019000100003.

Black Panther. 2018. Directed by Ryan Coogler. Marvel Studios.

Burger, Bibi, and Engels, Laura. 2019. "A Nation Under Our Feet: Black Panther, Afrofuturism and the Potential of Thinking Through Political Structures." *Image and Text*, 33: 1–30. http://www.scielo.org.za/pdf/it/n33/02.pdf.

Burroughs, Todd Steven. 2018. "Black Panther, Black Writers, White Audience: Christopher Priest and/vs. Reginald Hudlin." *Fire!*, 4 (2): 55–93. https://www.jstor.org/stable/10.5323/fire.4.2.0055#metadata_info_tab_contents.

Coates, Ta-Nehisi. 2016–17. *Black Panther—A Nation Under Our Feet*. Marvel Comics.

Coates, Ta-Nehisi. 2017. *Black Panther—Avengers of the New World*. Marvel Comics.

Coates, Ta-Nehisi. 2018–21. *Black Panther—The Intergalactic Empire of Wakanda*. Marvel Comics.

Cole, Teju. 2018. "On the Blackness of the Panther." *Medium*. https://level.medium.com/on-the-blackness-of-the-panther-f76d771b0e80.

Collins, Sibrina N., and Appleby, LaVetta. 2018. "*Black Panther*, Vibranium, and the Periodic Table." *Journal of Chemical Education*, 95 (7): 1243–4. https://pubs.acs.org/doi/10.1021/acs.jchemed.8b00206.

Guthrie, Ricardo. 2019. "Redefining the Colonial: An Afrofuturist Analysis of Wakanda and Speculative Fiction." *Journal of Futures Studies*, 24 (2): 15–28. https://jfsdigital.org/wp-content/uploads/2019/12/02-Guthrie-Redefining-Colonial.pdf.

Hahn, Steve. 2003. *A Nation Under Our Feet: Black Political Struggles in the Rural South from Slavery to the Great Migration.* Cambridge, MA: Harvard University Press.

Hanchey, Jenna N. 2020. "Desire and the Politics of Africanfuturism." *Women's Studies in Communication*, 43 (2): 119–24. https://www.tandfonline.com/doi/full/10.1080/07491409.2020.1745589.

Hodapp, James. 2019. *Afropolitan Literature as World Literature.* New York: Bloomsbury.

Hodapp, James. 2021. "Fashioning Africanfuturism: African Comics, Afrofuturism, and Nnedi Okorafor's *Shuri*." *Journal of Graphic Novels and Comics*, 1–14. https://doi.org/10.1080/21504857.2021.1965637.

Holbert, Nathan, Dando, Michael, and Correa, Isabel. 2020. "Afrofuturism as Critical Constructionist Design: Building Futures from the Past and Present." *Learning, Media and Technology*, 45 (4): 328–44. https://www.tandfonline.com/doi/full/10.1080/17439884.2020.1754237.

Marco, Derilene. 2018. "Vibing with Blackness: Critical Considerations of *Black Panther* and Exceptional Black Positionings." *MDPI*. https://www.mdpi.com/2076-0752/7/4/85.

Okorafor, Nnedi. 2019. "Africanfuturism Defined." Nnedi's Blog. http://nnedi.blogspot.com/2019/10/africanfuturism-defined.html.

Okorafor, Nnedi, and Araújo, André. 2017. *Black Panther—Long Live the King.* Marvel Comics.

Okorafor, Nnedi, and Romero, Leonardo. 2018-19. *Shuri—The Search for Black Panther.* Marvel Comics.

Opam, Kwame. 2017. "Wakanda Reborn: Tour Black Panther's Reimagined Homeland with Ta-Nehisi Coates." *The Verge*. https://www.theverge.com/a/marvel-black-panther.

Osei, Elisabeth Abena. 2020. "Wakanda Africa Do You See? Reading *Black Panther* as a Decolonial Film through the Lens of the Sankofa Theory." *Critical Studies in Media Communication*, 37 (4): 378–90. https://www.tandfonline.com/doi/full/10.1080/15295036.2020.1820538.

Posada, Tim. 2019. "Afrofuturism, Power, and Marvel Comics's *Black Panther*." *Journal of Popular Culture*, 52 (3): 625–44. https://onlinelibrary.wiley.com/doi/10.1111/jpcu.12805.

Talabi, Wole, ed. 2020. *Africanfuturism – An Anthology.* Chicago, IL: Brittle Paper.

Thompson Ford, Richard. 2018. "Black Panther: An Afrocentric Ethical Fable." Stanford Law School Blog. https://law.stanford.edu/2018/02/27/black-panther-afrocentric-ethical-fable/.

"US Government Lists Fictional Nation Wakanda as Trade Partner." 2019. *BBC World*. https://www.bbc.com/news/world-us-canada-50849559.

Wilderson, Frank B. 2020. *Afropessimism.* New York: Liveright/Norton.

Womack, Ytasha L. 2013. *Afrofuturism: The World of Black Sci-Fi and Fantasy Culture.* Chicago, IL: Lawrence Hill Books.

Zamalin, Alex. 2019. *Black Utopia: The History of an Idea from Black Nationalism to Afrofuturism.* New York: Columbia University Press.

12

Neoliberal Ideologies in *Menggapai Bintang* (*Reach for the Stars*)

Mohd Muzhafar Idrus, Habibah Ismail and Hazlina Abdullah

Introduction

This chapter examines some of the most popular graphic novels in Malaysia. Available from the beginning of 2010, they provide windows into some of the many issues at private and public levels, at home and in schools. However, this chapter aims to show examples of ideological work being perpetrated in the interests of a neoliberal view of the world through demonstrating how one of these graphic novels, *Menggapai Bintang* (*Reach for the Stars*), depicts young subjects dealing with day-to-day occasions such as going to school, participating in and outside classroom activities, and inquiring about one another. The term "neoliberalism," is often employed in its sociopolitical contexts and is most commonly used together with Foucault and his works on biopolitical configuration and his understanding of it as "concepts of the financialization of everyday life, of biopolitical forms, functioning as human, of subjectivity moulded into commodity forms" (Gupta 2019, 14). We wish to draw on this notion and recontextualize and broaden its scope to incorporate the cleavages of identity(ies) that are marked by socio-economic terms that by virtue of their social status, possess an identity, are inevitably seen as linked to one's "nationalistic institutions and power structures" (Gupta 2019, 8), and yet, for the most part, align their identities as "humans divided into segments with essentialist features" (Gupta 2019, 14). On one level, there is undeniably a "streamlined," linear link concerning nation and its subjects consistent with the tenets of particular notions of nationalism. On another level, however, markers or identities of subjects, signify socio-economic configurations in the reference that need "unpacking" within one's "everyday life" as represented in comics (Gupta 2019, 8).

The term neoliberalism, particularly from Foucault's viewpoint, is used in the following discussions. According to Claire Westall (2017), the penetration of neoliberalism distinguishes itself from the production of globalization in that it recognizes the "centrality of culture and cultural production to the cyclical continuity of capitalism, and specifically to the current circuit of capitalist accumulation, that of neoliberal capital" (272). This is also, by extension, applied to neoliberalism, and its impacts on cultural (re)production. By approaching culture from the perspectives of "material culture of capitalism" to use Westall's (2017) words, such scrutiny involves unpacking "the penetration or seepage" of commodity forms "into the normality of life" (Gupta 2019). To wit, the question remains: How have these ideological spectrums been constructed across Malaysia's graphic novels?

This chapter argues that, as readers engage with *Menggapai Bintang* comics within their national landscape characterized by Malaysia's diverse ethnicities, sociolinguistic variations, and cultures, readers' engagement with graphic novels at times perpetuates competitive, economically motivated "neoliberal capital" (Westall 2017, 272). By combining Fairclough's (1992) three-dimensional critical discourse analytical model, this chapter draws upon textual (texts), contextual (discursive practice), and interpretive analysis (social practice) to investigate the ways these graphic novels are currently understood. That is, by focusing on critical discourse analysis, we argue that many of these graphic novels build a dominant discourse that accords privilege to Western-imposed globalization by almost always relegating local cultures and values while prioritizing the needs of global commerce, business, and industries. In other words, these graphic novels stage many issues between local/global continuities and disjunctures while grappling with personal and public issues. The chapter begins by contextualizing Malaysia's graphic novels. After that, we provide a necessarily brief elaboration on how studies on graphic novels in postcolonial nation-states have so far been carried out and how pressing issues of these novels have been examined. Next, we situate Fairclough's concept of critical discourse analysis and how it is useful to illuminate ideological standpoints in these graphic novels. We discuss and analyze comic examples to argue how neoliberalism in comics through socio-economic and material wealth, still separate people of the masses into high and low classes. By pairing these theoretical concerns with close textual anlysis, we dissect *Menggapai Bintang* to examine the mechanisms used to expose interests, values, and power relations. In foregrounding neoliberalism in discussing these graphic novels, we demonstrate how these seemingly mundane tales of everyday Malaysian youths are in fact problematic neoliberal national narratives that elide and overwrite other more organic postcolonial ways of being present in much of quotidian Malaysian society.

Graphic Novels in Postcolonial Nation-(states): The Story So Far

Studies focusing on postcolonial graphic novels present contradictory and conflicting insights into them at personal and public levels. In other words, graphic novels that flourish within postcolonial nations contain wide-ranging experiences, rich in political and economic significance. As James Peacock (2016) points out, the commingling of private–public lives' interaction within socio-economic landscapes as expressed in graphic novels across postcolonial nation-states may serve to make visible "ideological constructions" and "hegemonic ideas about national identity and belonging" (445). Similarly, Aurélie Chevant (2017) explains that postcolonial literature could elaborate on "the evolution of historical, social, and cultural" manifestations that are previously ignored, and how they are currently understood. In her work, Chevant (2017), who studies the postcolonial graphic and textual practices, reveals how portrayal of native Vietnamese as "physically and psychologically dangerous," may threaten "the white colonizer" (82). Images of imperialism and power, thus, may lead one to construct and normalize binary opposition, between the natives and colonizer, and between the colonized and colonizer, as demonstrated in her study on graphic novels. By drawing upon Edward Said's notion of "geographical violence," Chevant continues, postcolonial literature appropriated through graphic stories may be conversant with human bodies, landscape, cultural meaning, and cultural production. "Space and power" Chevant (2017, 82) argues, bolster the question, how have space and power been articulated, shaped artistically, and reflected in graphic novels? What do they reveal? The examples given in this chapter are framed by (the malleable) socio-economic, socio-political systems that may elaborate human beings' practices and behavior. Perhaps it is necessary here to demonstrate a range of studies written about graphic novels within postcolonial settings, reviewed to sketch the field of inquiry and to position our work on the intersection of ideology and neoliberalism. While these readings are not in any way comprehensive, they provide a "window" into what it means to immerse in graphic novels and the ways in which these have come to be understood and analyzed from multiple lenses.

Célestin, Cloonan, Dalmolin, Lan, Lee, and Munro (2017), Santos and Sihombing (2016), and Ramone (2017) look specifically at postcolonial texts to study how nationalism and communal beliefs are interrelated. The fact that many postcolonial nation states have negotiated local and global cultural realities, Célestin et al. (2017), for instance, find out that complex webs of cross-discipline perspectives are interwoven, leading one to expect that postcolonial realities run the gamut in "cuisines, sports, film, including graphic novels" (2). Ramone (2017) seems to reach similar agreement. Like Célestin et al. (2017), Ramone examines the links between Francophone and Anglophone postcolonial writings, raising pertinent questions that cut across postcoloniality and the impact this has on neoliberal globalization, migration, and refugee crises. While acknowledging distinctions made between these two contexts, we shall demonstrate that neoliberalism is central to these writings because, far from being just a tool for scrutiny, they "unlock" the keys to reproduction of socio-cultural relations not only through investigating poetry, films, and theatre, but also graphic novels. Santos and Sihomning (2016) present an enterprising attempt at graphic novels from discourse analytical perspectives. Arguing that graphic novels do not necessarily receive much emphasis, their main argument is that various classifications of graphic novels such as manga and anime "visually resemble" (196) Southeast Asian culture; adapting local culture in comics. Santos and Sihomning (2016) problematize transcultural relations in Indonesia and Phillippines, highlighting the emphasis of politics and representation which reveal the needs for alternative "imagined national identities" (197). This is because during the post-war era, the two countries were devoted to their national culture, which highlighted their national aesthetics values and presented home-grown heroes who portrayed outstanding Indonesian and

Filipino qualities. The scenario changed in the 1990s when manga, a Japanese type of graphic novel, invaded the local comic cultures. Santos and Sihomning (2016) argue that because the two countries were once conquered by Japan during the Pacific War, the presence of manga comics in these countries has "triggered postcolonial sentiments that have led to a re-evaluation of the position of local comics in national culture" (197). It seems, in both countries, transcultural conflicts have arisen following the movement of manga and the mangaesque works (local comics resembling manga).

In relation to how nation-states negotiate local and global cultural realities in literary works, depictions of graphic novels in postcolonial literature reveal certain "stereotypes" about images of nation-states. Ty's (2018) work on Asian Canadian Literary Studies, reveals the way in which literature is "stored" through sinuous interweaving of worldly disjunctures. For instance, Ty argues that twenty-first-century works on Asian Canadian literature which among others include the experiences of Chinese, Japanese, and South Asian Canadians, diasporic colonies like India, Pakistan, Sri Lanka, and others, have shifted from merely autoethnographic accounts to stories that problematize sociocultural fragments, including, but not limited to domestic violence, environment, lesbian, queer, and oppressions. The genres, "memoirs, films, short stories, and graphic novels" demonstrate "marginalized groups" across, among others, "from British Asian Canadians diasporic writing from former British colonies" (1). Landis (2019) seems to demonstrate her concurrence with Ty's assertions about constructions within postcolonial literature. Using several visual narratives in Southeast Asian literature, Landis illustrates the influence of "identification," "imagery," and "refugee" in graphic novels. Specifically, Landis argues:

> Visual narrative is uniquely positioned to produce identification through its imagery and does so in such a way as to lend greater legibility to the movements and memories of refugee subjects.
>
> (88)

Landis explains that these visual narratives "activate" diasporic and refugee-related memories. Landis' focus on form and construction across Vietnamese and American graphic novels alerts us to the notions of home and nation. Both studies by Ty and Landis show that nation-state construction and its fragmentation play a considerable part in understanding how graphic novels exist and continue to gain popularity.

In his chapter, "The Postcolonial Graphic Novel and Trauma: From Maus to Malta," Sam Knowles (2015) analyzed the theme of traumatic experiences highlighted by several graphic novel authors such as Art Spiegelman (Maus—serialized from 1980–91), Josh Neufeld (A.D.: New Orleans After the Deluge, 2007–9), and Joe Sacco (Journalism). Spiegelman ventures into the issue of racism through the use of animal imagery. Among the bestial illustrations of racial disparity drawn included the Jewish people depicted as mice, Germans visualized as cats, and non-Jewish Poles seen as pigs. Neufeld's webcomic featured the devastation of Hurricane Katrina through the lens of different sociocultural individuals in New Orleans. Sacco, on the other hand, brought into play the issues of marginalization, belonging and trauma, as primarily experienced by people through immigration. Through the analyses of these graphic novels, Knowles (2015) highlights the issues of "postcolonial, marginalizing, 'othering', and politically oppressive situations" (88).

In their edited book, *Representing Multiculturalism in Comics and Graphic Novels*, Carolene Ayaka and Ian Hague (2015) put together a collection of articles that explore the issues of multiculturalism through the themes of "coexistence, interaction, integration, intersectionality, negotiation, power" (1). Through the combination of fifteen topics of various contexts, multiple issues and portrayal of multiculturalism are discussed. First, geographical bias often accompanies the way graphic novels are found and featured across American graphic novels. Second, this understanding of the way bias is presented to the readers of graphic novels strongly suggests a need to revise the (re)conceptualization of multiculturalism. By looking into words, phrases, and illustrations, graphic novels create and convey cohesive alliance with loyal fans of graphic novels, firming up the tight, often overlapping notions of representation, ethnicity, and diversity.

Within the Malaysian context, a number of studies undertaken examine homegrown graphic novels and comics that, nevertheless, adopt other frameworks rather than postcolonial lenses. In Malaysia, most comics and graphic novels are arguably influenced by Japanese manga or Japanese comics. Japanese manga and mangaesque works (along with their publication houses) retain their popularity from the late 1980s until now (Lent 2015). This is evident through the existence of publication houses like *Gempak Starz* which is considered as the "largest creator of comics and manga in the country" (Chiam 2016, para. 7). On top of that, is the annual organization of fan conventions that gather fans of Japanese manga including local mangaesque works and their live adaptation (anime), receiving consistent support from their Malaysian fans realized by the increasing number of attendees every year. For example, one of the most famous fan conventions, *Comic Fiesta*, since its inception in 2002 (Junid and Yamato 2019), received about 49, 000 participations at their event in 2014 (Yamato 2016). Such gatherings invited not only Japanese fans, but also artists and manga creators.

One of the most famous manga (comic) artists, known through her pen name, Kaoru, is the "first professional female cartoonist in Malaysia" (Chiam 2016, para. 7). She became a prominent household name at *Gempak Starz* through her manga by creating blended comic worlds that described manga-like-characters and storylines. However, her narratives are curated within "suspended reality" that is devoid of any attachment with specific place, culture or ethnicity (Chan 2018, 205). Chan, in her examination, argued that there is "a new wave of Malaysian made manga that roots itself in locally recognizable depictions of standard ethnicity, gender, and social class dimensions," with characters in one particular work by Dreamerz and Leoz (*Gempak Starz* artists), created within Malaysian-like-landscapes with characters actually wearing Malaysian school uniforms (205). These two styles of narrations and creations in graphic novels/manga, one with infused daily realities and the other with suspended reality, remain to the present in local Malaysian works. This, we argue, affects the identity constructions of characters and how these impact readers who "consume" these works.

Apart from examinations of the textual and visual style of the graphic novels, the most recent study to date by Iman Junid and Eriko Yamato (2019) investigated how Japanese manga and local narratives are reflected in the graphic novels by interviewing ten Malaysian Malay (manga/comic) artists. They also looked into challenges in comics production and issues of conflicting identities that contradict national identity. Their findings highlighted that the challenges of comics production include issues such as the "presence of nations, locals, and 'others'" (Iman Junid and Yamato 2019, 66). In creating comics and meaning-making within comics, identification of self and "others" is important, and, at the same time, these remain to be the most challenging part of local comic productions. Junid and Yamato (2019) recommend that more research should be published in order to present "insights into tension, confusion, and instability regarding variation in identification occurring daily in a localized and globalized society" (83).

In this chapter, we feel obliged to engage with the way postcolonial subjects are generally driven by social mobility and how their socio-cultural relations take shape as outcomes of these exchanges. While social relations are generally unified based on commonality and collegiality, the experiences by postcolonial subjects as demonstrated in the chapter, as we shall see, are not obligated to the same degree. These postcolonial subjects, differed in terms of their social status, are being encouraged to befriend their equals. Looking broadly, examples presented in this chapter reflect the increased dominance of a particular world-view or ideology with respect to how their day-to-day everyday experiences are "governed" by socioeconomic terms, relegating the importance of local cultures and values.

"Strategizing" Malaysia's Graphic Novels

This section places the chapter in a sociopolitical context. Specifically it differentiates how graphic novels in Malaysia are written and published in Malaysian context. The substance of this reading results from a complex articulation of authoritative laws, official provision, and segmentation about what can(not) be accessed, kept, and read by Malaysian readers. This combination of work which entails endorsements by the authority aims to "regulate" ideas and construction of knowledge even though their notions of authority in view of publication may differ from many Western-imposed notions of freedom of speech. Drawing from literature sourced from independent contributors, it is important to trace that these studies, by way of their emphases, take into consideration issues of graphic novels and Malaysia's media publishing. Many see the commingling of these laws of publication, provisions, and segmentation as largely due to what Marwan M. Kraidy (2002) termed as hybrid (re)conceptualization of cultural globalization, a seminal point in cultural globalization as it constructed a more globalized understanding cognizant of the complex underpinnings of culture, power, and global contexts. The extract below from Kraidy's (2002) *Hybridity in Cultural Globalization* accentuates this position of the way in which publication in Malaysia is structured according to a certain ideology of position and authority that sets up the reading position of readers:

I believe that hybridity needs to be understood as a communicative practice constitutive of, and constituted by, sociopolitical and economic arrangements... politically, a critical hybridity theory considers hybridity as a space where intercultural and international communication practices are continuously negotiated in interactions of differential power (Kraidy 2002, 317).

Kraidy's argument emphasizes the cognizance of the combination of Western-imposed globalization as much as it also draws on appropriating these global cultures and their effects on Malaysian readers. Just a few sentences later, Kraidy had also proclaimed, "if hybridity consists merely of observing, cataloguing and celebrating multicultural mixture, the inequality that often characterizes these mixtures is glossed over" (Kraidy 2002, 318). The maintenance of (un)official publication, arguments, and public consumption of publication especially in the Malaysian context remains the preoccupation of Malaysia's government inquiry. Therefore, the focus on generating diversity, plurality, and multiplicity within local and global levels by way of publication can be seen to reflect the desire to keep national and international threats at bay.

Publication of graphic novels in Malaysia involves publicly governed scrutiny of large entities. While many of these people in power "regulate" the content, they also recognize fellow institutions as existing side-by-side. Most of these entities, which include government and publication institutions, produce their own sets of constraints on publication. Many of these government agencies share similar provisions as to what can(not) be shared and disseminated. The two institutions relevant to understanding of the novel, *Menggapai Bintang*, include but are not limited to Malaysia's Ministry of Home Affairs (MoHA) (Idrus, Hashim, and Raihanah 2016, 2017) and Kadogawa Gempakstarz Group of Companies. The first, MoHA, refers to an official body of operations regulating "publication materials" (MoHA 2020) and how it affects national security, particularly on (de)registering graphic novels' International Standard Book Number (ISBN) in Malaysia. MoHA is often cited as the harbinger of measures of control, as can be seen in Malaysia's Prime Minister's 2019 speech, which emphasizes how this regulation can support greater economy, citing publication as central to political stability (MoHA 2019). Secondly, Gempakstarz publishes and distributes graphic novels in Malaysia as part of the country's initiatives to "globalize" Kadogawa materials across other Southeast Asia countries (Gempakstarz 2020). Distribution of Gempakstarz's graphic novels, in whichever language, was the cohesive collective streamlining of the content and its "compliance" with provision of local and international publication and printing of materials laws. This adhesion to printing and publication materials clearly prohibits publication, materials, and content that may disrupt Malaysia's sociopolitical spectrum. As a case in point, a graphic novel, *Ultraman the Ultra Power*, is banned for the "misuse" of the word, *Allah*, as it claims that the graphic novel misuses the term, Allah, to refer to a fictional Japanese action character (Lim 2014). While this example does not necessitate ultimate repercussions for all graphic novels for all genres available in Malaysia, this illustration on certain prohibitions against material for readers has led to diverse manifestations of regulations of graphic novels as they interact with global and local issues.

Thirdly, this transparent system between the elites and public conditioning the representation of literary textual productions make ideological constructions visible. A cursory investigation into the general "vision" of 2020 Malaysia's official Ministry of Communications and Multimedia (MCM) and its sister commission, Malaysian Communication and Multimedia Commission (MCMC), will reveal that their current, envisaged vision entails, "engaging the people's hearts and minds through Radio, Television and New Media Services" and "establishing a communications and multimedia industry that is competitive, efficient and increasingly self-regulating, generating growth to meet the economic and social needs of Malaysia" respectively, a far cry from 1970 MCM's vision of "promoting civic consciousness and fostering the development of Malaysian arts and culture." The content, including graphic novels, asserts Malaysia's political and social conditions that bolster "commercial and industrial practices" (Foo 2004, 29). The disparity between the ways in which literary textual productions are represented highlights the ideological constructions, both from the elite and public standpoints. This remains true to today, as Jaworska and Themistocleous (2018) argue, media publishing bears less significance of what the public audience want to believe; media publishing can be imbued with meanings as it is predominantly governed by political constituents (Idrus et al. 2016, 2017). To combine these readings, therefore, will (re)clarify our visions about significance of graphic novels in a postcolonial Malaysia, and encourage us to situate Malaysia's graphic novels within wider socio-political landscapes.

In the following section, using Fairclough's (1992) three-dimensional critical discourse analytical model, this chapter draws upon textual (texts), contextual (discursive practice), and interpretive analysis (social practice) to tease out our stories on *Menggapai Bintang* to make visible the presence of neoliberal ideologies. Informed by Fairclough's (1992) concepts, we examine how ideological leanings across the novel serve as modes "of action" that act "upon other actions" (789). Although the content and words employed by the novel at first sight might be picked up as bland and uncontentious, the ways in which they appear are never neutral, but present within themselves ideological fragmentations or differences (Holquist 1990).

Before examining neoliberalism in the comic, perhaps it is best to outline *Menggapai Bintang*. Set in everyday school, *Menggapai Bintang* explores the intricacies of establishing and sustaining friendship, simultaneously negotiating with issues about the self and others. The central characters, Joni and Mia, are friends and they work their way into a group in their bid to compete at a local singing competition. They are placed in a group together with Emilia. During the first singing rehearsal, the novel elaborates on Emilia's growing disappointment with Joni's singing as they prepare to head off to the competition. Joni, however, being introverted and reclusive, finds it difficult to face Emilia's rejection and hateful comments about her appearance and voice. *Menggapai Bintang*, in short, tells a story of Joni and Mia directed toward issues about working in teams and collaborating, and what their singing and friendship mean to each other. The issues involve a degree of sophistication as the characters navigate these issues in all of their rich socio-cultural complexity. In this sense, these young postcolonial subjects "have no fixed, essentialist meanings" (Bhabha 1994, 55). These young postcolonial subjects go back and forth dealing with issues that are "revisited and reinterpreted." It is in this sense that these images aim to glorify the notions that irrespective of how the natives reject Western-imposed globalization, their experiences can be defined as existing in a multiplicity of occasions, neoliberalism included. In other words, issues raised as a result of these depictions of postcolonial subjects question the notions of homogeneity and synchronicity. And they are not alone in this respect. As scholars, we will begin to ask the same question concerning who is able to say what and who gets to inquire what within certain kinds of conditions. Drawing on these complications, the graphic novels will lead us as readers to diverse manifestations of postcolonial subjects across "identifiable politically powerful economic elites at the expense of nonelites" (Venugopal 2015, 175).

How Is Neoliberalism Constructed in *Menggapai Bintang*?

This section elaborates some of the many stories in *Menggapai Bintang* that lean toward neoliberalism, by appropriating Fairclough's (1992) concepts. Neoliberalism and other ideologies, singly or in combination, build a dominant meaning of what it means to grow up in postcolonial Malaysia. These stories alert us to the ways in which local, cultural fragments are, among others, displaced and "silenced," and the possible reasons for relegating them. While marginalization of local, cultural issues signals over-reliance on Western-based globalization, the perceived "silencing" of "local," "multicultural" elements indicate their insignificance. Our approach with *Menggapai Bintang* is to displace these points, and provide insights into alternative discourses to make visible "hidden" agenda. By incorporating Fairclough's (1992 and 1998) ideological constructions, they will present insights into the preoccupation with social status and rank, as the ensuing discussions will show.

This story illustrates a kind of exchange which serves to highlight the hidden, implicit "privilege" attached to (bourgeois) class consciousness, although other issues concerning female adolescents become obvious in this example of "transaction." Cristina, their classmate, is portrayed as a rival to Sophia and Emilia's own "groups." Their social links do not enter into this exchange as equals, but Sophia and Emilia expect their friends to heed obeisance to their outfits and what results from this exchange. The inclusion of the words, "expensive," "poor," "sophisticated," and "reputation" make visible two important notions. Firstly, the words chosen in these dialogues give us insight into the minds of (early) postcolonial subject-readers. That is, the words chosen depict social status as an object of concern; words such as "expensive" and "poor" suggest that their lives depend upon quantity and sophistication, while those who are left behind are portrayed as needing to catch up. Secondly, the word, "sophistication" and "reputation" commingle perhaps to glorify a mindset that sees anything money-related as superior, and the sub-associated knowledge that might be derived from them.

252   Graphic Novels and Comics as World Literature

Figure 12.1 *Menggapai Bintang* Translation: Sophia (first page): Hey, are you blind? Our clothes are expensive, you know! You gotta pay if they get torn, you know? Cristina (first page): Stop being such a bully! It was an accident! Sophia (second page): Excuse me? How dare you … ! Emilia (second page): That's enough, Sophia. It's no use talking to them. They simply aren't sophisticated at all. Let's just go! Talking with these people will just drag us down to their level.

This claim about the "superiority" of those who are at a financially advantaged position is repeated in other narratives in *Menggapai Bintang*, in which "poor" and "image" are used to signal that this is a "team" plan.

As these words are expressed within the contexts of familiar school orientation, it evokes an "imaginary" field in which young postcolonial subjects can only materialize their futures and claim future rewards by understanding "who's who" and the notions of "us versus them," vis-à-vis a mentality that suggests money and social class are beyond anything. That is, the insinuation is that these young postcolonial subjects can only attain the lives and imagination desired if they are able to socialize with friends who are a step beyond them financially, a prospect that completely neglects the changing and challenging situations that surround them. Graphic novels, seen from this perspective, diminish the significance of the actual, everyday realities of being and becoming young postcolonial human beings. By using words such as "poor" and "image," indeed, the text evades these realities; taking a leap or being successful in the future is and can only be represented by these associations of "poor," "rich," and "image" that are considered desirable.

Figure 12.2 Mean Girls

The illustrations discussed above show that it is social status, affluent or not, that dominates postcolonial subjects' behavior. The above are merely a fraction of examples of belief in social status or "material culture" (Westall 2017). One would certainly establish similar narratives of material culture's dominance over one's social interactions and behavior. Yet, one needs also to be cognizant of the fact that because the preoccupation with material culture lives on to this day (through the publication of the graphic novel), it perhaps demonstrates that forces of material culture still operate to "segregate" one from the other. As Marwan Kraidy (2002) explains, these practices more often than not emphasize differentiations according to "differential power." Less powerful and less affluent subjects, as demonstrated above, are "divided into segments with essentialist features" (Gupta 2019, 8), as governing concepts about social "financialization of everyday life" (Gupta 2019, 8). Both Kraidy and Gupta's observations point to material culture as curtailing postcolonial subjects' behavior, and to a certain extent, their autonomy.

Conclusions

Our story is only a small part of many stories that can be shared about the role graphic novels play in the midst of neoliberalism and postcoloniality, including, but not limited to, the centrality of social and economic development culture around the world. Our study and those that occur in other genres are, in many ways, aligned in the sense that it tells that postcolonial subjects are being "sold" as part of larger, dominant corporate interests via graphic novels. It makes our study of producing Malaysian counter-discourse to the metanarratives of the spread of postcoloniality, globalization, and neoliberalism all the more urgent. Conversations about how postcolonial subjectivities are shaped by ordinary, daily experiences and problematization of what it means to capture and to live as postcolonial individuals can mediate their choices and consequences. And although one may argue that these graphic novels are packaged and sensationalized to provide reader hooks, they are, at the same time, commodified and exchanged (Teo 2000) reproducing "social inequality" (van Dijk 1993, 252–3). Indeed, they are not the casual, disposable fare that they may at first appear to be, but rather a comic bellwether attempting to naturalize neoliberalism as a way of being for Malaysian youths. By highlighting these comics' claims of being apolitical, this chapter has begun to defamiliarize neoliberalism in graphic novels in a Malaysian youth context and offer more rigorous postcolonial politics of reading and writing comics in the process.

References

Ayaka, C., and Hague, I. 2015. *Representing Multiculturalism in Comics and Graphic Novels*. New York: Routledge.
Bhabha, H. 1994. *The Location of Culture*. London: Routledge.
Célestin, R., Cloonan, W., Dalmolin, E., Lan, F., Lee, L., and Munro, M. 2017. "Reorienting cultural flows." *Contemporary French and Francophone Studies*, 21 (1): 1–7. https://www.tandfonline.com/action/showCitFormats?doi=10.1080/17409292.2017.1304614.
Chan, R.S.K. 2018. "Breaking Windows: Malaysian Manga as Dramaturgy Of Everyday-Defined Realities." *JATI-Journal of Southeast Asian Studies*, 23(2): 205–29.
Chevant, A. 2017. "Graphic Heritage: Exploring Postcolonial Identities and Vietnamese Spaces in the Francophone Graphic Novel." *Contemporary French and Francophone Studies*, 21 (1): 81–90.

Chiam, M. 2016. "Kaoru's Romantic Comics, or Shojo Manga, are Hits." *The Star* [Kuala Lumpur], July 29. https://www.thestar.com.my/lifestyle/living/2016/07/29/kaorus-romantic-comics-or-shojo-manga-are-hits (accessed December. 20, 2020).

Fairclough, N.L. 1992. *Critical Language Awareness*. London: Longman.

Foo, T.T. 2004. "Managing the Content of Malaysian Television Drama: Producers, Gatekeepers and the Barisan Nasional Government." PhD diss., Athens, OH: Ohio University.

Gempakstarz. 2020. "About Us," *Gempakstarz*, December 13. https://gempakstarz.com/about-us-malaysia-top-publisher/ (accessed December 20, 2020).

Gupta, S. 2019. "Indian Student Protests and the Nationalist-Neoliberal Nexus." *Postcolonial Studies*, 22 (1): 1–15.

Holquist, M. 1990. *Dialogism: Bakhtin and His Own World*. London: Routledge.

Idrus, M.M., Hashim, R.S. and Raihanah, M.M. 2016. "Globalization Re-Discovery of the Malay 'Local,' and Popular TV Fiction through Audience Narratives." *3L The Southeast Asian Journal of English Language Studies*, 22 (2): 31–48. https://doi.org/10.17576/3l-2016-2202-03.

Idrus, M.M., Hashim, R.S., and Raihanah, M.M. 2017. "Rediscovery of the Malay 'Local:' Youth and TV Fiction in Malaysia". *International Journal of Adolescence and Youth*, 22 (2): 210–25. https://doi.org/10.1080/02673843.2016.1154876.

Jaworska, S., and Themistocleous, C. 2018. "Public Discourses on Multilingualism in the UK: Triangulating a Corpus Study with a Sociolinguistic Attitude Survey." *Language in Society*, 47 (1): 57–88.

Junid, I., and Yamato, E. 2019. "Manga Influences and Local Narratives: Ambiguous Identification in Comics Production." *Creative Industries Journal*, 12 (1): 66–85.

Knowles, S. 2015. "The Postcolonial Graphic Novel and Trauma: From Maus to Malta." In Ward, Abigail, ed. *Postcolonial Traumas: Memory, Narrative, Resistance*. London: Palgrave Macmillan, 83–96.

Kraidy, M. 2002. "Hybridity in Cultural Globalization." *Communication Theory*, 12 (3): 316–39.

Landis, W. 2019. "Mapping the Nation and Reimagining Home in Vietnamese American Graphic Narratives." In Howard, Leigh Anne, and Hoeness-Krupsaw, Susanna, eds. *Performativity, Cultural Construction, and the Graphic Narrative*. London: Routledge, 88–102.

Lent, J.A. 2015. *Asian Comics*. Jackson, MS: University Press of Mississippi.

Lim, I. 2014. "Ultraman Book Ban: Phantom Publisher Forced Our Hand, Claims Ministry." *Malay Mail*. https://www.malaymail.com/news/malaysia/2014/03/08/ultraman-book-ban-phantom-publisher-forced-our-hand-claims-ministry/631015 (accessed December 20, 2020).

Menggapai Bintang. 2010. *Topik: Persahabatan*. Kuala Lumpur, Malaysia: Kadokawa Gempak Starz Sdn Bhd.

MoHA. 2019. "Ministry of Home Affairs's Monthly Assembly," *Ministry of Home Affairs*. http://www.moha.gov.my/index.php/en/maklumat-korporat22-4/speech/4268– (accessed December 20, 2020).

MoHA. 2020. "Main Function of the Ministry," *Ministry of Home Affairs*, December 13. http://www.moha.gov.my/index.php/en/fungsi-kementerian (accessed December 20, 2020).

Peacock, J. 2016. "'My Thoughts Shifted From the Past To the Future:' Time and (Autobio) graphic Representation in Miné Okubo's Citizen 13660." *Journal of Postcolonial Writing*, 52 (4): 445–63.

Ramone, J. 2017. *The Bloomsbury Introduction to Postcolonial Writing*. London: Bloomsbury.

Santos, K.M., and Sihombing, F. 2016. "Is There a Space for Cool Manga in Indonesia and the Phillippines?: Postcolonial Discourses on Transcultural Manga." In Mclelland, Mark, ed. *The End of Cool Japan: Ethical, Legal, and Cultural Challenges to Japanese Popular Culture*. London: Routledge, 196–218.

Teo, P. 2000. "Racism in the News: A Critical Discourse Analysis of News Reporting in Two Australian Newspapers." *Discourse & Society*, 11 (1): 7–49. https://doi.org/10.1177/0957926500011001002.

Ty, E. 2018. "Building Asian Canadian Literary Studies." *Oxford Research Encyclopedias*. https://doi.org/10.1093/acrefore/9780190201098.013.880 (accessed December 20, 2020).

van Dijk, T.A. 1993. "Principles of Critical Discourse Analysis." Discourse & Society, 4 (2): 249–83. https://doi.org/10.1177/0957926593004002006.

Venugopal, R. 2015. "Neoliberalism as Concept." *Economy and Society*, 44 (2): 165–87.

Westall, C. 2017. "World-Literary Resources and Energetic Materialism." *Journal of Postcolonial Writing*, 53 (3): 265–76.

Yamato, E. 2016. "Construction of Discursive Fandom and Structural Fandom through Anime Comics and Game Fan Conventions in Malaysia." *European Journal of Cultural Studies*, 21(4): 469–85.

13

"LONG LIVE the Waste!": Junk Food Bites Back in Jung's *Approved for Adoption*

Sheng-mei Ma

The Korean–Belgian artist Jung chronicles his adoption from Seoul, South Korea, by French-speaking Belgian parents at the age of five in his four-volume graphic novel *Couleur de Peau* (*Color of Honey* 2007–16) and its animated film adaptation (2014), both translated as *Approved for Adoption*. To grasp the adoptee's tortu(r)ous psychology, the graphic novel and the animation constitute a totality, despite their generic differences. Privileging one genre over the other is to miss the wood for the trees, to miss the person for either the panels or the film frames. That tortu(r)ousness manifests itself in the dropping of his surname Henin; in Jung's romanticized French title evoking "milk and honey," albeit sans milk or whiteness; and in the English rechristening that highlights Jung's caustic voice. Indeed, the satiric tenor runs through the graphic novel, erupting at the nadir when the foundling Jung found "Yum! Some leftover chicken leg... LONG LIVE the waste!" in a garbage can on the streets of Seoul (4). Yum or yuck, honey or hogwash, Jung the child's literal "junk food" inspires the adult to bite back artistically.[1] This biting back signals not only a lashing out against the motherland and the adoptive land but also an unwitting biting of his own tongue. To express his *ressentiment* against the French-speaking world, Jung is, nonetheless, indebted to its language, graphic medium, and cultural capital. Just as Jung the unwanted orphan sustains himself with salvaged trash, the adult artist proclaims "VIVE le gaspillage!," a sardonic riff on "Vive la France!," and "Vive la liberté!" Jung disavows and acknowledges the Francophone legacy at once. Jung's wordplay is but the tip of linguistic and cultural reservoirs that enable him to double-tongue throughout, while every move of the tongue reopens the old wound like a canker sore inside the minority's mouth and mind.

Adoptees, particularly interracial and transnational, are oftentimes haunted by the fact of biological parents' relegating of their social contract to any newborn, brought into this world without his or her express consent, and then given up for adoption by

---

[1] An intriguing echo is in Patricia Park's ethnic novel *Re Jane* (2015), which depicts schoolmates crossing "party [racial] lines" as junk food that we disdain and crave (283). Junk food is bad for us, but we love it anyway. Whitewashing damages self-esteem, but the urge to belong is irresistible to minorities coming of age. Loving and hating junk food symbolizes how minorities trash their "ethnic half," for lack of a better phrase, in hope of mainstreaming.

total strangers. In the worst-case scenario, a sense of abandonment, betrayal gnaws the adoptee's consciousness. Psychiatrist Paul M. Brinich puts it as "the unwanted child" ("Adoption from the Inside Out" 45). This is compounded by racial differences between the adoptive family and the adoptee. Maladjustment intensifies should the host society manifest patronage, prejudice, even racism. At the very least, the host society, SooJin Pate contends in *From Orphan to Adoptee* (2014), engages in "construction of the displaced Korean child as a social orphan—an ophan whose familial and national ties are severed in order to reincorporate him or her into the national and domestic American family" (2014, 74). In Jung's case, such "social orphans" derived from the social problem of, as Christopher Bagley reports, "a very high birth rate in Korea up to the 1970s meant that there were many 'surplus' children" (1993, 177). Consequently, adoptees confront the conundrum of value. On the one hand, if valued and loved, why were they cast out by their birth parents and home country? On the other, how to find their own worth when they are defined as much by emotional attachment to the adoptive family and nation as by physical difference from them? Those who look like them, in all likelihood, threw them away; those who do not look like them, in all likelihood, are not keen to countenance their loneliness, even pain, amongst the host family and country. Precisely because the subject matter of orphan turned adoptee is so fraught, even insufferable, Jung's graphic book and animation anchor the narratives in objective history, in romanticized Korean birth motherhood, and in an unflinching look back in rage at adoption. Jung navigates between fact and fury, between the blessing and the trauma of adoption, between graphic panels and film frames, between silent pages and filmic soundscape, between his dual names, between his book's French and English titles.

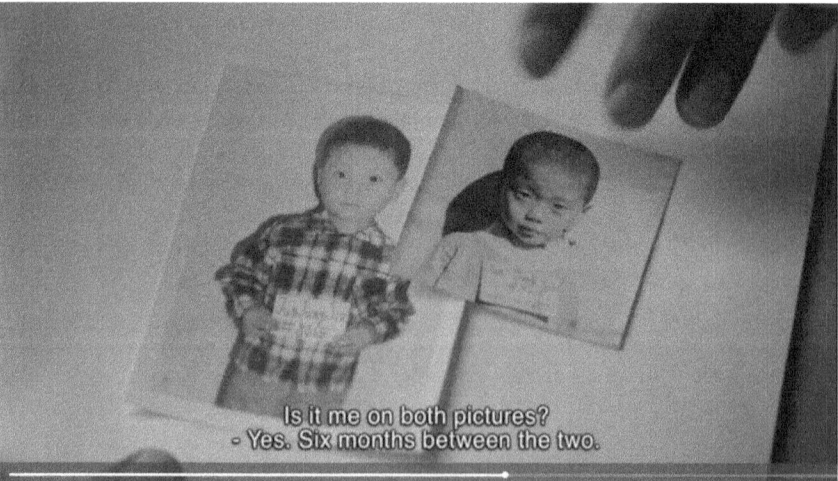

Figure 13.1 The animated *Approved for Adoption*'s adoption photo turned into the graphic novel cover.

Evident from the graphic book cover, Jung is a truncated name. Holding up a sign with "Jun Jung-Sik," "#8015," and "12-2-65" is a child with his innocent smile and bruises on the face and knee. Figure 13.1 shows the animation's actual photographs on which the book cover as well as the "BEFORE" and "AFTER" contrast on p.6 are based. The graphic book inserts a standard hyphen to his given name where there is none in the photos. The rawness of the past is being revised, "corrected" in its spelling.[2] On the graphic novel cover, he stands among adults walking past, none stopping for no one notices the boy barely reaching their hips. The original Korean name, like the midget boy, is halved, severed by adults who are supposed to care for him. The name "Jung" identifies the author, but the identification is itself incomplete, fractured. This (mis)naming saga continues in the proverbial rebirth of adoptees when they deplane from the womb of transcontinental flights into the arms of adoptive families. On their drive back from the airport, the Henins muse as to what to call him, from the children's "Igor" to the mother's variant pronunciation of Jung ("yung") as "Chung" or "Djung." The Korean name Jun Jung Sik (전정식, Jeon Jeongsik)[3] has a given name explained as "Straight Plant" by Korean expatriates in Belgium while Jung has long thought that it means "Bright Light." Whichever is accurate, the life this given name signifies is neither straightforward nor well-lit. After the children's Slavic fling, his name is redacted by the father as Jung with the "j" substituted by the German pronunciation of "j" as "y." This transposition suggests a father's psychological need—no different from the children's—to grasp the unknowable other from the Orient with what is the knowable other in his European frame of reference, hence Germanizing. Why a Spanish "h" for "j" is not elected is anybody's guess. German may simply be more immediate to Belgians than Spanish is. The mother's second choice "Djung" (jung) is in fact closest to the Korean pronunciation, but the French pronunciation is too "homey" for what the grandmother in the animation calls the "little Asian." The French sound thus comes across as a passing whim, dropped anon.

A collective naming of the new member of the family, such momentous labor of love always transpires with the newborn blissfully oblivious to it. In Jung's case, however, it verges on an initiation rite, like naming a new pet which/who happens to be the person sitting right next to oneself. Note that the five-year-old Jung would not have been cognizant of French names bandied about in the car. Only an adult artist's recollection in some bitterness—far from Wordsworth's tranquility—would recreate the car ride. This may account for the divergence between the graphic novel

---

[2] The book cover and the animation's photograph list Jung's birthday as either "12-2-65" or "December 2, 1965," in the order of month-day-year. This order contradicts the hand-drawn Holt Adoption Agency's document, which types "born 2/12/65" (5). In fact, all the documents fleetingly shown in the animation follow the order of month-day-year. On the back of the said animation photograph is typed "1970 10 14," the day Jung turned up at the Holt Orphanage. The hand-drawn document is the only one with "born 2/12/65" in the Belgian order of day/month/year. Is this yet another example of subconscious transposition of the European onto the Korean, no different from displacing European wheat fields onto Seoul, South Korea, in the reunion reveries with Jung's birth mother? Ironically, in this hand-drawn adoption document that yields both the French and English title, what is allegedly the representation of the Other's dating system in Asia is in fact that of One's own in Belgium.

[3] I want to thank my Independent Study student Samantha Manges for calling attention to this.

and the animation. In the panels, the naming process ends before it starts. The fanciful "Igor" (vol. 1, 45) gives way to an introduction to his new family: siblings Catherine, Erik, Coralie, Gaelle, and another adoptee Lee Sung-Sook, renamed Valérie, soon to join the Henins. This seguing from "Igor" to a family portrait demonstrates how a factual catalog of siblings gives the graphic artist agency in naming rather than being named. Further creative control accrues in the graphic novel's "stand-alone" Jung, unproblematized by the film's divergent ways of saying that name. In this cast of family members, revealingly, the parents are not named. The motive remains unclear: either Jung avenges himself by depriving them of their names; or as any child does, he simply thinks of them as mom and dad; or the anonymity protects those who are portrayed on occasion in an unflattering, even racist, light.

Instead of the skeletal treatment in the graphic novel, the animation elaborates on the prolonged debate over naming. This rechristening does not come about until Jung's re-visitation in the animation with the added detachment of his co-director Laurent Boileau. While speech or thought balloons and the narrator's box do layer soundscape into graphic novels, the animation's film sound makes possible alternative pronunciations of "Jung." The parents' trying out of different consonants for "j" cedes the graphic artist's control to other characters, yet this concession manages to satirize both parents, one of whom insists on the wrong pronunciation, the other chances upon his Korean name, only to drop it. The mistake has never been corrected, as though it is no longer of consequence. With all its flaws and agony, the maladjustment of adoption gives birth to art. Subsequently in the film, the mean grandmother arrives and calls him "Joong" on purpose, among other names, to separate him from her biological grandchildren. The grandmother's malicious misnaming, like the mother's fleeting thought, turns out to be the correct Korean pronunciation, whereas the father's Germanic tweak is less for the son than for his own peace of mind. Adoption as a transnational practice begs the question of saving the orphan for whose sake. Jung in the graphic novel sardonically thanks "Little Buddha" for rescuing him from adoptive parents who shunned him for his "blue black scar" (35). Mockery aside, Jung still seeks succor from Guanyin, Goddess of Mercy in East Asian Buddhism, who eases the story into Chapter 3 of Volume 1 (65).

An adoptee's raw, unmitigated rage against the world and fate is bandaged in Jung by matter-of-fact narration, by escapist romanticizing, and by sarcasm. *Approved for Adoption* wobbles on these three legs because each leg is of different length and shape, as it were. More alarmingly, these legs keep morphing into one another: history subverted by a snide remark; anger rounded off by self-indulgent reverie. This destabilizing in the graphic novel is compounded in the animation, where irony and ambiguity intensify in the juxtaposition between live action and hand-drawn segment. Jung's voiceover in thought balloons confides that comics have offered the teenager an escapist flight from adoption, only to return the forty-four-year-old artist live to the streets of Seoul. In a cyclical fashion, live action sequences in the animation come to "animate" graphic book panels, which, in turn, freeze moments in Jung's lived experiences.

Consistent with the overall ambiguity, the book's opening fluctuates between a fairy-tale and a historical order imposed onto Jung's troubled graphic memoir. The first panel casts an extreme long shot from a satellite: "I was born somewhere on our planet" (3), similar to the formulaic "once upon a time" opening. This soon historicizes through the devastation of the Korean War and the partitioning of the Korean Peninsula along the 38th Parallel, the backdrop to "the Holt Children Services Inc." (13), "the largest international adoption program," A. Silverman and W. Feigelman contend, which had arranged international adoption of Korean babies, Jung among them (1990, 188). Jung invariably injects such neutral information with extreme emotions, ranging from resentment to apology. The narrative voice swings from "Since 1958, Korea has provided more than 200,000 children, 50,000 for domestic consumption, and 150,000 for export" to "I shouldn't... it has saved them from misery." The sense that one should be thankful never quite overwhelms resentment, evident from the "fringe benefit" of travel and of "Coke in Europe" for the forsaken (16). This contextual bent surfaces again when the graphic novel introduces Belgium's north–south Flemish–French linguistic divide. Establishing shots for the ensuing story perhaps, such factual streak arrests emotions on the verge of cresting. For the same reason, Jung is prone to cracking a timely joke or two to avoid the narrative crack-up. Jung plays with the thin lines among the dry monotone of factuality, the straight-face deadpan, and thinly-veiled acerbity. The cosmic establishing shot, for example, zooms in on Seoul's street scene of a Jung joyous over "leftover chicken leg" (4). South Korea's trash sustains its castaway, an affective trauma that is, on the facing page, papered over by a reproduction of Holt adoption agency document. While this document removes the orphan from the peril of the street, it portends the complex trials awaiting Jung overseas.

Both the romantic title in French and its English riposte are extracted from this document that occupies an entire panel in the graphic novel: the French from the top "skin color—honey"; the English from the bottom "Child approved for adoption." However, a footnote states: "original text in English" (5). In other words, *couleur de peau: miel* is itself a French translation of Holt's original in English, whereas the English translation *Approved for Adoption* is the authentic officialese. Nonetheless, both Western languages are once or twice removed from the Korean child they purport to describe. Representing Jung in a positive light to prospective adoptive parents, the language of the document borders on the sentimental, the sole exception being the line "brought in by the police... a blue black scar between the nose and the eye. He fell." This scar led to Jung's fall from grace when a couple withdrew from adoption because "Luckily he was under warranty." The child Jung first mocks Holt's incompetence, volunteering that the file should have simply noted "bruise" (35). Jung's sharp tongue then retaliates against the couple, who may have been moved "by the Holy Spirit and have adopted a pet instead" (36). The next panel shows a prancing, well-groomed dachshund on a leash with the owner behind about to step on a pile of fresh dog poop. (Images of excreta and filth periodically soil Jung's art, chronic infections from junk food in Seoul and in his soul—Solid Seoul Food force-fed too early in life, causing irreparable internal damage.) Stinging words and graphics target not only individuals but also Christianity, which drives the assembly line of adoption (126) and certainly the middleman of the Holt Agency. But the artist's vitriol oozes, like pus, from a psychological festering that lies far deeper than the one on the skin, a secondary wound of having been passed over by foreigners on the heels of the primary wound of having been abandoned by Koreans. Self-defense mechanism disguises hurt as haughtiness. Rejected a second time as damaged goods, unwanted trash, a would-be adoptee feigns indifference, even superiority. The fact that Jung knows nothing about this couple from "USA? Norway? Australia? Germany?" renders his rhetorical revenge off-target, ineffective (36).

Ultimately, resentment against the world coincides with resentment against the self. Self-loathing motivates the characterization of a childhood and teenage Jung with serious behavioral problems: bullying female classmates, stealing school cafeteria tickets, forging school reports, and engaging in adolescent experimentation with sexuality. Such anti-social conduct is consistent with Bagley's findings of "the combination of overactivity, poor attention span and some impairment of spatial and numerical abilities" (1993, 87). The self-portrait of a lying, scheming Jung with no pang of conscience suggests overwhelming survival instinct from an early childhood of deprivation. The drive to fill the empty stomach parallels the drive to fill an empty heart for love and sense of belonging. In fact, the hunger for food constitutes as much a through line in Jung's art as the search for identity and love. Dumpster diving in Seoul turns into the adoptee's first transgression upon entering the Henin household: he immediately climbs on top of the table to consume a whole bottle of Coke. The mother's thought balloon indicates that she must "teach him some [table] manners" (47), while this very "street" manners has kept him alive. To flash back to the genesis of this "food chain": how to account for the discrepancy between the dumpster epiphany and the lack thereof? The graphic novel has a Jung overjoyed, raising high the leftover chicken leg, exclaiming "LONG LIVE the waste!" By contrast, Jung in the animation squats near the garbage, hugging himself, when the police officer finds and comforts him in a string of soothing Korean, untranslated as though irrelevant (Figure 13.2). Why the shift of emphasis from an ironic celebration of a foundling's agency to that of

Figure 13.2 The animated *Approved for Adoption* skips the graphic novel's "LONG LIVE the waste!"

his being found? To read the twin representations together: Jung the artist splits the child in two. The fighting Jung is the dream self of the fetal Jung, or the latter lurks behind a lifetime of swagger and bravado.

This theme of food proliferates from the Holt document's "hearty appetite" to the chicken leg to the Coke and, disastrously, to Jung's pilfering of a classmate's lunch tickets, triggered no doubt by the scramble for food in his Seoul years. The theft results in the mother's tempestuous outburst, once again in the family car with all five children in the backseat, that Jung is "a rotten apple... stay away from MY CHILDREN" (78). Both rites of passage—rechristening a new Henin and rejecting a defective one— proceed as the family are in transit, which to Jung would feel like a birth canal for a new life or an aborted one. The hurtful words readily bring back memory of garbage in Seoul, deepening Jung's self-abjection and alienation from his Belgian family (80).

Searching for identity away from his surrounding, the teenage Jung develops a crush on Japan as a symbol of power and beauty, after dabbling in Roman "legionaries and gladiators" and "the Gauls" (115–17). Samurai and swordsmanship, karate chop and kamikaze pilot, feed Jung's psychological void; he displaces his roots from Korea to Japan, fully conscious as an adult of his younger self's "cultural transference" (118). Akin to Eric Lott's thesis that blackface minstrelsy ridicules yet "tr[ies] on the accents of 'blackness' and demonstrates the permeability of the color line" (1993, 6), Jung embraces the most stereotypical *japonisme*, as much an act of self-empowerment as self-caricature. Assuming Japanese rather than Roman or Celtic masculinity in denial of the Korean adoptee's impotence subconsciously acknowledges his "unalienable Asianness." Yet this Orientalist obsession and growing defiance widen the gap with his disciplinarian mother, so much so that he leaves home for a half-way house. His self-hate reaches a suicidal pitch as he consumes bowl after bowl of rice and Tabasco sauce, making him throw up. Subconsciously, a self-loathing East–West "mongrel" stuffs himself with himself, namely, a dangerous mixture of rice from Asia and spicy Tabasco sauce from the American South, with the intention of purging himself, if not gutting himself. Tabasco sauce may well be a replacement for Korean kimchi, tongue-stinging "pickled cabbage, very spicy," part of the staple at the Holt Adoption Agency (18). A self-destructive Jung has turned his lifelong quest for food and identity on its head in hope of ending the pain.

Jung's story does not end tragically. His mother brings Jung home from the hospital, confiding in him that she has always reserved a place in her heart for Jung ever since the death of her firstborn. A reconciliation of sorts as Jung is nursed back to health, the fact remains, however, that Jung is a substitute for a loved one, which defines the very nature of adoption in filling a role, fulfilling a wish.[4] The animation concludes like an elegy for Jung's fellow Korean adoptees who have not made it, their lives cut short by themselves or other means, mental asylum included. The sense of mourning and guilt culminates in the last casualty "of a strange car accident": the 25-year-old Valérie,

---

[4] Paul M. Brinich contends that "the adoptive 'triad' (biological parent, adoptive parents, and child)" may reach a resolution by "keep(ing) these feelings of love and hate apart, with one set of feelings reserved for one point of the triad and another set reserved for the other point" ("Adoption from the Inside Out," 47). In Jung's works, maternal love gravitates to the romanticized biological mother, and resentment to the adoptive mother. Not until the very end of the graphic book and the animation does love cross into the adoptive family.

or Lee Sung-Sook, Jung's kid sister adopted after him, his mirror image from whom he had recoiled with secret shame and open hostility. Valérie's car crash recurs like repetition compulsion in the graphic book: vol. 2, 99; vol. 3, 133; vol. 4, 35. It is perhaps a tragic irony that Valérie's French makeover, with a brand new name untraceable to the old one, fails to transition her to a new identity, whereas Jung manages to do exactly that, despite living under a "pseudonym," a bastardization of his Korean name.

While rejecting Korea which rejected him, Jung immortalizes, beatifies one particular Korean: his birth mother, an imaginary victim forced to relinquish him by the misogynist, patriarchal Korean culture. Graphics accentuate what is cast as factual, contextual explication: a woman with a baby strapped to her back kowtows to the pants and shoes of a male (123). Thus, Jung orchestrates a series of dream sequences with the birth mother. These rendezvous open with the child's fetal posture, the body language of infantilized regression signaling an unrequited need for maternal love. The reverie then unfolds perennially in a wheat field, the birth mother appearing in traditional *hanbok* under a parasol, her face dimmed and blurred in the shade.[5]

Family reunions are not the only scenes unfolding in wheat fields. Anything that is intimately Korean comes through the golden ears of wheat as well. While assimilation compels Jung to shut off the Korean language and memory, the bottom panel of page 50 and the animation have Jung lying in the wheat field, eyes closed, three drawers—one of which identified as "Korean" in the graphic novel—pulled open from his forehead (see Figure 13.3). His closed eyes suggest that he fancies the heritage language is simply locked away and would return unbidden like opening a drawer. A children's game of shutting the eyes for magic to unfurl! The self-indulgent dreaminess about roots, however, clashes with the grotesque, macabre image, where Jung is reified as a chest

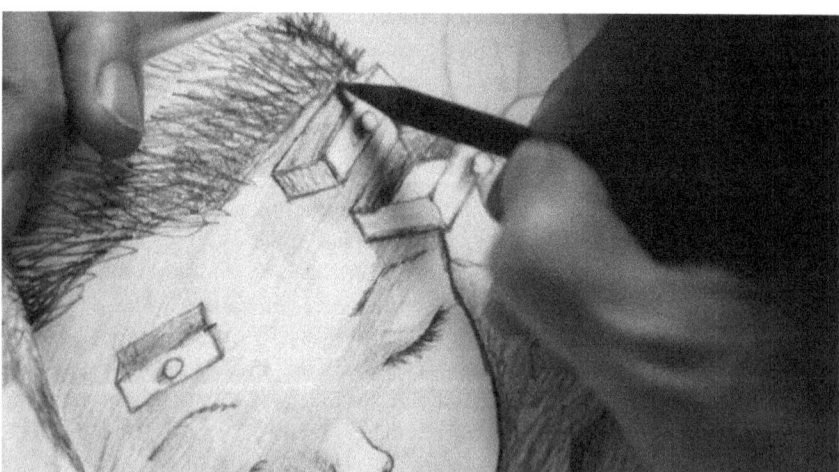

Figure 13.3 The animated *Approved for Adoption* portrays Jung's forehead drawers.

[5] The wheat field is also the setting for Jung's compunction of conscience that his adoptive parents do provide a home, so the Korean birth mother and the Belgian adoptive parents overlap via the wheat field, even if tangentially (136).

storing the past, its hard shell constituting a self-defense mechanism against alienation at the core of this adoption memoir. The wheat dreamscape jars internally in the same panel against the Gothic graphic, where forehead protuberances conjure up abnormal growths, crystalized in Frankenstein's monster's neck bolts and knobs. Page 51 goes on to state that the drawer also contains good memories like the woods behind the Henin house where the siblings play hide and seek. Is this why only one of the three drawers is labeled? But the hide and seek results in the painful and guilt-ridden memory of Jung shooting and hurting his younger sister Gaelle. The grove of childhood play and fun hides the siblings' secrets of nearly blinding Gaelle and Coralie relieving herself there. Pleasure and pain, joy and shame, are forever interlaced.[6]

Apropos wheat fields, Figure 13.4 from the animation, inspired by page 160 from the graphic novel, shows the child Jung walking among, and running his hand over, rows of ripening ears, which takes a page out of Ridley Scott's *The Gladiator* (2000) when General Maximus (Russell Crowe) strolls lovingly across his wheat field in a homecoming trance, only to find his wife crucified. The formulaic tracking shot, often in slow-motion and with soothing music, of fingers touching waist-high stalks is hypnotic, arousing nostalgia in a tactile, visceral way. This possible influence from a cliché scene from Hollywood films reaffirms the paradox at the core of the minority condition: to reconstruct ethnicity, Jung depends on the French language and Western cultural reference. Indeed, are there actually endless acres of wheat fields near Seoul, South Korea, so imprinted in a five-year-old's memory that he returns amidst the golden ears in the animation? Quite revealingly, one of Jung's maternal reveries is set in such a wheat field, from which he emerges to be accosted by his brother Erik (132). Wheat fields are displaced from the Henins' environment—their Belgian "backyard," so to speak—to imagined reunions in Seoul. This is quite unsettling since golden reprises the color association of Jung's yellow skin with "honey," echoing ironically the Henin family trait of "hair color... honey" (45). Despite the "family" resemblance of

---

[6] While Figure 13.3 draws from a panel with internal contradiction, another discord occurs between panels in this otherwise well-wrought, flowing graphic book, despite its heavy subject matter. Page 125 of Volume 1 illustrates a Viking ship flying the Korean national flag, which transports Asian adoptees to "the Scandinavian countries." The following panel shows the backside of a tall woman in a mini-skirt, her body iridescent, surrounded by sparkles and two lecherous men, one of whom has his tongue hanging out, nearly drooling. The caption states: "That puts an end to the myth of Swedish woman, tall and... BLONDE." To read between the lines—the panels, rather—one comes to the uncomfortable conclusion that Asian adoptees contaminate the Swedish gene pool, tarring Swedish blondes' luminosity. This idolizing derives from nonwhite males' quest for control in a white-dominated world by way of its "backdoor," namely, possessing white femininity, real or imaginary. The adolescent Jung, for instance, masturbates to pornographic centerfolds of *Pussy Kitten*, apparently Caucasian models (96–8). The animation has excised the explicit masturbatory reveries in the graphic novel. Volumes 2–4 of the graphic book contain many more male fantasies over white female voluptuousness. What the adolescent Jung does is no different from what men of color have done in general. Frantz Fanon analyzes the White Goddess syndrome in "The Man of Color and the White Woman" (*Black Skin, White Mask*, 1952). Black Panther leader Eldridge Cleaver opens *Soul on Ice* (1968) with the rude awakening of the "whiteness" of the pin-up girl he put up in his cell when the prison guard who had ripped it off told him to "get yourself a colored girl for a pinup—no white women" (21). I have discussed the deification and fetishization of white women in two chapters—"Interracial Eroticism in Asian American Literature: Male Subjectivities and White Bodies" and "Postcolonial Feminizing of America in Carlos Bulosan"—of *Immigrant Subjectivities in Asian American and Asian Diaspora Literatures* (Ma 1998).

Figure 13.4 The animated *Approved for Adoption* imagines the rendezvous with the mother in a wheat field.

the Henins' hair and Jung's skin, Holt's euphemism has already been doubly sabotaged by "lemon" and "yellow" (7) in Jung's modus operandi spiking pathos with bathos, tears with sneers.

Bathed in the golden halo of wheat fields, if also sepia and faded, Jung's dream vision with his birth mother means to leave a sweet aftertaste. This is yet another twist to junk food biting back. Jung rips Korea in half in order to romanticize his biological mother in opposition to the masculine Korea, creating a bittersweet childhood. Yet that sweetness is an artificial flavor manufactured in the image of European and Hollywood wheat fields. The human mind seeks to comfort itself somehow. When Jung (be)holds the photographs of the five-year-old in his adoption file, he, on the verge of tears, runs his thumb over the image several times as if in a loving caress, albeit minimalist with his fingers (Figure 13.5, also see vol. 3, 71–5 of the graphic book).

This is similar to what his fellow Korean adoptee Deann Borshay Liem pauses to do in her documentary *In the Matter of Cha Jung Hee* (2010) when she locates her own adoption picture.[7] These individual artists' heart-wrenching responses differ qualitatively from collective Korean culture's coping strategy of returning the "lost sheep" to the fold of Mother/land. For instance, the twenty-episode TV series *Hotelier* (2001) exemplifies this in the Korean adoptee (Yong-jun Bae) avenging himself against the world as a Harvard Business School-trained corporal raider, leaving a trail of downsized companies and laid-off workers. Bae's character mends his ways only when he returns to Seoul and falls in love with a female hotel manager. Absent the happy ending of Hotelier, the works of Jung and Liem hum a quiet lullaby for the orphans, all alone in recurring nightmares. Their art sings of itself and militates against the injustice of fate until it, too, falls silent, overcome by that which wells up from within.

[7] See Chapter 6, "Hyde-and-Seek in Asian Diaspora: Deann Borshay Liem's Negative and Ang Lee's Ventriloquy" in Sheng-mei Ma's *The Last Isle: Contemporary Taiwan Film, Culture, and Trauma* (2015).

Figure 13.5 The animated *Approved for Adoption* where Jung strokes his adoption photo with his left thumb.

References

Bagley, Christopher. 1993. *International and Transracial Adoptions: A Mental Health Perspective*. Brookfield, VT: Avebury.
Brinich, Paul M. 1990. "Adoption from the Inside Out: A Psychoanalytic Perspective." In Brodzinsky, David M., and Scheichter, Marshall D., eds. *The Psychology of Adoption*. Oxford University Press, 42–61.
Cleaver, Eldridge. 1968. *Soul on Ice*. New York: Ramparts.
Fanon, Frantz. 1952. *Black Skin, White Masks*. Trans. Charles Lam Markman, 1952. New York: Grove.
Hotelier. 2001. Directed by Yong-woo Chung, performances by Hwa-jeong Choi, Yong-jun Bae, Jin-hie Han. MBC. https://www.youtube.com/watch?v=DhNUWzfV3eA (accessed February 12, 2019).
Jung. 2007–16. *Couleur de peau: miel*. (Vol. 1–4). Belgium: Quadrants astrolabe.
Jung. 2014. *Approved for Adoption* (translation of *Couleur de peau: miel*). Vol. 1–2. Amazon.
Jung, and Boileau, Laurent, dir. 2012. *Couleur de peau: miel*. Cinedigm Entertainment Corp. https://www.hoopladigital.com/title/12136836 (accessed December 2019).
Liem, Deann Borshay, dir. 2000. *First Person Plural*. Mu Films.
Liem, Deann Borshay, dir. 2010. *In the Matter of Cha Jung Hee*. Mu Films.
Lott, Eric. 1993. *Love and Theft: Blackface Minstrelsy and the American Working Class*. Oxford University Press.
Ma, Sheng-mei. 1998. *Immigrant Subjectivities in Asian American and Asian Diaspora Literatures*. New York: State University of New York Press.
Ma, Sheng-mei. 2015. *The Last Isle: Contemporary Film, Culture and Trauma in Global Taiwan*. New York: Rowman & Littlefield International.

Park, Patricia. 2015. *Re Jane*. New York: Viking.
Pate, SooJin. 2014. *From Orphan to Adoptee: U.S. Empire and Genealogies of Korean Adoption*. Minneapolis, MN University of Minnesota Press.
Silverman, Arnold, and Feigelman, William. 1990. "Adjustment in Interracial Adoption: An Overview." In Brodzinsky, David M., and Scheichter, Marshall D., eds. *The Psychology of Adoption*. Oxford University Press, 187–200.

Contributors

Hazlina Abdullah received her PhD from the International Islamic University Malaysia, M.Ed. TESL from Universiti Pendidikan Sultan Idris and B.Ed. TESOL degree from the University of Warwick. She has gained vast teaching experience through her teaching career at secondary and tertiary levels. She is currently affiliated with Universiti Sains Islam Malaysia.

Shilpa Daithota Bhat is an assistant professor at National Forensic Sciences University, Gujarat, India. She has a PhD from Gujarat University. Her areas of interest are South Asian literature, diaspora and postcolonial theories, Canadian studies and children's literature. She was a visiting fellow, Oxford University; visiting fellow, McGill University, Canada, 2017; and international visitor, York University, Canada, 2015. In addition, she has several publications in peer-reviewed international journals and has authored/edited books.

Allison Blecker received her PhD from Harvard University in Arabic Literature with a secondary field in Comparative Literature. She is currently a Research Associate at Swarthmore College. Her dissertation, *Eco-Alterity: Writing the Environment in the Literature of North Africa and the Middle East*, is situated at the intersection of postcolonial studies, Arabic literature, and the environmental humanities. Allison is the co-translator of a collection of poetry by Nouri Al-Jarrah, *A Boat to Lesbos* (2018), and her English translations of Arabic poetry have appeared in *Banipal* and *Gathering the Tide: An Anthology of Contemporary Gulf Poetry* (2011).

Debadrita Chakraborty is a research scholar from Cardiff University researching on gender, sexuality, critical/cultural studies and de-colonial praxis. Her PhD research using gender and cultural theories explored the shifting nature of the construction and performance of South Asian masculine identities catalysed by major political and socio-cultural events in Britain as represented in British Asian Fiction. She holds publications in postcolonial and diaspora literature, critical race studies, gender and migration studies.

Dominic Davies is Senior Lecturer in English at City, University of London, where he is also the director of the BA English programme. He holds a DPhil and British Academy postdoctoral scholarship from the University of Oxford. He is the author of *Urban Comics* (Routledge 2019) and the co-editor with Professor Candida Rifkind of *Documenting Trauma in Comics* (Palgrave MacMillan 2020). He is currently co-authoring with Professor Rifkind a new book entitled *Graphic Refuge: Visuality and Mobility in Refugee Comics* (forthcoming with Wilfred Laurier University Press 2022/23).

Sandra Federici has been Editor-in-Chief of the bi-annual journal *Africa e Mediterraneo* since 1999. She has coordinated educational projects and exhibitions around comics by African authors. In 2017, she completed a PhD at the Université de Lorraine, in co-tutorship with the University of Milan, with a thesis entitled *L'entrance des auteurs africains dans le champ de la bande dessinée européenne de langue française (1978–2016)*, published in 2019 by L'Harmattan (Paris). A second article entitled "Je ne voulais pas d'histoires-calebasse" will appear in her book, *Entretiens avec les bédéistes africains* to be published by Sépia publishing house in 2022.

Dr. Jana Fedtke is Assistant Professor of English at the American University of Sharjah (United Arab Emirates). Her research and teaching interests include transnational literatures with a focus on South Asia; gender studies; and postcolonial literatures. Dr. Fedtke's work has been published in *Online Information Review*, *Journal of Further and Higher Education*, *South Asian History and Culture*, *Asexualities: Feminist and Queer Perspectives* (Routledge), and *South Asian Review*.

Camila Gutiérrez is a dual-title PhD candidate in Comparative Literature and Visual Studies at The Pennsylvania State University. Her research focuses on the aesthetics of shōjo manga in transpacific migration from Japan to the Americas and explores how this visual language helps women and gender nonconforming authors to articulate knowledge that is rooted in local, peripheral, and nonnormative lived experience. Additionally, Camila is a founder of the Liberal Arts Collective at Penn State and of the Mentoring for the Future program for BIPOC communities in graduate education. At Penn State, she has taught undergraduate courses in world literature, comics, video game culture, and virtual worlds.

James Hodapp is an assistant professor of English in the liberal arts program at Northwestern University in Qatar. His research has appeared in *The Journal of Graphic Novels and Comics*, *The Journal of Postcolonial Writing*, *African Literature Today*, *Critical Arts*, *English Studies in Africa*, *ARIEL: A Review of International English Literature*, *The Global South*, *The Journal of Commonwealth Literature*, and *English in Africa*, as well as in other journals and anthologies. He is the editor of *Afropolitan Literature as World Literature* (2020) from Bloomsbury Publishing.

Mohd Muzhafar Idrus (PhD) is an associate professor at Universiti Sains Islam Malaysia. His research interests include literature, ideological spectrums, and popular culture. He is a reviewer for a number of Taylor & Francis journals including *Critical Inquiry in Language Studies*, *Cogent Education*, and *Cogent Arts and Humanities*. His work has appeared in *Globalizations*, *Changing English*, and *Comparative Literature: East & West*.

Habibah Ismail is a lecturer at the Faculty of Major Language Studies, Universiti Sains Islam Malaysia. She has a doctoral degree in Linguistics (University of Sydney), focusing on gender issues in Malaysian sports news discourse based on media's examination of written and visual texts.

Jin Lee is an assistant professor of American and British Literature at Myongji University. Lee's interests in scholarship include Asian American literature, graphic narratives, trauma studies, and postcolonial literary studies and globalization. Her research has appeared or is forthcoming in *The Comics Grid: Journal of Comics Scholarship, American, British, and Canadian Studies Journal, Journal of Literature and Trauma Studies,* and *CLCWeb: Comparative Literature and Culture.*

Sheng-mei Ma (馬聖美 mash@msu.edu) is Professor of English at Michigan State University in Michigan, USA, specializing in Asian Diaspora and East–West comparative studies. He is the author of over a dozen books, including *The Tao of S* (2022); *Off-White* (2019); *Sinophone–Anglophone Cultural Duet* (2017); *The Last Isle* (2015); *Alienglish* (2014); *Asian Diaspora and East–West Modernity* (2012); *Diaspora Literature and Visual Culture* (2011); *East–West Montage* (2007); *The Deathly Embrace* (2000); *Immigrant Subjectivities in Asian American and Asian Diaspora Literatures* (1998); and memoir *Immigrant Horse's Mouth* (2023). Co-editor of five books and special issues, *Transnational Narratives in Englishes of Exile* (2018) among them, he also published a collection of poetry in Chinese, *Thirty Left and Right* (三十左右).

Dima Nasser is a PhD student in the Department of Comparative Literature at Brown University. She researches poetic visuality in experimental twentieth-century Arabic poetry and its formal and conceptual intersections with contemporaneous works of visual art. Her interests include word-and-image studies, graphic narratives, translation studies, and world literature. She has published with *African Literature Today* and *Kohl: A Journal for Body and Gender Research*. She is also a published academic translator working between Arabic and English, and has co-edited a volume of contemporary Arab women's writing from the region and the diaspora titled *Arab Women Voice New Realities* (2017).

Catherine Sly taught English in Australian high schools for many years. She later undertook a PhD investigating the literary merit of graphic novels. She continues to pursue her interest in visual literacy as an independent researcher. Currently, she is a writer and editor for the NSW Department of Education journal, *Scan*. Her publications on visual narratives include "EmPOWering 21st century readers" in *Picture Books and Beyond* (2014) edited by Kerry Mallan, "Crossing cultural boundaries with graphic novels" (2017), *Scan*, 36(4), "An eloquent silence: The value of wordless narratives" (2020), *Scan*, 39(7), and "Anthropomorphic or zoomorphic? – Fictional animals" (2021), *Scan*, 40(4).

Jasmin Wrobel holds a PhD in Latin American Studies from Freie Universität Berlin. She has been Junior Lecturer at Lateinamerika-Institut, FU Berlin and was

Guest Lecturer at Pontificia Universidad Católica de Chile and Tel Aviv University. She is Postdoctoral Researcher and Academic Coordinator at the Cluster of Excellence *Temporal Comunities: Doing Literature in a Global Perspective*, FU Berlin, and working on a book project titled "Body / Images—Foreign / Gazes: (Feminine) Territoriality and CorpoGraphy in Latin American Graphic Narratives." She is author of the book *Topographien des 20. Jahrhunderts: Die memoriale Poetik des Stolpens in Haroldo de Campos' Galáxias* (2020), editor of the volume *Roteiros de palavras, sons, imagens: Os diálogos transcriativos de Haroldo de Campos* (2018), and co-editor of the themed issue "Experimental Poetry Networks: Material Circulations" (2019 in *MATLIT*; with Pauline Bachmann). She has published articles in several international journals and compilations.

Index

'Abdel-Moneim Rakhkha, Mohamed 61
Abdelrazaq, Leila 123–44
Aboriginal and Torres Strait Islanders 187–212
Abouet, Marguerite 187
abstract imagery 65, 174, 176–7
abstract spaces 80
absurdity 66
Abū Naẓẓārah Zarqah (1877–1910) 62–3
accent/dialect 202–4 *see also* linguistic varieties
Achka, Hans Kwaatail 107
activism 86, 89, 125, 139–40, 145–6, 154, 167–71, 178, 185
Adéeḭkò, Adélékè 240
adoption 257–68
Adorno, Theodor 63
aesthetic influences 59, 61
aesthetics of sameness 83–4
Africa
  Francophone African comics 97–122
  Wakanda 229–42
Africa e Mediterraneo 116 n.6
African Book Collective 99
African Publishers Network (APNET) 99
Africanfuturism 235–8, 241
Africultures portal 99
Afrikatoon 108
Afrilivres 99, 102
Afrofuturism 235
Agamben, Giorgio 13, 14, 15, 150–1, 152, 155
Agence Internationale de la Francophonie 104
Ago Media 108–10
Agostini, Angelo 37
Akligo, Jo Palmer 105
Akoma Mba 106
al-Ali, Naji 123, 130
al-'Awadi, Zohdi 61
Alber, Jan 192

albums 58, 102, 104, 105, 114
Aldama, Frederick Luis 5
Alerte à Kamoto 112
Alf Layla w Layla 68
al-Hallaq, Eyad 140
alienation 36, 55, 60, 68, 71, 155, 170–1, 240, 263, 265
Alladayé, Hervé 104, 112
Alliance of independent publishers (Africa) 99
Allison, Marjorie C. 203
Almo Productions 112
Almond, Ian 4–5
Al-Udhari, Abdullah 134
Anderson, Reynaldo 236
Andrade Ecchio, Claudia 41
Angles, Jeffrey 85
Angoulême Festival 101–2, 110
animations 41, 135, 257, 258–9, 260, 265, 266–7
anime 82
anti-colonialism 6, 148
Apollinaire, Guillaume 69, 70
Appleby, LaVetta 234
Approved for Adoption (Jung) 257–68
Apter, Emily 11, 13, 127, 128
Arab-American literature 125
Arabic 55–73, 126, 127, 128
Araújo, André 229
archetypes 13, 61, 63
Argentina 37, 42
Arni, Samhita 215, 219, 220–1, 225
Art and Liberty Group 68
art history academy 63
As Aventuras de Nhô Quim ou Impressões de uma Viagem à Corte (Agostini, 1869) 37
As Aventuras de Zé Caipora (Agostini, 1883) 37
Asante, Godfried A. 240
Assem, Paulin Koffivi Mawuto 108

associations of authors 115–16
Astro-Blackness 236
Atelier Fond 114
atemporalization 178, 179–80, 182, 183
Auerbach, Erich 191
Auschwitz 14–15, 24
Australia 187–212
authorial transparency 21
autobiographical pact 42
autobiography 33, 34–6, 40 *see also* graphic memoir
avatars 22, 42
awards/prizes 38, 51, 58, 103, 118
Ayaka, Carolene 247

Ba, Cheikh 105
Bá, Gabriel 38
backgrounds, minimal 195
Baddawi (Abdelrazaq, 2015) 124, 125, 128, 129–36, 139, 140, 141, 142
Baetens, Jan 35 n.2, 128, 192
Bagley, Christopher 258, 262
Bakame 102
Bake, Julia 21
Bakhtin, Mikhail 205
Bal, Mieke 199
Ball, David M. 129
Bambara 104
bande dessinée 58 n.2, 76, 94, 118
Banerjee, Sarnath 146–7, 155–62
Baruti, Barly 97, 100
Bas Backer, Joris 42
Bathy, Asimba 113
Bayart, F. 118
BDB (Bande des Dessinateurs de Bamako) 116
Bechdel, Alison 2, 16, 33, 35–6, 37, 141
Benin 102, 104, 105, 111–12
bestseller lists 35
Bgoya, W. 102
Bhabha, Honi 251
Bhat, Harsha 220
Bhayroo, Shenid 238
biblical collections 100
bibliodiversity 103
Bidegaray, Alejandro 39
Bikar, Hussein 68

Bingo (1981–4) 100, 101
biography 150 *see also* autobiography; graphic memoir
biopolitics 151–3, 155–62, 163, 243
bird's-eye perspectives 13, 15, 19, 198
bishōnen 88
black, blocks of 93
black and white images 41, 65, 150, 167, 195
Black Lives Matter 140
black pages 58
Black Panther 229–42
black utopias 236
Blankets (Thompson) 35, 51
bleed pages 174, 177, 178, 180
blogs 17, 42, 61, 108, 117
body/corporeality 36, 37, 44–50, 200, 245
Bombasaro, Olivier 104
Bomboko, Dan 107
book fairs 108
book-bound comics 13, 17
Boom Latinoamericano 38–9
border crossing 2, 13, 20, 25, 126, 135
Border Diary (Abdelrazaq) 142
Borges, Gabriela 39, 40, 41
"born global" 2
Bourdieu, Pierre 97–8, 117, 118
Boys Love (BL) 80, 85–94
Bradford, C. 200
Brecchia, Patricia 39
Breccia, Alberto 38 n.6
Brennan, Timothy 14
Brezault, Alain 109
Brinich, Paul M. 258, 263 n.4
Brown, Chester 187
Burger, Bibi 240
Burroughs, Todd Steven 240
Burundarena, Maitena 39

Cailleaux, Christian 98–9
CairoComix 58
Calais camps 20
calligrams 69, 70
Cameroon 105–6, 112, 116
canons 2, 4, 5, 17, 27, 35–6, 75, 126–7, 135, 221
captions 19, 42–3, 63, 174, 194, 201

carceral spaces 11–14
carceral World Literature 11–13, 14, 17, 18–27, 28
caricature 61, 62, 201
carnival 205
Casanova, Pascale 14, 168
Cassiau-Haurie, Ch. 105, 107, 116
"catwalk effect" 78 n.22
Celestin, R. 245
censorship 58, 62, 80–1, 85 n.19, 151, 249–50
Chad 110
Chak, Tings 17, 22–5
character introductions 194
characterization 199–204
Chatterji, Roma 218
Cheah, Pheng 167, 168, 169, 172 n.8, 185, 191, 194, 201, 205, 209, 210
Cheung, Ysabelle 171
Cheurfa, Hiyem 128
Chevant, Aurélie 244–5
Chiam, M. 247
Chicks on Comics 42, 51
childlike expression 41, 44
children's book illustrations 102–6
children's comics 60, 61
child's perspectives 36
Chile 76, 77, 87, 90
Chitrakar, Moyna 215, 218, 219, 221, 225, 226
Chroniques de Lomé 109
chronology 60
Chute, Hillary 5, 11, 13, 15, 16, 17, 18, 27, 33, 34–5, 36, 44, 60, 64, 66, 150
close-ups 55, 78, 79–80, 88, 91
Coates, Ta-Nehisi 229, 230, 237, 239, 240
Cocobulles comic festival 108
Codex Zouche-Nutall 37
coffins of memory 15
Cole, Teju 231, 235
collaboration 58, 59–60, 104, 110, 116–17
collections of drawings 17
collective memory 131, 240
collectives 39, 51, 99, 103, 109–10, 116, 118
Collins, B. 200
Collins, Sibrina 234

Colombia 34, 41–51
colonialism, *see also* postcolonialism
  Africa 238–40
  Australia 191, 210
  bande dessine, 60
  India 223, 226
  Japanese 167, 168, 174, 177, 181, 184, 246
  and modernism 64
  and the publishing industry 99
  Wakanda 235
color, use of 68, 89–90, 194, 195
"comfort women" 167–86
comic anthologies 39–40
Comic Fiesta 247
comic magazines 39
comic strips 37–8, 100, 145
Comics and the Latin American City: Framing Urban Communities 34 n.1
Comics Grinder 17
comics journalism 13, 16–17
coming of age stories 33, 35–6, 41–50, 150, 191
comix 60
conferences 116
Congo 100, 107, 112, 114
constellational modernism 63–4, 71–2
consumerism 60
corporeality/body 36, 37, 44–9, 200, 245
correspondence pages 82
Corridor (Banerjee, 2004) 146–7, 155–62
Couleur de Peau (Jung, 2007–16) 257
counter-gaze 44
COVID-19 214, 220–3, 226
critical discourse analysis 244, 250
critical hybridity theory 249
critical literacy 146, 163
cross-cultural empathy 199–204
crowdfunding 117
cuadrinho 76, 94
culinary tradition 131–2, 138, 263
cultural animations 108
cultural assets 38
cultural capital 194
cultural diplomacy 116
cultural events 116, 119, 127

cultural fields 97
cultural globalization 248
cultural references 44, 59, 63

Dabley, Olvis 108
Dadié, Charles 105
Dago (Maïga) 102, 107
Daina, Samy 110
Damrosch, David 14, 80, 93, 125, 126, 128, 129, 135, 168
Danner, Alexander 213, 225
Darwish, Mahmoud 134
Davies, Dominic 5, 13, 14, 16, 18, 21, 22, 25, 27
Daytripper (Moon and Bá) 38
de Ilha, Crau 39
De Moor, Bob 100
de Teffé, Nair 39
Dearden, Lizzie 13
decolonial theory 5, 238
dehumanization 22, 172–3, 201, 234–5
Déjame que te Llame (Prado Bley) 77–80, 86, 93
Délestron 105
Delhi Calm (Ghosh, 2010) 146–7, 148–55
Delisle, Guy 187
Denson, Shane 5
Denzin, Norman 71
depth 66
development assistance 99, 108
Dewerpe, A. 118
dialogue 18, 22, 201 *see also* speech bubbles/balloons
Diarra, Igo Lassana 104, 105
Diarra, Yacouba 105
diaspora 125–7, 134, 141, 213–14, 223–4, 226, 237, 246
dictatorships 40
Dieme, Lamine 105
digital coloring 117, 151
digital printing 99
direct speech 18, 22 *see also* speech bubbles/balloons
Disney 76, 238
dissolving images 72, 80, 91
distant reading 127
documentary 64, 66

Dollase, Hiromi Tsuchiya 85 n.19
Domínguez Jeria, Paloma 41
Dominic, D. 161
Dorfman, Ariel 76
Doron, Assa 161
dōseiai 85
double-page splashes 13, 14, 18–27, 68
Doucet, Julie 36, 40
doujinshi 87
dramatis personae 194
dream-like imagery 174, 194, 265
drugs 25, 34, 44
Dubois, Jacques 98
Dunst, A. 145
Durand, Pascal 98
dystopia 145–65

Ebileeni, Maurice 126–7
ebooks 17
Ecuador 41–51
Edimo, Christophe 106
Éditions du Crayon Noir 112–13
Éditions Elondja 107–8
Éditions Fluide Thermal 112
editorial space 20
Egypt 55–73
Egyptian graphic text 61–4
Eisner, Will 3, 16, 35 n.2
Eisner Award 38
El Eternauta (Germán Oesterheld) 38
El Volcán: un presente de la historieta latinoamericana (Sainz and Bidegaray) 39, 40
Elikya, le petit orphelin 107–8
elision 85, 93
el-Telmissany, Kamel 68
Embury, Gary 13, 18
Engels, Laura 240
English
   Australia 194, 202–3
   India 146
   left-to-right reading direction 19
   Palestinian American community 125, 126, 128, 135
   reportage 17
   translation into 38, 43 n.11, 77, 87, 130

varieties of 202–3
Wakanda 237–8
Esale, Dick 107
Escaping Wars and Waves: Encounters with Syrian Refugees (Kugler) 11, 18–20
Estrellas de la Pampa (Prado Bley) 86, 87–94
ethics of attention 150
ethnography 125, 130, 133
Eurocentrism 1–4, 5
Evans, Kate 17, 20–2
exhibitions 59, 115, 116, 118, 123
expressionism 68
extradiegetic narrators 194

Facebook 105, 108, 117
fading 78
Fairclough, N.L. 244, 250, 251
Fall, Samba 102, 104
Fanon, Frantz 265 n.6
Fantagraphics 13, 38
fantastical imagery 68
fantasy 145
fashion drawings 78 n.22, 83
Feigelman, W. 261
female-female romance 82–3
feminist theory 34, 39, 41, 44, 51
Ferguson, P. 156, 159
Fernandes D'Oliveira, Gêisa 35 n.2
Festival International de la Bande Dessinée d'Alger 58
festivals 41, 58, 101–2, 110, 113, 116, 247
Fī shiqqat bāb el-loq (*The Apartment in Bab El-Louk*) 55–73
fields (Bourdieu) 97–8, 117–18
Fig Tree, The (Abdelrazaq) 135–7, 139, 142
film studies 71
First Nations Australians 187–212
first-person narration 42
flâneurs 155–62
flashback devices 58, 174, 196
floating text 78–9, 84, 91, 174, 178, 180, 182
Flore à tout prix 110
Floyd, George 140
Fludernik, Monika 192, 202, 203

folk poetry, illustrated 68
Fonkoua, R. 97
Fons, T.T. 106, 114
fonts 79, 201
Foo, T.T. 250
food and belonging 131–2, 138, 263
Footnotes in Gaza (Sacco) 141
Ford, Richard Thompson 240
forensically accurate drawings 24
foreshadowing 174, 177
formal vocabulary 60
Foucault, Michel 71, 147 n.1, 150, 151–2, 157, 160, 243
frame stories 204–5
frames 60, 68, 80, 92, 194, 196
France 59 n.6, 62
Franco-Belgian comic tradition 27, 58 n.2, 61–2, 76, 100, 118, 119
Francophone African comics 97–122
freedom of speech 58, 248
French 38, 70, 97–122, 257, 258–9, 261, 265
Frey, Hugo 192
Fujimoto, Yukari 78 n.22
Fun Home (Bechdel) 16, 33, 35–6, 37, 51
fundamental narrator role 194

Gabon 107
Galvão, Patrícia Rehder ("Pagu") 39
Gamberi, Valentina 218
gang violence 25
Ganzeer 56, 58–9, 69, 70
García Canclini, Néstor 35 n.2
Gardner, Jared 192
Gaviria, Paola, *see* Powerpaola
gaze 11, 26, 44, 55, 69, 71, 80
Gazzar, 'Abdel Hadi 68
Gbassman 108
Gbich! 108
Gempak Starz 247, 249
Gendry-Kim, Keum Suk 167–86
genre 27–8, 59–60, 66, 79, 93, 191, 194, 213, 225, 257
gentrification, cultural 16
geographical violence 245
Ghaibeh, Lina 61, 62
Ghosh, Vishwajyoti 146–7, 148–55

Giguet-Legdhen, E. 106
Girard, A. 102
Glidden, Sarah 141
"global" art 64
globalization 22, 142, 155, 168, 244, 248–9, 251, 254
global-local tension 34, 42, 76, 93, 244
glocalism 93
Gloeckner, Phoebe 36, 40, 141
glosses 129
Go Magazine 108
Go Média 108
Goethe 5, 168, 191
Gómez Gutiérrez, Felipe 45, 46, 50
Gonzalez, Carolina 87
González Rodríguez, Sergio 25
Goor mag 114
Goorgoorlou 113–14
Gorrora, Claire 15
grammar, comic 15, 60, 64
graphic essays 40, 98–9
graphic memoir 16, 33–53, 59 n.6, 129, 130, 257–68
graphic narratives
  cross-cultural 187
  Egyptian graphic text 60
  historical narratives 110, 148, 151, 177–8, 195, 260–1
  India 145–6
  Latin America 38, 42, 77
  and narrative theory 192
  South Asia 213
  World versus popular literature debate 35 n.2
"graphic nonfiction" 16–17
graphic nonfiction 16–17, 34–5, 36, 44
graphic novels
  Australian 187–212
  Baddawi (Abdelrazaq, 2015) 124, 129
  Couleur de Peau (Jung, 2007–16) 257–68
  Fī shiqqat bāb el-loq (*The Apartment in Bab El-Louk*) 59–60, 72
  Francophone Sub-Saharan Africa 97
  and graphic reportage 16–17, 27
  India 145–65
  Indigenous graphic novels 187–212

Malaysia 243–56
  as marketing term 35 n.2
  and postcolonialism 245–8, 252–4
graphic poetry 68, 69, 83
graphic reportage 11–31
Graphi-Culture Foundation 110
Grass (Keum Suk Gendry-Kim) 167–86
Greece 18–19
grey tone sequences 196
greyscale fades 78, 88, 91, 93
grids 19, 21–2, 25, 27, 60
grief 136
Groensteen, Thierry 78 n.22, 79, 92, 192, 194
Guerrero, Agustina 41
Guinea 103, 105
Gupta, S. 243, 244, 254
Guthrie, Ricardo 238
gutters 11, 15, 19, 21, 60, 91, 93, 196
Guyer, Jonathan 61, 62, 68
Gymnich, Marion 202
Gyr, Agnes 102

Hague, Ian 247
Hahn, Steve 239
Halen, P. 97, 98, 117
half-splash pages 15
Hanamonogatari 85
Hanchey, Jenny 237
Handala 123, 128, 130, 133, 136
Harvey, D. 146, 154
hashtag movements 39–40
Hebrew 126
Hemman, Kathryn 81 n.6
Henein, George 68
Hergé 100
Herman, David 192
Herodotus 49, 50
high culture versus low/popular culture 50–1, 59, 145
hijab 2 n.2, 37
Hillary, Simplice 108
historical narratives 110, 148, 151, 177–8, 195, 260–1
historicization 98
Histories, The (Herodotus) 49, 50
historieta 76, 94

Hodapp, James 33, 234, 237
Holbert, Nathan 234
Holmberg, R. 154
Holocaust 12, 13, 15
homelands 123, 126, 138, 141
homosexuality 83–94
Hotelier (2001) 266
Hoyos, Hector 77 n.3
human rights 12, 38
humanitarianism 12, 14, 18, 19, 20, 22
humor 156, 194, 204, 205–10
Hunt, Nancy Rose 114
hybrid creatures 62
hyperdensity 93
hyperframes 92

iconography 61, 63, 123, 201
identification 200
identity 123, 125, 130, 131–2, 134, 141, 210
identity predication 98
Idrus, M.M. 249
Ikeda, Keiko 83 n.14
Illanes, María Angélica 87
illustrated poetry 68, 83
IMPALA 112
India 145–65, 213, 222–3
Indigenous graphic novels 187–212
indigenous visual systems 75
informal production 110
Instagram 117
interdisciplinarity 59
Intergovernmental Agency for the French-Speaking Community 109
interior world 80, 91
intermedial dialogue 36
internal monologues 78–9, 91, 203
International Alliance of Independent Publishers 103 n.3
International Association of Francophone Libraries 99
International Board on Books for Young People (IBBY) 102
international cross-pollination 225
international law 12
International Youth Literature Festival 105
Internet 117 *see also* online publishing

intertextual references 36, 126
irony 66, 114, 156, 206, 207, 262–3
Ishida, Hitoshi 86
Issaka, Abou Abakar 110, 111
Ivory Coast 102, 103, 104, 105, 106, 108, 116
Iyegar, K.R. Srinivas 222

Jacquette, Elisabeth 56, 69
Jameson, Fredric 168
Jamieson, Teddy 17, 19, 20
Japan 2, 75, 76, 81–6, 246, 263 *see also* manga
Jaworska, S. 250
Jay, M. 102
jojōga (lyrical drawing) 82–3, 91
Jōmakan collection 82, 83 n.13
Jones, Charles E. 236
journalism 13, 16–17, 62, 66
Journées africaines de la B.D. 107
Jung 257–68
Junid, Iman 247, 248
juxtaposition 58, 60, 69, 84, 91, 195

Kahil Award 58
KanAd 108, 110
Kaoru 247
Kassaï, D. 104
KBenjamin 105
Keen, Suzanne 201
Kennedy, J.M. 201
Kiaer, Jieun 170, 172
King, Edward 35 n.2, 41
Kioko, Ndinda 1, 2
Knowles, Sam 246–7
Kojele, Alain 107
Kōji, Fukiya 83
Kominsky-Crumb, Aline 36, 40
Konaté, Moussa 104
Korea 167–86, 257, 258
Kotler, Mindy 170
Kouadio, Benjamin 104, 105, 106
Kouroublis, Panagiotis 12–13
Kraidy, Marwan M. 248–9, 253–4
Krisht, Aya 141
Kugler, Olivier 11, 12, 17, 18–20, 21
Kukkonen, Karin 199
Kyle, Richard 35 n.2

La grande épopée du Tchad 110, 111
La Lucha (Sack) 25–7
Labio, Catherine 16
L'Amour est Roi 108
Lamuka 116
Landis, W. 246
Langston, J. 204, 209
Lanterne 112
Larios, Delia 39
Latin America 33–53, 75–95
Latin texts 50
Lavado Tejón, Joaquín Salvador, *see* Quino
Lebanon 62
Leclaire, Gèrard 110, 111
Lee, Young-Jun 171
Lefebvre, Henri 153
left-to-right reading direction 19
leitmotifs 37
Lent, J.A. 247
Lent, John 61
Les aventures de Mamisha 107
Les refoulés du Katanga 112–13
Les sorcières 108
Lesage, S. 110
Let me Call you (Prado Bley) 77 n.4
LGBTQA groups 86
Libreville 107
Licar, Susana 39
Liem, Deann Borshay 266
Lim, I. 249
linearity 20, 59 n.6, 60, 66, 68, 83
Lingala 114
linguistic varieties 34, 44, 58, 62, 127, 202–3, 237
literary institutions 98
"literature," definitions of 16, 27–8
logosyllabic languages 37
López, María Luisa 39
López-Calvo, Ignacio 170
Lott, Eric 263
Lumbala, Hillary Mbiye 115
Lunsford, Andrea A. 133

Maamoul Press 125, 141
Macaire, Etty 106
Machado, Laluna 41
Madagascar 100

Mafalda (Quino) 37–8
Magabala Books 188
magical realism 191, 236
Maher, Donia 56, 58, 59, 69
Maïga 102
Malagasy comics 100
Malaysia 243–56
male-male romance narratives 77, 83
Mali 103, 105
Mandaville, Alison 170
Mandel, Naomi 14
manga 60, 77–87, 94, 187, 200, 209, 246–8
Map of Palestine (Abdelrazaq) 123, 124, 125
maps 123, 132–3, 194, 198, 230
Marco, Deriline 232
Marino, Dani 41
"Mariposa" (Abdelrazaq) 140–1
Marshall, Niní 39
Masioni, Pat 97, 100
Mattelart, Armand 76
Maus (Spiegelman) 14–15, 16, 17, 24, 27, 35, 36, 246
Mayan languages 37
Mazur, Dan 213, 225
Mbembe, Achille 147
McCausland, Elisa 41
McCloud, Scott 37, 60, 93, 174
McKenna, Brenton E. 187–212
McLelland, Mark 87
media cycles 18
Mehta, Binita 5
memory processes 36, 129–36, 148, 151, 196, 232–3 *see also* collective memory; graphic memoir
Mena, Erica 38
Mendel, Yonatan 132
Mendozza 108
Mendy, Alphonse 113–14 *see also* Fons, T.T.
Menggapai Bintang (*Reach for the Stars*) 243–56
menstruation 50
Merino, Ana 41
metaphor 80, 116, 150, 168, 205, 240
metonymy 182, 237
Mexico 25–7

Mfumu'eto 114–15
Mickwitz, Nina 13, 17, 21
migrant detention comics 20
migration 11–31, 223, 247
Mikkonen, Kai 192
Minichiello, Mario 13, 18
minimal backgrounds 195
missionaries 100
Mitchell, Timothy 64
Mitchell, W.J.T. 60
mixed media 60, 155
Mixtec 37
mobile phones 117
modernism 61–4, 68, 71
modes of circulation 6
modes of perception 60
Mongoproduction 100
Moon, Fábio 38
Moretti, Franco 93, 127, 168
Morton, S. 148
Mory, Diane 105
Moussa, Adji 110
Mufti, Aamir 4, 135
Mukherji, Pia 5
Mulheres e quadrinhos (Marino and Machado, 2019) 41
multiculturalism 93, 192, 194, 199, 203, 207–8, 210, 247, 251
multimodality 60, 69, 72, 210
multiple readings 204–5
multi-stylistic approaches 58
murals 59, 123

Nady, Ahmed 58, 59
Nakazawa, Keiji 27
narrative architecture 11, 13, 23
narrative coherence 26
narrative propulsion devices 13, 19, 22, 24
narrative theory/narratology 192, 199, 209
narrative/storytelling 60, 123, 128, 134–5, 140, 146, 187, 192, 194, 209
narrator roles 38, 42, 194
nationalism 61, 69, 146, 169, 236, 243
nature protection 105
Nayar, P.K. 146, 148, 163
necropolis, city as 148–55, 163
neocolonialism 167, 169 n.3, 231

neoliberalism 9, 81, 146–7, 154, 155–62, 243–56
nested narratives 204–5
Neufeld, Josh 246
Neumann, Birgit 185 n.10
newspapers 66, 97, 102, 105, 148
NGOs 116–17, 171
nonfiction, graphic 16–17, 34–5, 36, 44
non-linearity 20, 60, 66, 83
Noomin, Diane 40
Notas al pie (Vollenweider) 40
Nye, Naomi Shihab 131 n.2

obscenity 36
Oesterheld, Héctor Germán 38
Okorafor, Nnedi 229, 230, 234, 236–7, 238, 239, 240
Oliver, Kelly 11, 12, 13
Olvis Dabley Agency 108
On va où là? 108
on-demand printing 110
online publishing 17, 58, 61, 93, 110, 117
  see also webcomics
Opam, Kwame 230
Opening, The (Abdelrazaq) 135–7, 139
oral tradition 104, 128, 134, 192–4, 204, 223
Orbán, Katalin 16, 18
Osei, Elisabeth Abena 238
Otero, Sole 40
othering 203, 259
Oubrerie, Clement 187
overlays 88, 89, 177

Page, Joanna 35 n.2, 41
page count length 79
page layout 91, 92 *see also* bleed pages; frames; splash pages
pages of exception 13, 14, 18–27
Palestine 11, 123–44
Palestine (Sacco) 13, 14, 16, 17, 25, 141
panels 15, 60, 68, 174, 194–5, 198–9, 265
Panique à Kinshasa 113
panopticon 71
Pappe, Ilan 133
Park, Patricia 257 n.1
Parker, Emma 13

Parker-Royal, Derek 201
parody 66
Pate, SooJin 258
patriarchy 47, 61, 170–1, 213–14, 218–20, 222, 224, 264
Patua art forms 215, 218–19, 221, 225, 226
Peacock, James 244
Persepolis (Satrapi) 2 n.2, 16, 33, 35, 36, 37, 51, 59 n.6, 141, 187
perspective 66
photographic gaze 18
photography 65
Pindi, Gloria Nziba 240
Pinhas, Luc 99, 102, 103
Pinto, Cecília Alves ("Ciça") 39
place names 230–1
plot-driving conflicts 77
political cartoons 61, 62, 68, 97, 100
Poncho Fue (Otero) 41
popular comics 114
popular culture 50, 59, 68, 145, 200
"popular literature" 35 n.2
Posada, Tim 240
postclassicalism 192, 200, 209
postcolonialism
   Black Panther 240
   center-margin binary 2
   critical perspectives 6
   and cultural modernity 64
   decolonial theory 5, 238
   deoccidentalization 170 n.5
   and field theory 97
   and the graphic novel 245–8, 252–4
   India 146, 148, 226
   intersection with other theories 5
   Japanese 246
   Malaysia 244, 247, 250
   and masculinity 161–2
   South Korea 169, 178
post-underground comics 36, 40
Powerpaola 34, 39, 40, 41–51
Prado Bley, Pia 77, 81, 86, 87–94
Prakash, G. 150
preambles 194
precursors of comics 37
Prince, Gerald 199, 202–3
printing technology 110, 194

prizes/awards 38, 51, 58, 103, 118
proto-comics 37, 68
Prough, Jennifer 82
Proverbes sérieusement illustrés 108
publishing industry 98–103, 247, 248

quadrinho 76, 94
Qualey, Marcia Lynx 72
queer experience 75–95
queer sequential art 39
Quino 37–8
Quiñones, Viviana 103

race and ethnicity
   Indigenous Australian graphic novels 187, 191, 193–4
   Latin America 84, 89–90
   Malaysia 247
   racial justice 139–40
   transcultural adoption 257 n.1, 258, 260, 265 n.6
   Wakanda 232, 235–6
racism 39, 140, 150–1, 157, 206–7, 246–7, 258
Ramayana 213–27
Ramone, J. 245
Ranta, Ronald 132
reading direction 19
realistic imagery 62, 65–6, 100, 173, 174
Red de investigadoras e investigadores de narrativa gráfica (RING) 34 n.1
refugee camps 11–31, 130, 131, 133
refugees 125, 130–1, 134
religion 43, 215, 220, 260, 261
re-makes/reworkings 214, 220
Repetti, Massimo 114, 115
reportage 11–31, 129, 133
reworlding 191, 205
rhymed prose 62
Richman, P. 224–5
Rifas, Leonard 187, 201
Rifkind, Candida 11, 13, 18, 20, 24
Rilke, Rainer Maria 235
Riva, S. 112
River of Stories, The (Sen, 1994) 145–6
Rosenblatt, Adam 133
Ruisseaux d'Afrique 102, 103 n.4, 112

Saab, Zainab 141
Sabaaneh, Mohammad 140
Sacco, Joe 13, 14, 16, 17, 19, 21, 24, 25, 27, 133, 141, 246
Sack, Jon 17, 25–7
Sagar, Ramanand 214, 215
Sah Bi, Jess 102
Said, Edward 5, 25, 170, 245
Sainz, José 39
Saleh, Rania 61
Salmi, Charlotta 5–6, 27, 192, 200, 209
"Same Old, Same Old" (Abdelrazaq) 140–1
same-sex love 77, 80–1, 85
Sandten, C. 156
Santos, K.M. 245, 246
Sanua, Ya'qub (James) 62–3
Sapiro, G. 117
Sarma, Ira 155
Saroukhan, Alexander 68
satire 62, 66, 108, 114, 115, 257
Satrapi, Marjane 2 n.2, 16, 27, 33, 35, 36, 37, 41, 59 n.6, 141, 187
scene-setting devices 25
Schmitz-Emans, Monika 5–6, 27, 34, 191, 194, 197, 199, 200
Schodt, Frederik L. 187
Schröer, Marie 35, 36
science fiction 38
Scorer, James 38–9
Seggerman, Alex 63–4, 69
self-publishing 38, 42, 110–15
seme/uke binary 86–9
Sen, Orijit 145
Senegal 102, 104–5, 113–14
sensory experience 64–8, 70, 72
sepia tint 151, 194, 196, 266
sequential art 37, 39, 60, 68, 194
serializations 214–15, 223
Shammas, Anton 132 n.4
Shamoon, Deborah 81, 83
shared affect 150
Shin, Hyonhee 171
Shin, Jung-seop 171 n.7
Shoemaker, Adam 205–6, 210
shōjo manga 77–9, 80–94
short stories 85

Sihomning, F. 245, 246
Sikoué, Deubou 106
silent panels 209
Silverman, A. 261
Sindibād 61, 68
Singh, Sherry-Ann 220
single-frame works 68
Sisé, Mongo 100, 101
Sita's Ramayana 213–27
smart cities 230
Smith, Josh 171
social archetypes 61, 63
social class 62–3, 145, 247
social media 61, 105, 117
social movements 87
social realism 66
socio-cultural issues 146–7, 193, 215, 245, 246
sociology 97–122
Solano López, Francisco 38
Sonon, Hector 104, 105, 112
Souffle, Kan 108
sounds, depiction of 64–9, 70–1, 93, 200, 203, 260 *see also* speech bubbles/balloons
South Asia 213–27
South Korea 167–86, 257, 258
Southall Black Sisters (SBS) 224 n.8, 225
South-South exchanges 2, 6, 99
spaces of exception 13, 14, 18, 21, 24, 25, 155
Spateen, Taqi 140
spatial grammar 15, 60, 64
specialized publishers 107–17, 125, 188, 194
speech bubbles/balloons 13, 19, 60, 79, 91, 174, 178, 201, 260
Spiegelman, Art 2, 14–15, 16, 17, 24, 35, 246
Spivak, Gayatri 127, 169 n.4
splash pages 14, 15, 18–19, 49–50, 199
Stallybrass, P 205
state of exception 148, 150–1, 153
Stelfreeze, Brian 230, 233, 235, 237
stereotypes 1, 86, 103, 134, 201, 230, 234, 235, 246
sterilization camps 152

"Still Born" (Abdelrazaq) 135–6, 137, 139, 142
storytelling 60, 123, 128, 134–5, 140, 146, 187, 192, 194, 209
street art 59
style shots 88
stylistic approaches 36, 58, 201
subalternity 147, 154, 167, 169 n.3, 171
subversion 62, 205–10
suggestion 85, 91
superheroes 3, 110, 200, 234–5
surrealism 62, 66, 68–71
surveillance 24, 58, 66, 71
sustainability 229–42
sutairu ga overlays 88, 89
Suyong, Kim 171
Suzuki, Michiko 85
syllabi 127
symbolic capital 98
Syposz, Jessica 148

Tache d'Encre (Ink spot) 116
Takam Tikou 103
Takemiya, Keiko 85
Talabi, Wole 237
Tan, Shaun 187
Tara Books 221
Taruho, Inagaki 85, 86
Tebeosfera 41
television serials 213–27
temporal succesion 20, 58, 60, 174
temporal-normative dimensions 167–86
Teo, P. 254
Tessy, D.R. 111
textual worlds 87
Tezuka, Osamu 187
Themistocleous, C. 250
theoretical colonization 35 n.2
Thierry, Raphaël 103
Thompson, Craig 35, 36
Thorn, Rachel 78 n.22
thought bubbles/balloons 45, 201, 260, 262
Threads from the Refugee Crisis (Evans) 17, 20–2
time-lapse sequences 20
Tinta Femenina 33–53

Tintin 100
Togo 110
Tomsky, Terri 23
Töpffer, Rodolphe 75
Tounkara, Massiré 104, 105
Trait Noir (Black Line) 116
transculturalism 6, 80, 82, 94, 205, 245–6
translation
    Arabic comics 58
    Baddawi (Abdelrazaq, 2015) 125, 128–9, 135
    Couleur de Peau (Jung, 2007–16) 261
    into English 38, 43 n.11, 77, 87, 130
    and Global South comics 1, 2, 6
    Latin American comics 38, 77
    between universalism and particularity 127–9
    untranslatability 13, 128, 185
    Western comics in Egypt 61–2
translocality 6
transmedial references 34, 50
transnational Blackness 240
transnational genres 17
trauma 14, 33, 36, 40, 130, 240, 246–7, 258, 262
tropes 78, 80, 81–6
Trujillo, Marcela ("Maliki") 39, 40, 41
Tsai, Yi-Shan 79–80
Tshibanda-Kibwanga 112, 115
t-shirts 140
Turkmen, Sezen 206
Ty, E. 246
typography 203

UAE 62
Ubby's Underdogs trilogy (McKenna) 187–212
Ultraman the Ultra Power 249
underground comix 36, 40, 60
Undocumented: The Architecture of Migrant Detention (Chak) 22–5
universality 213, 214, 215, 219–21, 226
unsayable, the 15, 36, 185
untranslatability 13, 128, 185
urban dystopia 147
urban spaces 145–65, 230
Urry, J. 159

US comics tradition 75, 94, 200
USA, Palestinians in 124

Valmiki 219, 226
van Dijk, T.A. 254
Varughese, E. Dawson 145
Veld, Laurike in't 14
Venugopal, R. 251
verbal-visual duality 59–60, 69, 146, 148, 192, 193
Vergueiro, Waldomiro 35 n.2
vernacular language 62, 100, 114, 202–3
    see also linguistic varieties
vertical scrolling 91, 92
viewpoint 24, 55
violence, see also trauma
    gang violence 25, 44
    geographical violence 245
    India 148, 152, 153
    as narrative device 93
    Palestine 130, 131–2, 133–4
    same-sex couples 86
    state violence 12, 148
    and surveillance 71
    against women 36, 39, 40, 43, 219
virtual communities 93
Virus Tropical (Powerpaola) 34, 41–51
visual density 19–20
visual languages 37, 61
visual turn 35 n.2
Vollenweider, Nacha 40
von Rebeur, Ana 39
voyeurism 69–71, 134

Wakanda 229–42
Walcott, Derek 223, 224
Walkowitz, Rebecca 2 n.1
Wandja, Josephine Guidy 102
Wanly, Adham 68
war reporting 133
Ware, Chris 2
weather 26–7
webcomics 17, 77 n.4, 87, 91, 134
Weber, Hilde 39
Weizman, Eyal 12
Weltliteratur 5, 168

Westall, Claire 243–4, 253
White, A. 205
white space 68, 72, 93
Wilderson III, Frank B. 236
witness 18, 128, 129, 178, 181, 183–4
Wolof 114
Womack, Ytasha 235–6
women
    female artists 33–53, 221, 247
    female characters 207–9, 213, 215–25, 234
    feminist theory 34, 39, 41, 44, 51
    Korean "comfort women" 167–86
    La Lucha (Sack) 25
    Palestinian 125, 139
    shōjo manga 81–6
    violence against 36, 39, 40, 43, 219
    Wakanda 234
word-image combinations 83
workshops 116, 118
worlding 167, 168, 169, 185, 191, 192, 195
worldliness 1–2, 9, 27, 59, 93, 129, 191, 193
Worley, Will 13
Worth, Jennifer 37
WReC 14
Wrobel, Jasmin 40, 50

Yamato, Eriko 247, 248
Yang, Gene Luen 187
Yao crack en math (Sah Bi, 1985) 102, 105
yaoi 86
Yaoundé 106
Yates-Lu, Anna 170, 172
Yoshiya, Nobuko 85, 86
youth publishing 99
Yumeji, Takehisa 83
Yunan, Ramses 68

Zamalin, Alex 236
Zell, Hans 99, 103
Ziarek, E.P. 147
Zinsou et Sagbo album 111–12, 112 n.5
Zohoré, Lassane 104, 105, 108
Zöhrer, Michaela 21
Zoromé, Aly 104